ASSASSINS AND TEMPLARS

ASSASSINS AND TEMPLARS

A Battle in Myth and Blood

STEVE TIBBLE

YALE UNIVERSITY PRESS
NEW HAVEN AND LONDON

Copyright © 2025 Steve Tibble

All rights reserved. This book may not be reproduced in whole or in part, in any form (beyond that copying permitted by Sections 107 and 108 of the U.S. Copyright Law and except by reviewers for the public press) without written permission from the publishers.

All reasonable efforts have been made to provide accurate sources for all images that appear in this book. Any discrepancies or omissions will be rectified in future editions.

For information about this and other Yale University Press publications, please contact:
U.S. Office: sales.press@yale.edu yalebooks.com
Europe Office: sales@yaleup.co.uk yalebooks.co.uk

Set in Adobe Garamond Pro by IDSUK (DataConnection) Ltd

Printed and bound in the UK using 100% renewable electricity at CPI Group (UK) Ltd

Library of Congress Control Number: 2025939818
A catalogue record for this book is available from the British Library.
Authorized Representative in the EU: Easy Access System Europe, Mustamäe tee 50, 10621 Tallinn, Estonia, gpsr.requests@easproject.com

ISBN 978-0-300-28212-2

10 9 8 7 6 5 4 3 2 1

As the Assassins and the Templars would say, 'For Faith'

Contents

	List of Plates and Maps	ix
1	The Promise of Death	1
2	Assassins: Birth of a Legend	9
3	A Beginning and a Blueprint: Persia (1090–1100)	18
4	Assassins and Syria: In Search of a Home (1100–1113)	27
5	Assault on Shaizar: Mum's Army (1114)	50
6	Assassins: A State within a State (1115–1126)	61
7	Templars: The Ideology of Love and Death (1095–1129)	71
8	Templars: 'A Living Sacrifice' (1119–1129)	82
9	So It Begins: The Strangest Partnership (1126–1130)	97
10	Assassins: Home Sweet Home (1130–1162)	109
11	Templars: The Little Castle on the Prairie (1130–1169)	122
12	Fear and Loathing in Lebanon (1130–1162)	143
13	Sinan: The Old Man of the Mountain (1162–1170)	151
14	Ambushes and Ambassadors (1170–1174)	168

CONTENTS

15 Saladin Must Die: Assassins Take the Lead (1175–1176) — 179
16 Saladin Must Die: The Templars' Turn (1177–1191) — 195
17 The Death of Heroes (1192–1193) — 209
18 Contest for the Holy Land (1194–1248) — 221
19 Egypt, Saints and Sinners (1248–1254) — 229
20 Assassins: Holocaust and Horror (1255–1291) — 246
21 Templars: Death in the East (1255–1291) — 265
22 Afterlife: From Intimidation to Entertainment — 273
23 Ending and Beginning — 292

Acknowledgements — *294*
Notes — *297*
References and Further Reading — *317*
Index — *326*

Plates and Maps

Plates

1. The assassination of Vizier Nizam al-Mulk, from *Jami' al-tawarikh*, fourteenth century. Topkapı Palace Museum, Inv.H. 1653, f. 360b.
2. The gatehouse at Shaizar. Reproduced with kind permission of Dale Fishburn.
3. Baldwin II ceding the location of the Temple of Solomon to Hugh of Payns and Godfrey of Saint-Omer, from William of Tyre, *Histoire d'Outre-Mer*, thirteenth century. Bibliothèque nationale de France, Département des Manuscrits, Français 9081, f. 132r.
4. Masyaf castle, 1930s. From John D. Whiting, *Diary in Photos*, Vol. III, 1938.
5. Saladin, from a manuscript copy of *Kitab fi ma'arifat al-hiyal al-handisaya*, 1354. World History Archive / Alamy.
6. The death of King Amalric of Jerusalem. Bibliothèque nationale de France, Département des Manuscrits, Français 9084, f. 290v.
7. The Old Man of the Mountain training the *fidais*. British Library, MS Royal 19 D I, f. 70v. From the British Library archive / Bridgeman Images.
8. Tiles showing Richard and Saladin, thirteenth century. © Trustees of the British Museum.

PLATES AND MAPS

9. The port of Acre. Library of Congress, Prints and Photographs Division, G. Eric and Edith Matson Photograph Collection.
10. The Mongol siege of Alamut, 1256. Bibliothèque nationale, MS Supplément Persan 206, f. 149r.
11. A Mamluk leader, from the *Baptistère de Saint Louis* by Muhammad ibn al-Zayn, 1325–40. Photo © Musée du Louvre, Dist. GrandPalaisRmn / Hughes Dubois.
12. A Mamluk riding coat, first half of the thirteenth century. Metropolitan Museum of Art, Purchase, Director's Fund and Oscar de la Renta Ltd. Gift, 2008.
13. The attempt on the life of Prince Edward (later Edward I), 1272. British Library, Cotton MS Nero A IV, f. 110v. From the British Library archive / Bridgeman Images.
14. The fall of Tripoli, 1289. British Library, Cocharelli Codex MS 27695, f. 5r.
15. The execution of the masters of the Templars in France and the death of Philip IV of France. British Library, MS 27695 f. 6v. From the British Library archive / Bridgeman Images.
16. The legend of the Assassins. Bibliothèque nationale, MS 2810, ff. 16v and 17r.

Maps

1. The medieval Middle East (after Barber, 2012).	xii
2. The crusader states: The Latin kingdom of Jerusalem (after Barber, 2012).	xiii
3. The crusader states: Tripoli, Antioch and Edessa (after Barber, 2012).	xiv
4. The Assassins' castles in Syria (after Willey, 2005).	xv
5. The Assassins' castles in Persia (after Willey, 2005).	xvi

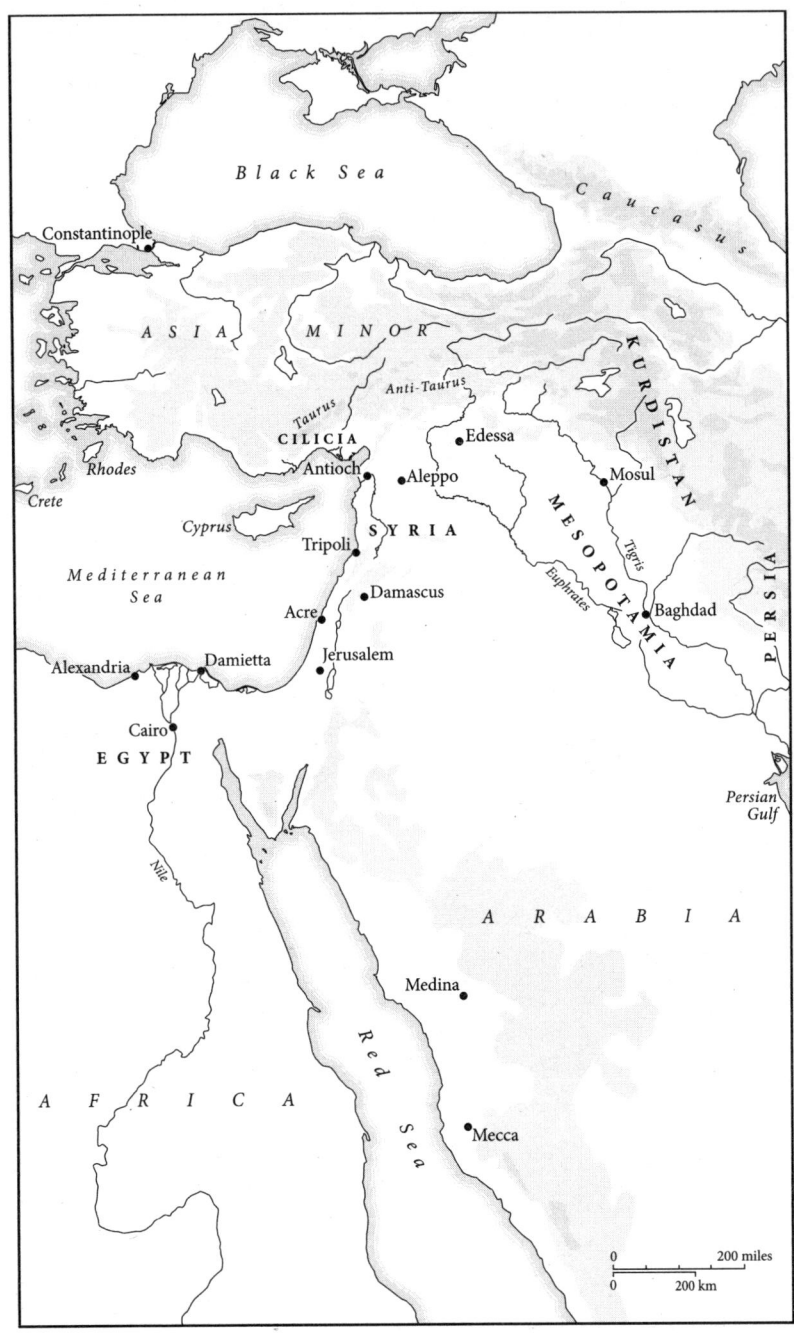

1. The medieval Middle East (after Barber, 2012).

2. The crusader states: The Latin kingdom of Jerusalem (after Barber, 2012).

3. The crusader states: Tripoli, Antioch and Edessa (after Barber, 2012).

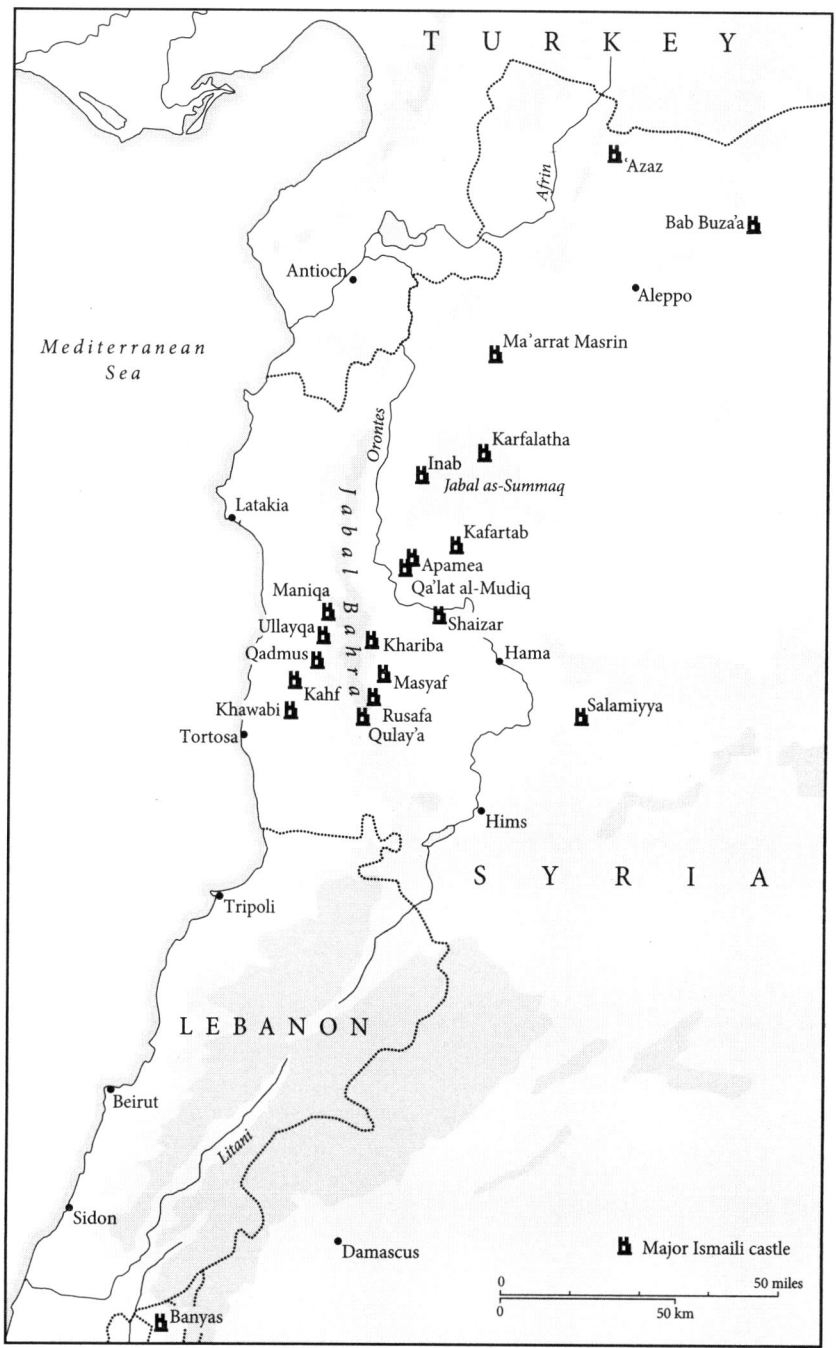

4. The Assassins' castles in Syria (after Willey, 2005).

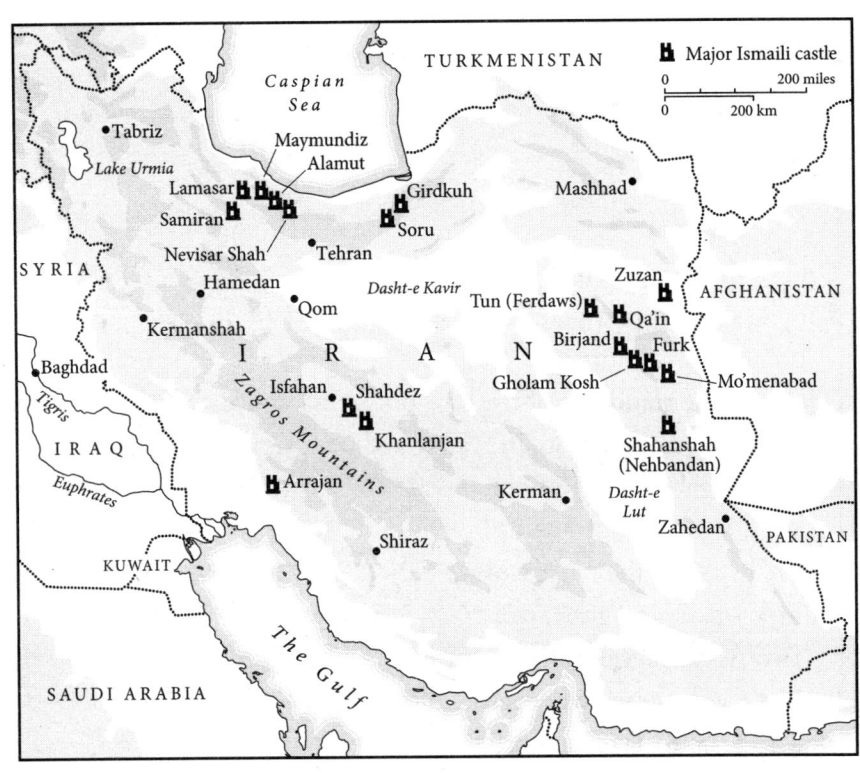

5. The Assassins' castles in Persia (after Willey, 2005).

1

The Promise of Death

In the thirteenth century, people thought you were doing pretty well if you made it past your fortieth birthday.

Philip of Montfort, the 'Old Lord' of Tyre, was, in his mid-sixties, elderly by the standards of the day, but he remained a respected leader of his people. So much so, in fact, that Sultan Baybars found him to be an irritatingly effective opponent. In 1270, he paid Philip the unwelcome and back-handed compliment of hiring the Assassins to kill him. When it came, the hit employed their classic techniques for covert murder – patience, guile, treachery and disguise.

Two Assassins were chosen for the task. They dressed as cavalrymen for hire – young men who were professional, confident and flamboyant. They rode up to Tyre 'on horseback, carrying Turkish arms and wearing belts of silver, in the manner of Saracen men-at-arms. They went straight to the Lord of Tyre and asked him for baptism'.[1]

Their request for conversion (and, more importantly, employment) was taken at face value. They were escorted to the lord of Tyre and his household, and he 'had them baptised'. One of the Assassins 'took his name and was called Philip', meaning that Philip of Montfort became his godfather. They were also introduced to Philip's nephew, Julian Grenier, the lord of Sidon. Julian, showing a similarly misguided sense of trust, 'had the other one baptised, and was his godfather, and he took the name Julian'.²

As with all good frauds, it is much easier to sell a lie that your victim wants to believe – and in this instance, the crusaders (or Franks, as they were often known) were far too gullible. They were always short of manpower, and there was a desperate hope that these resourceful, hardened men were genuine recruits. The Assassins, and their disguises, were extremely convincing. They were employed by Philip of Montfort and Julian of Grenier in their corps of light mounted archers, the famous Turcopoles. Even more impressively, they appeared so trustworthy that they were quickly made part of their new masters' households – opportunities for access were presented to them on an almost daily basis.

There were warning signs: rumours began circulating that an assassination attempt could be on the cards. Philip tried to take precautions and 'had his viscount seek out and monitor foreign people who came into Tyre'. But although the possibility of an attack had clearly been linked to the Assassins, the exact nature of the threat was unknown. More to the point, the Assassins' trademark long-term planning and fastidious commitment meant that they were already in place before the danger became apparent. In a stark vindication of the hit squad's professionalism, the new Turcopole 'converts' remained unsuspected.³

Nonetheless, the plot was nearly discovered. The two killers became friendly with an Arab-Christian valet in the household. Their new friend was almost as untrustworthy as they were, however. While he was rifling through their belongings one day, presumably looking for something worth stealing, he accidentally discovered a poisoned dagger, hidden in one of their quivers and 'wrapped in a cloth'. Confronted with the evidence, the Assassins confessed the plot to him.⁴

The valet was either brave or foolish. Or probably both. He tried to blackmail his new 'friends'. They offered him money to buy his silence, but brought forward the timing of the murder attempt, just in case he reneged on the deal. The Assassins 'promised to give him 100 old bezants by Sunday', to keep him quiet. With the prospect of a life-changing sum of money dangling in front of him, the native Christian acquiesced; but the murderers now knew that they needed to move fast.⁵

The attack was planned to take place simultaneously in two locations – multiple strikes were calculated to exploit the initial surprise and unpreparedness, and to maximise the resulting confusion. On Thursday, 14 August, Julian of Sidon left to travel to Beirut, accompanied by one of the Assassins, while the other remained in Tyre with Lord Philip.⁶

Exact coordination was inevitably difficult, however – this was an age before watches (still less, mobile phones). The attack in Tyre was launched first. With surprise on the Assassins' side, it started well. On Sunday morning, 'the Assassin came into the courtyard very early and went towards the lord's chapel [in the citadel of Tyre]. There he found Sir Philip of Montfort at the entrance to his chapel, on foot, speaking with one of his burgesses.' Suspecting nothing, Lord Philip spoke amicably with the Assassin. In a little detail which speaks volumes for the trust and affection that had been built up, he even gave him money to put into the collection plate for Mass.⁷

The Assassin spotted his opportunity. He 'took the money and went off to give it, and then he saw that there was no one in the chapel except for the Young Lord [Philip's son, John of Montfort] and one other knight, called William of Picquigny'. By inspecting the chapel in advance, 'Philip' the Assassin was also planning his escape route after the murder. Assassins were prepared to die in the course of their work – but, contrary to some later perceptions, they did not actually want to be part of a suicide mission unless there was no alternative. Fanatical killers were a scarce resource.⁸

The scene looked promising. The lord of Tyre had few people with him and, as they were in church, they were unarmed. There was unlikely to be a better chance.

Once the decision had been made, the act itself was shockingly fast and simple. 'On emerging from the chapel, [the Assassin] ran into the Old Lord, Sir Philip of Montfort, and stabbed him in the chest with the dagger.' A slightly OCD habit on the part of the elderly Frank almost saved his life. At the moment when he was attacked, 'the Old Lord was handling one of his rings on his finger on the other hand'. The Assassin's blow was partially absorbed, as it 'pierced the hand which was on his breast, and then he left the dagger in him'. But the wound was severe nonetheless.[9]

Leaving Lord Philip bleeding out on the floor, the Assassin 'put his hand to his sword and went back into the chapel to kill the other lord'. Philip's son was less resourceful than his father. John, 'who was in the chapel reading his book, turned to see what was going on. When he saw the Assassin coming in with a naked sword in his hand, he lunged towards the altar, which had a board painted with pictures of saints on the front of it, and he got behind it.'[10]

An almost comical game of chase ensued – the Young Lord was endearingly useless. The Assassin threw his sword at him to try to stop him escaping. Upsetting for future generations of art historians, but luckily for John, it stuck in the ornate altarpiece, penetrating so far 'that it could not be withdrawn'. The Young Lord panicked and hid behind the altar.[11]

John's companion, William of Picquigny, was similarly unarmed, but realised that more resolute action was needed if they were to get out of the chapel alive. He 'came up and grabbed the Assassin from behind, and told the Young Lord that he could come out. The Young Lord came out and took the Assassin by the hair with one hand, while with the other hand he tried to pull out the sword'. The hapless Young Lord couldn't even do this properly, however. As he overexcitedly struggled to grab the weapon, 'two fingers of his hand were injured'.[12]

While this farcical fighting was under way in the chapel, the Old Lord, Philip of Montfort, had struggled painfully to his feet. Brave to the last, he staggered across the courtyard of the citadel, leaving a trail of blood as he tried to reach his chamber. From there he directed his men to run and save John. He collapsed onto a stone bench just outside the doorway and told them: 'Go help my son in the chapel, for the Saracen is killing him!' The household sergeants ran to the chapel, cut down the

Assassin, 'and rescued the Young Lord of Tyre, who came to his father'. Philip was still alive, but died of his wounds soon afterwards – he outlived his assailant by only a few minutes.[13]

As an emotionally cathartic, but ultimately pointless, post-mortem punishment, the Assassin's corpse 'was drawn and hanged'. More practically, the garrison of Tyre immediately sent a fast boat to Beirut by sea, and a Turcopole messenger by land, to warn Julian and seize the other Assassin. Even this ended in farce, however. The Assassin got wind of this development, 'mounted his horse and fled to the Saracens and was safe, for it was only a very short distance from the Christians to the Saracens'.[14]

Few people emerge well from this sad and bloody story.[15] Everyone was refreshingly incompetent. The breach of security that allowed hardened soldiers who had only recently 'converted' to Christianity into the household is astounding, particularly given that there had been intelligence about the possibility of an assassination attempt – it speaks volumes for the professionalism and plausibility of the assailants. And the Young Lord was so frightened that he managed to wound himself, despite his opponent being pinioned by a companion. Similarly, the failure to capture the surviving Assassin in Beirut was unimpressive.

Even the performance of the Assassins was underwhelming. They had allowed themselves to be discovered by one of their new household companions, and that had bounced them into acting faster than they had anticipated. And the Assassin in Tyre proved unable to kill two unarmed men in the enclosed space of the chapel, despite having the element of surprise on his side.

Meanwhile, the passively treacherous valet who had discovered their conspiracy tried to sneak off, but was captured. 'He was questioned, and taken and tortured' – almost certainly not in that order – 'and he confessed that he had known about it.' The Assassins were beyond the reach of justice, so the valet bore the brunt of everyone's anger. While he was still alive, 'his tongue was torn out beneath his chin, and his right hand cut off, and he was drawn and hanged'.[16]

There were no happy endings.

Death and dictionaries

The death of Philip of Montfort was a single incident, yet it gives us a sense of the crazy, bloody world in which medieval Middle Eastern politics played out. And it introduces us to many of our main protagonists.

We have come across the Turkic-heritage Mamluks and their fearsome cavalry – it was these impressive warriors that the hitmen were impersonating. And we have encountered the crusaders, the European settlers and their descendants – they are still hanging on, by their fingernails, to the coastline of the Holy Land almost two hundred years after the end of the First Crusade.

Most importantly, however, we have met the Assassins. And the capital-A is important. An assassin, in modern usage, is a professional killer. An Assassin (or a Nizari Ismaili, as the members of the group are more properly known) is part of a Shiite religious sect who sought to defend themselves and to project power through political murder.

The two words are related, of course. The word 'Assassin' (or *hashishin*) was employed as a pejorative by those who were on the receiving end of their remorseless hit squads in the twelfth and thirteenth centuries. But it stuck. Eventually it entered the dictionary as a broader by-word for premeditated murderers or contract killers. And that inevitably colours their legacy and the way we look at them today.

The promise of death

This book looks at the history of the Assassins in Syria and the extraordinary relationship they had with the Templars. It seems strange to juxtapose these groups; but the relationship between the two is grounded in truth – and it is a stranger true story than many fictions. We will see how they both survived and inflated their own influence by creating corporate 'brands', at the heart of which were 'the promise of death'.

THE PROMISE OF DEATH

The Assassins and the Templars have become two of the most legendary groups of modern times. Although both have accumulated a huge deadweight of mythology and absurd conspiracy theories along the way, the roots of their intertwined story contain, oddly enough, much that is true and similar. The tactics were different, but their foundations were the same. The promise of unstoppable death might be 'in your face' in the form of a Templar charge. Or it could be unstoppable death 'in your back' in the form of an Assassin's dagger. But death was at the core.

Both groups were tiny in number, certainly compared to the military and political behemoths that they were frequently pitched against. But they were huge in terms of the effect they had on the world. And even beyond their parallel methodologies, they shared a strangely intimate relationship. Appropriately enough, they walked a remarkably intertwined path towards their own destruction and on into legend.

The histories of the Assassins and the Templars contain extraordinary anecdotes of death, passion and commitment – these were lives played out far beyond the parameters of our own comfortable existence. Both groups were legends in their own lifetime, and those legends have only grown over the intervening centuries. Their myths have inevitably become distorted over time – but they were often deliberately promoted and are not entirely without a basis in fact. This book is the story of the unlikely reality behind those equally bizarre legends.

These two highly committed groups – many might call them 'sects' – committed acts of violence that were in equal measure impressive and crazy, refined and shocking. They had, in their own way, similarly extreme ideologies. They were men with intellectual strategies founded on an ability to exploit our innate fear of death. And they knew that anyone who genuinely overcame that fear could pose a huge threat to those around them. Liberated from death, they were able to deal it out remorselessly and without fear of its consequences for them personally. Their actions would speak louder than the voices of their relatively small communities ever could.

ASSASSINS AND TEMPLARS

As we shall see, the Assassins and (to a lesser extent) the Templars lived isolated but parallel lives, both as individuals and as groups. But they also knew each other well – they had prosaic but hate-filled relationships as neighbours and trading partners, landlords and tenants.

Perhaps most surprisingly, however, they had far more in common with each other than they would have acknowledged.

2

Assassins: Birth of a Legend

> We are oppressed and not oppressors
> Letter from the Old Man of the Mountain to Saladin

During the crusades, the winning formula was to pour enormous amounts of money and energy into acquiring big armies. All the major players did it. The vast number of young, reckless men that this entailed was the underlying driver for two centuries of war and criminality. And those armies were also the basic building blocks upon which (almost) all power structures were built. But if the major players struggled to build these voraciously expensive and disruptive armies, how did the minor players, the ones without the big budgets or pulling power, survive?[1]

The short answer is that in most cases they did not. The majority of the smaller Turkic players and their city states gradually got rolled up into the bigger political entities that were forming around them – superstates, such as Saladin's Ayyubid empire or its Mamluk successors. The old ruling families survived as best they could, but only as vassals. Before long almost all of them were swept away. Almost, but not all.

ASSASSINS AND TEMPLARS

Playing a different game

The Assassins and the Templars often had an extremely fractious relationship. They had ostensibly nothing in common. They had vastly different reputations and cultural backgrounds. And yet in some ways they were strikingly similar.

Both groups, though they would not have deigned to recognise it, had a bizarrely similar cultural underpinning – overlapping objectives, similar strategies and strangely parallel defining characteristics. Each was outnumbered. Each was surrounded. And each possessed no significant technological advantage over their enemies. They had to resort to fanaticism, focus and reckless bravery to redress the balance.

Both groups had some of the characteristics that we normally associate with being a 'cult'. As we shall see, both of these 'cults' were formed around the promise of death. And both embodied the liberation, commitment and finality that accompanied such an acceptance. They looked for the death of their opponents and, although not wilfully suicidal, embraced the strong possibility of death themselves. Death was their promise, and that promise lay at the heart of their power.

Each group also found a vital role as 'state-builders'. This was an essential life raft for religious minorities in an often intolerant age – the Christian communities of the Middle East and the Nizari Ismaili Shiite minority, both nestling in the shadow of a potentially overwhelming Sunni empire, were always vulnerable. Both sects, Templars and Assassins alike, had, in effect, ambitions to create a state within a state.

Vitally for their image and the methodology of fear that they eventually became famous for, both were unusually structured – unlike most political entities in that time and place, they were *corporations*, rather than the more typical 'family-run businesses'. They knew that the death of a carefully chosen individual (a successful leader, say, a wife or a beloved child) would have a profound effect on the dynastically centred states of their enemies, while they themselves were impervious to such threats.

These ostensibly opposite, yet strangely parallel, groups kept bouncing off each other over a period of two centuries – and, up to the present day, they have become endlessly conjoined in our memories. Their reputations have each taken a similar arc, morphing from hard-nosed reality into absurd legends, and from champions of their communities into pantomime villains.

The methodologies they invented were different, but parallel. The Assassins' threat was death when you least expected it – poisoned daggers in the mosque, hidden murderers emerging from the shadows. The Templars' threat was death exactly when you did expect it – when you saw them charging straight at you there was no bluster, no war cries, just the power of death on horseback speeding onwards like an implacable force of nature.

The tactics might have been different, but the message – and the fear it provoked – was the same. Whether facing the Assassin hit squads (the elite *fidais*) or a squadron of Templar knights, you knew you had a problem – these were people you needed to take far more seriously than their numbers would otherwise suggest.

Assassins: From fragile to fearsome

Among the minor groups that most contemporaries in the medieval Middle East would initially have nominated as 'least likely to succeed' was a small, unpopular band of Shiite religious enthusiasts. For most of its early history in the Holy Land it lacked a clear territorial or political base. The band was small in number and without obvious economic assets. And its members were widely despised, viewed by its powerful Sunni Muslim neighbours as heretics and traitors. This obscure, and presumably doomed, breakaway sect later became known, by its enemies at least, as the Assassins.

The word 'Assassin' is used in this book purely because it is the name most readily recognised by western readers, particularly in the context of the period of the crusades. The term *al-Hashishiyya* (that is, 'Assassins') has often been used in a deliberately derogatory manner, particularly by the sect's opponents. Here, of course, it has no negative or defamatory intent. Other terms used to describe the sect's adherents by Muslim contemporaries – who were generally hostile sources – included, with varying degrees of negative connotation, religious terms such as *Batiniyya*, *Ta'limiyya* or *Malahida*. The more formal, and most correct, descriptor for the sect is Nizari Ismailis.[2] Whatever we choose to call them, however, the Assassins were the militant underdogs of the crusades. Surrounded by danger, they chose to transform themselves into a community of unique threat, rather than meekly succumb to the more overt violence of their enemies.

Against all the odds, the Assassins survived – and they did so by refusing to play the same game that everyone else was so swept up in. They knew that they could not raise big armies: the regional demographic arms race was pitched at such a level that they could not even begin to compete. So, rather than fail in doing the same as everyone else, they focused instead on succeeding by doing something very different. The Assassins instinctively grasped a profound (but not always obvious) truth. And they pursued that truth through to its logical conclusion. The concept behind their strategy of targeted murder was simple, yet powerful. As one anonymous Nizari poet wrote: 'By a single warrior on foot, a king may be struck with terror, though he may own more than 100,000 horsemen.'[3] The delivery of death by an individual was a political act that circumvented the need for large armies or riches. It was the perfect means of projecting political will for those who were too weak or too poor to do so in more traditional military ways.

Armies are threatening. They can occupy ground, defeat other armies or capture cities. But they are hugely disruptive for all concerned. Their employers require vast amounts of money, food and land to attract and sustain them. And they have to be prepared for the social pressures that these restless bands of armed strangers bring to bear on the communities they find themselves in. Even more importantly, these armies are, until the critical moment, rather abstract and impersonal. They are the playing pieces in longer-term campaigns – the generality of violence, rather than its pin-point application. What the Assassins understood was that they needed to project power in a way that was far more personal. And in a way that did not require the services of tens of thousands of irritatingly disruptive foreign soldiers.

Their solution was murder. Unstoppable murder.

The intimacy of death: Different game, different rules

It is an almost universal truth that individuals are afraid of violent death. Families are particularly vulnerable: no father wants to see his children butchered; no wife wants to have her husband killed in front of her. The genius of the Assassins lay in their recognition that anyone who could credibly play on those primal fears had no need of large, expensive, clumsy armies.

Violence was common in the Middle Ages – and was even more frequent in the crusader states, whose cities were teeming with mercenaries, garrisons and visiting military contingents. Even small towns and villages were highly militarised. All men were expected to have access to arms to protect their local communities – and, in extremis, to be conscripted at a moment's notice into the army for the defence of the kingdom, in the event of invasion or nomadic raids.[4]

This violence generally resulted in even bloodier outcomes for the same kinds of crime that we have today: more serious muggings, more stabbings during armed robberies, more violence in the course of drunken fights and so on. But it also helped in popularising some surprisingly modern political crimes. This era arguably had the dubious honour of having been a crucible for one of the most enduring manifestations of contemporary political violence – terrorism.[5]

The Assassins did not, of course, invent terrorism or the idea of political murder. That brutal way of ending an argument has existed since time immemorial. And political violence in the Muslim Middle East was already widespread. Muslim leaders of the time habitually wore chainmail shirts under their everyday clothing. This was not a fashion statement: they did so for a very good reason. They recognised that they were in mortal danger in what passed for 'peacetime', just as much as on the battlefield.[6] During the period 1114–46, for instance, the city of Aleppo had nine different Turkic rulers. Of these, only one gave up power of his own accord. Five were murdered, one died in battle and two were forced to surrender to their enemies. Politics in Syria was a bloody contact sport.[7]

Much the same was true of Egypt. In the reign of the caliph al-Amir (r. 1101–30), his vizier, al-Afdal, a long-standing enemy of the crusaders, was murdered in 1121. The next vizier was crucified, alongside his brothers, in 1128. His successor in charge of financial affairs of state was flogged to death soon after, in 1129. Even the caliph himself was murdered by a *fidais* squad in 1130. Blood was a form of political communication.[8]

This was no aberration. The violence in Egypt continued unabated. The period 1153–64, for instance, was a time when Fatimid Egypt was confronted by both Christian and Sunni Muslim enemies. It needed political stability more than ever. None was to be found. The country had no fewer than five viziers in that short period, four of whom were murdered. The fifth was killed while on the run, fleeing into the desert with as much of the state treasury as he could fit into his saddle-bags. Criminality and violence were the constant background rhythm of political life.

Politics in the medieval Middle East was violent in the extreme. Factions, in-fighting and deadly conspiracies were rife. But, in this supremely dangerous time and place, the Assassins perfected the art of institutionalised murder, and took it to its logical conclusion. Their murders were the result of conspiracy, intrigue and insinuation. Everything was secret up to the point of the hit. But beyond that point, the Assassins revelled in their notoriety. As some modern groups have similarly grasped, the 'spectacular' nature of a high-profile attack (and its visceral PR impact) was every bit as important as its substance.[9]

The Assassins made carefully targeted murder a central instrument of strategy. Without armies to do their bidding, they elevated individual death to become the primary expression of their power. Desperation drove them to this extraordinary, but logical, extension of the rules of power politics.

The 'Old Man of the Mountain' was the marvellously redolent honorific title first bestowed upon the Nizari leader Sinan in the 1160s, but later associated with all of the Assassins' leaders in Syria: leaders come and go, but the 'Old Man' remained seemingly immortal. Death, it implied, had no hold on such men. One such 'Old Man' wrote threateningly to a Sunni enemy, and in so doing summed up the essence of the sect's 'brand promise': 'You know', he purred menacingly, '. . . the quality of our men, what they can accomplish in an instant and how they seek the intimacy of death.'[10]

And with that knowledge came the Assassins' power.

How to make enemies and influence people

Their numbers were tiny. Their resources were negligible. But the Assassins punched far above their weight. They made a huge impact at the time. And even now their reputation reverberates around the more outlandish corners of history. How was any of this possible?

None of it happened by accident. A 'cult' is, in this case, better understood as an extreme form of 'branding'. A brand, above all, is about a promise. And the 'brand promise', in this extraordinary instance, was death itself. Creating the Assassin brand and the mystique that went with it required effort and dedication. But as the totalitarian regimes of the twentieth century also discovered, it is worth the effort: creating and controlling such a brand offers a powerful lever.

The Middle East in the eleventh and twelfth centuries was a crowded and extremely violent environment. The Assassins were a relatively small group of individuals, surrounded by much larger ethnic and religious groups, each of which was capable of deploying infinitely greater military and political resources. At such a time of supreme intolerance, small groups of 'heretics', operating without powerful protectors, were extremely vulnerable. The Assassins, with no army, no navy and no obvious homeland of their own, needed to establish an intimidating 'corporate identity' – an identity, moreover, that would allow them to survive in the midst of far larger predators. The identity they developed (and which emerged surprisingly quickly) was distinctive and effective – it was an identity founded on fear. Not fear in any abstract sense. The Assassins never had the numbers or the leverage to make vague threats about invasions or economic sanctions with any semblance of credibility.

Rather, the fear they sought was deeply personal. The Assassins' 'foreign policy' was simplicity itself. The implicit promise was clear cut and final: if you don't come to an understanding with us, you will die. If you persecute us, you will die. And if you attack us, you will die. We will penetrate any security you can erect around you. We can do this because we have men who are willing to die in the attempt, and who have the patience and skills to wait for years before launching their attack.

Almost all medieval societies were occasionally happy to see their enemies eliminated – the murder of military or political opponents was hardly new. But the Assassins, with far fewer military alternatives at their disposal, focused much more on it and took political murder to new levels of sophistication. This was not a strategy calculated to improve their popularity. As one contemporary Muslim historian unequivocally put it, the Assassins were 'rabble and scum, persons without intelligence'. He was clearly not a fan. And he was far from being alone in his view. The crusaders and the Turks – indeed all of Sunni Islam – disagreed on many things, but the Assassins were not one of them.[11] How did such a small group of highly religious individuals become so hated, so quickly and so universally?

It is possible to portray the Nizari Ismailis as a breakaway sect, certainly. But they can also be viewed as an eccentric, relatively minor community; as just another persecuted religious group in the medieval

Middle East (one among many); or as ordinary citizens – the elite devotees that made up their famous hit squads, the *fidais*, were, after all, just a tiny minority of the sect's population, most of whom were hard-working, law-abiding peasants, cotton workers or merchants.

All that is true. But there is a very different story, too. One which is partly based on the extraordinary cult that they used to further their ends. And one which is also the result of a compelling PR campaign – a campaign which they used to transform their activities, already remarkable, into something approaching legendary status. For the Assassins, legend meant leverage.

3

A Beginning and a Blueprint: Persia (1090–1100)

The origins of the Assassins are unlikely and obscure – something that is appropriate for any group with aspirations to, literally, cult status. With that obscurity, of course, often come preconceptions of ancient beginnings and of mysteries that have been lost in the mists of time. In fact, the Assassins were relatively newcomers, and barely pre-dated the crusader period in which they played such an intriguing part. And in the traditional way of religious sectarianism and revolutionary party politics, they were the product of a split from a faction that had already split.

Hasan and Persia: Birth of a new state

Ismailism is an offshoot of Shiism, which is in turn a branch of Islam that supported Ali, Muhammad's cousin and son-in-law, in his claim to be the religious and political leader of the Muslim community.[1]

The leaders of the sect can be regarded as belonging to one of two types. At the centre stood the imam – divinely inspired, infallible and the source of all authority and knowledge. He could be either a 'speaking' imam (one who was present and visible) or a 'silent' imam (who was believed to be hidden, particularly in times of secrecy or oppression). For much of the period we are discussing – that is, the twelfth and thirteenth centuries – the sect's imam was in the 'silent' category.²

The organisation and day-to-day leadership, however, particularly during periods when the Ismaili imams were silent or hidden, fell to the chief *da'i*, who was assumed to be the imam's immediate assistant and his conduit to the faithful.³ Thus, although the imam, or Mahdi, was seen as the rightful leader of the sect, below him the chief *da'i*, or 'Summoner', did the preaching and led the followers on the path to victory or martyrdom.⁴

In North Africa in 909, the 'hidden' imam felt the time was right to reveal himself. He proclaimed himself as caliph and al-Mahdi. His new state and the dynasty that went with it were known as the Fatimids, because of their descent from Fatima, the prophet's daughter.⁵

In 969, Fatimid troops conquered Egypt and built a new city, Cairo, as their capital. Their religious beliefs put them at odds with most of the other Islamic players in the region, such as the majority of the local Muslim Arabs and the later Turkic entrants from the steppes, who adhered to Sunni Islam.⁶

Egypt was at the heart of the new sect, but one of its most important leaders was born far away, in Persia. He was a man whose personal commitment to the cause was so profound, so severe and so implacable that he set the tone for the whole movement. This man was Hasan Sabbah, and he was to become the founder of the Nizari state in Persia.⁷

Hasan was born in the Persian town of Qom, in modern-day Iran, at some point in the 1050s. His family were mainstream Shiites, but – for reasons that are now obscure – he converted to Ismailism when he was aged seventeen. Hasan spent three years in Egypt learning more about his new religion and returned to Persia in 1081, eager to take on a leadership role.⁸

Hasan was no ordinary religious leader. He had qualities which allowed him to combine a life of learning with the practical skills required to run a military campaign and build a new state from scratch – even under the most difficult conditions. At the heart of this unique skillset (and at the heart of his new sect) was a ferocious commitment to the cause – a commitment that transcended family or friends or the usual ties, comforts and weaknesses that mark out most of our lives.[9]

The Persia that Hasan was born into was dominated by an alien elite – Turkic by ethnicity and Sunni Muslim by religion. This allowed him to effortlessly combine the role of nationalist warrior with that of charismatic religious leader. He started to gather followers around him. Soon his community was in revolt against what he saw as a foreign occupying force.

The turning point in Hasan's struggle came in 1087, when he happened upon an exceptional mountain castle named Alamut. Hasan decided (however implausible that must have seemed at the time) to make it the capital of his nascent state. Alamut was certainly a tempting prospect: it was imposing and easy to defend, perched on a mountain ridge almost 2,000 metres above sea level. But it also had sustainability, as it dominated a fertile valley, some 50 kilometres long, which stretched out below. This was, he realised, a miniature kingdom, and a base from which the Ismailis in Persia could grow.[10]

His plan to capture it was, as always with the sect, a long game and a ferociously far-sighted one. Hasan first prepared the ground by sending out teams of missionaries to convert the local peasants around Alamut. Hasan himself played an integral part in the plan, and in September 1090 he entered the castle disguised as a teacher. More of his missionaries were infiltrated into the castle. Men of the garrison began to convert to his new sect. Eventually the time came to take control. The lord of Alamut was offered the chance to join and become part of the community. He refused but, with his garrison suborned and confronted as he was by Hasan and his secret converts, he surrendered. The Assassins' first castle was handed over with a surprising lack of bloodshed.[11]

Hasan the charismatic preacher slipped seamlessly into his new role as military planner and state-builder. The walls of the castle were strengthened. Water storage was improved. Irrigation in the surrounding neighbourhoods was made more efficient. Everything was geared to the need for survivability in a siege. Hasan and his sect were here to stay.[12]

In the Daylami language, 'Alamut' meant 'the eagle's teaching'.[13] Hasan was already a brilliant strategist before he acquired the castle. But the eagle certainly taught him what elements his plan for state-building should contain: strong castles in remote mountain fastnesses; villages of converts to sustain the garrisons and missionaries; the application of power by stealth, rather than by brute force; and, above all, devoted followers who valued the needs of the sect above their own lives or the lives of their families.[14]

Hasan now had his blueprint. He used Alamut as a base from which to branch out still further. He and his followers captured or built many more fortresses in Rudbar and in nearby areas in Daylam. Against all the odds, he succeeding in creating what was, in effect, an Ismaili state in Iran – and one which was to become an independent splinter group from its roots in Fatimid Egypt.

His grasp of strategy was intuitive, but profound. Hasan realised that as followers of a minority belief system in an intolerant world, their best chance of survival lay in creating their own political structures and defences. And, although he never ousted the Turks from Persia, he succeeded in creating an Ismaili state, with a vast network of interconnected castles and villages, joined together in a religious and cultural struggle against their foreign overlords. Large parts of northern Persia joined his new Ismaili domains and declared independence from their Seljuk Turk overlords.[15]

Hasan was certainly a demanding companion by modern standards. He spent thirty-four years in his new headquarters at Alamut. And in all that time, he never left the castle, and indeed only left his living quarters twice – both times, as a treat, going up to visit the roof-top.[16] This ascetic lifestyle extended even to his family: his wife and daughters were sent away to earn a living by spinning. He wanted to prevent them becoming a distraction. And in this, he succeeded all too well – they never saw him again.

His two sons were treated even more harshly. One made the mistake of drinking wine and was killed for the offence. The other was executed for alleged involvement in a murder plot. He was innocent, but by the time the actual facts had been established it was too late – he was already dead. For Hasan, though, there was no regret. He proudly drew attention to his decision to kill his sons, and used it as the ultimate proof of his determination: the severity of his new sect was plain for all to see.[17]

This was an astonishing, almost terrifying, strength of will. But the disregard for the normal boundaries of family affection or the sanctity of life allowed Hasan, against all the odds, to build and administer a state – and to establish the sect's unique code of behaviour and operating principles. Even in its earliest days, the Assassins' new state was defined by blood and a ruthless fanaticism.

The strategy of the underdog

Like all good strategies, the plan was simple, but profound. It had the four 'Cs' – castles, conversion, carnage and chaos. With a remote network of mountain *castles* in your possession, you had safety and a place to regroup. From the security of those bases it was possible to launch *conversion* programmes, building up a greater base of followers who could provide economic support to the group. Using the targeted *carnage* of political assassination, you could sow fear and exert leverage far beyond the normal scope of your more obvious military assets. And selectively killing your opponents' leaders created *chaos*, leaving them continually off balance. This was a masterly strategy for an underdog.

The acquisition of remote but powerful castles, in areas that offered security and self-sufficiency, was an obvious centrepiece of the strategy. Using Alamut and the fertile Alamut valley as their model, Hasan and his successors expanded their reach in Persia. Missionary groups were sent to likely areas with a brief to target potential converts and attractive castles.[18]

A BEGINNING AND A BLUEPRINT: PERSIA

Ultimately, the way in which these castles were taken was irrelevant – achieving the objective was the only important thing. As one (admittedly very jaundiced) Sunni chronicler wrote:

> Hasan exerted every effort to capture the places adjacent to Alamut or that vicinity. Where possible he won them over by the tricks of his propaganda, while such places as were unaffected by his blandishments he seized with slaughter, ravishment, pillage, bloodshed, and war. He took such castles as he could and wherever he found a suitable rock he built a castle upon it.[19]

Hasan's plan was ruthless – and extremely successful.

As with all effective resistance movements, each base had its own semi-independent authority and a high degree of autonomy. But thanks to Hasan's force of will and the willingness of local commanders to accept orders from Alamut, the cohesion of the whole remained intact – the Assassins retained their unified sense of purpose and direction.[20]

Targeted murders were, in the absence of large armies, also vital. But they had an obvious downside – they were unlikely to foster affection. Assassination attempts, regardless of success or failure, generally triggered a massacre of anyone thought to be associated with the killers. For those who had suffered the attack, this was a blunt instrument of retribution, but one that brought instant gratification, regardless of justice or accuracy. Depending on location, the massacres could include Shiites in general, Ismailis in particular, or anybody who stood out as a foreigner.[21]

But the Ismailis were used to unpopularity and had been on the wrong side of massacres for some time. Sectarian rumours about Ismailis murdering travellers had led to the entire community in Isfahan being burnt alive in the town square in 1093. Other vicious massacres took place in Persia in 1101 and 1104. Ismailis, and particularly the Nizari Ismailis, were often disliked, and using murder as a political tool did not improve their reputation. But for Hasan, a man who had executed his own sons, the collateral damage was acceptable.[22]

This was brutal logic, but it was not entirely wrong. The overwhelming military strength of the Seljuk Turks, and their ferocious steppe cavalry, meant that they were unbeatable in circumstances of their own choosing. Subterfuge and targeted murders were the only ways in which the Assassins could project political power against their foreign overlords. There was little alternative if they were to deal with an enemy that possessed a vastly superior war machine.[23]

The first recorded attack took place in the late eleventh century, perhaps even before the capture of Alamut. A group of Ismailis went on missionary work in Isfahan. They tried a little too hard, however. As the hostile Arab chronicler Ibn al-Athir later wrote, 'they preached their message to a muezzin, a man from Saveh, who was living in Isfahan but he did not respond to their call. Fearing that he might report them, they killed him. He was their first victim. Suspicion [of involvement] fell on a carpenter, called Tahir.' Guilty or not, Tahir's punishment was harsh and public, as a visible way of deterring further missionary activity in the area. He was 'killed as a warning to the public and dragged by a leg through the markets. He was their first "martyr".'[24]

Planned political assassinations came soon after. Their initial target was suitably ambitious – the Seljuk commander in Persia, Vizier Nizam al-Mulk (1018–92). Hasan asked for volunteers to carry out the hit, and the challenge was accepted by a follower named Bu Tahir Arrani. A few days later, dressed as a Sufi (a form of Muslim mystic), the Assassin walked up to the vizier. The elderly Seljuk leader was being carried towards his harem in a litter. But his attacker dodged the guards, lunged towards him and slew him with a dagger. The 'spectacular' nature of the murder was fully recognised at the time. Hasan was reputed to have gloated that 'the killing of this devil is the beginning of bliss'.[25]

The effect of the murder on the Assassins' popularity among the local Sunni communities was predictable. As one contemporary charmingly put it, 'to shed the blood of [an Ismaili] heretic is more meritorious than to kill seventy Greek infidels [that is, Christians]'. The Assassins' age of bloodshed had started in earnest.[26]

But Hasan was never interested in winning popularity contests. By the end of his time as leader, the Assassins had achieved a position in Persia that was far more secure than they could ever have imagined. They had castles and mountain ranges of their own, supported by prosperous villages and converts. They had taken the fight against the Seljuk Turks to a new level and had empowered many provinces to rebel against their overlords. They had followers in the countryside, but also on occasion felt comfortable enough to act openly in major cities, such as Isfahan.

But then, just as things were going so well, factionalism kicked in.

From Ismailis to Nizaris

The Fatimid empire may have been founded in religious inspiration, but power gradually devolved, in the predictable and mundane fashion of everyday politics, to a secular figure. This man, usually a general, governed with the title of vizier.[27]

And, as if the splits from Sunni Islam and mainstream Shiism were not disruptive enough, in 1094 the Ismailis in Egypt split once more. The Fatimid caliph at the time, Imam al-Mustansir bi'llah, died, leaving his eldest son, Abu Mansur Nizar, as his heir. The vizier, who was responsible for most of the day-to-day administration for the regime, had a better idea, however. He launched a palace coup and took power for himself, ruling in the name of one of Nizar's more malleable younger brothers.[28]

Nizar and his men were understandably unimpressed by the new arrangements and civil war broke out. The following year, he and his army were defeated in battle by the vizier's forces. Nizar, still seen as the legitimate caliph by his supporters, was taken back to Cairo. There, in order to bring final closure to the uprising, he was executed.

That should have been an end to the matter. But his execution was a beginning, rather than an ending. In a manner which presaged their later steely determination, the new 'Nizari' supporters chose to regroup, rather than to disband. Unwelcome in Fatimid Egypt or Sunni-controlled Syria, they made their way to Hasan and his followers in north-west Iran.[29]

This left Hasan with a major problem. Which side should he and his people support in the civil war and religious schism? Typically, he made the radical choice. Rather than take orders from Cairo, he would do his own thing. Alamut was being developed into an informal principality, and the war against the Seljuks was proceeding well. Hasan and his followers in Persia decided to support the Nizari branch of Ismailism. They severed relations with Egypt.[30]

This was a turning point for the sect. The strains of geography and the lack of Fatimid political influence in Persia would inevitably have loosened ties with Egypt over time – but the schism made the split formal and final. The vizier al-Afdal's brutal personal ambitions had alienated most of the Ismaili communities outside Egypt. Hasan had already started to take a semi-independent path, but the Nizari imams of Persia were now officially in control of their own sect. The process of state-building had been driven by nationalism and was given a major boost by the acquisition of Alamut – but it now had a new religious imperative as well.[31]

Hasan continued in his position as leader of the Assassins until his death – he passed away at the age of about seventy in June 1124. His mausoleum in Rudbar became a major Nizari shrine and pilgrimage site until it was destroyed by the Mongol armies in 1266.[32]

Hasan never claimed to be the imam. The imam remained mysterious and hidden, so Hasan was merely his representative. But in practice Hasan was in charge.[33] Under his extraordinary leadership, the Assassins, a tiny, unpopular group that many considered heretical, waged a nationalistic, religious and revolutionary war against the Seljuk Turks in Persia. And they had established their own sect, free from the constraints of control from Egypt. But Hasan had also left a blueprint for his successors – a strategic plan that was designed to help them survive and grow in an increasingly hostile world.[34]

The time was right for them to branch out – to Syria.

4

Assassins and Syria: In Search of a Home (1100–1113)

They were lucky – probably far more than they realised. The westerners of the First Crusade and the Assassins arrived in Syria at a propitious time. The eruption of nomadic tribes into the region had shattered the status quo and changed everything.

In the middle of the eleventh century, a confederation of Turkic warbands appeared, led by the Seljuk family (newly converted to Sunni Islam). They had left their tribal steppe-lands north of the Caspian and Aral seas and moved to areas offering greater opportunities. First taking Persia, by 1055 they had taken Baghdad. Their leader adopted the suitably intimidating title of *sultan* ('power'). The settled lands of Christian (Byzantine) Anatolia, to the west of this new 'Seljuk empire', inevitably proved attractive, and in the course of the 1060s groups of nomadic warriors began to push into the heartlands of what we now know as Turkey, raiding and destabilising the local communities. The Byzantine authorities were on the defensive and struggled to keep the nomadic invaders at bay.[1]

Once they were established in Anatolia, other areas to the south, such as Syria and Palestine, became increasingly appealing targets. Small Turkic groups had been infiltrating into the area for several years, but in 1064 ʿAtiyya, the lord of Aleppo, made the catastrophic mistake of calling in large numbers of Turkic mercenaries to help him with the traditional problem of dynastic in-fighting. Predictably, the nomads soon turned on their employer, and other tribal bands started to come into the region, looking opportunistically for plunder.

Turkic incursions continued to ramp up. In January 1071, the Seljuk Sultan Alp Arslan led the first major expedition, taking an army across the Euphrates and heading south through Syria and on towards Egypt. Muslim historians knew the significance of this step. The 'reign of the Arabs', they wrote, had ended; the 'reign of the Turks' had begun.[2]

By the 1080s, nomadic warlords had taken over most of the Syrian city states and much of Palestine. But although it may not have always seemed so to those on the receiving end of their attentions, the west of the Seljuk empire was a fragile construct. To use a commercial analogy, it was more akin to a loose affiliation of family-run businesses than an efficiently functioning corporation. And this fragility provided opportunity.

False hope and descent into chaos

Within a few months this volatile mixture had exploded. Between 1092 and 1094, entirely coincidentally, something shocking and profoundly disruptive took place: almost all the major political leaders in the region died. The casualties included the vizier and the caliph-imam of Fatimid Egypt in the south; Malik Shah, the Seljuk sultan in the north; and almost everyone else in between. Absolute mayhem ensued. The western Seljuk empire imploded. Malik Shah's four sons and Tutush, his brother, all competed to grab as much land and power as they could. Just as the crusading movement and the Nizari presence in Syria were about to be launched, chance intervened to ensure that circumstances in this turbulent environment changed dramatically to benefit both the crusaders and the Nizaris.

Tutush became recognised as the pre-eminent Turkic ruler in Syria and his two sons were given the most important cities to govern –

ASSASSINS AND SYRIA: IN SEARCH OF A HOME

Ridwan was put in charge of Aleppo in the north, while Duqaq was given Damascus in the south: rival sons in charge of rival domains. Mirroring this divide, other parts of Syria were split into smaller and smaller entities, each run by the strongest local Turkic family.[3]

To cap it all, the arrival of the crusaders in 1097 in the midst of this already heady free-for-all ratcheted the chaos up still further. What became known as the First Crusade had originally been launched to help the Byzantines defend local Christian communities from the Turkic invasions. By the time the armed pilgrims from Europe arrived, however, the political landscape had changed beyond all recognition.

Helped by the unsettled conditions in the region, the crusade's success exceeded all reasonable expectations. After Jerusalem had been recovered and brought back into Christian hands, most of the original crusaders returned home, often traumatised, but glad to have survived their adventure. However, some remained to defend the Holy Land. They established four political entities, collectively known to modern historians as the 'crusader states': the Latin kingdom of Jerusalem in the south (geographically similar to what we call Israel); the county of Tripoli (largely modern-day Lebanon); the principality of Antioch (in what we call Syria and southern Turkey); and the county of Edessa, further inland.[4]

So, at the start of the twelfth century the entire region was disastrously fragmented. For the Assassins, Syria had become a region full of opportunity.

Faltering steps: Misapplying the Persian formula

There was already an Ismaili community in Syria at the end of the twelfth century, with a strong presence in the mountain ranges of the Jabal as-Summaq and Jabal Bahra. It is not entirely clear, however, where they stood with regard to the schism with Egypt. They were seemingly divided: some favoured Nizari Ismailism; others (probably the majority) took the more orthodox stance of continuing to support the Fatimid regime in Egypt. It was not until the 1120s that the Nizari branch of Ismailism became the fully dominant part of the sect in Syria.[5]

Hasan did everything he could to speed the process along. He sent emissaries to the Ismaili communities in Syria, ostensibly to advise on organisational issues, but also to influence and ensure that they took the Nizari path. Even more ambitiously, he wanted to take the fight to the enemy, creating bases from which to strike at other parts of the Seljuk empire.

The political fragmentation in the region was an obvious opportunity, but there were other reasons to hope for success, too. Geography was one. There were lots of mountains, deserts and inaccessible valleys in the area. Ethnic and religious diversity was a natural corollary of such a disjointed landscape. As well as scattered Christian and Sunni Muslim populations, there were many local pockets of Shiism. Syria had been under the control of the Fatimids for several periods in the preceding century, and they had inevitably helped foster large Shiite populations – some who were orthodox and some who were decidedly less so.

Alongside the existing Ismaili community in Syria, other dissident groups provided Nizari missionaries with grounds for optimism. The Druze of Mount Lebanon, for instance, were a group with roots in Fatimid Ismailism, and offered some possibilities. The Nusayris, or Alawis, in the area around Latakia, were another dissident sect that might be brought into the fold. There were rich pickings to be had in terms of potential converts, alongside enticing opportunities to establish mountain fortresses from which the Assassins could operate.[6]

So it is not surprising that by the early years of the twelfth century, coincidentally around the time the crusaders arrived from Europe, the Assassins began to shift their focus towards Syria. Leaders and missionaries were sent from their headquarters in Alamut to win new converts, galvanise the local population and set up local bases. As in Persia, the disunity and occasional unpopularity of the Seljuk Turk overlords created opportunities which the Assassins were quick to exploit.[7]

ASSASSINS AND SYRIA: IN SEARCH OF A HOME

The Nizari missionaries were – perhaps surprisingly – successful, and that was due in large part to what the sect had to offer potential converts. They had an attractive set of ideas to promote, appealing to both the emotional and the rational needs of people who often felt marginalised. To the pious, they offered respect for the Quran and adherence to the way of life it promoted. To the more intellectual recruits, they offered philosophy, often derived from neo-Platonic thinking. To those who were more spiritually inclined, they offered an emotionally satisfying faith founded on self-sacrifice. Above all, for those who were disgruntled and on the margins of Sunni society, they offered a focus with which to resolve their grievances – the Nizaris were a religious and political opposition movement into which they would be welcomed and find redress.[8]

They offered hope and confidence to the Syrian Shiite communities, who had been increasingly cut off from their absentee and ineffectual Fatimid government in Egypt. There were still some old loyalties to Cairo, but the Nizari war cry of religion and struggle against the foreign invaders had enormous resonance for many people – and it is this that helps explain how the Assassins were able to insinuate themselves into the region so effectively during the chaotic first decade of the twelfth century.[9]

Nizari missionaries embedded themselves quickly, propelled as much by the disunity and weakness of their enemies as by any inherent strengths. But coming from Persia, where the fundamentals of their new state were far stronger, they arrived with a false sense of capability. The similarities between the Nizaris' position in Persia and that of the sect in Syria were obvious: in both areas they needed to establish influence and security in order to survive. And the means by which to do so centred on the acquisition of mountain fortresses and local converts.

The differences were less obvious, but arguably even more profound, however. The fundamental disconnect was that the fight against the Seljuk Turks in Persia was a popular religious and nationalistic rebellion against hated foreign overlords – the Nizaris in Persia were a fledgling state at war, but they enjoyed popular support. But the situation in

Syria was far more complicated and opportunistic. It was also less well grounded in the support of the general population. There the Assassins were a sect struggling for survival, rather than a popular uprising. Most Nizari missionaries were Persian, so they were no less foreign than the Turks or the crusaders. This had profound implications for the way in which they operated in Syria, and made the process of establishing a Nizari state in the region much slower and more difficult.[10]

The strategy of seizing remote mountain fortresses and using them as bases for expansion had worked well in Persia – but, unfortunately for the Assassins, it proved more difficult to achieve in the highly militarised and crowded context of twelfth-century Syria. They were instead forced to explore an alternative political plan: urban infiltration. This involved making high-level converts and exerting political influence among existing (ostensibly Sunni Muslim) political structures and leaders – in effect, trying to operate as a 'state within a state'. The sect began to establish networks of followers in major cities like Aleppo and Damascus, ingratiating themselves with the local Turkic leadership and lobbying for a share of power.

There was a massive problem with this policy, however: the fundamental vulnerability of the small- or medium-sized family-run city states was that they were based around strong individuals, rather than strong institutions. The upside of this (from a Nizari perspective) was that these states were vulnerable – either to the threat of assassination or to having their leaders suborned. The downside was just as clear, however – when a compliant Sunni host died, he was often replaced by someone far less sympathetic. Without the demographic grounding of a large Nizari population, violent pogroms quickly followed. A dangerous 'riches-to-rags' rhythm was built into this precarious strategy.

Semper fidais: The Assassin elite

Perhaps because of the greater challenges they faced, it was in Syria that the Assassins perfected and professionalised their famous squads of elite killers – the *fidais*. The Assassins were enemies to be feared, and the best of their operatives were dedicated and highly skilled – the list of their victims reads like a *Who's Who* of the medieval Middle East. They were described either as fanatical and brainwashed (by their enemies) or as dedicated and skilful (by their admirers) – and, depending on your perspective, both simplistic characterisations were at least partly true. The Nizari *fidais*, or hand-picked elite, were extraordinarily focused and effective. They were the ninjas of the twelfth century and the special forces of their own tiny, but dangerous cult.

Then, as now, there were many lurid descriptions of the Assassins as drugged-up, deluded fanatics, twisted men who were eager to die for a twisted cause. But this was all part of the illusion, an essential element in the 'unstoppable death promise' that lay at the heart of the Assassin brand.

They were at the forefront of the Nizari Ismailis' high-profile assassinations in Syria, and they have scorched a trail through legend and history: if you see an 'Assassin' in a video game or movie, you are probably, more strictly speaking, looking at an artist's impression of a Nizari *fidais*. Inevitably, like all truly elite groups, they were only ever available in very small numbers. But given the focused nature of Nizari 'foreign policy', this was usually enough.[11]

They were trained to carry out dangerous missions on behalf of their leaders, often with only a slim chance of survival. Most of their attacks were on high-profile individuals and took place in very public spaces. Every member of a *fidais* team had to be courageous and committed to the cause.[12]

Dangerous or not, death lay at the heart of what the Assassins had to offer. In a rare display of humour, Sinan, the Old Man of the Mountain in the 1170s, responded to a threat from one of his many Sunni enemies, a general commanding vast armies, with the retort: 'Do you threaten a duck with the river?'[13] In this joke he encapsulated the core of the Assassins' power and the menace of their *fidais* volunteers. Their enemies were afraid of death and they could not stop the Assassins from bringing it to them when they least expected it. That was the Nizaris' power. But the Nizaris themselves were impervious to reciprocal threats. Their devotees were men who placed the needs of the sect above their own lives, and those of their families. If death was a river, the *fidais* were all too happy to swim in it.

Whether or not the *fidais* formed an official corps of 'elite operatives' from the beginning is not entirely clear. It is likely that arrangements were more informal in the early years, becoming more structured as time progressed. Some operated as medium-term 'sleepers' in the households of their enemies, learning their religious and cultural mores as they insinuated themselves into places of trust and influence. Even here, however, it is not certain that they had specialist training for their roles, such as foreign languages or weapons skills (though common sense would suggest these as obvious areas of attention in the run-up to a mission).[14]

The first attacks, such as that on the muezzin of Isfahan, do not seem to have been the result of a planned *fidais* hit, and what later became an elite core of killers probably did not formally exist at this stage in the sect's history. Perhaps in the early days, all committed followers might be called upon to carry out such dangerous tasks. Only later did death become a specialised art.[15]

Regardless of any moral judgements we might make, the *fidais* were not mindless fanatics. There was certainly a high level of personal motivation and, given the extreme dangers involved, this is not surprising – they believed that the act of murder on behalf of their sect was a pious, cleansing and holy act. But there is little evidence that they were promised an afterlife with ethereal virgins or any other pseudo-spiritual inducements. These accusations were probably later insults, invented by their many enemies and aimed at discrediting the nature of their commitment to the cause.[16]

Similarly, wild rumours circulated about the nature of the training the *fidais* undertook, most of which are likely to be untrue. It is unlikely, for instance, that *fidais* were given drugs (such as the almost eponymous 'hashish') to numb their senses before they carried out a hit. On the contrary, their missions were so difficult and so elaborate that being under the influence of narcotics would have created far more problems than it solved. A skilled Assassin needed to have his wits about him.[17]

The truth was more prosaic. The *fidais* were an elite force and existed only in very small numbers. They did not want to die unless it was absolutely necessary. Far from being drugged and anaesthetised, they needed to be sharp and aware when they went on their missions. And when an attack was under way, participants were prepared for death, rather than eager for it. Even the most passionate members of the sect looked for exit routes as they made their elaborate plans for murder. But regardless of whether they died or not, death was a possibility that they accepted. Assassin squads were prepared to give up their lives in the pursuit of their prey – and it was this relentless focus that made them such formidable foes.

Survival rates among the *fidais* when on active service were inevitably low. This was reflected in the honour which they were accorded within their communities. In much the same way as European villages contain poignant monuments recording the names of the glorious fallen, so too did Assassin castles – we know that they kept rolls of honour commemorating individual members of *fidais* teams and the missions that they had been sent on, and their memory was preserved in the chronicles of Alamut. They, too, shall not grow old . . .[18]

Not all Nizari fighters were *fidais*, however. Despite a strong preference for working in the shadows, the sect also required larger bodies of men. Castle networks needed garrisons. Supplies and envoys needed escorts. And they occasionally needed to conduct larger military operations.

The acts of individual Assassins were sufficient for the purposes of intimidation and to inculcate a climate of fear. But that was never going to be enough to establish the sect in prime defensive locations – and particularly not in the Syrian mountaintop castles to which they most aspired. To capture these, much larger groups of fighters were sometimes required. In these circumstances, they would call on other Nizari followers to fight – the militia would be summoned to temporarily boost their military capabilities, albeit at the cost of dramatically reducing the overall calibre of their fighting men.

The Assassins' efforts to take part in more conventional fighting were inevitably far less impressive than the lightning strikes of their murder squads. In 1100, for instance, a small army of Assassins ('three hundred of their leaders and champions') set out to attack a Turkic emir, Jawuli of Mosul. The attack went catastrophically wrong, however. A bloodbath ensued when battle was joined and 'only three individuals escaped. They climbed a hill and fled. Jawuli took their horses, weapons and such like as booty.' Interestingly, and in an ironic reversal of the usual tactics, this early defeat seems to have resulted from the presence of traitors in the midst of the Assassin army – we are told that the followers of Jawuli 'sought out the [Nizaris], pretending to be with them and of their views. They remained with them until they were trusted.' Then, when the fighting started, and the Nizaris were fully committed, 'Jawuli's men in their ranks turned against them and put them to the sword.'[19]

It was risky to extend the reach of the *fidais* by getting them to take militia volunteers under their wing and undertake more conventional military actions. It might work in Persia, where the population was largely on their side and the war against the Turks had the characteristics of a popular uprising; but it was far more difficult to do in Syria.

It was the *fidais*, small in number but high in impact, who were the stars of the sect – and it is they who remain the iconic figures at the heart of the Assassin legends.

Aleppo and Ridwan: Creating a base

The rich, vibrant cities of the region were tempting. They had money and markets, power and people. Here, the Assassins' leaders must have thought, lay real possibilities for long-term religious and political stability. Aleppo was the clear target for the first Assassin leader in Syria – a man named al-Hakim, but better known, somewhat esoterically, as the 'doctor-astrologer'. Even in these early days, the Syrian Assassins had a knack for creating a suitably unusual reputational presence.

Geography was helpful – one of the many advantages of Aleppo as a base for the Assassins was that it was close to the Ismaili heartlands of the Jabal as-Summaq and the Jabal Bahra. Even more helpfully, although its Seljuk rulers may have been Sunni, much of the local population was Christian or Shiite by inclination – the former were generally uninterested in Muslim in-fighting, while the latter offered a clear path for conversion to the cause. The Sunnis might have held power, but they were perhaps a minority in the city they ruled.

Just as helpfully, Ridwan, the Seljuk ruler of Aleppo from 1095 to 1113, seems to have been a man without strong religious convictions. Instead, he took far more interest in the all-too-tangible world of Turkic in-fighting. Ridwan was ostensibly Sunni in his beliefs, but in practice was theologically flexible. He had shown favour to the Shiite beliefs of the Fatimids in the early years of his reign and, as the ruler of a large non-Sunni population, maintained a high degree of religious tolerance. He may even have been a Nizari convert himself. But if that was the case, he did not, for entirely understandable reasons, advertise the fact too openly.

Ridwan's religious affiliations, or lack thereof, may also have been carefully calculated. He was vying for position against a plethora of Seljuk competitors. And there were new Christian entrants, such as the crusaders, coming into the unforgivingly bloodthirsty world of regional power politics. He needed all the support he could get. Perhaps he saw the ferocious commitment of the Assassins as the basis for a military force that he could rely on. These were brutal times, and whatever feelings of spirituality Ridwan had, they almost certainly existed alongside a healthy dose of political expediency.[20]

The Nizaris were certainly charismatic and persuasive. One chronicler wrote that the 'doctor-astrologer' had 'persuaded Ridwan of the righteousness of the sect of the Assassins so that they were allowed to recruit in Aleppo and he declared himself to be their patron and protector ... Ridwan, deaf to all the messages on this subject from other princes, never abandoned the beliefs of this sect.' Prosaically, and indicating one of the ways in which the Assassins infiltrated Ridwan's administration, it was said that if you wanted to 'harm an enemy you could always resort to them'. Paid killers willing to work for the state were an attractive and enduring asset.[21]

Whatever Ridwan's private beliefs, the 'doctor-astrologer' was certainly a valued adviser and a very public member of his entourage. Nizari missionaries were allowed to preach openly in Aleppo and make as many converts as they could. Ridwan even helped them build a new mission complex to accommodate the sect's expanding following. The Assassins began to relax and, in the eyes of hostile Sunni commentators at least, to behave in a proprietorial and arrogant fashion.[22]

These were heady times. Everything seemed possible. The Assassins had set up a highly successful base of operations at Aleppo and they began to influence Ridwan's decisions in their own interests. It seemed that Aleppo was on the verge of becoming the capital of a new Nizari state in Syria. All that was needed now was an opportunity to show the Assassins' Turkic sponsor just how valuable their support could be. And that opportunity was not far away.

The hit on Janah al-Daula

One of the first well-documented missions carried out by the *fidais* in Syria was against a warlord named Janah al-Daula. Many modern books about the Assassins are written from a Eurocentric perspective: they focus on the high-profile attacks that were occasionally made on the crusaders and their leaders. The assassination attempts on the lives of Christian rulers need to be put into perspective, however: in reality, most Nizari attacks were aimed at their fellow Muslims.

This should come as no surprise. The regional Muslim players were far bigger and more important than the crusader states. And the level of animosity between them was greater. The Christians may not have been fond of the Assassins, but they were generally uninterested in Muslim theology. They did not, unlike the Sunnis, have a visceral hatred of the Nizaris as 'heretics'. Ridwan, the ruler of Aleppo, was one of the first to spot the advantages of having the Assassins in your debt and in your entourage. He soon started to deploy his deadly new weapon against his enemies.[23]

Janah al-Daula, the atabeg (or governor) of Homs, was one of his main opponents. He was nominally a vassal, but had proved in practice to be irritatingly independent. Not coincidentally, he was among the first to receive a visit from the *fidais*. The atabeg, habitually suspicious, took tight security precautions. One day, in May 1103, he left the citadel of Homs to go to the great mosque for Friday prayers. He was taking no chances and made sure that he was 'surrounded by his principal officers with full armour'.[24] It was a good effort – but not good enough. An Assassin hit squad, consisting of a team leader ('a sheikh') and three *fidais*, was waiting among the worshippers. When 'the sheikh gave the signal they attacked the amir with their knives and killed both him and a number of his officers'. The *fidais* team was captured and killed on the spot, but that was not the end of the matter. Anyone who was nearby and looked like a foreigner was in danger. According to the Damascene chronicler Ibn al-Qalanisi,

> There were in the mosque at the time ten Sufis, Persians and others; they were suspected of complicity in the crime, and were straightaway executed in cold blood, every man of them, although they were innocent.[25]

As a telling indication of the precarious position of the regime in Homs (and its relatively small numbers), the Turkic population fled upon hearing the news of Janah al-Daula's death and moved back to the safer environment of Damascus. Ridwan was absolutely correct in seeing the hit as an easy way of destabilising the entire government – to his immediate advantage.[26] He understood what it was to have the Assassins on your side.

False start for a mountain home

The Assassins' leader, the 'doctor-astrologer', did not long outlive Janah al-Daula – he died (seemingly peacefully) just a couple of weeks later. His successor, Abu Tahir al-Sa'igh, had a similarly exotic nickname – he liked to be known as the 'Persian goldsmith'. The 'goldsmith' built on his predecessor's success in killing Janah al-Daula and capitalised on the goodwill this had bought them with Ridwan. He used this to try to persuade Ridwan to let them take over several strategically important fortified towns in the mountains south of Aleppo. Ridwan, impressed by the loyalty and usefulness of the Assassins, acquiesced. He was perhaps influenced in this by the aggressive nature of his crusader competitors in the region. Foremost among these was Tancred, the ruler of Antioch, a masterful and restless Norman warrior with seemingly infinite ambitions, matched only by his boundless self-confidence.

Many of the main battlegrounds between the crusaders and the lords of Aleppo were to be found in the mountains of the Jabal as-Summaq. The area was vital to all the local players. It stretched from the Ruj valley to the south-east of Antioch (one of the most important approaches to the city) and included the vital fortified towns of Kafartab, Albara and Ma'arrat-al-Nu'man.[27]

Fighting around this area was fierce: all parties campaigned with unstinting aggression and opportunism. Everyone needed to contest the mountain range and, if they could not control it themselves, they at least wanted to give responsibility for its defence to allies who could form a buffer zone on their behalf. This was where Ridwan felt he could use the Assassins. They were fierce and dedicated fighters and they would, he believed, be prepared to operate as vassals on his behalf. When the Assassins captured towns in the region, many of which had large Shiite populations, they proclaimed their allegiance to Ridwan –

the Nizaris emphasised that they were operating at least with his acquiescence or, more likely, with his active approval. And, from their perspective, working with Ridwan gave them the opportunity to create their own embryonic state, ideally situated in a volatile frontier zone.[28]

Once again, it is misleading to be too Eurocentric when looking at these events. The crusaders were involved; but in pursuing this strategy, the Assassins do not seem to have been operating in a specifically anti-Frankish or 'jihadist' manner. Like Ridwan, they were primarily acting in their own interests – in this case, carving out a mountainous buffer state for themselves in between the crusaders and the Seljuk Turks.

The old Graeco-Roman town of Apamea was an important target for both Ridwan and the Nizaris. Its lord, Khalaf ibn Mulaʿib, was an Arab Shiite (and probably an Ismaili). Unluckily for him, he seems to have kept his religious allegiances tied to the Fatimid regime in Egypt, rather than transfer them to the Nizari sect in Persia. Khalaf had taken Apamea from Ridwan in 1096, and his enemies said, conveniently enough, that he had turned his new property into a base for banditry. Now, in the form of the Assassins, the lord of Aleppo thought he had found a way to recover it.[29]

Early in 1106, the 'goldsmith' made plans to take the town. He extracted a team of local Nizari volunteers from Apamea and took them to Aleppo, where they were trained and equipped for their task. With the sect's typical sense of drama, particular attention was paid to creating an elaborate backstory – something that would allow them to ingratiate themselves with the regime in Apamea.

The plan was simple, but very effective – 'six of [the Nizaris], after having obtained a horse, a mule, some Frankish gear, a shield and a mail hauberk, went out from the region of Aleppo to Apamea with all that gear and those animals'. The team introduced themselves to the garrison commander in the citadel. They had killed a Frank, they claimed, and were giving him the knight's possessions.[30]

In a scenario which the Assassins played out many times over the next two centuries, the *fidais* claimed to want to fight for their target.

The team leader approached Khalaf and said, 'we came intending to enter your service . . . And so [he] treated them with hospitality and bade them stay.' The ploy succeeded. People believe what they want to believe.[31]

The team was given rooms in the citadel that were next to the city walls. Its members started to dig a hole in the wall. Their co-religionists in the town, led by a local judge named Abu'l-Fath, started to dig their way in from the other side, and broke through on 1 February 1106. The Assassins entered the citadel in force and began to effect regime change in the most primal way – hunting down the emir and his men.[32]

Khalaf did not die easily. As the hit squad approached him, 'he faced them boldly, but one of them dashed at him and drove a dagger into his belly. He then threw himself into the tower, trying to reach one of the harem apartments, but another of them delivered a second blow.' He was dead within minutes.[33] The rest of the garrison carried on fighting for a while, but they were demoralised by the loss of their leader. Khalaf's sons and their troops counter-attacked, but the Assassins 'seized the place from them and killed a number'. With the emir dead and the town in Nizari hands, Apamea became their first significant and semi-independent base in Syria.[34] The Assassins' success was short lived in the extreme, however.

Tancred, the Frankish regent of the neighbouring state of Antioch, knew an opportunity when he saw one. Apamea was clearly in a state of turmoil. He and his small army immediately set off for the town to see what he could extract from the fluid situation. Tancred had powerful leverage. Carried in chains in his army's baggage train he also had a brother of Abu'l-Fath, the local Nizari leader. When they got to Apamea, Tancred used his hostage to extract 'a fixed tribute, and having received payment of this sum withdrew'.[35]

But the money was just a taster. Having reconnoitred the town's defences and enjoyed a sample of its treasury in February, Tancred soon came back to bring it entirely under his control. He had inside help in doing so. Sometime earlier, one of the governor's sons had

ASSASSINS AND SYRIA: IN SEARCH OF A HOME

escaped from Apamea and fled to Shaizar. Once there, he had been arrested and held in custody, presumably while the ruling Munqidh family worked out which way the wind was blowing. Eventually he was released and tried to get Frankish military aid in an attempt to recover his old lands.

Now, a few months later, with the help of his new Turkic friend and an accompanying veneer of legitimacy, Tancred and his army surrounded Apamea once more. The Assassins, always few in number, were unable to withstand a conventional siege. The town surrendered to him on 14 September 1106. Abu'l-Fath seems to have offended the irascible Tancred in some way, and he was tortured to death. The rest of the Nizari population, including Abu Tahir, the 'goldsmith', ransomed themselves and fled, disappointed, back to Aleppo.[36]

Apamea was lost, but the battle for control of the Jabal as-Summaq continued. The strategically important town and citadel of Kafartab was another vital possession of the Assassins in the region. As always in this chaotic area, its recent history had been one of extreme shifts. The crusaders seem to have captured it in January 1099, soon after their arrival in the Middle East, but lost it shortly afterwards. They recaptured it after defeating Ridwan at the battle of Kella in the summer of 1100, but it was soon back in Muslim hands once more. After the disastrous battle of Harran in 1104, it seems to have been given to the Assassins by Ridwan as part of his efforts to shore up the region against encroachment by the Franks.[37]

It was the same story as with Apamea, however. The Assassins were strong enough to take over the town – but not strong enough to hold it. Aggressive as ever, Tancred marched in and took it in 1110.[38] Sarmin, the base of the unfortunate judge Abu'l-Fath and (like Kafartab and Apamea) a town with a significant Ismaili population, was likewise recaptured soon afterwards. By 1111, it was back in Frankish hands, and held by someone with the suitably French name of 'lord Bonable'.[39] The short-lived dream of a Nizari principality in the Jabal as-Summaq was dead.

The death of Mawdud (1113)

Despite these setbacks, Ridwan continued to use the Assassins to further his own ambitions. They were reliable troops – or, at the very least, were more dependent on him than the rest of the population of Aleppo. Importantly, they provided him with military muscle, as well as access to their assassination teams.

Mawdud, the ruler of Mosul (1108–13), was high on the ever-shifting list of Turkic rivals that Ridwan wanted to see dead. Annoyingly from his perspective, Mawdud was an inspiring and effective general. He had been commissioned by the caliph of Baghdad to unite the local Turkic-run states in Syria, and to wage Holy War against the crusaders. Mawdud had proved embarrassingly good at one part of his job – attacking the Franks. But he found that getting the local Muslim warlords to act under his command was like herding cats. Both Ridwan of Aleppo and Tughtigin, the ruler of Damascus (r. 1104–28), were less than enthusiastic about giving up their freedom. They didn't much like the Franks, but they liked being forced to 'unite' by outsiders even less.[40]

Ridwan had used his Nizari auxiliaries against Mawdud and his irritatingly effective troops in the past. When an expedition was launched by Baghdad in 1111 to try to enforce Muslim unity against the crusaders, he had refused to take part. Instead, he had used the Nizaris to shore up his position. When his unwelcome Turkic 'allies' arrived, 'they had expected that either . . . [Ridwan], lord of Aleppo, would himself come out to join them, or else his officers would join them by his command'.[41] But Ridwan had other ideas. He 'shut the gates of Aleppo, took hostages from the townsmen into the citadel' – an interesting indicator of his popularity among his own subjects – 'and organized his troops, with the armed bands of the [Nizaris] and the loyal citizens, for garrison duty to guard the city wall and prevent the citizens from ascending it'. He also set loose his men to 'seize whomsoever they could from the fringes of the army', in order to encourage Mawdud to move on as quickly as possible. This was hardly the spirit of jihad that Baghdad had hoped for.[42]

Like Ridwan, Tughtigin of Damascus was a long-standing supporter of the Assassins, and for much the same reasons. He, too, may have had some religious sympathies for their cause; but more cynically (and probably more realistically), he helped them because he knew he could rely on them to do his dirty work. So, however attractive the prospect of Muslim unity might have looked from the elevated perspective of Baghdad, the Assassins and their local patrons all had good reason to prevent the creation of a centralised and orthodox Sunni Muslim state in Syria. Mawdud would have to go. And the *fidais* were the men who could make that happen.

On 2 October 1113, fresh from more victories against the Franks, Mawdud was a feted guest of Tughtigin in Damascus. Security was tight. As he left the Great Mosque, he was surrounded by the best bodyguards that money could buy – his security team on the day were described as 'Daylamites, Turks, Khurasanis, men-at-arms and armour-bearers, with weapons of all kinds, fine-tempered blades and keen thrusting swords, rapiers of various sorts and unsheathed daggers'. The procession was so tightly surrounded that it was as if they were walking 'in the midst of a tangled thicket of intertwined spikes'. Maximum measures for his protection were in place.[43]

However, no amount of protection could guarantee your safety if the Assassins were determined to get to you. When Mawdud and his men 'entered the court of the mosque', wrote Ibn al-Qalanisi, 'a man leapt out from among the crowd . . . approaching the emir Mawdud as though to call down a blessing upon him'. But there were no blessings. Instead, he 'seized the belt of his riding cloak with a swift motion and struck him twice with his dagger below the navel'. The thrust, calculated to ensure that the knife entered Mawdud's body under his armoured shirt, was all too effective.[44]

The murderer did not survive the attack. Given the need to keep the identity of the man who commissioned the act secret, perhaps that was always the plan. Anyway, 'as the Assassin struck his second blow swords fell upon him from every side and he was struck with every kind of weapon'. The frustration of Mawdud's guards was taken out on the corpse. Belatedly, the head of the Assassin was cut off and paraded round for identification purposes – but no one recognised him. What remained of his body was burnt.[45]

Tughtigin was close to Mawdud during the attack, but remained suspiciously unharmed – they were said to be 'hand in hand' when the Assassin struck. Tughtigin just carried on walking ahead. In a surreal but strangely plausible moment that spoke of the shock of the incident, the wounded Mawdud tried to act as if nothing had happened. Instead, he just struggled to keep up with his all-too-nonchalant host. Despite his wounds 'Mawdud, controlling himself, walked on until he was close to the north gate of the mosque. There he collapsed.' Ibn al-Qalanisi, as a Damascene chronicler writing about the ruler of Damascus, claimed – highly dubiously – that Tughtigin was very upset by his death. Few others were so sure.[46]

The Franks took a keen interest in the affair, as they had been increasingly worried by Mawdud's military successes. Writing later in the century, the historian William of Tyre claimed that the attack 'was not done without the knowledge and consent of [Tughtigin]. For rumour declared that [Tughtigin] distrusted the power of that leader and feared that he might deprive him of the kingdom.'[47]

The contemporary chroniclers Fulcher of Chartres (a well-informed companion to the king of Jerusalem) and Albert of Aachen similarly suggested that Tughtigin was behind the plot, and that his 'deception became common knowledge among the Turks'.[48] Even King Baldwin I of Jerusalem, tough and blunt as ever, was said to have written to Tughtigin immediately after the murder. He pointedly commented that 'a people that has killed its main prop on its holy day in its house of worship truly deserves that God should destroy it'.[49]

Not everyone knew whom to blame, however. The Syriac Orthodox chronicler, Gregory Bar Hebraeus, had his own version. The information he had was that 'some people have thought that [Ridwan], the lord of Aleppo, sent the [Ismaili]. And others think that it was [Tughtigin] himself who incited the murderer . . . and that he promised him gifts to do this, because he was afraid for his city by reason of Mawdud.'[50]

Ultimately, it could have been either or even both of them. Tughtigin was close at hand, and hence the prime suspect. But Ridwan, who died just a few weeks later, may have had a hand in it. However, it is also conceivable that the Assassins, who were highly motivated to delay any form of Sunni Muslim unity, may have undertaken the act on their own – or that they had approached either Ridwan or Tughtigin to offer their services for cash and favours. With so many enemies and just a mutilated corpse as evidence, no one really knew who was to blame. And this deliberate air of uncertainty only added to the fear which the death created.

Either way, the assassination was extremely successful from the perspective of the local Turkic rulers (and incidentally, of course, the crusaders). The caliph of Baghdad was forced to look elsewhere for a leader to pursue his jihadist offensive against the Franks. He chose an emir called al-Bursuqi (atabeg of Mosul, 1113–26) as his new general. Al-Bursuqi, however, was a far weaker figure and no match for the wily local Turkic ruling families or the aggressive Franks.[51]

The Assassins, too, must have been delighted at the continuing fragmentation of Sunni power – Mawdud's death was a coup for the Nizaris in Syria.

The end in Aleppo: Counter-revolution and rebuff

The Nizari influence over Ridwan was profound, but greatly resented. Inevitably, the Assassins' success – and the ruthless methods they used to achieve that success – did not endear them to others. Resentment became suspicion, and suspicion turned to persecution and pogroms. It was a prescient reminder that being a successful minority group is not without danger.[52]

Ridwan died on 10 December 1113. The new government in Aleppo, led by Alp Arslan al-Akhras (Ridwan's son) and Ibn-Badi (the chief of police) was far less supportive. The government was initially 'afraid of them [the Nizaris] because of their numbers' and because of the implicit threat they posed. But not afraid enough.[53]

Alp Arslan was encouraged to take a hard line against the Nizaris by the caliph of Baghdad: he had been deeply unimpressed by the way in which these 'heretics' were so obviously undermining his jihad against the crusaders. The caliph wrote to Alp Arslan, bluntly saying that 'Your father disobeyed my orders with regard to the Assassins; I would like to think that you, who are my son, will exterminate them.'[54]

The decision was made to destroy the Assassins in Aleppo. As the chronicle of Damascus delicately put it, it was decided to 'use rigorous measures against them and root them out'. The order was given for a massive wave of simultaneous arrests and killings. In the traditional way of such things, the leaders were rounded up first. The 'goldsmith' was arrested and executed. Ismail the Missionary, the brother of the 'doctor-astrologer', and other members of the Nizari leadership were swiftly put to death.[55]

With the sect decapitated, a more wide-ranging massacre ensued. The remainder of the Nizaris 'were imprisoned and their properties were confiscated . . . and some were executed'. This was a time for the settling of old scores. It was said that 'about 200 people were arrested . . . [while] others were thrown from the heights of the citadel or had their throats cut'.[56]

The pogrom was shockingly bloody, but some Nizaris 'escaped, fled to the Franks and dispersed throughout the country'. Relations between the Shiite minority sect and their Sunni neighbours were now so poor that taking refuge with the crusaders was seen as preferable to staying as 'heretics' within an Islamic state.[57]

It probably didn't seem so at the time, but the pogroms had reinforced the wisdom of the Nizaris' underlying strategy. It taught them that if they were not loved by their neighbours, they could at least make them fearful. The Assassins might not have armies, but with *fidais* warriors in their ranks – men prepared to commit almost suicidal acts of violence against the enemies of their sect – their influence could be leveraged far beyond their numbers.

That strategy was proving difficult to implement in practice, however. The sect realised that it needed its own independent region if it was to survive. But the Nizari push to create a network of castles and fortified towns in the Jabal as-Summaq had clearly failed. And their attempt to create an urban centre for their nascent state (in the form of surreptitiously establishing their own government in Aleppo) had ended in disaster.

The survivors of the pogrom in Aleppo were now destitute and homeless. The Syrian Assassins' 'foreign policy' had reached a crossroads. The search for a fortress on which they could centre a new state became paramount. And, as luck would have it, there was one obvious candidate: a castle that was close to hand and ripe for the picking – Shaizar.

5

Assault on Shaizar: Mum's Army (1114)

The Assassins were the most feared and implacable group of killers in a region already notorious for its violence and lawlessness. But in 1114 they met their match – in the unlikely form of a group of middle-aged women who decided they were not going to be pushed around anymore.

The Assassins were famously mysterious, and deliberately so. But we are fortunate that a very intimate account of one large-scale Nizari attack has survived. It was based on conversations with those survivors who were lucky enough to make it through the ordeal. And it was recorded by one of their relatives.

Audacity was a vital ingredient in the Assassins' success – their actions were often so outrageous that they took their opponents completely by surprise. Normally their operations were focused on just one or two individuals, but on rare occasions they could be far more ambitious – even, on one memorable occasion, attempting to take over an entire principality in an elaborate *coup de main*.[1]

In the aftermath of the anti-Nizari pogroms in Aleppo in 1114, most of the survivors took the hint and fled. Ibrahim al-Ajami, commander of the castle at Balis, ran. He and his followers took refuge in the Arab principality of Shaizar, in central Syria. The town itself was on an important crossing point of the River Orontes. Even more usefully, it had an extremely formidable citadel. Relaxing in the safety provided by his unsuspecting hosts, Sultan, the lord of Shaizar and the Banu Munqidh clan, Ibrahim sent word out to the scattered Nizari communities of the region. He told them that the town was ripe for the taking – it would, he suggested, make an excellent base for their activities in Syria.

Ibrahim's plan was to launch a surprise attack in the middle of the Easter holidays. He would kill his Sunni hosts and capture both the town and the castle. As well as the practical benefits the attack would offer the sect, the treachery involved was probably justified – in his mind at least – by the need to take revenge on more orthodox Muslims for the atrocities recently committed against the Nizaris. Assassins from the nearby towns of Ma'arrat Masrin, Apamea, Sarmin and Ma'arrat al-Nu'man all rallied to the cause. They moved surreptitiously to Shaizar to prepare for the assault.[2]

They pretended to integrate into the local community, but quickly began to finalise their secret coup. When it came, it was clear that the 'attack had been organised a long time before', despite the fact, as one contemporary chronicler bitterly noted, that the ruling family 'had shown every kindness to these men when they came on their errand of mischief'. A betrayal of hospitality on this scale was shocking in an Arab society.[3]

The attack on Shaizar (1114)

We have an extraordinary account of the attack on the town, written by one of the local princes, Usama ibn-Munqidh, and based on eyewitness testimony. Usama was born in Shaizar on 4 July 1095, coincidentally just a few months before Christian troops in Europe started to gather for the First Crusade.

Ownership of Shaizar changed many times after the Muslim invasions of the seventh century, and the town had been a late addition to the Islamic dominions. It became a strategically important centre on the border between two warring empires – the Byzantines and the Fatimid Egyptians. It was recovered by the Christians in 999, when Emperor Basil II managed to dislodge the Fatimids and installed an Armenian garrison of his own. The Armenians, who had an excellent track record of fortifying rocky hilltops, probably carried out much of the work that turned Shaizar into a formidable (and desirable) fortification.[4]

The Byzantines managed to hold on to the town for most of the eleventh century, but their military position was significantly diminished after the catastrophic defeat at Manzikert in 1071. In 1081, the local authorities, led by the civilian bishop of al-Bira, finally gave up the struggle. Usama's family, the Banu Munqidh, took over.[5]

When Usama was born, Shaizar had been in Muslim hands for less than fifteen years. Consequently, in the early twelfth century the population was very mixed. A large number of the peasants – probably the majority, particularly in the outlying villages – were still Christian. But there were many Muslims in the area, both Shiite and Sunni. Importantly, as we have seen, there were also Nizari Ismaili refugees, people who had fled from repression first in Apamea in 1106 and then in Aleppo, earlier in 1114.

And there were further, potentially dangerous splits even within these groupings. The ruling dynasty of Shaizar, the Munqidhs, were ethnic Arabs, rather than the Turkic newcomers who ruled most of the neighbouring regions. Both groups were Sunni Muslims, but there were always tensions between the two. The Munqidhs, led by Usama's uncle, Sultan, were proud of their Arabic roots. Usama, for instance, was keen to point out in his memoirs that he did not speak Turkic.

The different communities seem to have rubbed along together relatively harmoniously – but the fault lines were always there. In an emergency, in a battle or in a siege perhaps, whom could one really rely on?

The Nizaris had ambitious objectives, and from their perspective Shaizar had many advantages. Most obviously, it had the potential to act as the centre of an independent principality, providing a safe haven from which the sect could expand. It occupied a commanding position on the regional road network, and was an important crossing point on the River Orontes. Both of these advantages could be used to drive revenues and create strategic leverage.

The walled town was imposing enough in itself, but its fortress was particularly formidable. The ruins we see today post-date the crusader period, but the old castle that Usama and his relatives occupied was a serious obstacle to any invading force. Strong Byzantine and Frankish armies, lavishly equipped with catapults, siege equipment and cadres of miners, tried and failed to capture it on several occasions during the twelfth century. The Assassins, bold as ever, with a tiny force and no siege equipment, thought they could do better.

In March 1114, the Easter celebrations of the local Arab Christians were taking place in one of Shaizar's neighbouring villages. The Christians of the town left to participate in the festivities. Perhaps not coincidentally (given that the celebrations would probably have included alcohol), they were joined by most of the other men of Shaizar, including the Muslim garrison and the male members of the ruling Munqidh family. Only the old men who were unable to travel and the town's women were left behind. The Assassins were never going to get a better chance – and they took it.

A force of about a hundred Assassins rushed the citadel. According to the chronicler Ibn al-Qalanisi,

> on the Easter day of the Christians a company of the [Assassins] . . . made an assault on the castle of Shaizar when its garrison were off their guard, and having seized it and driven out many of its defenders, they closed the gate of the fortress, mounted to the citadel and captured it together with its towers.

The initial assault was wildly successful: the Assassins could relax a little and start to negotiate a formal handover of power.[6]

Only one male member of the ruling family remained behind to negotiate with: Sultan's son (and Usama's cousin) Shabib. With the

Assassins in control of the town and much of the castle, Shabib felt he had no option other than to start surrender talks with their leader. A meeting was held outside the citadel. The leader of the Nizari assault teams, 'Alwan ibn Harar, was surprisingly magnanimous, certainly by the standards of the sect. This was partly, perhaps, because the Munqidh family had been so accommodating to the Assassin refugees – but, more pragmatically, it was also because he wanted to conclude the mopping-up operations before the regular garrison had time to return. He made it clear that he was prepared to offer good terms in order to get the last remaining Munqidhs and their few household servants out of the castle quickly. 'Go back to your home,' said 'Alwan, 'carry off whatever you can and get out of here. You won't be killed. We've already taken the castle.'[7]

But the Assassin leadership had misjudged the situation and over-played its hand. Pausing to negotiate had broken the momentum of the assault. And although Sultan's son was prepared to talk, his aunt (Usama's mother) was not. When Shabib showed his willingness to surrender, she persuaded him not to. She deliberately shamed him by putting on the male combat kit of 'a mail hauberk and a helmet, with a sword and shield'. The matron was prepared to fight for the family's honour, she said, even if he would not. 'And so,' Usama wrote causti-cally, 'she prevented him from running away.'[8]

The only male of the dynasty in the castle was clearly lacking in backbone. The rest of the men were out partying: Usama, although he does not emphasise it, was one of the absentees. He tried to imply that they had been out on patrol, or raiding – in his memoirs he merely wrote, in the blandest way he could contrive, that the Nizaris had 'gained possession of the fortress of Shaizar while our bravest fighting men [himself included, of course] were out riding beyond the town'. Other sources make it clear that they were, in fact, enjoying the Christian festivities and accompanying entertainments.[9]

The women stepped in to take control – they were calmer, braver and more determined than the men in the face of the Assassins' assault.

Much later, when Usama got back, he searched for his swords and his armoured tunics, only to find them gone. His mother, it transpired, had used them to arm an impromptu female militia within the citadel, proudly saying that she 'gave the weapons to whoever would use them to fight for us'. In a homely but telling aside, we also know that Usama's mother gave her new troops the blades, but not the scabbards: always a careful leader of the household, she had decided that those were too richly decorated for mere retainers to be trusted with.[10]

Even old women went into the breach. An aged servant named Funun 'covered herself with her veil, took up a sword and went into battle'. Usama later wrote that the brave old lady 'kept at it until we were able to climb up and overpower the enemy'.[11]

And if that militia had failed to stop the attack, the women were prepared to make even more extreme sacrifices. As the Assassins approached, Usama's sister was placed on the balcony of their house, teetering on the sheer drop to the Orontes below. After the event, Usama's mother proudly said that 'I made her sit here on the balcony while I took my seat just outside. That way, if I should see that the [Assassins] had reached us, I could push her off, throwing her down to the valley.' The explanation offered by the splendidly haughty Munqidh matron was that 'I would rather see her dead than see her a prisoner of peasants.'[12]

The Assassins had made the mistake of not rushing on to capture the few remaining chambers in the castle – the women were still fighting and time was running out. The Munqidh cavalry had been summoned back 'when the alarm was sounded in the fortress' and the shamefaced garrison eventually returned from the Easter partying. Later chronicles tried to put a braver gloss on things, claiming that 'the Banu Munqidh, lords of the castle . . . climbed up to them, and shouting *Allahu Akbar* engaged the [Assassins] until they forced them back into the citadel'. But the reality was far more embarrassing.[13]

Instead, they arrived at the foot of the citadel and called up to those trapped in the chambers above them. Once again, however, the men were ineffectual. Usama's tutor, the scholar Ibn al-Munira, was up in the citadel's mosque, and had a panic attack on a scale that outshone even the poor performance of Sultan's son. The Munqidh troops shouted to him 'Dangle a rope down to us!' But in his confused state he was too flustered to do anything. Seeing that he was wearing a turban, the increasingly frustrated troops called up 'Well, dangle down your turban-cloth!' But even this proved too complicated for the shocked old man. After a while, the relief forces gave up trying to communicate with him. They went instead to find someone who had their wits about them, and who could lower some ropes. When the troops eventually recaptured the castle, they found the tutor wandering around naked, and more confused than ever.[14]

The defenders who had the sense to let down the ropes proved, once again, to be the women of the household. They helped pull the relief forces up into the citadel and showed them where the enemy were. Usama, normally boastful and bullish, was forced to acknowledge that it was only the resolute actions of the Munqidh females that saved the day. One had to admit, he wrote rather patronisingly, that 'courage for the sake of honour is more intense [among women] than such courage among men'. Proving that mansplaining is not a modern invention, he also pointed out, as if events had not already made it obvious, that women could 'possess disdain for danger'.[15]

Once the Munqidh household troops began to enter the castle, their superior numbers and heavier equipment inevitably began to tell – the Nizaris were hunted down and destroyed. Killing cornered fanatics was never going to be easy, however. With nothing left to lose, they fought with extraordinary and desperate bravery.

Even Usama, a teenager at the time, was nearly killed in the vicious room-to-room fighting that ensued. 'One of them came at me with a long knife in his hand,' he later wrote,

> while I had one of my swords. He charged at me with his knife, but I struck him in the middle of his forearm as he grasped the handle

of the knife, its blade held back close to his raised arm. A length of four finger-widths was cut from the blade of the knife and his forearm was cut in half, clear [sic] off.[16]

The Assassin was dead, but it had been a close thing. As usual, he had been brave – outnumbered and armed only with a dagger, the Nizari warrior still attacked first, rather than trying to back off or escape. From that day on, Usama carried his chipped sword blade with him as a badge of honour. 'The traces of that knife-blade remained ever afterwards on the edge of my sword,' he later wrote. 'An artisan in our town saw it and said, "I can get rid of that dent there." But I said, "Leave it as it is. It's the best thing about the sword." Even today, when someone looks at that sword they know it is the mark of that knife.'[17]

Similar stories were unfolding throughout the citadel, as the Munqidh troops spread out in search of the intruders. The fighting was grim and deeply shocking in its violence. A cavalryman named Hammam the Pilgrim 'encountered one of the Ismailis in a portico in the residence of [Usama's] uncle'. The Assassin

> had a knife in his hand and Hammam had a sword. The [Assassin] charged at him with his knife, but Hammam struck him with his sword above the eyes. He cut through the top of his skull and his brains fell out, spattering and spreading out on the ground. Hammam then threw the sword from his hand and vomited up everything in his stomach, stricken with nausea at seeing those brains.

Like Usama's opponent, this Assassin was brave and desperate; but armed only with a knife, he had almost no chance of getting out alive – he just wanted to take one of the Munqidhs with him.[18]

Even when completely trapped, and far beyond hope, the Nizaris refused to give up. Another of Usama's cousins, Abu 'Abdallah ibn Hashim, saw an Assassin 'in a tower of my father's home, wielding a sword and shield. The door was open and a great crowd of our comrades stood outside it, but no one dared to go in.' It took a foolish man to be the first to go against an Assassin. One soldier was ordered to go in, 'but the [Assassin] did not waste any time and struck the man, injuring him, and the man came back out, wounded'.[19]

Another soldier entered the room and was likewise wounded. Hashim ordered yet another man to go in, but the Assassin had the courage to say what everyone else must have been thinking. 'Hey hang-behind!' he shouted. 'How come *you* don't come in here? You send everybody else in, but you just stand there. Get in here so's you can get a look!' Despite the embarrassment and dishonour, Hashim still declined the kind offer. The Assassin eventually had to be brought down by another member of the garrison.[20]

The Shaizari soldiers were understandably cautious, and should have finished him off by archery – presumably, as Shaizar was primarily recaptured by hand-to-hand fighting, they had no bows to hand at that moment. One of the few instances in which we have archaeological data for a comparable situation (a room in the fortress of Chastellet where Templar troops were cornered by Saladin's men) shows that the defenders were eventually picked off by short-range archery fire – the attackers, very wisely, decided to keep their distance from such desperate and fanatical fighters.[21]

Most of the Nizaris were dead at this point, but rumours circulated that there might be some Assassins still alive in the lower buildings of Shaizar. After the attackers in the citadel had been killed, the Munqidh troops went in groups through the town to hunt down any remaining stragglers. Usama and some of his men tentatively 'crossed over to an empty, darkened stable and went inside'. They discovered that 'there were two armed men there and killed them both. We also found one of our own comrades who had been killed, but he was lying on top of something.' Usama's soldiers lifted up the body, only to find that underneath was another Assassin 'who had wrapped himself up in a cloth like a shroud and covered himself with the dead body of our comrade. So we lifted off the body of our comrade, and killed the man hiding underneath him.'²²

In a further twist to this strange war story, it transpired that the 'dead' Munqidh soldier under whom the Assassin was hiding was only wounded. The Assassins had 'stabbed him with their knives until they thought he was dead', but the stab wounds on his neck and on his body eventually healed and, against all the odds, the man survived.²³

The citadel and town were thoroughly scoured. The 'men of Shaizar attacked [the Assassins] in increasing numbers, put them to the sword, and killed them to the last man'. Harshly, but perhaps understandably given the Nizaris' track record and reputation, the rest of the Ismaili population in the surrounding villages were deemed guilty by association. They 'were put to death, and a strict watch was kept against a repetition of this attempt'. The Nizaris must have known that betrayal of hospitality on such a scale could have only one punishment.²⁴

The young prince Shabib emerges very badly from the story, but it is worth noting that Usama was not an entirely unbiased observer. On the contrary, he was keenly jealous of his cousin and of the position his rival held as heir to the principality of Shaizar – a position which Usama seems, without much substance, to have felt was more rightfully his. Perhaps not surprisingly, Usama portrayed his cousin as a weak man lacking in leadership skills, while his own branch of the family – and particularly his mother – are shown as the heroes (and heroines) of the piece.

The self-serving and violent Usama, who by his own admission had committed his first murder while still a child (knifing an unarmed family servant to death for irritating him), did not last long in Shaizar. He was soon thought to be too dangerous to be allowed to remain in close proximity to the ruling family – he and his brothers were exiled.²⁵

Thus Usama began his long and often precarious career as an itinerant diplomat, international fixer and, luckily for us, wheedling memoirist.

The Assassins in Syria always played a high-stakes game. With them, it was all or nothing. Death or defeat. Victory or rout. And that mesmerising, binary commitment resonates through the ages.

But it is the Munqidh women who come across most forcefully in the incident – strong women seem to have been the norm in Usama's family. And it was not just Usama's mother: his grandmother, too, was a powerful character. Even when she was a hundred years old, the strong-willed matron refused to sit during prayers (a robust constitution seems to have run in the Munqidh family, as Usama himself lived well into his nineties). One day, Usama later wrote, she gave him a massive dressing-down for his grandstanding and braggadocio. She was forthright (and entirely correct) in warning Usama that he should be more careful, and that his insensitive, violent behaviour was going to alienate his uncle, the clan leader. Her grandson ignored her advice and duly suffered the consequences of exile.[26]

The Assassins also ignored the women and met their match at Shaizar. In storming the Munqidh citadel, some of the world's most fearsome and fanatical killers were outwitted by a small group of middle-aged matrons.[27]

6

Assassins: A State within a State (1115–1126)

The Assassins in Syria continued in their attempts to establish a safe base for their unpopular sect. They had no choice. But unlike their co-religionists in Persia, there was no definitively obvious homeland in prospect – they did not have that luxurious possibility.

There was no easy geographical vacuum to be filled in the relatively compact, febrile political landscape of the medieval Middle East. So, by necessity, they simultaneously sought to integrate themselves into positions of high authority within the leading states of the time, while also taking every opportunity to carve out a defensible place of their own on the peripheries of the great powers.

The Assassins had a clear set of priorities: short-term revenge and then in the longer term a new home. The assault on Shaizar had been an utter failure, so they turned briefly to their favourite (and far more successful) preoccupation: vengeance.

A signature dish served cold

Even while struggling to set up a new state, the Assassins found time to settle old scores. They never forgot. They never forgave. Those who had persecuted them in Aleppo and beyond were about to find out what it meant to have the Nizaris as enemies.

Ibn-Badi, the corrupt (and appropriately named) Aleppan police chief, had presided over the massacre of the Assassins in 1113. He knew he had been marked out for death and lived his life in as near-total security as possible. But eventually even he had to break cover. And when he did, the Assassins were waiting.

In 1119, Ibn-Badi was exiled from Aleppo and fled towards Mardin. As he crossed the Euphrates, a coordinated attack was unleashed. The *fidais* had been tracking him, and as he 'set foot in the little boat which would take him to the . . . other side of the river, two Assassins attacked him and rained many blows upon him'. He was wounded, but his sons leapt on the Nizari assailants and killed them.[1] Unluckily for Ibn-Badi, however, the attack was not over yet. He died along with one of his sons because, with typical Nizari remorselessness, 'as he was transported to the castle, [another] of the Assassins threw himself upon him and killed him; as for the Assassin, he threw himself in the river and was drowned'. Casualties among the *fidais* were high, as always. But the point had been made.[2]

The Nizaris' old Ismaili enemy in Egypt, the Fatimid vizier al-Afdal, also received his reward for opposing them. In December 1121, he was cut down while on a procession at the end of Ramadan. Although rumours suggested that his death was due to the usual toxic internal politics of the Fatimid regime, we know from independent Nizari sources that the hit was, in fact, carried out by 'three comrades from Aleppo'.[3]

The death of al-Afdal at the hands of the Assassins was one of their greatest successes; but it went unnoticed by most contemporary historians, because the attack had been mounted in such secrecy. There was plenty of time for quiet congratulations and cheery partying back in Persia, however. When news came of the vizier's death, the Assassins recorded that 'Our Master [Hasan, at Alamut in Persia] ordered them to celebrate for seven days and nights, and they entertained and feted the comrades' who had killed him.[4]

Once again, despite the Eurocentric tendency to focus on the attacks that the Assassins' made on the crusaders, in fact usually they were just pursuing their own interests – in this case the pursuit of revenge. As it happens, the ensuing chaos in the Egyptian government was of great help to the Franks: it contributed significantly to their efforts in capturing the Fatimid coastal city of Tyre, which fell to them in 1124. But that was beside the point.

Revenge was an integral part of the brand. No matter how long it took, vengeance was vital. It was logically essential, as well as emotionally satisfying: killing old enemies was gratifying in itself, but more importantly, it reinforced the implacable, remorseless nature of the Assassins' promise of death.

The assassination of al-Bursuqi (1126)

Despite the failure at Shaizar, Nizari missionaries continued their quest for security and converts. They regrouped and were soon ready to try again. A senior Persian Nizari named Bahram was chosen to succeed Abu Tahir, the 'goldsmith', who had been executed at the beginning of the Aleppan massacres. In the immediate aftermath of the pogroms, Bahram went underground. He 'lived in extreme concealment and secrecy, and continually disguised himself, so that he moved from city to city and castle to castle without anyone being aware of his identity'. Eventually, however, he felt confident enough to turn his attention south, towards Damascus.[5]

Like many Nizari missionaries, Bahram was certainly not lacking in energy or focus. Ibn al-Qalanisi, the author of the Damascus chronicle, wrote that he 'grew so formidable that he became a factor to be reckoned with in Aleppo and Syria . . . [H]e appeared in Damascus . . . with a letter containing strong recommendations on his behalf.' It is interesting to see that even at their weakest, the Assassins were feared – Bahram, we are told, 'was received with honour', but only 'as a measure of precaution against his malice and that of his organisation'.[6]

He did not waste any time in gathering new converts around him. He 'moved about', in the disapproving words of one Sunni commentator, from place to place and gained a following among the ignorant and witless mob, and foolish peasantry, men lacking both intelligence and religion, who sought in him and his party a means of protecting themselves and injuring others.

Even when seen through the lens of those who despised him, it is clear that Bahram was a man of powerful charisma.[7]

The charm offensive worked – Bahram and his followers found favour with Tughtigin, the tough Turkic overlord of Damascus. Perhaps not surprisingly, this favour was bought with more than just an engaging personality. The Assassins may (or may not) have already helped Tughtigin by killing his rival Mawdud in 1113. But either way, Bahram continued to offer the support, and blood, of his followers – together, they made efforts to strengthen Tughtigin's regime in the city and help see off his enemies.

Support came, for instance, from the Nizari militiamen who helped Tughtigin to fend off a crusader attack on Damascus. Ibn al-Qalanisi, despite his contempt for the Assassins, wrote that in January 1126, in the face of a Frankish threat, 'there were assembled . . . a great host', which included 'the armed bands of the [Nizaris], noted for courage and gallantry, from Hims and elsewhere'. This support was greatly appreciated. It also found expression in even more specific forms of bloodshed.[8]

On 26 November 1126, extremely conveniently for Tughtigin, al-Bursuqi, the Seljuk Turk lord of Mosul, was killed by a *fidais* team while attending prayers in the city's Great Mosque. Al-Bursuqi had been the replacement for Mawdud after he, too, had been killed by a *fidais* team in 1113. As the caliph of Baghdad's generalissimo in charge of leading the jihad against the crusaders (and, they must have suspected, Nizari 'heretics'), he had many enemies. As was so often the case, it is not entirely clear who ordered, or commissioned, the hit.

The Assassins themselves wanted him dead. They knew that the caliph of Baghdad, as the leader of Sunni orthodoxy, had been one of the main instigators of the shocking pogrom launched against them in Aleppo – and being the sultan's servant in Syria would have been more than enough to mark al-Bursuqi out for death. But the internal politics of the Seljuk empire were shockingly poisonous. He had many enemies of his own. Even at the time, no one could be entirely sure why the attack took place.[9]

We may not know everything about the *why*, but we have a lot of evidence about the *how*. From a selfish point of view, we are fortunate that al-Bursuqi's murder was so spectacular. It achieved a very high level of coverage in the local chronicles, Christian as well as Muslim. This has given us an unusual level of insight into several different aspects of what happened during a Nizari hit, and it is worth looking at these contemporary accounts in some detail.

It is clear that the Assassins were determined to kill al-Bursuqi whatever the cost – their commitment was total, and they must have realised that the consequences would inevitably be similarly bloodthirsty. The *fidais* were not to be squandered lightly. Although they did not seek suicide, their missions were intensely dangerous. Because their survival was not to be expected, hit squads typically consisted of around three men. That was usually enough to get the job done. The attack on al-Bursuqi was different, however. Up to ten *fidais* were deployed, of whom all but one were killed on the spot or tortured to death after the event.

The murder itself was savage and thorough. It had to be, if it were to have any chance of success: in the first place, al-Bursuqi was heavily armoured and surrounded by professional bodyguards. Despite this, however, the *fidais* were able to separate him from his men for a few seconds, and it was perhaps the need to do so that dictated the unusually large size of their team. The chronicler Kamal al-Din wrote that, as al-Bursuqi arrived 'at the foot of the pulpit, eight men clad as dervishes attacked him, knives in hand . . . and [although he] was surrounded by a numerous bodyguard, the Assassins got ahead of his escort and riddled him with wounds, so that he died the same day'.[10]

Armour was the other main problem. Al-Bursuqi's chest and torso were heavily protected, and even his arms and legs, under his outer clothing, probably had some form of defensive covering. This still left two main areas of vulnerability, however, and it was on these that the *fidais* focused their attention. As al-Bursuqi was at a public event, his neck and face had to be on show. And because he was wearing trousers, a mail shirt could be expected to end just above the groin.

The Christian chronicler Michael the Syrian wrote that the initial dagger thrust did not harm al-Bursuqi, since he was, very sensibly, wearing a breastplate or mail shirt. While the first Assassin was being hacked down, however, he cried out to his other companions to strike below the shirt, and they stabbed al-Bursuqi in the lower abdomen. The great man died humiliated, according to Michael, of wounds to the groin.[11] Ibn al-Qalanisi, in his detailed account of the murder, wrote that other Assassins also shouted out 'strike his head above', presumably changing their target to his face and neck, and confirmed the kill.[12]

The *fidais* had been correct in identifying the need to go in en masse. Quite apart from the wall of bodyguards who surrounded him, al-Bursuqi was a formidable opponent in his own right. He fought back against the Assassins and 'with his own hand killed three of his attackers'. He did not go down quietly.[13]

As so often, hindsight sought a dramatic story to accompany a dramatic ending. The murder, it was later said, had been preceded by portents of death, covered in a suitably pious carapace of respectability. The evening before his death, some said, al-Bursuqi dreamt that 'he was attacked by a pack of dogs of whom he killed three but was savaged by the others. Those of his household to whom he told this dream advised him to stay indoors and not to go out for some days, but he declared that he would not for anything miss Friday prayers.'[14]

The *fidais* might be compared to a 'pack of dogs', but the job was meticulously planned. The hit squad had been in place for some time, waiting for the right opportunity to present itself. The man who had sheltered them – a cobbler – eventually broke under torture and told the authorities that 'they came to kill [al-Bursuqi] several years ago, but they had no opportunity until this present time'.[15]

The northern crusaders, who had the closest relations with the Nizaris, may also have had advance warning of the hit through their intelligence networks. Ibn al-Athir mentions that 'the lord of Antioch sent to [al-Bursuqi's son] to tell him of the killing of his father before the news reached him [from elsewhere]. The Franks had heard it before him because of their intense interest in learning about Muslim affairs.'[16]

As usual, the aftermath of the affair was a bloodbath – the victim, the *fidais* and scores of innocent civilians were all butchered. The consequences for the local Ismaili (and, more broadly, Shiite) community could also be profound. In the immediate aftermath of any attack, innocent bystanders who were unlucky enough to be in the wrong place at the wrong time, and particularly those who were unfortunate enough to 'look Persian', were habitually killed. In this instance, the blood flowed copiously. The chronicler Matthew of Edessa wrote that after the murder, 'al-Bursuqi's servants killed [the *fidais*] and others whom they found in the city dressed in the same manner – all in all eighty men'.[17]

Even those who had been associated with the *fidais* were subjected to the most appalling tortures. According to Ibn al-Athir,

> an enquiry about those [Assassins] and a full investigation into their background took place. It was said that they had been apprenticed to a cobbler in the Iliya Lane. He was summoned and promised generous treatment if he confessed, but he did not . . . His hands, his feet and his penis were cut off and he was stoned to death.

For the Assassins, the collateral cost of the attack was appalling – but felt to be acceptable.[18]

But there was one survivor of the raid – a young *fidais* who somehow managed to escape the carnage. A story was told – possibly apocryphal, probably defamatory – about how this Assassin was received by his loved ones when he returned home. 'All those who attacked [al-Bursuqi]', wrote the chronicler Kamal al-Din,

> were killed except for one youth, who came from Kafr Nasih, in the district of 'Azaz [a town to the north of Aleppo] and escaped unhurt. He had an aged mother, and when she heard that Bursuqi was killed and that those who attacked him were killed, knowing that her son was one of them, she rejoiced, and anointed her eyelids with kohl, and was full of joy; then after a few days her son returned unharmed, and she was grieved, and tore her hair and blackened her face.[19]

This is certainly unfair. The *fidais* were not suicidal and they were expected to escape if they could. But there may be a grim germ of truth to Ibn al-Athir's hostile views. Having a reputation for an unswerving dedication to the death of their enemies was the Assassins' main strength. It was the source of the fear upon which their political leverage was founded – the sect had every reason to encourage such extreme legends, whether they were literally true or (more likely) false. Above all, they needed to be feared.

Banyas: New power, new principality?

At the end of 1126, just a few weeks after his rival al-Bursuqi had been murdered by the Assassins, Tughtigin, the ruler of Damascus, made the sect an extraordinary gift. For their support, he rewarded the Nizaris with their biggest prize to date – the important fortified frontier town and castle of Banyas. The Nizaris once more had the basis of their own principality.[20]

Banyas was no minor acquisition. As subsequent military events proved, it was a strategic hotspot on the frontier between the Franks of the Latin kingdom of Jerusalem and their Turkic opponents. Straddling the important military and trade route between Damascus and Tyre, it was, like the Jabal as-Summaq, vital to both sides. Neither could afford to lose it.

For Tughtigin and his regime, control of Banyas was necessary to safeguard the food supplies of Damascus. The geographer al-Muqaddasi called it 'the granary of Damascus' and wrote how water from the nearby river was used to irrigate cotton and rice fields. Militarily, it helped control the main invasion routes used by the crusaders to attack the fertile Hauran region that the population of Damascus depended on. And from the Franks' perspective, the stakes were similarly high: if Banyas was in enemy hands, it posed a continuing threat to the Christian settlements in Galilee, and made any attack on Damascus far more difficult.[21]

Banyas was a vital strategic asset and Tughtigin was no sentimental old fool. Entrusting it to the Assassins was a supreme token of his confidence in them. But he had good reason to reward them. They had shown themselves to be brave, ferociously dedicated and effective, and had supported his regime against all comers. In making them his vassals and giving them the lordship of Banyas, Tughtigin was creating a buffer state against the continuing attacks of the crusaders – and he was placing it in the hands of those in whom, he thought, he could place the greatest trust.

The fact that the 'heretical' Assassins were isolated from much of the population of Damascus was an added bonus for Tughtigin – it made them more dependent on his favour and, he would have hoped, all the more trustworthy. The atabeg was himself a Turkic foreigner who had his own suspicions about the loyalties of the local Damascenes. He inevitably sought, in the traditional way of dictators, to create divisions and rivalries among his followers, constructing an intricate balance of distrust which left him safe as the overarching manipulator.

Regardless of the realpolitik involved, however, the chronicle of Damascus was disapproving and sceptical about this shocking turn of events. In doing so it was probably just expressing a much broader sense of disquiet among the Sunni population as a whole. Bahram and his lieutenants, Ibn al-Qalanisi wrote, had 'requested of [Tughtigin] a castle in which to take refuge and a fortress in which to defend himself. [Tughtigin] accordingly delivered up to [Bahram] the frontier fort of Banyas.'[22]

Once there, Bahram was joined by what Ibn al-Qalanisi uncharitably described as 'his rabble . . . and vile scum, whom he had seduced by his lying and his false pretensions, and had won over to his side by his intrigues and deceits'. The Assassins, he wrote, 'set about killing all those who opposed them, and supporting all who gave them assistance'. They were never going to be popular in Damascus – but that was not the point of the exercise.[23]

Bahram moved swiftly to crystallise the opportunities provided by his new acquisition: the fortifications of Banyas were strengthened; new buildings were erected as residences for the Nizari elite; and converts from the surrounding areas were brought in to man the newly improved castle. Banyas was to be the proud headquarters of the Assassins' new principality in Syria.

Even in Sunni Damascus, this new and increasingly visible manifestation of Nizari power continued – the sect was given a 'palace' or 'mission-house' as an imposing centre for its activities in the city. The work of converting local Sunnis was ramped up. Critics were silenced by fear – or, for those more vocal, by increasingly violent attacks. Damascus was ripe to become another base for the Assassins.[24]

But for now, we must leave the Assassins. They are in the ascendant. Their star is on the rise in Damascus. And their new principality in the Golan Heights, centred around the castle of Banyas, is beginning to take shape.

7

Templars: The Ideology of Love and Death (1095–1129)

It is time for a brief interlude. For not far away, in Jerusalem, another star is being born – a star that will have a profound effect on the Assassins and on the way they are seen in the modern world. It is an unlikely new 'partner' – more a nemesis perhaps, but also operating in strangely similar ways. This new actor will hack out an approach to life that mirrors much of what the Assassins have already learnt and made their own. This is another small but deadly band of committed warriors – the Templars.

Ironically, and although neither knew it, Nizari Ismailism was born at almost the same time as another extraordinary movement was created far away in western Europe. A few months after the Egyptian schism of 1094 that led to the founding of the Assassins, a meeting took place that would lead to the founding of the Templars. At Clermont, in the duchy of Aquitaine, Pope Urban II gave a speech and issued a call to arms that reverberated around the Mediterranean. The wars of the crusades had started, and would rage across the Holy Land for two hundred years.

The consequences for both groups would be profound.

The First Crusade

For years, the Byzantine empire had issued urgent appeals for military aid. The Muslim (or at least nominally Muslim) Turkic tribes that ravaged Anatolia at the end of the eleventh century posed a dire threat to what remained of the Christian Middle East. Plans varied greatly in detail and realism, but the idea of an expedition to help these fellow Christians had long been simmering in the west. The time had come to put that idea into practice.

The decisive moment arrived on 27 November 1095. At the close of the Church Council in Clermont, Pope Urban II gathered a crowd in a nearby field and proclaimed the call to arms. He urged knights from across Christendom to journey eastward, go to the aid of their beleaguered brethren and liberate the Holy Sepulchre in Jerusalem (the tomb of Christ) from Muslim control.[1] From this small, almost eccentric, beginning, the crusading movement was born.

The call to arms embodied crucial elements that would be at the core of the nascent idea of the Templar order – the need for devout Christian knights to fight for the cause; the idea of a defensive war to reclaim the ancient heartlands of Christianity; and the paradoxical notion that a religion grounded in love might still resort to violence for self-defence. Though the birth of the Templar order would be two decades in the future, its essential purpose lay in the foundations of the crusading movement and was evident from the start.

The crusaders reached the Levant in 1097. There they encountered largely Christian populations, long subjugated and demilitarised by Muslim rulers. The Franks pushed their way into a complex and chaotic world, where Muslim disunity provided an unexpected advantage, making the establishment of what became known as the 'crusader states' temporarily feasible.

The first Muslim incursions had surged into the Middle East from the south in the seventh century, overwhelming Egypt, Palestine and Syria, and subjugating their predominantly Christian inhabitants. The

Byzantine empire had contested these territories, and a tenuous balance emerged. But this fragile equilibrium was shattered, as we have seen, by the further invasion of Turkic tribes from western Eurasia in the eleventh century.[2]

The Shiite Fatimid Egyptians and Sunni Turkic warlords were in perpetual conflict, exacerbated by profound cultural, racial and religious antagonism. Even among the Turks, internal divisions and mistrust prevailed. Each warlord prioritised his own interests, viewing the crusaders as a temporary nuisance or a potential ally, depending on shifting alliances and circumstances. The Europeans were not unique intruders, but merely new players in the volatile politics of the medieval Middle East.[3]

But this disunity was fleeting. It masked the crusaders' fundamental weaknesses. When the Sunni Muslim states began to coalesce, the true balance of power would become glaringly apparent, both to the Franks and, coincidentally, to a local group of which they were probably only dimly aware – the Assassins.[4]

The military predicament

The First Crusade, an improbable venture at the best of times, saw fractious crusader armies, supported by rudimentary logistics, march through Europe, across the Byzantine empire and down through Anatolia, Syria, Lebanon and Palestine. Despite the crazy odds stacked against them, the crusade succeeded. On 15 July 1099, Jerusalem – the Holy City and birthplace of Christianity – was recovered.

This was a beginning, however; not an end. The First Crusade had been remarkably successful, but these victories only ushered in a new set of challenges. Most crusaders returned to the west, believing that their vows had been fulfilled. Few grasped that saving the Middle East for Christendom was an ongoing process, not a one-off event. And holding territory on the fringes of Europe proved far more difficult than temporarily recapturing it.[5]

ASSASSINS AND TEMPLARS

Some men stayed behind to defend the Holy Land; but the crusader states they created were chronically undermanned and under-resourced. Their survival depended on massive levels of external military aid, unprecedented since the fall of the Roman empire. And while the First Crusade was successful, subsequent crusades – sporadic military expeditions – proved far less effective for defence. Sustaining this fragile foothold would require substantial support from Europe.[6]

Crusading was always a deeply flawed way of delivering military aid to the east. Reinforcements from the west continued to arrive, but these crusaders were usually just well-meaning and transient visitors, pious military tourists with no enduring stake in the region. They would arrive, acclimatise, visit holy sites and then return home, often leaving those they came to help vulnerable to reprisals.

What was needed was a standing army, rather than random interventions – permanent, high-quality soldiers with which to man castles and counter invasions. The military challenges were extraordinary, demanding equally extraordinary solutions. Standing armies were a distant memory in medieval Europe, yet the survival of the European settlements in the Middle East depended on reviving this concept.

The fragmented and inefficient nature of west European states at this time meant that only the religious authorities – primarily the papacy – were capable of channelling the necessary resources to the Holy Land. Even during the siege of Jerusalem, there had been discussions among the crusaders about the wisdom of establishing religious control of the new states – having a priest in charge, rather than a general. The idea was eventually rejected as impractical, to the point of being crazy. But ironically, the concept of the Church providing resources for Christendom's defence was not entirely without merit – in some ways it was an insightful and imaginative response to the strategic challenges facing the crusader states.

Establishing an ecclesiastical state was not feasible, especially amid ongoing military emergencies. Nonetheless, the leaders of the First Crusade had stumbled upon the core issue: if the newly acquired territories were to be defended, a mechanism was needed that could merge spiritual devotion with military power, and European resources with the needs of the Christian Middle East.[7]

The solution to this remarkable challenge emerged almost by chance, evolving so gradually and organically that many contemporaries did not fully grasp what was unfolding around them. It began modestly – as a practical idea, rather than a grand strategic vision. So unassuming was its inception that contemporary European chroniclers in Jerusalem, men who exchanged friendly nods with the key figures, scarcely mentioned it. But the idea of the Templars was born.

The foundational story

There was a sensible side to the Templars. A side that was diplomatic. A side that created a professional services conglomerate. A side that had excellent logistics skills. But there was another version of the Templars, too – a version whose stock in trade was death.

The Templars were formed sometime around 1119 and had several 'founders'. Their exact origins are obscure. No one at the time realised how significant they were to become, and no contemporary chronicler thought them interesting enough to mention the manner of their founding.[8]

It seems, however, that there were two senior knights among the original volunteers, of whom Godfrey of Saint-Omer, from Picardy and, even more significantly, Hugh of Payns, from Champagne, were the most prominent.

Walter Map, archdeacon of Oxford, wrote a story later in the twelfth century about a certain 'Paganus' (the Latin form of 'Payns') in his version of the Templars' origins story: 'There was a certain knight called Paganus,' he wrote, 'who went on pilgrimage to Jerusalem. There he was told that . . . the pagans were in the habit of attacking the Christians.'[9] 'Paganus', convinced that he was doing what his God would have wished, 'devoted all his expenditure to the cost of horses and arms.' He did not stop there, however. He drew others into his cause, and began to turn a personal quest into a small organisation of like-minded soldiers. Paganus persuaded 'all such pilgrims as were men of arms either to surrender themselves for life to the service of the Lord in that place or at least to devote themselves thereto for a time . . . He prescribes chastity and sobriety.'[10]

The narrative is fanciful and legendary. But it also contains the germ of a true story. The Templars were formed out of a necessity to protect travellers to the Holy Land, at a time when the crusader states were immensely vulnerable. They combined religious fervour with military prowess and a desire to help the cause by force of arms. And they did so by becoming a unique religious order with vows of chastity and poverty.

Their goals at this point were fairly limited – and necessarily so, given that they were just a handful of men. They seem to have operated as the security team to protect the relics at the Holy Sepulchre and, even more importantly, to help escort pilgrims up the supremely dangerous road from the port of Jaffa to Jerusalem. It was probably at the reforming Council of Nablus of January 1120 that they took vows before the patriarch to dedicate themselves to this work to the exclusion of all else.[11]

The brothers were helped in their early days by the local clergy in Jerusalem. Many of them later came to regret the decision, due to what they felt to be the order's arrogance and access to unprecedented privileges. The chronicler William of Tyre certainly suggests, rather bitterly, that the Templars had been greatly helped by the patriarch of Jerusalem, Warmund of Picquigny, and that they had promised obedience to him. William also emphasised the role played by King Baldwin II of Jerusalem, who gave them their first headquarters in his palace in the al-Aqsa mosque on the Temple Mount in Jerusalem. In doing so, he not only gave them a building, Baldwin also inadvertently gave them their iconic name.[12]

Michael the Syrian, a native Christian chronicler, similarly emphasised the role played by the king. Baldwin knew all too well just how much the Holy Land needed military assistance. He was said by Michael to have persuaded the first Templars that the kingdom needed warriors more than it needed men devoted solely to a life of piety and quiet reflection. Instead, wrote Michael, he wanted Hugh of Payns and his men to form a hybrid religio-military organisation and use it 'to serve in the knighthood, with those attached to him, rather than becoming a monk . . . in order to guard these [holy] places against robbers'.[13]

The Templars, like the *fidais*, were formed to protect their beleaguered community. But it was not just in their political and military manoeuvring that the Assassins and the Templars were to find so much in common. They were both exploring extreme ways.

Recruitment and brand-building

During the first decades of the twelfth century, the Templars took an extraordinarily parallel path to that of the Assassins. This was no coincidence – their direction was propelled by many of the same underlying reasons. Like the Assassins, the Templars were few in number, often isolated and unpopular. And, like the Assassins before them, they instinctively came up with ways to generate a 'multiplier-effect' for their tiny forces.

The decrees of the Council of Nablus were issued on 23 January 1120. But the Templars showed little early promise and were not initially successful. They needed to branch out and achieve international recognition if they were ever to reach critical mass. A decade after their inception, there were still only nine brothers in the order.[14] Their resources were completely insignificant, relative to the scale of the military need in the Latin East. There was a real possibility that the order would just peter out.

Something needed to change – and that change could not take place in the impoverished, distracted Latin East. If they were to survive, the Templars would have to fire the imagination of the warrior classes back in Europe. The turning point came in 1127.

In that year, Hugh of Payns, backed by his royal allies in the Latin East, set out on a high-stakes fundraising and recruitment drive in western Europe. It was a daring move, pulling many Templars away from the Holy Land at a time when every man was needed on the front line. But the potential payoff was enormous – the possibility of transforming the Templars from a handful of provincial enthusiasts into one of Christendom's most powerful international organisations.

Hugh brought five of his toughest knights with him on tour – men who could impress and charm in equal measure. These were figures with whom the western nobility and their kings could relate. Battle-hardened but pious knights were the perfect ambassadors for the cause. Hugh was betting everything on this one shot – taking his vision of a new and militant Christianity straight to the heart of Europe's courts and palaces.[15]

A second delegation, led by the nobility of Jerusalem, was also sent back to Europe. It was aimed primarily at offering Fulk, count of Anjou, the hand in marriage of Melisende, heiress to the throne of Jerusalem. But even here there was a huge Templar involvement.

Fulk was a great supporter of the order and was probably an associate Templar brother himself. He had already paid for the maintenance of a hundred knights in the Latin East, and was working hard to persuade others to help the cause, too. In approaching him, the Templars knew that they were working with a willing ally. Fulk and his men signed up for a new expedition. In May 1128, they took the cross at Le Mans and prepared to head east to help the Templars and the king of Jerusalem in their fight to defend the Holy Land.[16]

Constructing an ideology: Death and love in the east

It was not just men that the Templars needed, however. They were desperate for ideas and structures, legitimacy and doctrine – a powerful ideology with which to inspire the new volunteers and focus their commitment.

TEMPLARS: THE IDEOLOGY OF LOVE AND DEATH

All crusaders expected to have to fight on occasion. All the Frankish settlers in the Holy Land knew that they might be called upon to defend their community. Warfare and the prospect of violence were, however unpleasant, at the heart of the crusading movement. And in fighting for their religion, all crusaders were aware of the possibility of 'martyrdom', at least in the loose, overarching sense of being prepared to die for the cause.

But the Templars were different. They took the idea of death and made it their own. With this new military order, the idea of martyrdom became a centrepiece of ideology, rather than an abstract possibility. On one level, this should not be too surprising. The brother knights were the first military order, and throughout the crusades they remained unusual in their exclusive devotion to the art of war. Their Hospitaller rivals, for instance, were similarly elite warriors, but their role also had an emphasis on caring for the sick. With the Templars, there was a simple unity of purpose – the ever-present possibility of violence and death was at the heart of what they stood for.

The formative years of the Templars were (like the Syrian Assassins) the 1120s and 1130s. And it was in this strangely fluid time that the unique ideology of the Templars was formed – a time when survival hung in the balance, but simultaneously everything seemed possible.[17]

As we have seen, there were many 'founders' of the Templar order – ecclesiastical, political and military men all played their part. There were devout knights, such as Hugh of Payns and the local clergy in the Holy Land, including the patriarch of Jerusalem. Even the king, Baldwin II, with his profound understanding of the urgent need for military aid, was intimately involved.

But in terms of ideology at least, the way the Templars thought and the way they operated as a group was largely the product of one man. A man who stood head and shoulders above all the rest and who turned a small military unit into an extraordinary idea – Bernard of Clairvaux.[18]

Bernard (later Saint Bernard, after his canonisation in 1174) was born into the Burgundian nobility in 1090, just before the crusading movement began. In 1113, he joined the new reformed Benedictine monastery at Cîteaux (home of the Cistercians) and his charismatic example was so compelling that many others joined him, too, eventually including his brothers and several other family members. Shortly afterwards, in the summer of 1115, Bernard was sent with a group of twelve monks to establish a new community at Clairvaux.

At some point in the following decade, Bernard seems to have become interested in the defence of the Holy Land. This was not just a theoretical interest, however. He saw potential in the strange new order of Templars, and decided to use it as the vehicle for putting his ideas into practice. Bernard was the man who gave this embryonic new army its unique rules and philosophical grounding.

Structure was the first priority. Between their foundation in *c.* 1119 and Hugh of Payns' recruiting trip to the west in 1127–9, the Templars had operated in an informal way – they got by with a loose structure, a tiny number of men and minimal international recognition. All that was about to change.

A council was convened at Troyes in January 1129, at Bernard's instigation, to regularise the Templars' organisation and consolidate their official standing. Hugh of Payns seems to have visited England and Scotland in the summer of 1128 as part of the recruitment drive, but he came back for the culmination of the lobbying campaign, giving a presentation at the council. Bernard himself was ill, but was under considerable pressure (much of it no doubt self-imposed) to attend.[19]

Interestingly, he had been engaged in the recruitment process even before Hugh's mission to the west set off. As Bernard wrote bluntly to Pope Calixtus II, in a letter dated to late 1124 or early 1125, 'the necessities [in the Holy Land] are fighting knights, not singing and wailing monks'. The Council of Troyes was just the culmination of an extensive and coordinated lobbying campaign.[20]

Heavily influenced by Bernard and by the oral presentation of the equally charismatic Hugh of Payns, it was at this council that the 'Rule' of the Templars was passed. This was a set of instructions which were, in effect, an operational guide for the young order. They became an essential part of the 'welcome pack' for new Templar volunteers. This gave the order credibility and standing – vitally, they now had the official sponsorship of the Church.[21]

Not only had Bernard played a pivotal role in writing the Rule, but it was also around this time that he composed his famous treatise, De laude novae militiae ('In praise of the new knighthood'), for the order. He also sent many letters of advice and guidance to the Templar brothers. Bernard was not a fighting man, but he was in many ways the intellectual founder of the order.[22]

In writing De laude Bernard was clear from the outset that violence could only be condoned if the cause was just, and that any unnecessary bloodshed must be avoided. It was, he wrote, only permissible to kill non-Christians if there was no 'other way of preventing them from harassing and persecuting the faithful'. This was to be purely defensive warfare, with no question of forcible conversions or of attacking people merely because of their religious beliefs.[23]

But this 'new knighthood' was definitely a departure from previous practice. In an age of crusading, the sharp and often artificial dividing lines between the violence of the secular world and the quiet reflection of the cloister were being challenged. Bernard was keen to emphasise how, in the hands of this new hybrid elite, the old distinctions could be swept aside.

The Templars, he wrote, represented

> a new kind of knighthood and one unknown in ages past. It indefatigably wages a twofold combat, against flesh and blood and against a spiritual hosts of evil in the heavens . . . [W]ho would not consider this very worthy of great admiration, even more so since it has hitherto been unknown?[24]

The Templars and 'the new knighthood' were now officially an army, and one to be reckoned with.

8

Templars: 'A Living Sacrifice' (1119–1129)

The Templars now had a structure. And they had the outlines of an ideological positioning. But how would it all work in practice? How would members of a religious order, dedicated to peace and acting according to the precepts of a religion founded on non-violence, behave on a battlefield? The answer was love.

The Templars thought that their death for the cause would be an act of love – a profound devotional undertaking in pursuit of what they believed to be a just war and a just cause. The new ideology of the 'new knighthood' allowed them to argue that even violence and death, in pursuit of this just cause, could be condoned.

The brother knights saw themselves as agents of peace. They were fighting for Christ, the Prince of Peace, and sacrificing themselves to defend the oppressed Christian minorities of the Middle East. If the cause and the intention were good, then their deaths would not be in vain. And if the men were righteous, so their deaths would be pleasing to God, and their combat would be dedicated to the cause of peace – just as Christ himself was the embodiment of peace and love.[1]

And much the same was true of the Assassins, of course. Both saw themselves as the defenders of their faith and of their respective communities – minority groups surrounded by hostile neighbours. They were both founded on polarity and irony.

Violence for peace

Irony to our eyes, perhaps, but not to theirs. In a faintly Orwellian way, war was, for them, an instrument of peace. And violence could be an expression of love. The quiet, menacing dedication of a Templar battle line was, to those involved, the ultimate Christian expression of devotion and self-sacrifice.

The theology of religiously endorsed violence was strongly espoused by Bernard of Clairvaux. It remained a central feature of what the brothers believed it was to be a Templar. This core belief was so strong that many Templars thought of Bernard as the founder of the order – and while this may not have been technically accurate, he was certainly their ideological founder.[2]

The Templars were warriors fashioned as agents of peace. But this seeming paradox had its own internal logic. They were expected to fight in order to re-establish a state of righteousness that had been disturbed by the Muslim invasions of the previous centuries. Bernard explicitly argued that the Templars were not in the Holy Land to be oppressors, but they should be prepared to 'march into battle in order to bring about peace'.[3]

The value of a Templar's earthly life was not to be measured in wealth or shallow, showy displays. Its real value lay in the contribution it made to the cause of God. A life lived according to the will of God created a path to eternal life, and made everlasting salvation feasible. A Templar who was committed to the cause of God through his actions already (in the harsh, but expressive words of Bernard) 'wished to die', so that he could achieve a higher level of existence. There was much here that an Assassin *fidais* could relate to.[4]

The Church believed that Christ's death and sacrifice gave humanity the gift of the remission of sin: it created a path to everlasting life. But those who undertook the work of God on crusade or in the military order took a virtuous fast track to that redemption.

Martyrdom (or giving up your life for your faith) was, in this context, literally a spiritual elevator. It raised a Templar up, creating a shortcut through the mundane and cluttered decisions of life – it led instead to an instant means of conveying the devout brother knight to a better, eternal existence. There was no more moral confusion, no more shades of grey. This was a binary philosophy, one in which even the most simple, illiterate brother could see what he needed to do. Like the Templars' famous piebald standards, the choice between life and death was now an issue of black or white.[5]

A Templar in combat, according to this ideology, was fortunate to have the most profound opportunity laid open for him – he just needed to be brave enough in the instant to grasp it. To die in battle for the cause of Christ was to imitate His death and sacrifice on the cross. As Bernard wrote, 'when such a knight is himself killed, we know that he has not simply perished but has won through to the end of this life.'[6]

From a modern perspective, this ideology (and that of the *fidais*) seems practical enough. It served to motivate and reward good 'behaviour' (in this case, combat skills) and acted as a recruiting tool for what was rapidly becoming one of the most dangerous jobs in Christendom – endlessly fighting against enormous odds beyond the furthest reaches of Europe. But it was far more than that.

Saint Bernard, like the Templar volunteers themselves, was genuinely pious to a degree that we can barely comprehend in the twenty-first century. The promise of martyrdom was, for them all, real. The practical benefits (creating a more effective fighting force for the defence of the Christian Middle East) were just a happy coincidence, co-existing alongside the deeper truths of martyrdom and salvation.[7]

Walter Map, who, like William of Tyre, was no fan of what he saw as the overweening arrogance of the order, told two stories about the Templars and their famous willingness to accept death in the service of their religion. Both contained an inner truth.

TEMPLARS: 'A LIVING SACRIFICE'

In the first, a prominent Templar knight was captured. His Muslim captors subjected him to torture and mock executions. Faced with the choice between apostasy and death, the Templar knight chose death. Impressed by his bravery, his captors set him free, in exchange for 'a pagan youth whom the Christians held captive'. Sadly for all concerned, the young Muslim captive died of natural causes before he could be returned to his people. Given that he had tried to conduct the hostage exchange in good faith, the freed Templar was absolved of any need to return to his captors. Both the king and the patriarch of Jerusalem tried to persuade him to stay. Entirely committed to his honour and his cause, however, the Templar was having none of it, and insisted on going back. His own people eventually went to the extraordinary step of imprisoning the knight to stop him surrendering. Undeterred, the Templar managed to escape and travelled back to his Muslim captors, as he had promised to do. The Muslim leader was so impressed by the Templar's display of good faith, and by his willingness to accept death rather than dishonour, that he set him free once more. The knight returned to his comrades in Jerusalem with his honour intact.[8]

The other story, full of dark medieval humour, again spoke to the Templars' bravery and commitment to death in preference to the 'easy' option of apostasy. Walter wrote:

> About that same time, a [Templar] cleric was being shot with arrows by Saracens to make him deny his faith. One who had already [converted to Islam] was present, and kept taunting him with his folly in believing, and at every shot kept saying, 'How do you like that?' To which the other made no answer. At last seeing him still constant, he smote off his head with a single blow, and the words, 'How do you like that?' The severed head, speaking with its own lips, at once replied, 'Now I like it very well.'[9]

Walter was drily forced to admit that 'these, and others like them, were the experiences of the first Templars'. The stories, despite their obviously legendary features, still contained the essence of what, it was thought, made an exemplary Templar.[10]

Inevitably, some leading Christian thinkers had misgivings about the validity of using violence. Certainly, the apparent paradox of monks of peace serving as agents of war was too extreme and jarring for easy acceptance by all Christians. There was some criticism of the Templars on philosophical grounds, even from the earliest days of the order's existence. Peace and non-violence was the intellectual default position of Christianity.[11]

But most recognised that matters in the material world were rarely clear cut. Even Saint Augustine argued that the use of violence could be justified, albeit only under very special circumstances. For Bernard of Clairvaux, the life and purpose of a Templar knight was unique. The brothers of the 'new knighthood', he argued, waged a war which was spiritual and intangible. But they did so alongside the all-too-tangible forces of evil, as he saw it, in the form of enemies who endangered the safety of the newly recovered Holy Land. This was a conflict that spanned both the material world and the next, and one in which spiritual strength and military prowess blended comfortably together.

The Templars' objectives, both as individuals and as a group, reflected this blended duality. The key corollary of that logic was that no Templar needed (in theory at least) to feel afraid of death – he was, even in the midst of violence, a martyr and hence about to enter into a better and everlasting life.

Much of De laude is devoted to discussion of a succession of 'holy places', such as Bethlehem, Nazareth, Bethany and so on. This is incongruous to our eyes. Why do you need a lengthy religious travelogue in the middle of a pamphlet extolling the virtues of a military order? But for Bernard and the Templars, there was no such tension – the material geography of the Holy Land was important in its own right; but more fundamentally, it was also a reflection of a far more important spiritual landscape and a series of sacred spaces.[12]

TEMPLARS: 'A LIVING SACRIFICE'

This ability to see the material world as a mere shadow of the spiritual one naturally helped inform the central concept of martyrdom through the purifying fire of combat – a few seconds of violence, undertaken in a just cause, provided a quick and glorious pathway to everlasting union with God. As Bernard wrote in De laude when discussing the Holy Sepulchre: 'Christ's life has provided a pattern for living for me, but his death, a release from death. The one prepared life, the other destroyed death.'[13]

Geography, spirituality and a climactic act of war made a strange but seamless combination.

Death and the example of Christ: 'A living sacrifice'

The Templars perfected the papal idea of the Christian knight, the Milites Christi – warriors who combined devotion and spirituality with the sacrifice of death. They believed that Christ had shed blood for mankind and, taking a very literal view, thought that His actions needed to be copied.[14]

Most Christians focus on Christmas and Easter – the birth and resurrection of Christ and the redemption this represents for humanity. But the Templar brothers, whether on the front line in the Middle East or stationed in the rural commanderies of the west, had a very different perspective: they showed instead a remarkable level of devotion to the *death* of Christ.

The Templars at worship placed a particular emphasis on the Crucifixion. This was, after all, the ultimate martyrdom. Perhaps not surprisingly, the brothers made a special effort to collect pieces of the True Cross, relics which spoke directly to their veneration of Christ's death, sacrifice and rebirth.[15]

From the very beginning, attention was drawn to the brothers' willingness to follow Christ's example in embracing sacrifice, even martyrdom, for others. In a papal charter of 1139 (Omne datum optimum), Pope Innocent II praised the Templar martyrs. 'As true Israelites and most instructed fighters in divine battle,' he wrote, 'filled with the flames of divine charity, you carry out in deeds the words of the Gospel, "Greater love no-one has than this, that a man lay down his life for his friends."'[16]

Good Friday, rather than Christmas or the celebration of Christ's resurrection, was the highlight of the order's liturgical calendar. The death of Christ was a particular act (and day) to be 'celebrated'. It was on this day, and by this act of sacrifice, that death was both embraced and overcome – all in the cause of love and peace. The death of Christ was the shining and inspiring example to the Templar brother knights of how the horrors of violence could be transformed into virtue and salvation.[17]

The more obvious emphasis on Christ's birth or resurrection, extremely popular in less warlike parts of the Church, played a far more subsidiary role in Templar devotion. Instead of mangers and shepherds, the unveiling of a representation of Christ crucified was the highlight of many Templar ceremonies. Martyrdom had quickly become the most visible and important way in which a brother knight could express his love of God.[18]

Theoretical ideas of martyrdom were also reinforced in more tangible ways. Much of medieval devotion, particularly among less intellectual clerics, such as the Templar brothers, was of a very literal nature. Templar dedication to the possibility of martyrdom was therefore experienced in many forms of tactile and visual worship. Where there were Templars, there were crucifixes. Both the cross and the passion of Christ were frequently referenced in the Rule of the Templars, as well as in their worship.[19]

Even at the very end, during their later trials, Templar brothers often made reference to Christ's example. The Templar Brother Berengar of Collo, for instance, bluntly suggested that the reason the Templars wore a red cross was because the brothers were proud to shed their blood fighting 'against the Saracens of the Holy Land and other enemies of the Christian faith elsewhere'.[20]

Death lay at the heart of what it was to be a Templar.

TEMPLARS: 'A LIVING SACRIFICE'

Martyrs and Maccabees

So the brothers were not just God's army on earth, but also His martyrs, destined for triumph in the afterlife. Entirely understandably in this context, the inspiration of the early Christian martyrs played a major role in Templar ideology.[21]

This ideology played out in practice, as well as in the abstract. Taking the example of the Templar church in Montsaunès, in the foothills of the Pyrenees, for instance, sculptures were commissioned by the brothers in *c.* 1200–20. They pointedly depict the dramatic martyrdoms of St Paul, St Peter and St Stephen. Other Templar paintings in the church, probably dating from *c.* 1220–50, also reflect a time of physical loss, but (so the brothers believed) of spiritual triumph as well. The elaborate decoration is unusual, but in the context of the death of two Templar masters in this period, both of whom were born nearby in southern France, the church-mausoleum makes more sense: despite defeats on earth, these works of art were created to remind the Templars that they could still look forward to the glory of triumphant martyrdom in the afterlife.[22]

The prospect of martyrdom for a Templar knight was widely recognised and greatly admired. It was clearly an important reason why many donors felt the order deserved their support. When Bishop Raymond of Vichiers gave a donation to the order in 1134, for instance, he stressed that it was at least in part because of its members' willingness 'to lay down their lives for their brothers'. Similarly, Ulger of Angers' donation to the order (made in *c.* 1128–49) was specific in citing the Templars' willingness 'to give their lives or to shed their blood'.[23]

It was not just the bravery of the early Christian martyrs that inspired the new order, however. Even death had to have religious ritual attached to it.

The Templars occupied a strange ground between clerics and knights. There are debates about whether they were, in a strictly technical sense, monks or priests; but they were certainly pious men, bound by strict religious rules. According to James of Vitry, they were expected to go through a process of ritual purification on the eve of battle, by holding 'vigils, fasts, and prayers during peace, so they would be ready to lay down their souls in battle for the defence of the Church'. Martyrdom required care and preparation, and not just on the battlefield.[24]

Bishop James also wrote, with the easy optimism of one who did not put his life on the line, that 'the knights of Christ ought to be completely pure and holy, always ready to die and not for a day risk to be in a state when they would not have courage to die'. They needed to be ready at all times, to go into situations 'where the crown of [the] martyr is expected'. Such a task, he suggested, was possible because only the spiritually unprepared 'have reason to fear and a single just man can defeat many impious'. The Milites Christi needed to be good Christians, as well as good soldiers.[25]

Inspiration was not confined to Christian saints, however. A group of pre-Christian martyrs who died rather than renounce their faith during a revolt against their Hellenistic overlords became known as the Maccabees. As Bernard of Clairvaux was careful to point out, these were the only Old Testament martyrs who merited a feast day (1 August) in the Catholic calendar. The Maccabees became role models for many of those who joined the First Crusade, and it was perhaps not surprising that Bernard, in his unofficial role as Templar ideologue, brought their memory to bear as he shaped Templar doctrines of martyrdom.[26]

Bernard praised Judas Maccabeus, because he had promised that God would help a handful of men to overcome a multitude. The theme of the historical virtues of martyrdom was echoed by Pope Celestine II in 1144, when he described the Templars as 'the new Maccabees'. A senior Templar envoy to the French court in 1164, writing of military disasters in the east, did not feel any incongruity when he compared the commitment of those fighting in the east to the bravery shown by Mattathias, the father of Judas Maccabeus.[27]

The association with biblical martyrdom was thought to be so rousing that a speech attributed to Gerard of Ridefort, as he led his doomed squadron into the massacre that became known as the battle at the Springs of the Cresson in 1187, makes the connection clear. 'Remember your fathers the Maccabees,' Gerard was reputed to have said as they rode to their death,

> ... [and] know that your fathers were victors everywhere not so much by numbers or in arms, as through faith, and justice, and observance of God's commands, since it is not difficult to triumph either with many [men] or few when victory is from heaven.[28]

Like the Old Testament Maccabees, the 'new knighthood' was designed to restore what was, in theory at least, the old peace in the Holy Land, and they were prepared to die as martyrs in doing so.

'By far the better thing . . .'[29]

The Templar ideology of heroism and martyrdom, often in the face of an inevitable death, continued to resonate across the crusades. Writing in the thirteenth century, James of Vitry clearly felt that the willing martyrdom of the Templars provided inspiration both for crusaders and for future generations:

> During the siege of Ascalon [in 1153], a number of Templars were captured by the Saracens, and hanged above the city gate. When the king of Jerusalem, and the other Templars, saw this, they were about to relinquish the siege in despair, but were dissuaded from this by an eminent man of great faith, Master of the Templars, who declared that their martyred brethren had preceded them, and gone to God, in order to deliver the city to them. The result proved the truth of this, for the city was captured, contrary to all expectations, just two days later.[30]

The story had been slightly garbled in transmission. We know that the master of the order had already been killed in combat, or executed alongside his comrades. His body was probably among the corpses dangling from the walls. But the heart of the tale was true: the Templars had indeed rushed bravely into the city, and their deaths seem to have inspired their comrades. Ascalon, the scene of intense frustration and bloody fighting over a fifty-year period, fell only a few days after the Templars' sacrifice.

They remained famous for embracing martyrdom, even as the crusades in the Middle East petered out. Once, it was said, a crusader knight was captured by the Muslims. While the other prisoners were held for ransom, the Templars in the group were, as usual, singled out for execution. Unfortunately for the knight (and in an interesting aside that says much about the no-nonsense way in which the Templars dressed), he was thought to be a brother in the order because he was so scruffy, 'bald and bearded'.[31]

Confused by his dour appearance, his captors took him aside to be killed. They 'said to him: "You are a Templar." He denied it, but they insisted upon it, whereupon, fired with zeal for the faith, he exclaimed: "In the name of the Lord, I am a Templar", and was slain like the rest.' The story, apocryphal or not, reveals an inner truth – the Templars were renowned, both by their friends and by their enemies, as people who were not afraid of death.[32]

For the Templars, the idea of martyrdom was never an abstract concept. It affected every aspect of their spirituality. Even more tangibly, it often improved their military efficiency and fighting prowess. Perhaps most importantly of all, however, it gave them a reputation – a brand – that was feared and respected. And it was that fear which gave such a small group of men political and military leverage beyond mere numbers.[33]

Templar brothers, like the Nizari *fidais*, had a dedication to death that was convenient for their leaders and for their community – but it was also an expression of piety that was deeply and sincerely felt.

TEMPLARS: 'A LIVING SACRIFICE'

Suicide, martyrdom and social boundaries

Much of Templar ideology was based on the idea of victory through death – that martyrdom was the pinnacle of a Templar's life and that it brought him instantly into close communion with God. But there were always tensions in that ideology – and not just the obvious one of justifying the use of violence in a peace-loving philosophy.

Suicide is deeply frowned upon in Christian belief. It was therefore imperative that a Templar's death should not be contrived – to actively seek death for its own sake would be suicide, and suicide would result in perpetual torment. As it had been outlawed by the Church, brothers who deliberately sought death as a way of achieving instant salvation would, on the contrary, condemn their souls to eternal damnation. Suicide on Christ's behalf was an ideological impossibility.[34]

Bernard of Clairvaux made a point of stressing that intention was the vital distinction between suicide and martyrdom:

> Indeed, danger or victory for the Christian are weighed by the focus of the heart, not the fortunes of war. If he fights for a good cause, the outcome of the battle can never be evil; and likewise the result can never be considered good if the cause is evil and the intention unrighteous.[35]

A knight could go into battle, even against apparently insuperable odds. He could look forward to a full communion with God in death, if he fought bravely in a just cause. But it was never acceptable to seek a suicidal ending. Like Christ in the crucifixion, the Templar knight was expected to embrace death, but not to actively seek it.

Strangely, this found resonance with the Assassins. The *fidais*, like Templar brother knights, were trained to be totally committed in their actions. But they were also expected to fight their way out after undertaking their mission, if at all possible. They were implacable, unstoppable, but not suicidal. Both groups of men, *fidais* and

Templars alike, were too precious a resource to be squandered unnecessarily.

Once again, however, there were important distinctions to be made. The issue of death, and the acceptance of death as a Templar norm, expressed itself in different ways. Sometimes the internal logic of enforcing that acceptance could be taken to absurd lengths. And it also applied to different parts of the order in different degrees.[36]

It is important to remember that a Templar army was not composed exclusively of brother knights. As with the *fidais*, the Templar brothers were small in number. They made up only a tiny part of any 'Templar' force. Templar knights (and *fidais*) were both supported by much larger numbers of doctrinally sympathetic, but less personally committed workers, peasants, foot soldiers and so on. For every knight there were dozens of sergeants, mercenaries, Turcopoles, squires and workers.

The initial Rule inevitably focused on the brother knights of the order; but even from the earliest days there were many other volunteers. Some knights were allowed to serve for a set time limit (milites ad terminum), while others could join as married men (affiliated as fratres conjugati). But most of the fighting men in a Templar unit – the sergeants and all the other helpers – were barely mentioned.[37]

This had practical, as well as social implications. The knights were bound by a higher level of ideological commitment than the sergeants and other troops. And nowhere was this more apparent than on the battlefield. Noblesse oblige, of course, and the Rule of the Templars laid down very different levels of expectation: sergeants were not expected to fight on the front line and, unlike the knights, were allowed to retire when wounded.[38]

We know, for instance, that only about 10 per cent of the front-line troops in the garrison of Safad (Saphet) in the early 1240s were Templar brothers. If artisans, slaves and other ancillary staff in the castle are included, the proportion falls below 5 per cent. This inevitably had a huge impact on performance – and on ideological commitment.[39]

TEMPLARS: 'A LIVING SACRIFICE'

The Templar castle of Gaston provides an extreme example of how this might affect behaviour and performance. In 1268, the castle was surrendered by its garrison to the Mamluk sultan, Baybars. This was a disaster. The fortification, occupying a strategic location in the Amanus mountain range, was one of the most important castles in the Latin East.[40]

Gaston and its surrounding lands had been given to the Templars in the 1130s and was at the heart of their first important 'marcher lordship'. But by the late thirteenth century even Gaston had become vulnerable.[41]

In May 1268, Sultan Baybars captured the nearby city of Antioch in just two days. This left the castle of Gaston in a hopeless position – desperately undermanned and isolated. As there was no relief force to send, the master of the Templars sent a messenger to collect the brothers together if they had already surrendered, or to instruct them to surrender the castle if they had not already done so. In the event, the garrison had already abandoned the castle by the time the messenger arrived. But, and this was the ironic part, they were still forced to confess when they got back to the order's headquarters in Acre that they had done so without permission.

A strange, almost Kafkaesque dispute ensued. Some in the order wanted the garrison punished for breaking the rules. Others said that this was inappropriate, as the castle was clearly indefensible and orders for its surrender had already been sent out. Presumably to save face, they reached a compromise. The brothers of the Gaston garrison were given a moderate punishment. But – and this was the face-saving device – the punishment was for their failure to destroy everything in the castle as they left, rather than for the loss of the castle itself.[42]

But the malaise facing the garrison went deeper than mere forms of words. One Templar brother had broken ranks – he turned renegade and absconded to Baybars, informing him that the brothers were teetering on the edge of surrender. Even worse, the loss of the castle had also been partly prompted by a threatened revolt – other members of the garrison, and particularly the Templars' sergeants, wanted to surrender because, they said, 'they did not wish to die'. The brothers were in a desperate situation. The behaviour of the 'other ranks', understandable as it was, rendered a difficult position entirely untenable. Templar armies tended to fight to the last knight, rather than the last man.[43]

This was just as true of the Assassins. The Assassins' *fidais* were backed up by much larger numbers of peasants, followers and ancillary troops in castle garrisons. Where larger numbers were required, as with the efforts to take over Apamea (1106) or Shaizar (1114), the quality of the assault squads was inevitably much diminished. The dilution of training, quality and commitment was clearly shown in the much poorer outcomes of these attacks.

One man's commitment is another man's fanaticism. And even in a Templar army, for every celibate man who was willing to embrace death, there were ten others who were keen to go home and instead embrace their wives and children.

9

So It Begins: The Strangest Partnership (1126–1130)

Before our brief interlude with the Templars, we left the Assassins happily insinuating themselves into power in Damascus and carving out a place on the borderlands of Galilee.

But the influence that they achieved through their relationship with Tughtigin was ultimately fragile and unsustainable. Probably even counter-productive. They were, after all, a small and irritatingly clannish group which was – their detractors felt – little more than a heretical secret society.

The acquisition of Banyas had been a major breakthrough. But the Assassins struggled to build on their new base. Like the crusaders, they did not have the numbers to create a solid state – that was true in Damascus, where they exerted influence without popular support; but it was also becoming self-evident in Banyas itself.

Hubris and hiatus: Failure in the Golan (1126–8)

Getting the title deeds to Banyas was a good start, but the Assassins needed to make their position there more secure, if they were to create a semi-independent state. Life with Tughtigin as an overlord and protector was fine as far as it went – but they knew he would not live forever.[1]

Banyas was to be the centre of the Nizaris' principality in Syria; but other castles and lordships were also in their sights. Ibn al-Athir wrote that, alongside the conversion and missionary programme in Damascus, Bahram had also 'gained several fortresses, including, for example, Qadmus'. So far, so good.[2]

The Assassins moved quickly to quash all opposition in their new domains. Perhaps too quickly. They overstretched themselves. They started to crack down on all opposition and conducted increasingly intrusive raids into the surrounding countryside. Many of the locals in the neighbourhood, including large numbers of tough, semi-nomadic Bedouin tribesmen, were underwhelmed by their new landlords.

Bahram and his followers established themselves in Banyas, and other followers of the sect from across the region quickly gathered there, eager to find a place in the new, semi-independent principality. Once fully installed, they relaxed and began to enjoy themselves. They carried out enthusiastic banditry (or so it was said by their Sunni detractors) 'against lonely travellers on the highways, whom they seized with violence and used despitefully, and with the slaying of men outrageously and unjustly'.[3]

Their reputation was not helped by the bullish way in which they tried to gain converts. 'In all directions,' wrote Ibn al-Qalanisi with his usual undisguised loathing of the Assassins, Bahram 'dispatched his missionaries, who enticed a great multitude of the ignorant folk of the provinces and foolish peasantry from the villages and the rabble and scum, persons without intelligence to restrain them from mischief'.[4]

This verdict may include a large dose of Sunni prejudice; but as was often the case with the Nizari sect, the unpopularity was at least partly self-inflicted, brought about by their own extreme actions. Aggressive as ever, and turning to murder as a preliminary negotiating stance, rather than as a last resort, they had not been afraid to make enemies.

Eventually they got too cocky – they just couldn't help themselves. They tried to impose their rule too aggressively. Inevitably, there was a falling-out with one of the local Bedouin chiefs, for reasons that are

SO IT BEGINS: THE STRANGEST PARTNERSHIP

obscure (even to contemporaries). Whatever the reason, Bahram lulled the Bedouin leader into a false sense of security and, it was said, after luring him 'into his hands, he put him in fetters and killed him in cold blood'.[5]

The murder of their chief, in defiance of all codes of honour and hospitality, was unlikely to improve relations with the dead man's family and followers – the Assassins may have calculated that the murder would leave the Bedouin leaderless and cowed, rather than angry and seeking revenge. If so, they were wrong.

They had seriously underestimated their opponents. The Bedouin were fierce warriors, almost as dangerous and clannish as the Assassins themselves. The dead chief's family and tribe gathered to take action against their enemies. Trying to take the initiative, the Assassins moved out of their fortress to head them off. Bahram and his men 'marched out from Banyas' and headed off towards Wadi al-Taym, where the Bedouin were mustering.[6]

Their actions were observed, and the Bedouin, about a thousand in number, took them completely by surprise – as only nomads can. They

> charged upon them when they were in their camp and off their guard. Shouting the battlecry, they took them unawares, and before the horseman could mount his steed or the footsoldier could seize his weapons, death overtook the greater part of the [Assassins].[7]

The blow fell so quickly that it caught Bahram completely unawares. He and his bodyguard were in his tent and 'on hearing the uproar and shouting they had leapt up to seize their weapons, but the men of [Wadi al-Taym] rushed upon them with their keen swords and death-dealing daggers and killed the whole company'.[8]

In the frenzied slaughter that followed, Bahram's head and hand were cut off, and his body was hacked to pieces 'by swords and knives'. To prove the victory beyond all doubt, one of the Arabs 'took these, along with his ring, to [Fatimid] Egypt'. It seems that Bahram's Bedouin were Ismailis, but not Nizari supporters. Sectarian differences may have been at the root of the dispute between the two groups. Once they had arrived in Fatimid territory, the gruesome trophies were exhibited and passed around as evidence of the triumph. The remnants of the Assassins' militia fled back to Banyas, entirely understandably, 'in a wretched state'.[9]

The Assassins' dream of a frontier state in the Golan was severely dented.

Muslim enemies and crusader allies (1126–9)

The Assassins were not the only ones with an eye to the main chance in Damascus and the Golan. For the crusaders, the city was the biggest prize in the Latin East – the great regional centre, a major population hub and the enduring Muslim opponent of the Latin kingdom of Jerusalem.

It had been a thriving Christian provincial city at the time of the Arab invasions, but Damascus had been overrun in 634 – and despite early efforts by the Byzantine military to recapture it, it remained in Muslim hands.

But if the city could be recovered, it would free up vital lands – lands to attract knights from the west to defend the Holy Land and colonists for settlement. It would bolster the eastern flanks of the crusader states. It would help stem the flow of nomadic tribes into the region from the north and sever communications between Muslim Egypt and the Seljuk Turks in Syria and beyond. Damascus was a vital objective – and the crusaders understandably strained every sinew to try to capture it.[10]

King Baldwin II of Jerusalem prepared for the task meticulously, building up experience, ramping up intimidation, gathering military resources and making probing raids whenever the opportunity presented itself. In the autumn of 1125, he launched a tentative attack into Damascene territory, and in 1126 he carried out an even more serious

SO IT BEGINS: THE STRANGEST PARTNERSHIP

invasion. Trying to gain further momentum, and sensing that Damascus might topple if pressure were applied, he also sent diplomatic missions to the west in 1127, to call for help.[11]

The objective of the mission was well understood by contemporaries. Hugh of Payns and the other ambassadors were

> sent by the king and the chief men of the kingdom to the princes of the West for the purpose of rousing the people there to come to our assistance. Above all, they were to try to induce men of influence to come to help us besiege Damascus.

And as we have seen, there was another motive. Hugh was also undertaking a hugely successful and high-stakes fundraising and recruitment drive in western Europe – his charm offensive to convert the Templars into a truly international force.[12] History was converging in one very small area.

Things were looking grim for the Assassins in Banyas; but they were about to get even worse. Tughtigin, their main supporter in Damascus, died in February 1128, at around the same time that the overconfident Nizaris were being hacked to death in the Golan and Bahram's body parts began their involuntary road trip around eastern Egypt. Tughtigin's son, Taj al-Muluk Bori, became the new atabeg of Damascus.[13]

Ismail the Missionary, Bahram's successor as leader of the sect in Syria, tried to carry on business as usual in Damascus – under the circumstances there was little alternative. He must have hoped that Taj al-Muluk would continue his father's reliance on Nizari loyalty. And there were reasons to hope that that might indeed be the case.

Despite Tughtigin's death, the Assassins still had supporters in Damascus – their cause in the city was buoyed up by the support of the pro-Nizari vizier, al-Mazdaghani, who remained in post to provide stability during the transition of power. The vizier made it clear that he 'maintained towards Ismail the same policy as he had observed towards Bahram'. Perhaps he had spiritual leanings towards the Nizaris – but, as always, most commentators viewed his support more cynically. The vizier, it was said, was thought to be aiding and abetting the Assassins, not because of any genuine affection for the sect, but out of fear – 'in order to guard himself against their malice and out of desire for his own safety'.[14]

Regardless of motivation, the vizier could not protect them forever. The situation was becoming increasingly fragile and luck was not on the Assassins' side. Their critics became bolder. Rumours of plots and treachery were everywhere and 'the complaints of the people, men of rank and commons alike, continued to multiply'.[15]

Feeling – entirely correctly – that their days were numbered, Ismail opened up negotiations with the Franks – these negotiations may even have involved discussions about launching a coup and handing over control of Damascus to the crusaders. Or perhaps they involved operating in some form of condominium with the Franks, as they had in effect done with the Seljuk Turks (in the form of a loose partnership with Ridwan in Aleppo and Tughtigin in Damascus). Profit-sharing arrangements between crusaders and local Muslims, particularly in frontier zones, were surprisingly common at this time.[16]

For their part, the Assassins were not particularly anti-Christian – as a 'heretic' minority, surrounded by more orthodox Muslim states that hated and persecuted them, the Nizaris never had that luxury. They could also be surprisingly open-minded about spiritual matters – far more so, in fact, than many of their Catholic or Sunni neighbours.

Indeed, in the absence of major conflicts of interest, there were few inherent reasons why the Assassins and the crusaders should be enemies. The Franks were infidels, of course, but they did not have any specific animosity towards the Assassins. If they had a vague awareness of Muslim sectarian in-fighting, they were probably not interested, beyond the potential it offered for diplomatic and military advantage – they certainly saw no intrinsic advantage in persecuting Islamic 'heretics'.

The crusader kings of Jerusalem and the Assassins had long-standing diplomatic connections and they seem to have communicated amicably

SO IT BEGINS: THE STRANGEST PARTNERSHIP

enough. Sometimes they even coordinated their military activities. The princes of Antioch, northern neighbours of the Assassins in Syria, generally maintained good relations with the sect. And, in a very tangible affirmation of trust, Nizari refugees fleeing from pogroms had long been happy to find safety in the crusader states.[17]

The Sunni chronicler Ibn al-Athir was convinced that the Assassins and their allies were in league with the crusaders:

> In due course, al-Mazdaghani contacted the Franks to surrender to them the city of Damascus and for them to hand over the city of Tyre to him. This was agreed between them and they settled on a date, a Friday which they named. Al-Mazdaghani agreed with the [Assassins] that on that day they should seal off the gates of the mosque and not allow anyone to leave, in order that the Franks might come and seize the city.

It is not clear how advanced these negotiations were, but later events suggest that Ismail and his people had been in diplomatic contact with the crusaders for some time.[18]

We shall probably never know the full truth. Tyre belonged to the crown, so it is not inconceivable that the revenues of the city might have been used as part of the king of Jerusalem's negotiating stance. And King Baldwin was so desperate to take control of Damascus that he would have given any possible deal due consideration. But whatever discussions were in train with the crusaders, they came to an abrupt and bloody end on 4 September 1129.

Taj al-Muluk made a decision that shocked no one. He decided that he wanted to be his own man. He no longer wanted to rely on a vizier who would associate him so closely with the unpopular Nizari 'heretics'. In an act which showed that local politics need not always be boring, al-Mazdaghani was murdered very publicly after a town council meeting. Taj al-Muluk himself gave the signal to strike, and the murderer struck [the vizier's] head several blows with his sword and killed him. His head was then cut off, carried with his dead body to the ash-heap at the Iron Gate, and thrown upon it, that all the people might see the act of God upon one who plotted and sought other helpers than Him.

Just for good measure, 'his body was burned with fire some days later, and reduced to ashes strewn by the winds'. Unpopularity in medieval Damascus had tangible consequences.[19]

The Nizaris had overplayed their hand – they were on their own once again.

Pogroms and betrayal

Word spread instantly. The vizier's death was taken as a signal for a widespread pogrom. The Nizari communities within Damascus and its territories were destroyed. Thousands of people were left dead in a particularly vicious eruption of sectarian violence. More importantly for the crusaders, the possibility of a negotiated takeover of Damascus, if it had ever really existed, was gone.

Taj al-Muluk, according to a more than usually sanctimonious Ibn al-Athir, 'proclaimed about the city, "kill the [Assassins]", and 6,000 of them were put to death . . . Thus God saved the Muslims from their wickedness and turned their plotting back upon the infidels.'[20]

The Damascene militia, assisted by people unkindly described as 'the mob and the refuse of the city', led the attack. The entire Nizari community was targeted, and local gangs were unleashed with official approval. They 'pursued [the Nizaris] into their dwellings, fetched them out of their places, and dispatched them all either by dismemberment with swords or by slaughter with daggers, and they were thrown out on the dung-heaps'. Pent-up resentment burst forth in the most violent fashion.[21]

Old friendships and loyalties counted for little when the chips were down. Even those who had taken refuge with their rich and powerful

SO IT BEGINS: THE STRANGEST PARTNERSHIP

friends – people 'who hoped for safety through their intercession' – found themselves cut adrift. All Nizaris were 'forcibly seized and their blood was shed without fear of consequences'. There was a temporary but complete breakdown of law and order in Damascus.[22]

The Nizari leader in the city, Shadhi the Freedman, was among those captured: he and his lieutenants were crucified on the walls of Damascus for all to see. The death toll of the massacre by the Sunni militia and crowds in Damascus was (very implausibly) put as high as 20,000 in one account. But whatever the exact number, the Nizari population in Damascus and the surrounding districts was effectively gone. The Assassins' short-lived hegemony in southern Syria had come to an abrupt end.[23]

News of the disaster soon reached Ismail the Missionary, Bahram's successor. Luckily for him, he was based out of harm's way in Banyas. But even this refuge was fragile. The Nizaris were still a minority in their own town, and a none too popular one at that. When he learnt of events in Damascus, Ismail was said to have 'feared that its populace might rise against him and his followers'.[24]

The citadel of Banyas had been strengthened, but most of the garrison had been killed in combat at the battle of Wadi al-Taym, the previous year. Given the Nizaris' small numbers and the lack of any credible relief force, it was ultimately indefensible. In the absence of any alternative, Ismail made the hard choice quickly, and 'sent to the Franks, promising to deliver up Banyas to them, in order to seek safety with them'. The castle was duly handed over 'and he with a number of others came into their hands and slunk away from Banyas into the Frankish territories'. Sunni commentators were pleased to suggest that when they got there, they experienced only 'abasement and wretchedness'.[25]

Ismail's dreams for the Nizaris lay in tatters. A broken man, he died just a few weeks after leaving Banyas, in late December 1129. The chronicle of Damascus created a suitably undignified end for their enemy, and noted with unconcealed satisfaction that he died 'smitten by the disease of diarrhoea'. But it is significant that the Assassins' good relations with the Latin kingdom of Jerusalem extended to the new Frankish garrison in their old castle in Banyas – Ismail was allowed to be buried in the castle grounds, an act which implied that Nizari pilgrims would be welcome visitors.[26]

What remained clear, however, was that the sect's urban strategy in Syria was now at an end. If thriving, populous places such as Damascus or Aleppo were not available, then they would have to look more closely at the old Persian model – they turned once more to the attractions of remote valleys and unassailable mountain castles.

The drive on Damascus

The pogrom in Damascus immediately triggered the long-prepared attack by the Templars and the other crusader forces. The Frankish army set off for Damascus in October 1129. This timing was highly unusual: no one started a major campaign in enemy territory in winter. And for good reason: roads became more difficult and fodder for horses became scarcer. Supporting a large army in enemy territory became a logistical nightmare. And with the collapse of Ismaili power in Damascus, the chances of a negotiated surrender were much diminished.

The assault seems to have been deliberately delayed during the course of the summer, while negotiations continued with the Nizaris (and possibly the vizier, al-Mazdaghani) to engineer a peaceful surrender of the city to Frankish forces. The wave of pogroms against the Nizaris definitively ended the dialogue, however. It forced the Franks to take action, regardless of the season and the normal rules of campaigning.

As Ibn al-Athir later wrote,

> when the Franks heard of the killing of al-Mazdaghani and the Ismailis at Damascus, they were very dismayed and regretted that they had not been able to achieve the take-over of Damascus. The disaster fell upon all of them. They all gathered, the king of Jerusalem, lord of Antioch, lord of Tripoli and other Frankish [rulers] and their

counts and also those who had come by sea for trade or for pilgrimage. They gathered in a great host of about 2,000 knights and of infantry beyond counting. They marched to put Damascus under siege.[27]

King Baldwin seems to have calculated that the opportunities outweighed the risks, and that his enemies would be as badly affected by the weather conditions as his own army. Certainly, the force he could field was formidable by Frankish standards. Many members of the army were experienced in this kind of warfare, having participated in recent successful sieges, such as the capture of Tyre in 1124. And the armies of Jerusalem, Antioch, Tripoli and Edessa were joined by a new Templar contingent, together with Fulk of Anjou's men and other crusaders.

But King Baldwin had to move quickly. Damascus was destabilised after its civil unrest, the Templars were gathered and he had well-motivated troops to hand, freshly arrived from the west. If he delayed, Damascus would soon recover and the unemployed crusaders would drift off back to Europe during the spring crossings in April.

To help with the preparations, the Christian armies exploited their new base in the Golan to the full. Having 'joined forces they halted at Banyas, where they established a camp and set out to collect supplies and provisions for their stay'. That was the end of the good news, however. Possession of Banyas was extremely useful, but the emphasis on the need for reprovisioning, because of the time of year, was ominous. The Frankish army had not yet left Christian territory, but the chroniclers noticed that foraging was already becoming an issue.[28]

The crusader army marched towards Damascus in the slow, tight formation needed to ensure protection against increasing numbers of enemy light cavalry. In the face of deteriorating weather conditions and dwindling food supplies, however, the Templars and the rest of the Frankish army ground to a halt near Darayya, about 10 kilometres south-west of the city.[29]

A loose siege of the crusader field camp began. The army was loath to retreat, but it did not have the strength to move forward. This stalemate could not last. In the middle of winter it was impossible to sustain an army in a fixed location. The precariousness of the crusaders' position was clear to all. Food was increasingly scarce. Foraging parties failed to return to camp, as they were surrounded and destroyed by enemy scouts. The Franks 'realised that the position was now such that they could not possibly hold on, knowing as they did that the Turkish troops far outnumbered them'. They had no choice but to turn back.[30]

The end of the campaign was anti-climactic. Damascene troops pursued the crusaders for a while and 'the rearguard of the fugitives was overtaken by the *'askar* [regular cavalry], who killed a number of persons separated from the main body'. But apart from a few stragglers, the exhausted Christian army was able to escape unscathed.[31]

The Templars' mission back to Europe had been a triumph and turbocharged the military role of the order for the next 170 years. They had been able to motivate 'many bands of noblemen' from across Europe to follow them back to the east. Their small armies had travelled far and mustered for the assault on Damascus. But in the event, they were lucky even to be able to withdraw in moderately good order back to Jerusalem.[32]

Both the Templars and the Assassins had seen their ambitions for Damascus come to naught.

As their Sunni tormentors rounded on them once again, the Assassins had taken a course of action that was not only ostensibly unthinkable, but also strangely portentous in terms of their future dealings with the Templars: they had turned to the crusaders for help.

The events of 1126–30 had been tumultuous – the secret negotiations between the Assassins, the Templars and the other Frankish authorities; the step-change in Templar strategy and recruitment that was partly sparked by the opportunity to work with the Assassins to seize Damascus; the shocking pogroms that destroyed the local Ismaili networks and derailed those plans; and the way in which the vital frontier castle of Banyas had been handed over to the Franks.

The bloody events of those pivotal years set the two groups on their strangely parallel paths for the next 150 years.

10

Assassins: Home Sweet Home (1130–1162)

The Assassins had taken a pounding. But the implacable nature of the sect, and its members' grim ability to show patience in the way they delivered death to their enemies, was demonstrated in classic style in 1131.

Taj al-Muluk of Damascus had turned against the Nizaris. In 1129, he had ordered the massacre of the sect's many followers in Damascus. After the pogrom, he knew that he was a prime target for the *fidais* death squads, and he increased his security accordingly. It was not enough. As always with the Assassins, events proved that no one was untouchable.

Retribution

Taj al-Muluk did not have long to wait for his new security arrangements to be tested in the most dramatic way. Ibn al-Qalanisi, a Damascene himself, wrote a wonderfully biased but fascinating account of the attack. In 1129, when news of the disaster in Damascus 'reached their fellows at Alamut', he wrote, the Assassins 'were filled with sorrow for them'. Grief was easily expressed in the traditional way. They sent 'two simpletons from Khurasan, to whom they gave instructions to devise some means of gaining access to Taj al-Muluk and to kill him in his palace when an opportunity should offer.'[1]

This small *fidais* squad 'reached Damascus in the guise of Turks . . . and made their way to some acquaintances of theirs among the Turks, whose good offices they asked to enable them to enter the employment [of the emir] and have a regular salary assigned to them'. Presumably helped by bribery, they eventually hit the jackpot – both men were selected to become members of his bodyguard.[2]

In classic *fidais* style, the team was 'thought to be completely trustworthy, since they had been guaranteed'. They watched for an opportunity to strike. The moment came on 7 May 1131. Taj al-Muluk left his castle to go down to the baths, surrounded by his guards, moving slowly in tight formation. The baths themselves were easier to secure. The public was removed and there were few exits and entrances to worry about. When he had finished, the security team formed a phalanx around him once more, and escorted its leader back to the citadel. They arrived without incident. Job done. Or so they thought.

The bodyguards relaxed. When Taj al-Muluk 'had reached the gate of his palace in the citadel of Damascus, all the members of his cortege . . . who were guarding him dispersed and left him'. The *fidais* saw their chance.[3]

Their attack was made more difficult by the fact that their victim was mounted, so they had to stretch to get to exposed, vulnerable areas. Difficult, but not impossible. As he rode past, 'one of them struck him with a sword, aiming at his head, but only dealt him a wound in the neck which did not penetrate into it, and [the other] struck him in the flank with a knife'. Taj al-Muluk jumped from his horse and ran for his life. In the meantime, his guards 'mustered in increasing numbers against the two Assassins and hacked them to pieces with swords'.[4]

Taj al-Muluk survived the attempt, but died of his wounds the following year. His ending was exactly the kind of death that the Assassins would have chosen – long, difficult and extremely disruptive. The pain 'dragged on until he grew weary of life and longed for death;

his weakness and the wastage of his body and strength increased, his end drew nigh, and his hopes of restored health were disappointed'. He died on 6 June 1132. It was said that in Damascus 'all hearts were filled with sorrow at his loss and all eyes with tears at the fate which had befallen him'.[5]

This attack was revenge in its purest form – the Nizaris had no chance of rebuilding their place in Damascus. But they had settled in for the long term: they had patience and were prepared to play a waiting game. Above all, they were determined to show that no one, however important, however well protected, could become their enemy without facing consequences.[6]

The Bedouin tribe who had killed Bahram and his Nizari warriors at the battle of Wadi al-Taym were even harder to get to. An isolated tribe with tight-knit familial relationships, they were difficult for any *fidais* team to penetrate. Even so, once sufficient time had passed for them to let their guard down, it proved possible. In 1149, some twenty years after Bahram's death, an Assassin squad managed to exact revenge. They found a way to get past the security of the Bedouin chief, Dahhak ben Jandal, and killed him. Revenge, and death, might be slow – but, in true Assassin style, it was inexorable.[7]

Castles in the mountains

Indefatigable as ever, after the loss of Banyas, the Assassins just picked themselves up and started to rebuild. Far from being beaten, in the years that followed they established a substantial and largely independent principality in the Lebanese mountains to the north-east of the county of Tripoli, planting the seeds of their new home in the cracks between the fractious states of Antioch, Tripoli, Shaizar, Aleppo and Damascus.

The Assassins had faced appalling rebuffs in Syria. They had tried to take over some of the most desirable real estate in the region, and had been killed for their ambition. In Aleppo and Damascus they had been subjected to ruthless massacres that had destroyed their urban bases and devastated their nearby rural communities. In Shaizar, they had tried to take over a heavily fortified town on a vibrant river crossing, only to get the same result – their men had been wiped out and their co-religionists in the town and neighbouring villages butchered during the inevitable reprisals. They needed to try something new. Something less ambitious perhaps, but a way to create a 'principality' of their own, where they could be free from persecution by their many enemies.

Their plan this time was less far reaching and far less dramatic – but all the more effective as a result. They decided to take over some of the least desirable castles in the region, in some of the most inhospitable places. And they also changed their methods. They began to use money and charm, as well as violence and manipulation, to make it all happen.

The combination of more limited objectives and more palatable methods worked. Between 1130 and 1141, the Assassins succeeded in doing what they had tried – and failed – to do over the previous three decades: they built up a formidable network of highly defensible castles in the middle of a crowded region. The dream of a Nizari state in Syria became a reality.

They took over large parts of what we would today call the Jabal Ansariyya, but which was known in the twelfth century as the Jabal Bahra (or Bahra Mountains). Importantly for the Assassins' new plans, the Jabal Bahra, situated between the Sunni principality of Hama and the Mediterranean coast, already had a substantial Shiite population. This was not a high mountain range by the standards of their previous efforts. It was, for instance, less than half the height of their mountain bases in Persia. And inevitably, there were many enemies close by. There was no vacuum in the Mediterranean coastal area of Syria. But it was the best, perhaps only, strategic option available to them, and they grasped it with both hands.[8]

The centre of the network of fortifications that the Assassins eventually established were the major castles of Masyaf, Kahf and Qadmus, surrounded by other castles such as Khariba, Rusafa, Khawabi, Ullayqa and Maniqa. Smaller forts were also built to help control approach roads around this impressive network.[9]

None of this came about by accident. There were two broad phases to this extraordinary spurt of Nizari state-building – the first in the early to mid-1130s and the second in the early 1140s. Both were propelled and enabled by military weakness in the nearby crusader state of the county of Tripoli.

The early 1130s were tough times for the county of Tripoli. Calling it a 'county' perhaps makes it sound more grand than it really was. The eastern frontiers of the small crusader state had always been vulnerable to attack by its Muslim neighbours. Much of its territory was in a relatively thin strip of land along the coast of Palestine and Syria, lodged uneasily between the Latin kingdom of Jerusalem to the south and the principality of Antioch to the north. This made any idea of a 'defence in depth' unfeasible – as a result, the county of Tripoli was dangerously fragile, even by the low standards of the time.

Inland, much of the population consisted of independently minded mountain folk. Regardless of their religious affiliation (there was a large Muslim presence, but many of them were Christian), they had their own interests to pursue. They could not always be relied upon in a crisis. To make matters worse, the county was almost surrounded by Muslim states. Shaizar was in the north-east, Hama and Homs to the east and Baalbek to the south-east. Threats were everywhere.[10]

Even before the Muslim states began to coalesce under the influence of the new generation of Turkic strongmen and their fierce nomadic mercenaries, the local Frankish military were overstretched. This was (just about) sustainable when the Muslim states were disunited and under-resourced, as the counts of Tripoli could play one off against the other. But when they were united and well supplied with Turkic cavalry, the county had to rely on the other Franks in the region for help.[11]

The crusaders' Sunni Muslim enemies exploited this weakness ruthlessly. Strong leaders such as Zengi of Mosul (r. 1127–46) were continually probing, raiding and invading the eastern borders. Contemporary chroniclers noted with disdain, for instance, that Count Pons (1112–37) was the first leader of Tripoli who did not feel strong enough to take the fight to the enemy by launching attacks on Muslim-held Homs.

And, as if that was not bad enough, Pons foolishly chose this moment to pick a fight with his neighbour, King Fulk of Jerusalem, which escalated into civil war. The conflict that followed only ended when Fulk was forced to march north to meet Pons in battle at Rugia, and the uprising was put down with much unnecessary bloodshed. The frontiers of Tripoli were in perennial danger of collapse, even without the self-inflicted disaster of such foolishness.[12]

For much of the 1130s until his death in 1143, King Fulk of Jerusalem was on campaign, helping to shore up the borders of his Frankish allies in Tripoli or even further north in Antioch. He knew, regardless of how ungrateful his neighbours might be, that the critical threats to the crusader states would be played out in the north, rather than the south.[13]

It was in this complex and shifting environment along the Jabal Bahra that the Assassins saw, and seized, their opportunity – they took what turned out to be the first steps towards the creation of their state in Syria. The Assassins bought the castle of Qadmus in 1132 from its Sunni Muslim ruler, the lord of Kahf, while Count Pons of Tripoli was preoccupied with his foolish and self-indulgent war with King Fulk. The castle was set in the west of the mountain range, at a commanding height and with excellent views of the surrounding countryside. It lay at the heart of what was to become the Assassins' giant fortification complex in the Jabal Bahra.[14]

Although it was only a medium-sized castle, the strategic position of Qadmus made it a natural command centre and one of the Assassins' main bases in the region. The Nizaris quickly made improvements to the castle, putting it in much better shape to withstand a long siege, and adding extensive new storage chambers, remnants of which still survive today. The imposing transformation of Qadmus was reflected in the views of those who saw it. The Jewish traveller Benjamin of Tudela, for instance, writing of his journeys in *c.* 1165, thought it impressive enough to be described as the Assassins' 'principal seat'.[15]

Soon after they acquired the castle, in October 1133, an army of nomad mercenaries commanded by Zengi, the atabeg of Mosul, invaded the county of Tripoli – shockingly, they even penetrated as far as the suburbs around the city of Tripoli and the Mediterranean coastline. These profound military problems were almost catastrophic for the county of Tripoli, but they gave the Assassins the opportunity to fan out still further. The acquisition of Qadmus may not in itself have been enough to secure a safe home for the Assassins, but it was a good start. Having strengthened Qadmus, the Assassins looked for other properties with which to expand their power base.[16]

Their next major acquisition was the even grander castle of Kahf, sold to them by the son of the same lord of Kahf who had given them Qadmus – the family may have been ostensibly Sunni, but it clearly had Nizari leanings. Locked in a spectacularly bitter succession dispute, the castle's owner preferred it to go to Nizari 'heretics', rather than end up in the hands of his cousin. Again, not coincidentally, it came into their hands through negotiations and an attractive financial offer, rather than the far blunter and more risky instrument of violence.[17]

This extremely isolated (and still hard to find) castle had been built around 1120. It became a major centre for the Assassins and was developed as a palace for their leadership. We know, for instance, that it was a base for diplomatic activity with the Franks in 1197 and possibly, in the thirteenth century, with King Louis IX of France and his crusaders.[18]

The scale of the fortifications is immense, and may have extended to 2 or 3 kilometres in length. It was built on a rocky spur whose sheer cliffs provided a strong natural defence. Any assault on Kahf would have been extremely difficult, because of the fortifications. And even an extended siege was problematic – the castle had its own natural springs and artificial canals to bring water into the garrison.[19] There are signs of at least seven water cisterns, many of which were interconnected, and several bath houses. The sophistication and complexity of the water storage system in the castle hint at its importance as a political and cultural base for the Nizaris, as well as its more obvious function as an impressive fortification. The main bath house seems, from a surviving inscription, to have been built in 1172, during the government of Sinan, the original Old Man of the Mountain, and there have always been suggestions that he was buried in Kahf, rather than the more famous Assassin castle of Masyaf.[20]

In 1136–7, soon after the acquisition of Kahf, local Nizaris also managed to expel the Frankish garrison at Khariba and eventually took control of it for themselves, despite fierce opposition from the Sunni lord of nearby Hama. The sect's castle network had at last achieved critical mass.[21]

With security on the borders of Tripoli deteriorating further, the Assassins continued to expand. They captured their most important fortification, the huge castle at Masyaf, just to the east of Qadmus, in 1140. With this impressive castle as the de facto capital of their small, mountain-refuge state, the Assassins could regroup, consolidate and perfect the extraordinary practices for which they are now so famous.[22]

The early history of Masyaf is largely unknown. The crusaders seem to have been in control of it in 1103. But the Assassins were by now so well established in the region that they did not always need to use charm to get what they wanted. Ibn al-Qalanisi, admittedly not a fan, later wrote disapprovingly that they 'seized' the castle in 1140 'by means of a stratagem'.[23]

Masyaf controlled a strategically important position at the intersection of the road from the crusader-held Mediterranean port of Baniyas (not to be confused with the fortified town of Banyas on the Golan Heights) to Sunni-held Hama, and of the road north up from Homs towards Aleppo in the east and Latakia on the coast. The walled town of Masyaf, which lies at the foot of the Jabal Bahra hills, was impressive enough in its own right – it originally had four gates, three of which can be dated by inscriptions to later refurbishments in the 1240s.[24]

But the castle of Masyaf was even more imposing. Set about 20 metres above the plain, it was, like the famous crusader fortress of

Kerak, built on a rocky promontory some 150 metres long. The buildings within had their own majesty – they were at least six levels high, standing up to 50 metres tall. The main entrance to the castle was suitably intimidating, too. It could be approached only by walking along a vulnerable path and climbing a steep external staircase, which was exposed to archery fire from the defenders. Anyone who survived that journey found himself confronted by the horrific prospect of attacking a heavily fortified barbican. This was a formidable base.

Masyaf, like the better Templar castles of the period, was concentric in nature. It used multiple layers of defence to seal off any breakthrough of the outer walls by attacking forces. The inner citadel formed a castle within a castle, and allowed fire to be rained down on anyone who penetrated the initial layers of defence.[25]

The castle was built on solid rock foundations, so there was little chance that it could be taken by mining – the Assassins were all too aware that this was a speciality of Sunni Muslim siege experts, such as those employed by Zengi and his successor, Nur al-Din. As with Kahf, the complex water systems speak to the sophisticated long-term planning behind the design of the fortifications. We know of four or more wells in the lower levels of the castle, for instance, and the water raised from these wells was stored in huge water cisterns. There was even enough spare capacity for the luxury of substantial bath houses.[26]

It is indicative of the smaller numbers of the Nizari garrisons that their castles seem to have had no posterns (concealed exits) within them. Byzantine and crusader castles that were built on this scale tended to have garrisons which were large enough, and aggressive enough, to use posterns as places from which to launch sorties against enemy besiegers. In Nizari fortifications, however, their much smaller garrisons tended to settle in for a purely defensive siege. The Assassins never had numbers on their side.[27]

But fortifications could make up for lack of numbers. Masyaf was a huge castle in its own right, but it was at the centre of a growing number of such fortifications. Like the crusaders, the Assassins used their castles as an expensive but essential 'force-multiplier' – a way of empowering and conserving their more limited military forces.

The Assassins eventually created a fortified area that was almost impregnable to all but the most determined besieger. The number of castles and forts in the region that they had bought, captured or built was huge, particularly given the relatively small area involved – estimates range from twenty-four up to around seventy fortifications. They were so well positioned, and so closely packed together, that any attacker would inevitably face enormous difficulties. This was the formidable centre of a new Nizari state.[28]

The economics of security

The Assassins now had their home – a network of strong mountainous castles and a safe base from which, if necessary, their *fidais* teams could operate. But there was something strange about the way the *fidais* were deployed.

Having established an independent homeland, the obvious course of action for the famously clannish Assassins would be to withdraw from their Sunni neighbours – these were, after all, people who detested and persecuted them. The Assassins were determinedly intellectually self-sufficient. This, surely, was the Syrian Nizaris' chance to say goodbye to fractious interactions with the more judgemental elements of mainstream Islam – they could now lower the shutters and keep themselves to themselves.

And yet that did not happen. On the contrary, time after time, we now find the Assassins touting for business among their Sunni neighbours, only too happy to trade the deadly services of their murder squads for cash payments and political advantage. How did they get drawn into a series of escalating murders, settling other people's old scores?

Historians have often either ignored this seeming contradiction, or claimed that it did not actually happen. Instead, they argue, a lot of the 'contracts to kill' ostensibly taken out on behalf of Sunni clients were either obfuscations by the sect or fabrications by its enemies.[29]

But it is important to remember what the successful underpinning of a viable medieval Middle Eastern state looked like. Most players had several compelling economic advantages on their side. Some possessed huge tracts of fertile land. Others had ports or access to other trade routes, which produced high levels of taxable income. Some also had large cities with economically active urban populations producing attractive revenue streams. Almost everyone, including the cash-strapped crusaders, had one or more of these assets. But the Assassins had none.

Security in the medieval Holy Land was eye-wateringly expensive. Defence cost money – and, sadly for them, the essence of the Assassins' solution to their defence problems was to hole up in places that would cause them economic problems. Building a castle was cripplingly expensive. We do not have any surviving financial accounts for Nizari castle-building; but taking the example of the Templar construction project at Safad, south of the Assassins' heartlands in Syria, we can see what a huge undertaking it was. Unlike the Nizaris, the Templars could call on external resources (from Europe) to help. And, nearer to hand, the castle itself was said to be able to draw on the revenues of 260 villages to support its maintenance. But even so, it was still, literally, a monumental effort.

Building castles was a money pit. An anonymous pamphlet, written in 1260–6, tells of the shocking amounts of cash that had to be poured into such a project. Building work at Safad began in the 1240s, and we are told that in the first couple of years 'the [Templars] spent on building the castle of Safad, in addition to the revenues and income of the castle itself, eleven hundred thousand Saracen bezants, and in each following year more or less forty thousand Saracen bezants'.[30]

And that was just the beginning. Garrisoning and maintaining a major castle was a never-ending financial drain. 'Every day,' the same pamphlet recorded, victuals are dispensed to 1,700 or more and in time of war, 2,200. For the daily establishment of the castle, 50 knights, 30 serjeant brothers, and 50 Turcopoles are required with their horses and arms, and 300 crossbowmen, for the works and other offices 820 and 400 slaves. There are used there every year on average more than 12,000 mule-loads of barley and corn apart from other victuals, in addition to payments to the paid soldiers and hired persons, and in addition to the horses and tack and arms and other necessities which are not easy to account.[31]

It is clear that even in the most fertile and productive countryside, castle-building was a devastatingly expensive commitment. Safad was no ordinary castle, of course: it was the medieval equivalent of an aircraft-carrier. The Assassins' castles tended to be simpler, and with smaller garrisons. But they were building a huge network of such fortifications. There were dozens of castles in places that were, by their very nature, mountainous and hard to access – not the most economically desirable real estate. As one western visitor wrote, in a fairly matter-of-fact way, the land around their castles 'is not particularly fertile, unless one lives off beasts'.[32]

The costs they were incurring must have been prohibitive, especially for a group with very limited sources of income. If we are looking for a reason why the fiercely independent Nizaris of Syria often demeaned themselves by acting as hired killers for their hated Sunni neighbours, we probably need look no further.

The Assassins were never rich. Like the Templars, their mystique was a fertile source of stories about treasure and other febrile imaginings. But the truth, in both cases (and particularly with regard to the Nizaris) was far more prosaic – building and maintaining large castle networks was not cheap. They both struggled to get by.

The chronicler Juwayni was present in the final days of the Assassins' vast fortress of Alamut, the capital of their state in Persia. He was involved in gathering their property together and assessing its value.

ASSASSINS: HOME SWEET HOME

Juwayni made a point of rummaging through their library (he had, after all, a professional interest in such things) and looked over the other valuables they had collected. But, other than for a historian, it is clear that these were slim pickings. Their new overlords were underwhelmed.

The last Nizari leader 'offered his treasures [to the Mongols],' wrote Juwayni, 'as a token of his allegiance. These were not so splendid as fame had reported them but, such as they were, they were brought out of the castle.' Even these choice items were not deemed worthy of being sent to the khan, however. Instead 'the greater part thereof was distributed by the King among his troops'. To the victors, the spoils – but the spoils, in this case, were barely worth having.[33]

The Assassins may have been as fierce as mountain lions – but they were also as poor as church mice.

11

Templars: The Little Castle on the Prairie (1130–1169)

The two mightiest armies in Europe were on the march. But their path was full of horror. These were skilled fighting men, but they were walking from Europe to the Holy Land, and encountering Turkic tactics for the first time – their experience counted for very little. In theory at least, they understood broadly what they would be facing. But the armies of the Second Crusade provide a case study in how not to conduct an orderly fighting march in the face of the enemy.

The German army of Conrad III had split up and been largely destroyed by the Seljuk Turks in October 1147, at the second battle of Dorylaeum. The French forces, led by King Louis VII, one of the west's most prominent crusaders, were in imminent danger of following the Germans along the same self-destructive trajectory. At the most basic level, they did not even know how to organise their march properly – and the Turks were not the opponents to let such sloppy behaviour go unpunished.

Luckily, there were Templar veterans present to try to instil some sense of 'best practice'. But its practical application left much to be desired. The need for a strong force in the vanguard, and another in the rear, was understood, at least in theory. But the French army of the

Second Crusade consistently underestimated the need for flank guards to protect the baggage train in the middle of the long, strung-out column.

Even more worryingly, the French king was inexperienced. Control was weak. What passed for discipline was lax in the extreme. There were far too many high-ranking nobles present, each with his own loudly voiced, overentitled and underinformed opinions. Orders were interpreted as suggestions; suggestions were ignored. Decision-making on the march often looked more like a poorly moderated group discussion, rather than the expression of firm strategic direction that was so plainly needed.[1]

The English commentator John of Salisbury, writing after the event, suggested that the French army had 'neither military discipline nor a strong hand to dispense justice and correct faults, [and had] lost all hope of ordered strategy'. Everyone was wary of criticising an anointed king too overtly, but the experienced leadership that a successful fighting march required was clearly lacking. And the arrogant independence of some of the greater nobles would ultimately lead to near disaster.[2]

Chaos and crusade (1147–8)

As they approached Mount Cadmus in early January 1148, the vanguard was under the command of 'a certain nobleman from Aquitaine called Geoffrey de Rancogne', who, together with Count Amadeus II of Maurienne, King Louis's uncle, petulantly decided that standing orders could be ignored. Not understanding – or not caring about – the difficulties that the rest of the army would have in keeping up, he chose to press on in defiance of instructions.[3]

As light began to fail, the entire column became increasingly disoriented. Units jammed together in confusion. The army was hardly a shining example of the military arts even in daylight; at dusk, it began rapidly turning into little more than a disorganised mob. In the chaos that ensued, the king was almost killed and elements of the French army were routed.[4]

Minds were focused by the imminence of destruction. The leaders knew they might not be so lucky next time. As he should have done at the outset, the king decided to give tactical command of the army to those who had the best understanding of how to deal with Turkic harassment – the Templars.

The order maintained a small, but elite task force within the army. It had contributed a contingent of some 130 men when Louis set off from Paris in 1147, presumably alongside larger numbers of their other retainers and hired troops. More importantly, they also brought their understanding of how to handle Turkic horse-archers. Putting their battlefield experience into practice, the Templars had performed extremely well on the march. Unlike many of their brave, but ill-disciplined colleagues, they were still in good fighting condition.

The Templars immediately put simple but effective organisational structures in place. They defined a clear chain of command. Sub-commanders were nominated and assigned clear roles in different parts of the marching column. Each was given standardised numbers of troops. Extraordinarily – and a sign of just how desperate the situation had become – everyone in the army was forced, on oath, to become a temporary lay-brother of the Templars. An oath was not something taken lightly in the medieval world – all were now subject to the order's rules and famously strict military discipline.[5]

The reorganisation was accompanied by a crash course on how to deal with Turkic cavalry. The discipline of the French host was tightened up. Archers and crossbowmen were deployed where the Templars knew they were most needed. Flanks were more assiduously protected. But the very basic nature of the remedial action that was now put in place speaks volumes for how disorganised the French had been before the Templars took control.

The French looked ungainly and amateurish compared to the more rigorous approach of the warrior monks. The Templars had learnt their trade on the hard training grounds of the Middle East, and it showed. The contrast was clear – a European army, however large, and however prestigious its leaders, lacked the cohesiveness that was needed to fight large Turkic forces while on the move.

The Templars had made clear their willingness to die for the cause. William of Tyre wrote that it was under Pope Eugenius III (1145–53), probably as a result of their discipline and service during the Second Crusade, that the Templars were given the right to wear a distinctive red cross on their surcoats. This simple symbol was given in recognition of their willingness to shed their own blood, and ultimately give up their lives, in the defence of the Latin East. Interestingly, James of Vitry, who lived in the Holy Land for many years, wrote of this red cross explicitly not just as a sign of bravery and sacrifice, but as a symbol of the Templars' acceptance of martyrdom.[6]

This was a turning point in the military history of the crusades – and it was the moment when the Templars transformed themselves from a small group of absurdly ambitious ecclesiastical bodyguards into mounted martyrs, leading the fight for the Christian Middle East.

A new knighthood for a new army

Injecting better-quality military practice was at the heart of what the Templars offered. This was particularly true in terms of the tactics needed to defeat light-cavalry horse-archers – a supremely dangerous type of warrior, almost unknown in western Europe. The military orders were not just making European troops better at what they already did. They also used their new professionalism to change the entire way in which Europeans waged war in the Holy Land.[7]

The poor performance of the armies of the Second Crusade was just one example of a much bigger problem. It was important to ensure that men on their way over from the west adapted as quickly as possible to the strange local conditions that they would meet when they arrived.

As well as their more obvious presence on active duty in the east, one of the many benefits of having a Templar organisation in the west was that the order could start to influence military best practice even before the crusading forces arrived in the east. Painful experience showed that new troops from Europe, and particularly the knightly class, were overconfident. They were also woefully unprepared for the horrors that steppe cavalry could inflict on a battlefield.

Crusaders were essentially tourists – however brave or skilled, they were still just passing through. Using crusading manpower for strategic purposes was difficult. Unhelpfully, there were just as many problems associated with its tactical use. Faced with very different styles of warfare in the east, travellers from the west could not be expected to adapt fully during the few months they were on pilgrimage. The amateurishness of new arrivals could be an active embarrassment. And the lacklustre performance of new (ill-acclimatised and only temporary) crusaders was often repeated during the twelfth century.

The role of the new Templar troops should not be exaggerated. They were never a fully 'professional army' in the way that we would use the term. But they had better resources, and the more 'corporate' focus of the new warrior monks allowed them to take a longer view. At their best, they could rise above the compromises and complications of local issues. The Templars also had the opportunity to develop and implement military best practice across large bodies of men – and this was a highly unusual luxury in the medieval world. They could identify the tactics that were most successful. And they could, by their example and training, introduce these new tactical responses into the west's crusader armies.

It is hard to be definitive about the key points in time when these innovations were put into practice – with the partial exception of the Rule of the Templars, there are no surviving strategy papers or planning documents. But whenever we see military innovation, we find the Templars at the forefront of change.[8]

When radical new concentric castles with multiple layers of walls were being built in the Holy Land, it was the military orders who took the lead.[9] As Turcopole horse-archers (Christian light cavalry) were recruited to deal with enemy horsemen, it was again the Templars who were in the forefront – they employed these archers in large numbers and created the senior position of 'Turcopolier' officers to command them. And as professional crossbowmen began to be recruited into Frankish armies during the twelfth century, so the order became a major employer of their services.

Famously, of course, whenever a determined and coordinated charge was called for, the Templars were those entrusted with taking the lead. They led by example – these were men who combined unit cohesion with bravery, and discipline with an aggressive spirit. Ironically, given their supposed fanaticism, whenever restraint was most called for, the Templars were there, too. The command of the tail end of a fighting column, always the most dangerous position and the one most susceptible to severe provocation, came to be given almost invariably to the military orders – only they had the discipline needed for the task.[10]

The military sophistication of the Templars, and the burdens being placed upon them, had clearly grown enormously over the previous two decades.

'We do not think you will find us alive'

Those burdens were only to increase. As the chronicler William of Tyre put it, with a bitter understatement bordering on black humour, as the Second Crusade petered out in 1149–50 the military situation in the Holy Land 'became manifestly worse'.[11]

The Christian East was certainly in need of help – the frontiers of the crusader states had come under intense pressure, and the growing strength and professionalism of the new Templar forces were sorely needed. The rulers of the crusader states welcomed any help they could get. They quickly learnt how to work in tandem with the Templars – and the Templars increased their military expertise, holdings and influence in the region accordingly.

Like the Hospitallers, the Templars seem to have established their own landed estates on the dangerous frontiers of the crusader states from an early stage in their development. When Alfonso-Jordan, count of Toulouse, confirmed the position of the order in his county in 1134, he made reference to extensive lands which it had already received 'in eastern parts from the king of Jerusalem, the prince of Antioch, and the count of Tripoli'.[12]

As Alfonso-Jordan was part of the ruling family that controlled the county of Tripoli, he was well positioned to give an accurate assessment of the Templars' status in the Holy Land. The order's archives have been almost entirely lost, so it is hard to produce definitive data. By way of comparison, however, detailed studies of land holdings in the lordship of Caesarea show that many of the villages in the lordship were owned by the Hospitallers by 1149. We do not have the exact data for the Templars, but there is no reason to think that their holdings would have been significantly less. We do know, for instance, that they owned more castles in the lordship than their Hospitaller rivals. Significantly, by the middle of the thirteenth century all the castles in the lordship were owned by the military orders.[13]

Although we lack many details of the process, it is clear that the Templars continued to take on huge financial and personal burdens throughout the late 1140s and 1150s. They fortified and manned entire stretches of the vulnerable frontiers in Palestine and Syria. Expansion was propelled by urgent need. All this took place within the context of a deteriorating political situation in the east. The crusader states' Muslim enemies, whose disunity had allowed the Franks of the First Crusade to gain a foothold in the Middle East, began to coalesce under the ruthless leadership of a series of Turkic warlords. Foremost among these was Zengi, atabeg of Mosul. He was a brutal but effective leader, and a deadly enemy of the crusaders – it was he who first captured a major Frankish city.

Zengi and his armies arrived outside Edessa, capital of the northernmost of the crusader states, at the end of November 1144. As always, the appalling lack of manpower was an issue. The defenders were mainly local Christians, fighting alongside a small number of Franks. They were highly motivated, but the city was acutely undermanned. The scale of the fortifications was impressive, but on their own they could not stop the besiegers indefinitely.

On 14 December 1144, Zengi's miners dug under the town walls, causing catastrophic damage. As the defences collapsed, so Turkic troops broke in and a violent massacre began. The usual ethnic cleansing ensued. The surviving Armenians and other native Christians were permitted to return to their homes, but the European prisoners were all executed. On 23 December, after a siege of twenty-eight days, the citadel and its garrison surrendered on terms. The entire county of Edessa east of the Euphrates collapsed in a matter of weeks.[14]

The disasters kept piling on. On 29 June 1149, the armies of Nur al-Din, Zengi's equally brutal successor, invaded the principality of Antioch. The northern Frankish army intervened, but failed to turn the tide. It was badly cut up at the battle of Inab; and in the case of Prince Raymond, this was quite literally so – his head and right arm were chopped off and presented as trophies to be sent on a triumphal, but increasingly unhygienic, tour of the Muslim courts of the Middle East. The loss of life at Inab was enormous – the defeat, wrote one Templar officer, meant not only the death of the prince, but also 'all his barons and men'. Antioch, the last remaining bastion of crusader power in the north, was on the verge of complete collapse. And in an ironic aside, Prince Raymond and his Templar friends at Inab died fighting alongside some extraordinary allies – the Assassins.[15]

In 1148, Nur al-Din, Zengi's successor in Aleppo, had abolished the Shiite forms of prayer that had traditionally been used in the city. This was in effect a declaration of war on the Nizaris. Perhaps finding themselves unable to get close enough to murder their enemy, the Assassins chose an unusually conventional way of taking their revenge. Showing once more their lack of qualms at cooperating with the crusaders, the sect formed a military alliance with their Frankish neighbour, the prince of Antioch, in his campaigns against Nur al-Din. The battle casualties at Inab included the commander of the Assassin contingent and most of his men.[16]

ASSASSINS AND TEMPLARS

We do not know how the Assassins reacted to this catastrophe, but the Templars lost so many men that they were in a state of shock. Unfortunately, the master, Everard des Barres, was absent at this time of crisis. He had gone back to France to organise a new crusade, and he was with King Louis when news of the disaster arrived.

Templar troops from other areas of the Holy Land were mustered as part of the relief column being formed to stave off complete disaster in the north. The commander of these troops was Andrew of Montbard, the seneschal of the Temple (*c.* 1148–54). Before he set off on his dangerous ride north, Andrew sent a letter back to the west to let everyone know how quickly the situation had deteriorated. But most of all, he asked for immediate help: he desperately needed men and money from France, Britain and all the other Templar provinces.

Andrew was the senior military commander in the master's absence, and became master of the Templars himself soon after. He was probably one of the order's very earliest recruits, and by the middle of the century he was one of its most experienced warriors. The seneschal was also the uncle of Bernard of Clairvaux, the man who had been the order's intellectual architect. This was not a man who would panic unduly.

But even such a hardened veteran was clearly shaken by the rapid collapse of the military situation in the east. As he wrote to the master,

> Our brothers joined up with the king of Jerusalem to go to the immediate help of Antioch, forming an army of 120 knights and up to a thousand well-armed squires and sergeants. Before we had crossed the bridge of Tyre we received a loan of 7,000 Acre and 1,000 Jerusalem besants to pay for their equipment.

We are, he continued,

> in desperate straits through lack of knights, sergeants and money [and] we entreat you, father, to return to us quickly with enough

arms, money, knights and sergeants to enable us with God's help to come to the aid of your eastern Mother Church.[17]

In the master's absence, his officers had almost bankrupted the order to gather a small army with which to ride to the help of their fellow Franks. The Templars' manpower in the Holy Land was so stretched that only a tiny number of men could be spared to go back to summon more help from the west. 'Do not be surprised that we are sending you such a small number of brothers' with this message, wrote Andrew:

[I]f only we had you and all the brothers living in the regions beyond the sea with us! Many of those who were in our army are dead, which is why we need you to come to us with those brothers and sergeants you know to be fit for the task.[18]

The seneschal was resigned to the likelihood that he and his surviving men would be dead by the time reinforcements arrived. He wrote a moving conclusion to his note, almost a farewell to his comrades in the west. It serves as a soldier's summary of much of the Templar ideal, and the sacrifices they were continually expected to make:

No matter how quickly you come, we do not think you will find us alive, but come without delay . . . It is time for us to honour our vows to God, that is sacrifice our souls for our brothers and for the defence of the eastern Church and the Holy Sepulchre.[19]

In the event, Andrew and many of his men survived. Antioch was saved – for the moment at least. But the Templar bloodletting continued unabated – and the new revenues and volunteers from western Europe were sorely needed to fill the gaps in the ranks.

The Templars were now an essential part of the military backbone of the Latin East. Fractured, impoverished and vastly outnumbered, the crusader states could not have survived long without the military orders' continuing help and commitment. As the Muslim powers became more consolidated, and as the strategic situation in the east deteriorated over time, so the influence and responsibilities of the Templars grew. Alongside the Hospitallers, they stepped up to meet the demands of defence as best they could. There was no one else with the resources to do so.[20]

A palatinate in the north

An ideology of death was demanding. But it was also, perhaps strangely, satisfying: it offered instantaneous certainty. For the Templar knights, as with the members of a *fidais* squad, the path was clear – once you bought into the ideology, you knew exactly what to do.

There were tactical manoeuvres and moments of bravery ahead. But whether it was the fierce commitment of a charge or the nerve-racking moments leading up to an assassination, the big decisions had already been made. For the individual at the cutting edge, and particularly for men who were not necessarily intellectually inquisitive, this made a lot of sense. They understood their role, and they did it supremely well.

The respective groups had deeper issues to consider as well, however – issues of corporate survival, macro-economics and complex, shifting political relationships. Alongside their more obvious roles as ferociously dangerous operatives who specialised in the tactics of death, the Templars and the Assassins both needed to be thoughtful state-builders. And the castle networks of the Assassins found a striking parallel in the awesome fortifications and 'principalities' built by the Templars.

The Templars, just like the Assassins, were perennially short of manpower. And, for the same reasons, both groups needed to create their own defensible network of castles and lordships. But where the ideal Nizari castle was hard to find and isolated, the Templar enclaves had to be in the forefront of defence – manning the frontiers and protecting the vulnerable civilian settlements that lay beyond.

TEMPLARS: THE LITTLE CASTLE ON THE PRAIRIE

The north and north-east of the crusader states were always particularly vulnerable to attack. It was from this direction that large numbers of Turkic cavalry entered the region – tribesmen drawn down from the Eurasian steppes by the prospect of plunder and profitable employment as mercenaries by the Muslim states of Syria.

Units of tough Templar troops were deployed in large numbers in this region to try to stem the flow. On the borders between Cilician Armenia and northern Syria in the early 1130s, the order set up what was effectively its own 'state within a state'. It built and garrisoned a string of castles along the Amanus mountain range, trying to restrict movement through the two main mountain passes – the Syrian Gates and the pass of Hajar Shughlan.[21]

Raymond of Poitiers (the man who lost his head at the battle of Inab) had been established as prince of Antioch in April 1136. He soon conceded the rights to large swathes of land in the Amanus mountains to the order. We do not know what castles, if any, the Templars already held in the principality at that time. But a stream of letters back to the west testifies that they soon had significant military interests in the region.[22]

There had been a long Byzantine military presence in the area. It is likely that the order mainly occupied and improved existing fortifications, rather than building its own castles from scratch. The Templar castle of Gaston was the linchpin fortification in what became a powerful network, positioned to try to defend the north of the crusader states and, more broadly, to stem the flow of nomadic tribes into the area. Built some 26 kilometres north of Antioch, and positioned to guard the Syrian Gates, it helped control the northern approaches to the principality. The Templars had another castle, Darbsak, at the northern entrance to the pass. These castles were masked by two further fortifications known to the crusaders by the wonderfully incongruous names of La Roche de Roussel and La Roche Guillaume.

The Templars may have been a vital part of the Frankish armies, but they also had an independent streak. They soon had to be treated as more or less reliable allies, rather than subordinates. John Kinnamos, for instance, a Byzantine official, noted that the Templars and the Hospitallers formed separate elements within the Frankish army during the siege of Antioch in 1137. He wrote that the Byzantines eventually called off the siege by coming to terms with the prince of Antioch's troops, who were described as being distinct from the '*frères*' of the military orders and from the contingents supplied by native Christians. Even from their earliest days, the Templars were doing their own thing.[23]

The Templar network helpfully provided Antioch with a screen towards the north; less helpfully, it also meant that the Templars became semi-autonomous marcher lords on the fringes of the principality.[24]

Galilean frontiers

As in the north, the early years of Templar military activity in the Latin kingdom of Jerusalem were hardly encouraging. Many of the order's early interventions were enthusiastic, but dogged by failure. Its members were still learning their craft and had failed to achieve critical mass in their recruitment drive or in their castle-building activities. This was partly because of the severity of the casualties they had suffered. In 1129, many of the volunteers whom Hugh of Payns had brought back from Europe were killed while on a foraging expedition, as the campaign against Damascus unravelled in dramatic fashion.[25]

Yet another disaster unfolded a decade later, in 1139. While the field army of the Latin kingdom of Jerusalem was away on campaign in the Transjordan, Turkic mercenaries from the Fatimid garrison in Ascalon launched a large incursion into Frankish territory. The raiders attacked the Frankish settlement of Thecua, just south of Bethlehem, and killed those who had not already evacuated the village and taken refuge in the nearby caves.[26]

News of the attack reached the Templar master at the order's headquarters in Jerusalem. Accompanied by 'some of his brethren and by a few knights of various ranks who had remained at Jerusalem, he immediately made all speed' to rescue the civilians at Thecua. The enemy cavalry retreated in the face of this mixed force, and the Christian forces started to relax.[27]

But as soon as it was clear that discipline had begun to break down among the impromptu Christian relief forces, the raiders turned on them. The result was a bloody rout. The Fatimid troops

> fell unexpectedly upon the bands of Christians . . . [who] tried to flee. But escape was practically impossible, because the place was rough with rocks and almost pathless. Some perished by the sword, and others were hurled headlong from precipices. From Hebron . . . even to the boundaries of [Thecua] the Turks pursued and wrought terrible massacre upon the Christians.[28]

The engagement had been a fiasco, and casualties were accordingly high. As ever, more men died in the rout than in the battle itself:

> Many noble and famous men fell on that day. Among others who perished was the illustrious Knight Templar, Eudes de Montfaucon. His death caused universal sorrow and mourning. The victorious enemy returned in triumph to Ascalon, rejoicing over the destruction of the Christians and the spoils which they carried with them.[29]

Despite this setback, the flow of resources and reinforcements gathered pace. It was no coincidence that one of King Fulk's Angevin compatriots, Robert of Craon, was chosen to replace Hugh of Payns as Templar master when he died (in c. 1136). Robert was described as being 'a man of pious memory in the Lord; an excellent knight and vigorous in arms, noble in the flesh and in his conduct'. He and Fulk, a king continually drawn into military firefighting in the north of the crusader states, seem to have got on well, and helped establish the military prominence of the Templars in the Latin kingdom of Jerusalem.[30]

With royal support, and more volunteers from Europe, the professionalism and the resources of the Templars quickly improved. From the middle of the twelfth century onwards, the Templars were actively encouraged to build castles and defensible enclaves around them – in effect, creating their own militarily sustainable lordships and de facto marcher principalities.[31]

In the 1160s, once much of the initial glut of castle-building and garrisoning in the north had been absorbed, the order turned its attention to the vital, and vulnerable, frontier zone with Syria – the flashpoints with the Turkic rulers of Damascus in the Transjordan (which the Franks called the Oultrejourdain) and Galilee. It is hard to know whether this was a result of Templar ambitions or, probably more likely, because no one else had the men or money to do the job. Either way, the defences, once again, needed shoring up.

Philip of Milly, lord of the Oultrejourdain, gave the order his castle of Ahamant (Amman), along with Belqa and lands in the Buqaia, when he joined the order in 1166. In northern Galilee, the Templars acquired the castle of Safad in 1168. After the massive (and hugely expensive) upgrading programme for the castle, it became one of the cornerstone fortifications of the crusader states.[32]

Defence on this scale was not just about the 'glamorous' front-line activities: logistics, support and defence in depth also had a vital part to play. Accordingly, the Templars created a central administrative presence to help sustain their frontier 'principalities' in the Latin kingdom of Jerusalem. The castle of La Fève was built, probably to act as a central supply depot and training centre. It was conveniently located at the intersection between the Acre–Bethsan road and the Tiberias–Jerusalem way. Its importance was shown by its large garrison, which included 50–60 knights, and a much larger number of other personnel. The castle's central location was so useful that it was used twice in 1183 by the field army of the entire kingdom as its muster point.[33]

Caco, another Templar castle just 6.5 kilometres to the east of La Fève, also had a relatively large garrison of some thirty brother knights, alongside all the other ancillary staff. Between them, they gave an exceptional 'reserves and depot' capacity for the order's frontier zones with Egypt and Syria. However much strain the Templars were under, they were increasingly indispensable for the defence of the kingdom.[34]

Southern frontiers: Gaza and Ascalon

Gaza, in the Latin kingdom of Jerusalem, became another Templar 'principality' – and the order gradually took over much of the defence network of the Sinai desert, facing the Fatimid Egyptian caliphate.[35]

After decades of attacks from the Fatimid garrison at Ascalon, the Franks were keen to go back onto the offensive. By 1150, King Baldwin III and the Templars felt confident enough to start building a castle at Gaza, south of Ascalon, cutting its overland supply lines. From that time onwards, the base could only be reprovisioned by the Egyptian navy, using Ascalon's notoriously dangerous shipping facilities – ships either had to be beached or stay offshore and discharge their cargoes onto smaller vessels. The weakness of the garrison was obvious.

Gaza was entrusted to the Templars as a means of piling pressure on the fading Fatimid forces in Ascalon. In the early spring, 'when the interior of the fortress was partly finished, the king and the patriarch returned to Jerusalem. They left at Gaza the Knights of the Temple, to whose care the castle was committed.' The order was keen to demonstrate that it had the aggression and resources to maintain a high level of pressure along the whole southern border with Egypt. But being stationed in the castle also put its members in great danger. Egyptian soldiers based in Ascalon were in their rear and potentially blocking their own supply lines back to Christian-held territory.[36]

Fatimid reinforcements were shipped in to Ascalon in a last desperate attempt to disrupt the castle's construction. When the main Christian army marched out of the building site, it left the Templars to complete the final 'fitting-out'. The Egyptian forces saw their opportunity. They 'appeared in large numbers before the stronghold at Gaza and made a furious attack on the place, where the townspeople had fled through fear of the enemy'. After several failed assaults, however, 'the officers in command saw that their efforts were useless and left for Ascalon'. The battle seems to have been bloody, but, from the Fatimid perspective, unsuccessful.[37]

More was to follow. The Egyptians were acutely aware that they had to destroy Gaza, ideally before it could be completed. To do so, they needed help. Nur al-Din, a Sunni Muslim who was no great friend of the Shiite Fatimids, sent a nominal force of thirty horsemen, commanded by an emir; but he also allowed the Egyptians to recruit 860 unemployed Turkic cavalrymen from his lands (an interesting indication of the large numbers of steppe mercenaries in circulation, just waiting for job opportunities).

The next major assault on the town was launched soon afterwards, probably in early 1152. This attack was no more successful than the first, and the Muslim forces were repulsed by the Templar garrison. The brother of Usama ibn-Munqidh, the famous Shaizari diplomat and raconteur, died in the debacle, much to the shock and sadness of his family.[38]

The Templar garrison of Gaza was eager to prove itself and

> from that day the strength of the foe was apparently weakened and their power of injuring decreased until gradually they ceased to harry the lands around them . . . They feared the ambuscades arising from the fortress lying on the way and stood in great awe of the knights [Templar].[39]

But this was just one part of the broader Templar attempt to set up a de facto principality along the border with Egypt. Templar patrols, and their Bedouin auxiliaries, were soon making their presence felt. As William of Tyre later put it, Gaza 'served as a fortified boundary at the south and was a great protection to that district against the Egyptians'.[40]

The endgame for Ascalon was fast approaching. In 1153, the combined forces of the Latin kingdom of Jerusalem and the Templars put the city under siege. At a pivotal moment, fire broke out and damaged part of the city's walls. First in line as ever, the Templars surged into the breach.[41]

About forty brothers managed to hack their way into the heart of the city, but the main army lagged behind. The narrow gap they had exploited was sealed off before their comrades could follow. The besieging forces outside the walls now had to wait in grim frustration as the Templars, having battled their way through the congested streets, made a desperate stand in the town square. They fought hard, but inevitably were wiped out. Master Bernard of Tremelay, who had only been in post for a few months, had led the attack and died alongside his comrades. The bodies of the fallen knights were hung from the city's battlements as a grotesque taunt to their attackers.[42]

Despite this grim episode, the sacrifice of the Templars had not been in vain. The reckless bravery of the assault and the weakened condition of the walls was now obvious to the defenders. Ascalon fell to the Franks just a few days later.

The incident contained two crucial warnings for the brother knights, however. The first was the staggering cost in lives. Although the Templar forces contained many men – including squires, sergeants and Turcopoles – it was the brother knights who bore the brunt of the fiercest fighting. The forty dead knights constituted a large proportion of the Templar forces available in the field.

The second lesson was far more insidious. Beyond the physical carnage, there lurked another dangerous problem – the Templars' reputation. Despite their gallantry, they were not universally admired. Collecting funds for the war effort drew accusations of greed. Their elite status and martial prowess was interpreted by some as arrogance and pride.

In the wake of the failed assault on Ascalon, William of Tyre, a member of the local clergy who resented the order's privileges, did not celebrate the Templars' courage. Instead, he seized the opportunity to condemn them, alleging (entirely fancifully) that their assault was motivated by a desire to hoard the spoils for themselves. It was left to native

Christians to recognise their efforts and single them out for praise – as Matthew of Edessa wrote, 'many of [the Franks], including the Templars, came to merit the martyr's crown' in the siege. The Templars, despite their bravery, were beginning to discover that the admiration they might have expected was not always forthcoming.[43]

Overstretch and exhaustion

There were certainly victories. But the pressure was unremitting. When Banyas, the crucial ex-Nizari castle on the north-eastern frontiers of the Latin kingdom of Jerusalem, came under attack in 1157, a Templar army joined the Frankish relief forces. Far from helping, however, the joint expedition was almost completely destroyed – on 19 June they were ambushed by Nur al-Din's armies at Jacob's Ford on the Upper Jordan. Although the king managed to escape, the Templars were particularly hard hit – Bertrand of Blancfort, the master, and eighty-seven of the brother knights were captured and imprisoned in Aleppo. Embarrassingly, Bertrand's captivity only came to an end in 1159, after Manuel, the Byzantine emperor, lobbied for his release.[44]

There were survivors, but the dual fiascos at the siege of Ascalon (1153) and the battle of Jacob's Ford (1157), alongside the other 'normal' but cumulatively shocking attrition of skirmishes and illness, meant that most of the order's fighting brethren had been lost within a couple of years. The need for reinforcements from the west once again became urgent.

Despite a rapid growth in their military capabilities, the Templars were still in danger of becoming overstretched. Raising armies and building castles was cripplingly expensive. Men needed to be trained and shipped out from the Templar network in the west on a continual basis – and the order geared itself up for this unremitting military and logistical challenge.

Just taking the period 1149–53 as an example, we find the Templars sending an entire army to the principality of Antioch with the king of

Jerusalem, in order to shore up the fragile Christian communities in the wake of Nur al-Din's ferocious invasions (1149); garrisoning the pivotal new castle at Gaza, on the border with Fatimid Egypt (1149–50); taking on the main role in defending the southern frontiers of the Latin kingdom of Jerusalem (1150 onwards); and leading a bloody assault on the city walls of Ascalon during the Frankish siege of 1153.

Being at the forefront of the fighting put huge pressure on the order. Everyone was at risk. Casualties among the Templar brothers were heavy, and that was reflected even in the life expectancy of the masters themselves. Just looking at the 1150s, for instance, it is clear that leadership of this elite group was a front-line role.

As we have seen, Master Bernard of Tremelay died at the head of his doomed band of knights as they hacked their way into Ascalon in the final days of the siege of 1153. Similarly, Bertrand of Blancfort had been master for just a year when he was captured, along with eighty-seven of his men, in June 1157, on campaign in Galilee. A later Templar master, Odo of Saint-Amand, was also captured in 1157, released, and then recaptured in battle twenty years later. He died in a Muslim dungeon soon afterwards.[45]

The order paid in blood for its military prominence.

'A miserable, lamentable state'[46]

While pressure in the northern crusader states was mounting, in the south the last real opportunity to build a long-term future for the crusader states was gradually unfolding: during the 1160s there were sustained and increasingly desperate attempts by crusading armies to bring Egypt, and the huge income produced by the Nile, back under Christian control.[47]

But the frontiers were a continuing drain on the order's men and money. Nur al-Din inevitably took advantage of the absence of the main Frankish field army in Egypt to attack the northern crusader states. He confronted the armies of Antioch and Tripoli at Artah on 10 August

1164. In the ensuing battle, he destroyed them almost completely. Many of the local Frankish knights were killed and all the leaders of the north were captured. The count of Tripoli, the prince of Antioch, the titular count of Edessa, even the local Byzantine commander – all were taken prisoner.

Inevitably, the Templars had been in the thick of the fighting. Their place in the front ranks meant that they bore a disproportionate share of the casualties. In a series of dispirited letters written in 1164, Geoffrey Fulcher, the preceptor of the Temple and Bertrand of Blancfort, the master, called out for help. They told of the disastrous battle and its consequences. No fewer than sixty brother knights had died fighting alongside Prince Bohemond of Antioch and his men, together with large numbers of Templar sergeants, squires and Turcopoles. Only seven Templar knights survived the catastrophe.[48]

To make matters even worse, while the disaster unfolded, the bulk of the order's surviving troops had been called off to campaign in Egypt. Its much-depleted garrisons in the north were left to cope as best they could. There was now, for all practical purposes, no significant Christian army in any of the crusader states – and almost no mobile Templar forces left in the field.[49]

This was just one of many setbacks. Over a relatively short period of time, several strong frontier castles fell into Nur al-Din's hands. In the absence of the main crusading armies, outnumbered Frankish garrisons, with little prospect of relief, were becoming cowed and demoralised.

In the middle of the twelfth century, Richard of Poitou, a Cluniac monk (died *c.* 1174), wrote that if it had not been for the efforts of the Templars, the Holy Land would have been lost long ago. Although much of the charter evidence has since disappeared, the military contribution of the Templars was increasingly clear, even to contemporaries.[50]

But just when they were needed most, the Templars had reached breaking point.

12

Fear and Loathing in Lebanon (1130–1162)

The borders of the county of Tripoli were a military nightmare.

In the 1140s and 1150s, the Templars had been pushed to within a sword's breadth of complete collapse. The frontiers of Antioch were under continual pressure. The armies of the Latin kingdom of Jerusalem were overstretched, as they tried to defend against attacks from Damascus. The drain on the order's manpower was shocking.

But there was one area of even greater vulnerability. Crucially for our story, there was a strip of territory that was uneasily close to both the new homelands of the Syrian Nizaris in the Jabal Bahra and their Sunni Turkic enemies. This was the fragile, complicated crusader state whose loss would create a deadly wedge between the remaining Frankish settlements – the county of Tripoli was strategically vital, but chaotic, deadly and hard to defend with the available military resources. Only those comfortable with the imminent prospect of a violent death could thrive in such a dystopian environment.

This was the perfect setting for the Templars and the Assassins to bounce off each other – and for over a hundred years they played out an edgy, grotesque parody of landlord–tenant relationships along these dangerous mountain frontiers.

Tripolitan frontiers

The county of Tripoli had always been hard to defend, and the Templars had shed much blood in attempting to do so. In 1137, they had participated in the campaign to defend the castle of Montferrand in the county of Tripoli against the armies of Zengi, the atabeg of Mosul. The crusading forces were heavily defeated, with only eighteen Templars surviving the carnage.[1]

But the collapse of the county of Edessa in 1144 made an already difficult job almost impossible. The gradual consolidation of Muslim power forced the counts of Tripoli to undertake a radical defence review along their eastern frontiers. The ability of the local Frankish lords to hold onto their lands was looking increasingly doubtful.

This should have been good news for the Nizaris – and it was, at least to an extent. It had allowed them to move into the Jabal Bahra and build their castle network more easily. Chaos did not create a vacuum, but it had at least opened up opportunities.

But there was a problem: the region was too crowded and too volatile for things ever to stabilise fully. Ironically, it was the gradual centralisation of power by Muslim strongmen that changed the nature of the relationship between the Assassins and their crusader neighbours – and the Templars.

The increasing military threat forced the counts of Tripoli to take a hard look at the defensibility (or otherwise) of their eastern frontiers. Zengi was making significant inroads. He had captured the important fortified towns of Montferrand and Raphaniya in 1137. The long-term defence of the Tripolitan frontiers clearly needed more professional, more consistent, resources.[2]

The Templars and the Hospitallers were the obvious solution. Only they had the money to build castles and garrison key fortifications without any immediate payback, other than the fulfilment of their desire to defend Christendom.

FEAR AND LOATHING IN LEBANON

This solution to the defence of the county of Tripoli – and it was only a decision born of desperation – was far less satisfactory from the Assassins' perspective. Successive counts were forced to give much of their marcher lands (and the castles and estates that went with them) to the military orders. Where there had been chaos, there was now order; and ominously for the Assassins, that order was being imposed by 'corporations', rather than by noble families.

The Hospitallers gradually took over the defence of much of the north-east of the county. The first major grant took place in 1142, but its stipulations were so detailed and so far-reaching that it must have been the subject of extensive discussions for some time before. The Hospitallers were given what was, in effect, their own principality, including the fortress that was later rebuilt as the iconic Crac des Chevaliers. Their role was to create a defensive bulwark against the threat of Sunni Muslim troops operating out of Homs and Hama.[3]

By the late 1140s and early 1150s, however, the military situation had deteriorated still further, and the Templars had to step in to take up a greater share of the burden of defence.

In 1152, in a telling indication of the changing balance of power within the crusader states, the Templars were given land in the coastal Tripolitan lordship of Tortosa to build a castle. The previous secular owner, Reynouard of Maraclea, had been unable to defend his castle from Muslim troops when they invaded; and when they left, he no longer had the money to rebuild it. The Templars stepped in because they were the only ones with the resources to do the job.

Aware of the increasing threat to the area, they built it bigger and better. The new Templar castle at Tortosa was said by the early thirteenth-century pilgrim Wilbrand of Oldenburg to have been defended by no fewer than eleven towers, as well as by a huge keep. This was a military commitment that most members of the nobility could only dream of.[4]

Interestingly, the new Templar fortifications at Tortosa, which date to the late 1150s and 1160s, trialled many of the design features that were later to be incorporated into the 'classic' crusader castles of the 1170s and 1180s. They featured the double layer of walls of what later became known as a concentric castle; each line of walls was protected by a moat; and there were other defensive features. The Templars were developing a blueprint for a new generation of state-of-the-art (and hugely expensive) fortifications. In the absence of sufficient manpower for large field armies, these castles would be needed very soon.[5]

The Templars had been the natural choice when it came to finding new owners for Tortosa. Their castle of Chastel-Blanc, up in the mountains, was built shortly beforehand – this too was a formidable fortification and part of a broader network of castles. From the top of Chastel-Blanc, the garrison could see another important Templar castle at al-'Arimah and the famous Hospitaller castle at Crac des Chevaliers in the distance – the quantity of the fortifications spoke volumes about the intensity of the threat.

As in Antioch, this Templar presence was more than just military. The order had created what amounted to its own mini-province in the south of the county of Tripoli. It controlled the population, the villages and even the churches. The benefits it brought to the local Franks were immense – without military help from the Templars and the Hospitallers, the entire county was barely a going concern. War in the Holy Land was being pushed to a level where most of the old crusader nobility were barely able to compete. Like it or not, the military orders were the only organisations able to step in and take up the slack.

The massive programme of frontier castle-building meant that the Templars were almost unrecognisable from their early days. They had started as a fledgling operation, supplying small contingents to other people's armies. They had fought in battles in which they had very little control over the final outcomes. But now they had become hugely influential warlords in their own right. They had their own networks of castles, garrisons and armies – and they had become marcher lords in the county of Tripoli, uncomfortably close to their new neighbours, the Nizaris.[6]

Frustration and blood

The Assassins knew that the Templars – disciplined and ferocious warriors – would make far less congenial neighbours and landlords than the distant and impecunious counts of Tripoli. They were not happy with this new arrangement – and they had tangible ways of expressing their feelings on the matter. It was, the Nizaris thought, the fault of the count of Tripoli, the man who had invited the military orders onto his lands. The Assassins could not turn back the clock, and there was little to gain by taking personal revenge on the counts of Tripoli for doing so. But, as usual, revenge was a central feature of the Nizaris' 'foreign policy'. Their anger and frustration was unstoppable. If they could not take their revenge on the Templars, they could at least strike back at Count Raymond II of Tripoli – the man who had installed these mortal enemies so irritatingly close to their domains.

In 1152, they expressed their disapproval in the way they knew best. As Count Raymond was 'entering the city gate [of Tripoli], without thought of evil mishap,' wrote one Frankish chronicler,

> he was struck down by the swords of the Assassins at the entrance to the gate between the barbican and the wall and perished miserably. With him was slain also that distinguished nobleman ... Ralph de Merle, and one of his knights, both of whom had chanced to be with the count on that journey.[7]

Across the Middle East, killing innocent foreigners was the traditional response in the immediate aftermath of such an attack – it was emotionally satisfying, it gave vent to an underlying xenophobia and, importantly, once a victim's property had been plundered, it was also very profitable. As news of the count's murder spread,

> the whole city [of Tripoli] was roused. The people flew to arms and without discrimination put to the sword all those who were found

to differ either in language or dress from the Latins. In this way it was hoped that the perpetrators of the foul deed might be found.[8]

But the real culprits were, of course, long gone.

The Templars, whose presence in the region had triggered the attack, now felt free to go on the offensive – from this time onwards they started to raid the villages and Nizari settlements in the mountains, and only refrained from doing so when the Assassins gave them an annual 'protection money' payment of 2,000 gold coins. A dangerous and long-standing precedent had been set.[9]

Cults and corporations

Most importantly for these new and deeply unsatisfactory arrangements, the Templars were an organisation, rather than a dynasty. This dramatically reduced the leverage that the Assassins could exert.

This strange dynamic persisted for over a hundred years. Even in the middle of the thirteenth century, when the crusader states were a mere shadow of their former glory, the Assassins were still paying tribute to the military orders. As one Christian memoirist wrote in the 1250s,

> the Old Man of the Mountain made tribute payments to the Hospital and Temple because they had no fear of the Assassins. The Old Man could not gain anything by having the master of the Temple or the Hospital killed because he understood clearly that if he had one of them killed, another man, just as able, would immediately replace him. Because of this he was unwilling to lose any of the [*fidais*] when he had nothing to gain by it.[10]

The military orders were the only groups among the crusaders who did not buy into the Assassins' assiduously cultivated 'cult of death' image. They did not take their PR campaign seriously – to a large extent, that was because it takes one to know one. The extreme, death-dealing Muslim Nizari sect seems, on the surface, unlikely to have had much in common with an order of devout Catholic monks. But the groups were far more similar than either would have cared to admit.

The Templars had their own branding issues to contend with, and their own intuitively crafted reputational strategy. Like the Nizaris, they were a tiny, but larger-than-life group: at their core, mirroring the impact of the *fidais*, were the brother knights – a small number of dedicated individuals, whose reputation spread far beyond their obvious capabilities. Much of this, as with the Nizaris, was because of their well-deserved reputation for fanaticism. Stopping a small number of highly motivated individuals is extremely difficult: both 'cults' exploited this strange truth and thrived on their 'living legend' status.

The Assassins and the military orders, particularly the Templars, had one other vital characteristic in common – their corporatist outlook. And it was this 'corporatism' that made the Templars so dangerous. Not being a 'family firm', they were hard to intimidate; and if power was not a personal or familial asset, then the ability of the Assassins to hurt an individual was irrelevant. Even if individual Templar masters were killed one after the other, power still resided in the order's governing chapter, which allowed it to make relatively seamless new appointments.[11]

The logic underpinning the Assassins' power was that leaders were relatively easy to coerce or blackmail – provided you could persuade them that they were personally vulnerable. The military orders, however – Hospitallers, as well as Templars – were the glaring exception to this logic. They were led by individuals, rather than families; by appointees, rather than warlords. And their governing structures were based on merit, discipline and obedience, rather than on family ties. If you killed the master of the Templars, there would be another one, operating the same policies, in place by the end of the evening. As the Templars were not susceptible to personal threat, they were impervious to blackmail. In fact, the military orders had the men and the castles to turn the tables on the Assassins and impose their own demands.

ASSASSINS AND TEMPLARS

The similarities of outlook between the two groups sometimes meant that they were able to maintain an uneasy *modus vivendi*: a tense truce usually existed between them. The southern reaches of the Jabal Bahra were the heartland of the Syrian Nizaris from the mid-1130s onwards, and remained so for most of the period of the crusades.[12]

But the Assassins and the Templars were never going to be cosy companions. The Templars usually had the upper hand – they had resources flowing in from Europe to strengthen their position, and they were impervious to the usual threats and intimidation that lay at the heart of the Assassins' power. This was quantitatively reflected in the hard currency of cash. Poor as they were, the Assassins regularly paid tribute to the military orders, but the military orders never paid anything to the Assassins.

From the early years of the Nizari state, based around Masyaf, the Templars assumed a supremely dangerous role: as blackmailers of the world's most famous extortionists.

13

Sinan: The Old Man of the Mountain (1162–1170)

An odd-looking man, bedraggled and deep-down weary, rode into the Nizari village at the foot of their castle at Kahf. It was early in the day, before it became too hot. A good time to travel. But he was dressed in a most spectacular and eccentric fashion. People called out, shouting for their families to come and see the stranger. Children ran out excitedly into the street to see what was happening.

They didn't know that the stranger had been travelling across the Middle East in secret. He had spent months hiding in the shadows. Living rough in the countryside. Hustled into alleyways. Sleeping in storerooms for his own safety. But today that all ended.

Unprepossessing to our eyes, but designed to make an impact, he turned up at Kahf wearing self-sewn shoes and a striped head-dress made of Yemeni wool. He flamboyantly rode a white donkey. There was an undeniable theatricality about the man, but it was possibly all more self-conscious than he would have cared to admit.[1]

He was called Sinan. But he became better known by a nickname: 'The Old Man of the Mountain'.

The Assassins were facing increasing intimidation by the military orders, and were encountering ever more hatred from their Sunni enemies. But they were fortunate in one vital regard – the highly capable

Rashid al-Din Sinan, their most famous leader, became ruler of the de facto Nizari Ismaili state in Syria in 1162. Under his guidance, the Assassins were able to stabilise their new network of mountain fortresses and perfect their unique way of dealing with far bigger and more powerful neighbours.[2]

Persecuted in Aleppo and Damascus, they turned in on themselves. Their setbacks, and the hatred which had been directed towards them by their fellow Muslims, confirmed their natural instincts – that they should become ever more separate from those who clearly detested them.

Sinan, decisive as ever, guided this change. He concluded that they should rather make their mark on the world by perfecting the art of fear, rather than by love. For a small group, doctrinally and geographically isolated, this was a logical (if not entirely admirable) strategy – it allowed them to survive and to exert influence far beyond their obvious resources. Most importantly, he made them a force to be reckoned with.

Sinan the man

Like the heroes of so many semi-legendary stories, Sinan's origins were mysterious. But there are clues. The twelfth-century historian al-Husayn records a fascinating conversation with Sinan – and on this rare occasion the normally enigmatic leader seems to have spoken openly about his early life and his rise to power.

He was born at some point around 1131–5 into a Shiite family in a village near Basra, in modern-day Iraq. His upbringing was comfortable and his father was said to have been 'one of its notables'. The young Sinan was going to become a schoolmaster. So far, so ordinary. But he chose to reject a quiet life: he converted to become a Nizari Ismaili.[3]

He argued with his family and was forced to leave quickly. There was a rift that he was happy to leave unclear. 'Something occurred between me and my brothers which obliged me to leave them,' he was later

SINAN: THE OLD MAN OF THE MOUNTAIN

reported to have stated vaguely, 'and I went forth without provision or a mount.'[4]

Showing the traditional fervour of a Nizari convert, he moved to Persia, and studied philosophy and religious texts at the sect's headquarters in remote Alamut. Significantly for the future of the Assassins in Syria, while he was there he became a close confidant of the future reformist imam, Hasan II (r. 1162–6). The Assassins' leader at the time, Kiya Muhammad, saw something in Sinan and he raised him as one of his own. As Sinan recalled, 'he put me in school [to train with his sons, one of whom was Hasan II] and gave me exactly the same treatment as he gave them, in those things that are needful for the support, education, and clothing of children'.[5]

Hasan II took power as imam without opposition in 1162. Tellingly, one of his first acts was to send his trusted schoolfriend Sinan to represent his interests in Syria. Hasan and Sinan had a radical reformist agenda to pursue – the mission to Syria was an important one. Sinan later said that Hasan 'ordered me to go to Syria. I set forth . . . and only rarely did I approach any town. He had given me orders and letters.' The journey was convoluted and secretive. Danger was everywhere. When he finally got to Aleppo, Sinan recounted that he 'met another companion and delivered him another letter, and he too hired me a mount and sent me on to Kahf'.[6]

Sinan travelled to the Assassins' huge castle at Kahf, presented his credentials and 'stayed there until Shaykh Abu Muhammad, the head of the [Assassins in Syria], died in the mountain'. The sect's leadership in Syria at this time was in a state of flux and internecine conflict – and it was this chaotic situation which at least partially explains Hasan's need to put his own man on the spot. Sinan quietly built up a power base of his own.[7]

The successor to Shaykh Abu Muhammad was not approved of by Hasan and his leadership team in Alamut. One of the local Nizaris, a man known as 'the chief Fahd' (a local leader, or *rais*) plotted against the successor 'and sent someone to stab him to death as he was leaving his bath'. The man who had murdered him was executed, conveniently ensuring his silence. Fahd was arrested for his involvement in the murder, but was released from custody suspiciously quickly, on orders from the top. Sinan was conveniently on hand, of course, and stepped in to ensure an orderly transfer of power that was acceptable to Hasan and the leaders in Alamut.[8]

Even his enemies were impressed by the mysterious and charismatic new leader. As one Sunni commentator later wrote, Sinan may have been hated by his opponents, but 'the Ismaili sect followed him as they had followed no one else, and he was able to achieve what no other had achieved'.[9]

Building the Nizari state in Syria

Sinan's role was not merely doctrinal: there were many difficult practical matters to deal with if the Nizaris' new home was to be made secure.

The Assassins already had useful castles in the Jabal Bahra, but there were tough times ahead. Sinan immediately set out to make them even stronger. As the Sunni historian Kamal al-Din wrote, 'he built fortresses in Syria for this sect; some were new and some were old ones which he had obtained by stratagems and fortified and made inaccessible'.[10] He made major improvements to the defences of Khawabi and Rusafa and captured Ullayqa, just north-west of Qadmus, as a way of rationalising and extending his territories. Interestingly, and perhaps as a deliberate statement of intent, he seized it from the control of the Hospitallers.[11]

Improving the infrastructure was vital, and Ullayqa is a good case study of how this was done. Built in a suitably intimidating spot, on a limestone cliff almost 800 metres high, the castle had room for a bath house and two wells inside its fortified village, with the citadel sited some 40 metres away on the top of the hill. Storerooms were built, as in other Nizari fortifications, to allow the garrison to withstand a long siege.[12]

SINAN: THE OLD MAN OF THE MOUNTAIN

But Sinan looked after the human infrastructure, as well as the buildings. He made sure that the men were in just as good shape as their castles. Under him the *fidais* teams became an even more professional and fearsome weapon – more formalised, better trained and increasingly highly motivated.

The Assassin garrisons and villages were necessarily scattered, given the deliberately inaccessible nature of their castles. But Sinan went to great lengths to ensure that his leadership was seen and felt throughout the Jabal Bahra. Unity within the sect was to be imposed as tightly as possible. A fourteenth-century Ismaili history, for instance, mentions that he used to spend his time travelling between the four castles of Kahf, Masyaf, Qadmus and Ullayqa. He was said to stop in each place to improve the defences of the castles and, just as importantly, to heal internal frictions within the fractious Syrian Nizari community.[13]

Improving communications was an essential part of both these tasks. From a charmingly intimate aside, we know that he also set up mountaintop pigeon towers to send messages from one remote fortification to another. Pigeon-post had been used by the sect's Sunni enemies for some time – Zengi and Nur al-Din both adopted such a system. But Sinan used his tiny new messengers to make the already strong network of Assassin castles even better connected.[14] This was the state-building, rational side of Sinan. But there was another side too.

Sinan as mystic

It is always tempting to try to create a revisionist view of the Assassins in general, and of Sinan in particular. We might describe them as being victims of their enemies' black propaganda, for instance – and that is undoubtedly partly true, regardless of the extent to which they encouraged this process. And we must always query the factual basis of the stories told by their Sunni persecutors. The Assassins had many enemies and, as committed radicals, were not afraid of making new ones. Fear, after all, was their stock in trade.

It is also the case, however much one might try to normalise their reputation, that there was a genuinely mystical, revolutionary and extremist aspect to much of what made them so unique. Sinan was an extraordinary figure: he was highly intelligent, a great leader and capable of acting with profound strategic insight. But that did not stop him from also being a man of a deeply esoteric, mystical and, some would say, even 'magical' disposition.

Sinan was always different. Efforts to create a deeply enigmatic persona seem to have dated back to the very beginning of his rule. The main Nizari source for his life, an early fourteenth-century biography, was written by the scholar Abu Firas. While acknowledging that Sinan had been accused of indulging in dark and magical arts, he inevitably goes to some lengths to emphasise his orthodox Islamic credentials. 'Many common ignorant fools', he wrote,

> think that it is thanks to his knowledge of magic that the Lord [Sinan] practised these marvels. Well, he confounded them all and reduced them to silence, not by science or magic but by the force of truth and conviction, by his demonstrations and by the quotations which he pronounced from Qur'anic verses.[15]

Severely undermining his own case, however, even Abu Firas could not stop himself from launching into a list of Sinan's occult achievements. He paints a picture of the Nizari leader as a man who was regarded as mysterious and enigmatic – and, we might suspect, one who went to great lengths to make sure he was seen as such. Abu Firas was proud, for instance, that Sinan was a clairvoyant, and that he had famous powers of telepathy. He could prophesy the future. It was claimed that he could reply to letters before they had been received. Despite being a man whose power rested on the ability to kill, and who was the subject of many murder attempts by his own people, he was said to be so charismatic that he never needed a personal bodyguard.[16]

Stories of telepathy and clairvoyance were repeatedly ascribed to Sinan by Abu Firas – so much so that it is clear that the Old Man's mystical powers were a central part of his authority and, in the eyes of the twelfth-century Nizaris, something to be extremely proud of. Abu Firas boasted of the way in which Sinan could answer 'yes' or 'no' questions without the question itself being voiced. In an echo of his close personal connection with the murder squads, he was also said to have known when a *fidais* had died, long before the news had officially reached the Assassins' fortresses.

Some of this mystique must have come from his unique personality; but much also seems to have been carefully crafted. He was never seen eating, for instance. He did not say much, but deliberately adopted strange poses. He would remain motionless for hours, his lips moving mysteriously, but making no sound. There were rumours among his own people that he did not even cast a reflection when looking into water.[17]

In this context, it is not surprising that Sinan seemed strange to his Sunni enemies and to Frankish observers alike – but one cannot help feeling that this was something which he was not too unhappy about. His image of arcane power was a useful tool of intimidation and was at least partly deliberately manufactured.

'Resurrection'

With a new and charismatic radical in charge, the stage was set for revolutionary change. Philosophically, Sinan was at the extreme end of an already edgy sect. But in 1164 something happened to propel him, and the Syrian Assassins, even further along the spiritual spectrum.

The Assassins were not generally viewed with affection, but they always had their own mystique. Part of that mystique derived naturally from the path they were obliged to follow. They dealt in death, death by murder, because they had no other way of protecting themselves and pursuing their interests. But the other part of their reputation was created by the exoticism of mystical religious extremism. In particular, the Nizari 'Resurrection'.

The 'Resurrection' of 1164 was not an invention of the Syrian Assassins – it originated with their co-religionists in Persia. And, in theory at least, it did not last long – just a few short years. But its effect was profound. The stories it generated were so striking, so arcane (and, incidentally, so useful) that they stayed with the Assassins not just for their entire existence in Syria, but on down through the centuries.

On the seventeenth day of Ramadan, 1164, Hasan II, the leader of the Assassins and Sinan's mentor, made a revolutionary announcement: he proclaimed that the spiritual rebirth of the Nizari Ismaili believers had already taken place.[18] There is still some mystery about what actually happened and why. Hasan was said to have gathered his people together and then

> from the top of the pulpit he presented a clear and eloquent epistle, and at the end of the address he said, 'The imam of our time sends you blessings and compassion, calling you his specially selected servants. He has lifted from you the burden of the obligation of the sharia [the traditional body of Islamic law] . . . and has brought you the Resurrection.'[19]

Perhaps some thought they had misheard the great man. But this was a deliberate and radical step. As one anonymous commentator put it, 'the ties and chains of Sharia restrictions were taken from the necks of the faithful'. The Assassins had taken a radically different path to the rest of Islam.[20]

Hasan II was serious about his new ideas. He expected everyone to conform. Disagreement was punishable by death. It was announced that in this new 'time of the Resurrection if a man complied with the letter of the [sharia] Law and persisted in physical worship and rites, it was obligatory that he be chastised and stoned and put to death'.[21]

SINAN: THE OLD MAN OF THE MOUNTAIN

On one level, this sounds like an obscure doctrinal footnote. Or, if one were an Assassin, perhaps a cause for quiet satisfaction and celebration. In fact, however, it was a massive change for the entire sect.

Most profoundly, particularly in the eyes of their Sunni enemies, many believed that this 'Resurrection' meant that the existing precepts of Islam no longer held good. Sinan, as Hasan's boyhood friend and acolyte, seems to have gone along with this change wholeheartedly. In fact, with hindsight, Sinan may have been sent to Syria by Hasan with the eventual proclamation of 'Resurrection' already in mind – the two radical leaders may have been working towards achieving the same secretive doctrinal objectives all along.[22]

If the rest of Islam had previously seen the Assassins as an extremist group, this doctrinal volte-face only served to confirm their prejudices. A contemporary Sunni commentator wrote, with undisguised shock, that he had

> heard that [Sinan] allowed them to defile their mothers and sisters and daughters and released them from the fast of the month of Ramadan, and they called themselves 'Sincere' [or possibly 'Pure'].[23]

Similarly, the author of the Bustan al-gami records (under the slightly later date of 1165–6) that the Assassins 'changed their doctrine and drank wine, practised incest, drank during Ramadan by night and by day, destroyed their mosques and castles and abolished prayer'.[24]

It would be easy to discount such lurid stories as Sunni propaganda. But there was clearly more to it than that. Even those with no obvious axe to grind thought that the Syrian Nizaris had now gone beyond 'heresy' – many outsiders felt that they had created their own new religion. Word of this dramatic 'Resurrection' spread widely in the Middle East, and not just among the Assassins' Muslim detractors. The crusaders knew about it and, despite their habitual lack of interest in Islamic doctrinal disputes, still thought it extraordinary.

A contemporary Frankish chronicler wrote, for instance, that for about four hundred years [the Nizaris] have followed the law and traditions of the Saracens so strictly that by comparison all other peoples seem as prevaricators and they alone the complete observers of the law.

With the arrival of Sinan, however, the chronicler identified a major shift away from Muslim orthodoxy. Their new leader, he felt, had come

> to despise the beliefs which he had absorbed with his mother's milk and to abominate the unclean tenets that deceiver. He instructed his people also in the same way and made them cease observing the superstition of the prophet. He tore down the places of prayer which they had been accustomed to use, absolved them from fasting, and permitted the use of wine and pork.[25]

Word was starting to get out that the Assassins were increasingly isolated as a religious group. John Phocas, a Byzantine soldier born in Crete, left an account of his trip to the Holy Land later in Sinan's tenure as leader. He, too, was aware that something had happened which thoroughly distanced the sect from the rest of Islam. The Assassins, he wrote, 'are a Saracen race, and are neither Christians nor of the Mohammedan persuasion. Rather they are a sect on their own.'[26]

Benjamin of Tudela, a Jewish traveller from Muslim Spain, was similarly in the area in *c.* 1165, just after the 'Resurrection' had taken place. He was not anti-Nizari by disposition. Benjamin noted with satisfaction, for instance, that there were several Jewish communities in the Jabal Bahra that were on good terms with the sect and even served in the Nizari militia.

Despite this, however, he clearly thought that the 'Resurrection' had changed Syrian Nizari doctrines so much and had moved the sect's members to such an extreme position that they were no longer part of the Muslim faith. 'They do not believe in the religion of Islam,' he wrote, 'but follow one of their own folk, whom they regard as their prophet, and all that he tells them to do they carry out, whether for death or life. They call him the Sheik Al Hashishim, and he is known as their Elder.'[27]

Just to emphasise the point, Benjamin commented elsewhere in his book that the Assassins 'do not profess the Mohammedan religion, but live on high mountains, and worship the Old Man of the land of the Hashishim'. Writing soon after Sinan had taken the castle of Ullayqa from the Hospitallers, Benjamin also correctly noted that 'they are at war with . . . the Franks, and with the ruler of [Tripoli]'.[28]

Although Benjamin may not have been aware of it, the term *hashishin* was a deliberate slur – but it cannot be dismissed as a western 'legend'. It was widely used as a pejorative descriptor by the Assassins' Sunni enemies in the course of the twelfth and thirteenth centuries. By the time of Benjamin's trip, the sect was clearly routinely being referred to as *hashishin* (or other variants of the same name). This was hugely effective as an insult (as the word combined connotations of being down-market and debauched, as well as ignorant and foolish). But it was also a crude way of devaluing the almost incomprehensible commitment and extreme actions of the *fidais*.[29]

Given that he mentioned conflict with Tripoli, it is clear that Benjamin was writing about the Assassins' heartlands of the Jabal Bahra. But the biggest problems with what passed for Nizari 'orthodoxy' in this tumultuous period seem to have been among those villages that were furthest away from Sinan's personal influence.

Some of the Assassin communities in the Jabal as-Summaq were moving towards semi-independence. By the 1170s, they had adopted an even more extreme version of the 'Resurrection'. 'In the year 572 [1176–7],' wrote Kamal al-Din,

> the people of the Jabal as-Summaq gave way to iniquity and debauchery, and called themselves 'the Pure'. Men and women mingled in drinking sessions, no man abstained from his sister or daughter, the women wore men's clothes, and one of them declared that Sinan was his God.

This was certainly one way of interpreting the 'Resurrection'. But they had gone too far.[30]

The Sunni authorities in Syria reacted predictably. In Nur al-Din's lands, vigilantes attacked Ismailis. The Aleppans sent an army against them. But the Nizari extremists retreated further into the mountains, where they dug in and holed up, in the traditional way of millenarian cults.

Eventually the excesses of this Nizari branch became too embarrassing even for Sinan himself. He knew his Sunni neighbours were never going to be friends, but he did not need to antagonise them unnecessarily. He washed his hands of his overenthusiastic co-religionists. Sinan showed no compunction in putting down their 'heresy within a heresy'. He first persuaded the Sunni troops to withdraw. The Nizari community leaders from the Jabal as-Summaq were summoned to fortresses such as Masyaf and Kahf, ostensibly for doctrinal discussions. They were then slaughtered with ruthlessness and much bloodshed.

Sinan the 'Old Man': Perfecting the brand of death

Sinan was astute and played his cards extremely well. He made alliances where they were useful, but was never afraid of making enemies. The bold move to take the castle of Ullayqa from the Hospitallers, soon after he took over in Syria, was a calculated way of showing his strength of purpose to the military orders – and it was one of the opening salvoes in their long-running conflict.[31]

Sinan also became detached from the Assassins in Alamut, particularly after the death of his friend and mentor, Hasan II, in 1166. He trod an increasingly independent path, and this did not go down well at 'head office': there were several attempts on his life by *fidais* teams sent from Persia. All of them were either killed or, in a forceful display of Sinan's charisma, turned and converted into his own men.[32]

Sinan had a genius for branding. Under his direction, even the language of hierarchy was twisted in the interests of an intimidating PR angle. He became known, ominously, as 'the Old Man' and the loyalty of his adherents was said to be total. Word of their scarily distinctive command structure travelled far. Even the Frankish chroniclers wrote that the Assassins' 'subjection and obedience to [Sinan] is such that they regard nothing as too harsh or difficult and eagerly undertake even the most dangerous tasks at his command'.[33]

Calling Sinan the 'Old Man of the Mountain' was originally a personal honorific. But – like 'caesar' or 'sultan' – it quickly became a job title, used to signify whoever was the Assassins' leader in Syria. It had the effect (important for a sect that dealt in murder) of creating a sense of transcending death itself – regardless of who was in charge at any particular moment, there was always an Old Man of the Mountain.

The mystery of an ominous title had a gratifying impact on the Nizaris' image. As one thirteenth-century Frankish chronicler wrote, 'near and far, all kinds of people went in terror of this prince, for he often used to have people killed without right or reason'. Sinan would have been delighted at this supreme back-handed compliment and the far-reaching fear it encapsulated.[34]

The *fidais* were central to this fear. Sinan improved the effectiveness and commitment of the death squads, and their threat was made ever more explicit. One of the confidants of the Sunni historian Kamal al-Din wrote to him to say that 'he had come across some sheets of the history of Shaizar in which he saw a letter from Sinan to [the] lord of Shaizar'. In the letter, Sinan offered condolences on the death of the lord's brother, but couldn't help adding a couple of lines of poetry which have an eerily portentous and threatening ring to them:

Death does not tread with heavy foot
Save on the shoulders of the great and mighty.

Coming from the head of the Assassins in Syria, this was a profound observation about the paradoxical vulnerability of the powerful.[35]

The 'death cult' image that Sinan had so fastidiously cultivated was a huge success. It grabbed the imagination of the Assassins' enemies and took hold there. Gregory Bar Hebraeus, a Syriac Orthodox historian, wrote that

> Sinan was held in fear by all the kings of the Arabs and Franks. And he forged knives (or daggers), and on each one of them was [engraved] the name of one of the kings. And when he gave a knife to one of his own men, even though it were in the heart of the sea, he would go and fulfil his will.[36]

A Byzantine traveller in the area was similarly transfixed by the Assassins' unique methodology of death. The *fidais* were, he wrote, at Sinan's command

> sent to the rulers of great nations [to] kill them with the sword. They too die in the adventure, for they are outnumbered when they have undertaken the deed, and this martyrdom they believe to be the way to immortality.[37]

Arnold of Lübeck, another Christian contemporary, also wrote that the

> Old Man so deceives the men of this land by his tricks that they worship him, and believe him to be none other than God himself. He also most wickedly promises them the hope and expectation of eternal joy, so that they choose rather to die than to live, for often many of them, standing on an exceedingly high wall, on his wish or order jump off it and die wretchedly through breaking their necks.[38]

The PR programme was working.

It is highly unlikely that Sinan ever read the words of Bishop Arnold. But he would have been quietly pleased if he had. The way in which the Assassins were viewed was a travesty of their true belief systems, but they probably did not mind too much – it just showed what a long and intimidating shadow the diminutive cult had cast.

Ensuring the obedience (and fierce motivation) of the *fidais* was at the heart of this compelling, but clearly embellished and semi-legendary methodology. Sinan, wrote Arnold,

> claims that they are most blessed who perish while shedding human blood in seeking revenge. And when any of his followers choose such a death, by treacherously killing someone, that they may die more happily while carrying out this revenge, he hands them the daggers for this deed as though they are consecrated, and then makes them drunk with a certain potion, through which they are roused to ecstasy or madness . . . Thus he strives to hold them ready forever to carry out such deeds.

This was power indeed – and, even better, power that was understood and exaggerated by those that Sinan needed to impress.[39]

Even Emperor Frederick Barbarossa had heard of Sinan's authority, and the distorted stories about the allegedly 'brainwashed' killers that were used to conduct the sect's eccentric approach to foreign policy. A German envoy, Burchard of Strasbourg, was sent to the Holy Land in 1175. He wrote home in suitably lurid but impressive detail about those he lyrically called the 'lords of the mountains'. The Assassins, he claimed, 'have a lord among them who strikes the utmost fear into all the Saracen princes near and far, as well as among the nearby Christian barons, since he is accustomed to slay them in an extraordinary way'.[40]

A garish form of mind control was a satisfying (and demeaning) explanation for the sacrifice of the *fidais*. The Old Man, wrote Burchard,

> has many sons of his peasants brought up from the cradle in these palaces, and they . . . must obey every word and command of the lord of this land. If they do this, then he will grant the joys of

paradise to them . . . and they never see any other man apart from their instructors and teachers, nor are they told anything else until the moment when they are summoned into the presence of the prince and ordered to kill someone . . . Then the prince gives each of them a golden knife, and sends them to slay whatever [other] prince he wishes them to kill.[41]

Once again, murder was correctly identified as the primary driver of Nizari power, and as the ultimate expression of devotion both to the cause and to the Old Man himself. 'For instance,' wrote the Frankish chronicler William of Tyre soon afterwards,

if there happens to be a prince who has incurred the hatred or distrust of this people, the chief places a dagger in the hand of one or several of his followers; those thus designated hasten away at once, regardless of the consequences of the deed or the probability of personal escape. Zealously they labour for as long as may be necessary, until at last the favourable chance comes which enables them to carry out the mandate of the chief.[42]

It is easy to discount evidence from outside the sect. Just as Sunni comments are often discarded as tainted propaganda, so too Frankish views are often characterised as being ignorant and coloured by a western fascination with eastern 'exoticism'.

The evidence provided by William cannot be so easily ignored, however. He was born in the Middle East and spent most of his life there. He wrote extensively about the Islamic world (in works now sadly lost) and almost certainly spoke and read Arabic. He held high office in the government of the Latin kingdom of Jerusalem and had access to confidential state papers. And he spent much of his life in Tyre, in modern-day Lebanon. His views of the Assassins need to be taken seriously.

SINAN: THE OLD MAN OF THE MOUNTAIN

Where does reputation end and legend begin? And where does PR start and the rumour mill take over? As so often, the Templars and the Assassins travelled a similar arc. Everyone benefited from the Assassins' having (and creating) a 'legendary' reputation. Their enemies used 'legendary' tales as a way of denigrating and isolating them. But it is also true that the fear and terror the Assassins generated were at least partially deliberate. As one Nizari poet put it, proudly glamorising the sect's main weapon, a single *fidais* may strike fear into the heart of the most powerful king.[43]

It was in this context, and largely during the rule of Sinan, that the extraordinary 'legends' of the Assassins arose. They sprang partly from their success: the murder of the great and the powerful, even when under the highest levels of protection, was shocking enough in itself. But these tales were encouraged and embellished wherever possible.

The Assassins were the masters, as well as the victims, of propaganda.

14

Ambushes and Ambassadors (1170–1174)

The small party of Arab and Persian travellers was strung out along what might have been called a road, but which was, for all practical purposes, just a dry and increasingly rocky path. They were on the lower foothills of the Lebanon mountains and were slowly working their way home, treading wearily up the tightly winding slopes. Social standing and the geography of their ascent were matched in a strange symmetry, from the highest to the lowest.

At the front of the group were the well-groomed and clearly expensive horses – animals that befitted the status of the diplomats who were riding them. These were men at ease with themselves and their world, looking ahead, quietly confident – and thinking about the discussions that had taken place over the previous days. Their measured voices would occasionally rise above the rhythmic clattering of their horses' hooves, working through the possible responses to what they had heard, the different strategies and permutations, to arrive at the most satisfactory outcomes. There was much to reflect on, but their discussions had been promising.

Behind them, riding on nags and each leading a small packhorse, were their retainers and squires. These were men focused on the practical work of the day, looking around for any possible trouble, particularly with the animals, and trying to keep the small convoy moving.

AMBUSHES AND AMBASSADORS

At the very end of the group were the lowest in the social hierarchy, dirty and poorly dressed – young mule drivers with their surly charges, and the old men who were used to fetch the water and the firewood.

The party rounded a sharp corner. From behind the outcrop of an overhanging rock face, a dozen heavily armoured knights charged down towards them. Surprise was total. With only a few short, but seemingly endless, seconds before the heavy cavalry hit them, each man in the column acted instinctively.

The men at the rear turned to run, leaving anything of value as far behind as possible. The squires dropped the reins of their packhorses and began to peel off from the path, scattering left and right, at first stunned, but acting on reflex in the face of the chaos that was about to careen into them.

The riders at the front of the group, completely unprepared and closest to their attackers, had no chance. They reached down to grasp their swords, but did not even have time to get them out of their scabbards. The knights hurtled into them, elemental and frightening, horse flesh and rider merging into a single unstoppable force.

The fight – or more accurately, massacre – was over in a few seconds. No one was seeking to take any prisoners: swords flashed and screams rent the air – the sound of wounded men who knew they were about to die.

When it came, the aftermath was unnaturally quiet – a momentary silence laden with sweat, adrenaline and relief. The leader of the ambushers took off his helmet, revealing a grizzled and sunburnt face. Shockingly, a livid scar seared its way across his cheek, up towards a missing eye, and the permanent reproach of a weeping, crudely stitched-up socket. The knight searched through the papers of the dead envoys, took out the contents of their diplomatic pouches and stuffed them into his saddle-bags. His job that day was done.

In the lawless, mountainous marcher lands of the Middle East, such violence was all too common. But this was different. This was a moment when two legends collided – with bloody consequences.

The Templars and the Assassins.

ASSASSINS AND TEMPLARS

The Assassins' embassy to Jerusalem (1173–4)

Like the princes of Antioch, the kings of Jerusalem were open to pragmatic suggestions of alliance with the Nizaris – there was always the tempting possibility of bringing them into an anti-Sunni alliance that would benefit both parties. In the early 1170s, discussions between the sect and King Amalric of Jerusalem were well advanced. The Assassins went so far as to hint that, with the appropriate incentives, they might even convert to a form of Christianity – or at least that is what some of the Franks chose to believe.

The famous Frankish chronicler, William of Tyre, was a thoughtful commentator and a close confidant of the king. He had been used by Amalric on high-level diplomatic and intelligence-gathering operations in the past and is likely to have been party to these sensitive discussions. As the archbishop of Tyre, he also lived near to the Assassins' lands and would, at the very least, have heard first-hand accounts of their activities.

William left a detailed record of the negotiations. Manpower was a long-standing problem for the crusaders and, correctly or not, the Assassins were believed to be numerous enough to be serious allies. 'In the province of Tyre', William later wrote, lived the Assassins, 'numbering some 60,000 or more, as I have often heard said, who possess ten castles, each with surrounding villages'.[1]

Sinan's charismatic leadership was also well known, even to the Franks. William was suitably impressed. 'In our times,' he gushed,

> they happened to appoint an eloquent man with a subtle, very sharp brain. Unlike his predecessors he began to collect the gospel books and the apostolic law. He pored over these in lengthy and continual study and for a while had put a lot of effort into following the whole of Christ's miracles and commandments and even the apostolic doctrine.

His people, wrote William, 'call him simply the Old Man'.[2]

AMBUSHES AND AMBASSADORS

According to this account, Sinan had

> sent to our lord the king [Amalric] a wise man by the name of [Abdullah]. This man, skilled in discussions, eloquent and fully conversant with his leader's religion, carried secret propositions, the first and foremost of which was that if the brothers of the Knighthood of the Temple who possessed castles on the Assassins' borders were willing to forgo the two thousand gold pieces that were paid annually by his people somewhat like a tribute, and henceforth show brotherly affection, the Assassins would join the Christian faith and accept baptism.[3]

The king agreed to all this and, keen to strike a deal, even said that he would fully compensate the Templars for their loss of income. The Assassins' ambassador stayed at the royal court for some time, finalising the wording of the agreement. All that needed to happen now was for the final document to be ratified by Sinan. The Nizari delegation was given Frankish bodyguards and guides and set off back home. A historic deal was close.

But it was not to be. Just as the party was leaving the king's territory, shortly after the royal escort peeled off back to home, the Templars struck. Hand-picked men from the local garrisons sprang an ambush. The members of the Assassins' negotiating team were relaxed, feeling safe and confident. At this moment, when they were at their most vulnerable,

> some of the Knights of the Temple rushed upon the party with drawn swords and killed the envoy. The latter . . . was pursuing his journey without caution, in full reliance upon the king's safe conduct and the sincere good faith of our nation.[4]

This was a shocking act, shattering the implicit promise of royal protection. In a deeply religious age, breaking an oath meant putting one's immortal soul in danger, as well as one's credibility as a leader. The incident was serious enough to bring the entire kingdom to the brink of civil war – and 'by this crime', wrote William, the Templars 'brought upon themselves the charge of treason'.[5]

They had gone too far. The king exploded

> with violent anger. Almost frenzied, he summoned the barons and, declaring that the outrage amounted to injury against himself, he demanded their advice as to the course of action to be adopted. The barons were of one mind that such wickedness should not be passed over.

Two of the king's nobles – the marvellously named Seiher of Mamedunc and Godescalous of Turout – were sent to the Templars to demand redress for the outrage.[6]

Odo of Saint-Amand, the master (c. 1171–9), responded in a deliberately insulting way, calculated to infuriate an already angry king. He merely replied that he had given the guilty man a penance to fulfil and was going to send him to Rome – until then, the master 'forbade anyone . . . to lay violent hands upon the said brother'.[7]

The actual perpetrator was a striking figure – a grizzled Templar veteran called Walter of Mesnil, described as 'an evil one-eyed man . . . a totally worthless man'. It was clear to everyone that he was the closest thing the order had to a contract killer – and that he was only acting on orders. The king and his advisers were sure that the ambush and murder 'was done with the cognizance of the brethren'.[8]

The Templars had deliberately derailed the process of forming an alliance with the Assassins. Their motives in doing so are not entirely clear: the sums of money involved – 2,000 gold pieces – were (relatively) small, and King Amalric had anyway agreed to compensate them for the loss of revenue. The reason probably lay in the precedent it might have set and, perhaps more importantly, the bad blood that undoubtedly existed between the order and the Assassins.[9]

William of Tyre, who was personally involved in the matter at this point and had reviewed the correspondence, was shocked on his king's behalf. He wrote that Odo of Saint-Amand had 'added other remarks [in his letter to the king] dictated by the spirit of overweening arrogance with which he was possessed'. William was party to the details, but, frustratingly for us, decided that 'it is unnecessary to record them'.

These 'remarks' were almost certainly a deliberate and massively insulting provocation – and William did not record them because they were too embarrassing to commit to vellum. The Templars, always confident to the point of hubris, were of the opinion that they had a semi-independent, self-governing principality on the borders of the county of Tripoli – and this was where the massacre took place. The king of Jerusalem, Odo was clearly implying, should mind his own business.

William's evidence is given independent corroboration by the account of an English cleric, Walter Map, written in 1182. In it, Walter suggested that the negotiations had indeed been far advanced and that the Assassins' envoy had been

> despatched to the Patriarch [of Jerusalem] to bring back priests and deacons who would be able to baptise them and give them the full sacraments of the faith. This pagan was ambushed en route by the Templars of the city and killed . . . When the Old Man [of the Mountain] learnt about the ambush, under the influence of the devil, he put a stop to his new Christian devotion . . . This was deplored by the patriarch and the king, but neither could exact revenge on the Templars.

Shockingly (and doubly so because it contained an element of truth), Walter finished by suggesting that 'the king could not [punish them] because he is smaller than their little finger'.[10]

That was a rare insult, particularly given that Amalric was huge – the obese king was described by one who knew him well as being 'taller than many . . . [and] excessively fat, with breasts like those of a woman hanging down to his waist'. But, man-boobs or not, 'small' Amalric was furious beyond measure. Even on a good day, famously short-tempered and lacking in bonhomie, he was unlikely to top anyone's list of an ideal companion for a beach holiday.[11]

But this outrage, following so closely on the murder of the Assassins' emissaries, pushed him to new levels of apoplexy. The Latin kingdom of Jerusalem was outnumbered and surrounded by enemies. Saladin was making inroads on an almost daily basis. The crusaders needed all the friends they could get, even in the most unlikely of places. The Templars, in their pique and arrogance, had ruined all that.

Betrayal and bitterness

Relations between the Templars and King Amalric had been frosty for several years. This was no minor matter – and there was a shocking history behind that breakdown. In the summer of 1167, Nur al-Din had launched an overwhelming attack on an allegedly 'impregnable' cave castle in the Transjordan. The castle was garrisoned by the Templars – a fortress literally hewn into the side of a mountain.[12]

Nur al-Din's army besieged the castle. It was quickly (embarrassingly quickly), 'surrendered . . . by the brothers of the Knights Templars, into whose care it had been given'. The garrison of the supposedly 'impregnable' cave castle seems to have felt, perhaps with some justification, that its position was hopeless. Isolated and surrounded, the defenders did not know that King Amalric of Jerusalem had gathered a relief force – and the castle surrendered while Frankish troops were rushing to its aid.[13]

Amalric was notoriously bad-tempered and tetchy. He was famous for lacking 'a genial temperament and was far too taciturn. He was entirely without that gracious affability which princes need . . . Rarely did he speak to anyone unless compelled by necessity or unless, perchance, annoyed by being addressed first.' Amalric was a man with many good qualities, but if he had not been the king, it is unlikely that he would have had a full social calendar. Perhaps he was depressed – being king of Jerusalem was one of the world's most difficult and thankless jobs. But he was hard to like.[14]

When he heard of the surrender, Amalric was incandescent. He regarded the Templars' behaviour as a dereliction of duty of the most egregious kind. He was sick of losing castles before he could relieve them. This was a shockingly poor performance from the normally reliable Templar brothers. Amalric put up with their arrogance because they were good at their job. But if they could not even do that job properly, what was the point of them? The brother knights in command of the garrison were arrested and put on trial.

The outcome of this trial was almost as shocking as the loss of the castle. 'Infuriated at [the] news' of their submission, William of Tyre wrote drily, 'the king caused about twelve of the Templars responsible for the surrender to be hanged from a gallows'.[15]

When Amalric launched a vital, but ultimately unsuccessful, invasion of Egypt soon afterwards, in 1168, relations between the Templars and the monarchy were still extremely strained. Although the order had played a central role in all the previous campaigns, Master Bertrand of Blancfort (in post 1156–69) now refused to take part – the Hospitallers had to take up the slack instead, and almost bankrupted themselves in doing so.

There were several reasons why the campaign was not popular. The perennial rivalry between the Templars and the Hospitallers did not help. Logically, it was also the case that the Templars had become far too thinly spread. They did not have the resources to defend so much of the vulnerable borders of the Holy Land and simultaneously go on campaign into Egypt.[16]

But there was a deeply emotional aspect to the issue as well. The affair of the 'impregnable' cave castle in 1167 and the subsequent executions had left both parties feeling bitter and aggrieved. The loss of the castle had been shocking for the king. And the hanging of the Templar brothers in the aftermath of the fiasco had not been forgotten by the order. The garrison had made the wrong decision and would probably have been severely punished by the Templars themselves – but the imposition of royal justice still rankled.[17]

If Walter of Mesnil's derisory 'penance' was meant to placate Amalric, it failed in the most spectacular fashion. Perhaps it was calculated to be insulting. Either way, the king, irascible enough at the best of times, went ballistic. Fighting almost broke out when Amalric 'went himself to Sidon on this matter, and found the master with many of the other brethren, including the culprit himself'. Royal troops stormed in and 'the king caused that man guilty of treason to be dragged forcibly from the house [of the Templars in Sidon] and had him sent in chains to [the royal city of] Tyre, where he was cast into prison'.[18]

Walter was lucky. He survived, but only because King Amalric died shortly afterwards, in July 1174. The affair was glossed over by the order and the new king – neither party had an interest in prolonging the toxic aftermath of the massacre of the Assassins' envoys. Walter, the Templars' killer of choice, disappeared into history.

Wishful thinking?

Amalric, we are told, made fulsome apologies to the Assassins and, importantly for him and his people, 'was able to clear his own honour'. But the chance of a deal had passed. William of Tyre knew that, at the time of his death, Amalric was planning to make complaint to Rome about the conduct of the Templars.[19]

In some ways this entire story sounds implausible. Surely the Assassins, fanatical in the defence of their religion, were not seriously contemplating discussions with the Christians about a change of spiritual allegiance? Were the Franks just deceiving themselves? Possibly, but only up to a point. There may well have been an element of wishful thinking, but William of Tyre, one of the more rational medieval chroniclers, was extremely well informed. When he wrote his account of the episode, he was also acting as the royal chancellor and thus was in

1. The assassination of Vizier Nizam al-Mulk. The elderly Seljuk commander in Persia, Vizier Nizam al-Mulk, was being carried towards his harem in a litter when his attacker dodged the guards, lunged towards him and slew him with a dagger. The 'spectacular' nature of the murder was fully recognised at the time. Hasan was reputed to have gloated that 'the killing of this devil is the beginning of bliss'.

2. The gatehouse at Shaizar. It was here at Shaizar, a formidable (and desirable) fortification in central Syria, that the Assassins met their match in 1114 – in the unlikely form of a group of middle-aged women, who decided they would no longer be pushed around. Calmer, braver and more determined than the men in the face of the Assassins' assault, it was only the resolute actions of the Munqidh females that saved the day.

3. A new headquarters for a new knighthood. King Baldwin II of Jerusalem gave the Templars their first headquarters in his palace in the al-Aqsa mosque on the Temple Mount in Jerusalem. In doing so, he not only gave them a building, Baldwin also inadvertently gave them their iconic name.

4. Masyaf. The Assassins captured their most important fortification in Syria, the huge castle at Masyaf, in 1140. This became the de facto capital of their small, mountain-refuge state.

5. Saladin. In 1169, a Kurdish adventurer named Saladin made his bloody entrance into the politics of the Middle East. The mutual antipathy between him, the Assassins and the Templars changed the destiny of them all.

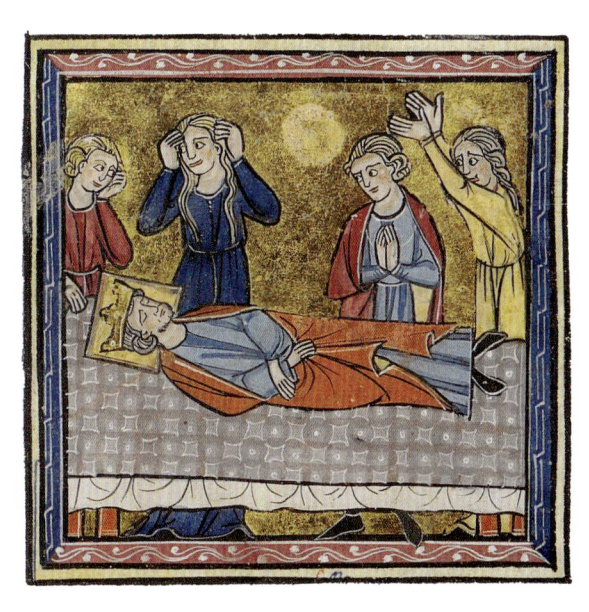

6. The death of King Amalric of Jerusalem. Brother Walter of Mesnil and a Templar hit squad killed Assassin ambassadors who were concluding an alliance with the Franks. Walter was lucky. Despite being arrested, and hugely guilty, he survived – but only because the furious King Amalric died before the Templar could be brought to trial.

7. The Old Man of the Mountain training the *fidais*. This Frankish imagining of what an Assassins' training course looked like fails to convince. But the artist had little to go on – there is scant evidence about how their famous skills were acquired.

8. Saladin must die. These beautifully evocative tiles bring the threat of a Templar charge to life – Frankish knights, focused on a single target, were a very personal, and almost unstoppable, force of destruction.

9. The port of Acre. In the thirteenth century, Acre was the capital of the Latin kingdom of Jerusalem. It was here in 1250 that the Templars made a memorably menacing threat to Assassin emissaries: if the envoys hadn't been under the king's protection, they said, they 'would have drowned them in Acre's filthy waters'.

10. Alamut. The great Assassin castle of Alamut in Persia was besieged and captured by the Mongols in 1256. The Sunni historian Juwayni was with the Mongol army. He took a few choice manuscripts from the castle's famous library – the rest were thrown onto a bonfire.

11. Mamluk emir. An image of what a Mamluk leader wanted to look like: dressed to fight – and to survive. A more downmarket version of this dress code was a typical disguise for Assassins seeking to ingratiate themselves into Frankish society. The rabbit, between the figures on the left, is justifiably scared.

12. Dressed to kill. Beauty and elite menace effortlessly combined in a Mamluk riding coat.

13. The attempt on the life of Prince Edward (later Edward I), 1272. One of the *fidais* attacked Edward in his chambers at night. The prince was off guard, unarmoured and unarmed. The Assassin wounded him, but with an impressively quick recovery Edward 'knocked him senseless to the ground'. Longshanks stabbed him in the face before he could regain consciousness.

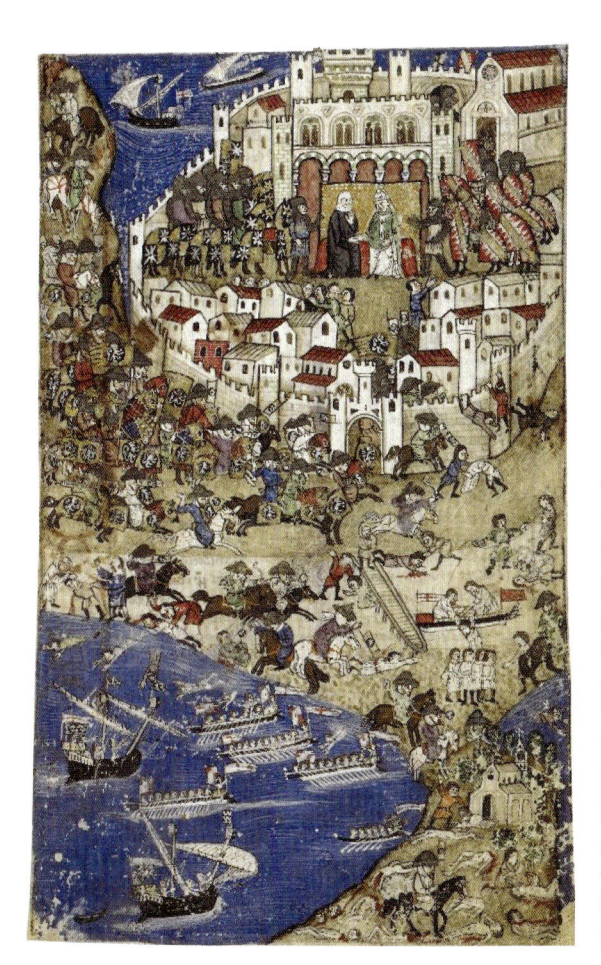

14. The fall of Tripoli, 1289. The Templars had obtained some forewarning of an attack on Tripoli through their network of spies and contacts. The Frankish authorities in the city could not bring themselves to believe the worst. But even if they had, there was little they could have done. The Latin East was collapsing.

15, left. The execution of the Templars in France and the death of Philip IV of France. King Philip of France set in place the events that led to the destruction of the Templars. His death was seen by many as ironic or, for those more superstitiously inclined, as the culmination of a curse.

16, below. The legend of the Assassins. The *fidais* were brave and highly committed members of their sect. For their enemies, this devotion could be explained, and devalued, by portraying them as drug-addled patsies – fools seduced by lurid promises of drugs and sex, both now and in the afterlife. Another legend was under construction.

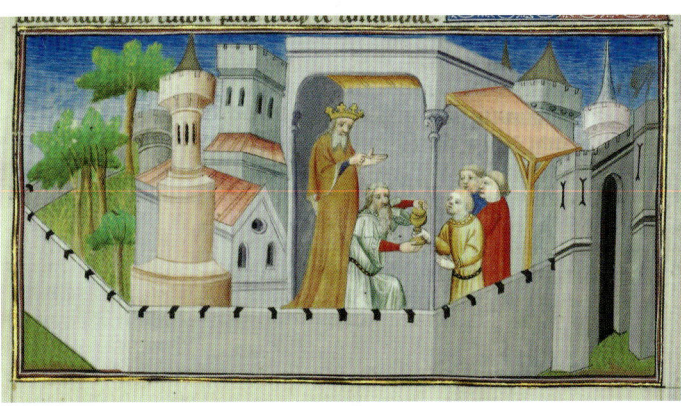

charge of the kingdom's archives – if anyone was in a position to get to the truth of the matter, it was William.

And strangely enough, there were certainly some grounds to encourage him to think that the Syrian Nizaris might genuinely be considering conversion, or at least some form of religious convergence.

As we have seen, the Assassins had become increasingly unorthodox in their forms of worship. The 'Resurrection' of 1164 had changed religious practice in the sect, and represented a substantial break with sharia law. This upheaval, of which William of Tyre was well aware, had resulted in the sect's followers being allowed access to alcohol and pork, and feasting rather than fasting during Ramadan – shockingly, it had also led to the destruction of many mosques.

As one of the Christian Syriac chroniclers of the time commented,

> although the Ismailis were considered Arabs, they were a peculiar tribe that belonged neither to the Arabs nor to the Turks, in religious doctrine or traditions. Concerning Christ, they said that although he was the one about whom the prophets prophesied, yet he was not the saviour . . . They have always vilified Muhammad and do not accept his book (the Quran).[20]

There was at least some theological flexibility to be found in the Nizaris. With their mutual Sunni enemies, there was none.

Tantalisingly, the Old Man of the Mountain also made no secret of his interest in other religions, including Christianity. Optimistic Franks could be forgiven for thinking that this open-mindedness – which outraged the Assassins' Sunni neighbours – presaged a move towards Christianity. The Assassins, of course, may also have encouraged such thinking as part of their negotiating strategy.[21]

Alternatively, the talks may just have been to establish a religious rapprochement (rather than a full conversion) and a military alliance between the Assassins and the crusader states against their mutual enemies – the Turkic-run Sunni Muslim states of the Middle East.

But the Templars wanted the negotiations to flounder, and took radical action to ensure that happened. We will never know how the discussions might have played out – or what terms, if any, might have eventually proved agreeable to both parties.

Just a few weeks after the death of Amalric (and, coincidentally, at almost the same time as Nur al-Din died), Raymond III, count of Tripoli, was appointed regent of Jerusalem. Raymond's father had been murdered by the Assassins. He clearly had no interest in cosying up to Sinan, or in pursuing Amalric's dreams of a closer alliance with the Assassins. The Franks and the Nizaris might still be fighting on the same side against their common enemy, but a more formal and coordinated alliance was now out of the question.[22]

Whatever the exact details of the negotiations, however, one thing is clear – even the Assassins, scary as they were, were terrified of the Templars. They were prepared to go to great lengths to find someone who could help rid them of their nemesis.

15

Saladin Must Die: Assassins Take the Lead (1175–1176)

Thirteen men. Unlucky for someone.

They were dressed to kill – which in this case meant that they looked exactly like everyone else. Part of the background. They moved closer and closer. No pushing, no shouting, just heading for their target. But their progress was checked. There was a shout from behind as they walked on with studied nonchalance. Someone recognised a familiar face. An acquaintance, not a friend. They had no friends.

A puzzled expression, then a simple question: 'What are you doing here?' There was a moment of indecision. It felt like an eternity, but it lasted barely a second. Should they try to bluff their way through? Or, cover blown, should they literally carve their way through to the target?

The chosen answer was simple and shocking – an explosion of flashing weapons and violence as the *fidais* team erupted into the tent where their victim sat, unawares and at the centre of a very different kind of attention, surrounded by generals, lackeys and bodyguards. Blood sprayed everywhere as daggers and swords did what daggers and swords do.

ASSASSINS AND TEMPLARS

Saladin and a Sunni empire

The Assassins and the crusaders of Jerusalem in close alliance? Rumours of a political and even religious rapprochement between Shiite extremists and the devout Catholics of the crusader states? How was any of this possible? The reason why the Assassins and the Franks came so close to a formal partnership was simple – the threat posed by one man.

In 1169, a Kurdish adventurer named Saladin made his bloody entrance into the politics of the Middle East and changed the course of history.[1]

He had gone to Egypt as one of Nur al-Din's junior commanders. Good fortune and ruthlessness allowed him to take power, not least by killing the leadership of his Egyptian hosts. Once installed, he refused to hand the new province over to his erstwhile master. Instead, over the years that followed, Saladin succeeded in bringing all of Muslim Syria under his control.

Relations between the Assassins and Nur al-Din, a devout Sunni Muslim of Turkic heritage, had inevitably been difficult. The chronicler Abu Firas wrote a story of a time when the *fidais* managed to penetrate his security while he slept. They left a dagger by his head, on which was engraved an unambiguous and suitably menacing greeting: 'If you do not leave tomorrow night, this dagger will be stuck in your belly.' Perhaps not surprisingly, when he died in 1174 Nur al-Din was said to be planning a major attack on the Nizari strongholds.[2]

But Saladin was a far greater threat. His empire was so much bigger – under him, for the first time, the main Muslim powers in the region were forcibly dragged, often kicking and screaming, into a single regime.

Saladin, as a usurper desperate to shore up his shaky image as a legitimate ruler, found it useful to pose as the champion of Sunni orthodoxy. The idea of a 'Holy War' against the crusaders and the Nizari 'heretics' was an attractive tool to help further his ambitions. It gave him a PR shield, behind which he could destroy his Sunni rivals, while simultaneously claiming that he needed to do so in order to bring overwhelming force to bear against the outsiders. Saladin spent 80 per cent of his reign fighting his Sunni neighbours, but his propaganda machine glossed lightly over that embarrassing truth: both Assassins and Franks slipped easily and conveniently into the role of scapegoats. They were the unifying bogeymen of his self-justification.[3]

Usurper or not, Saladin's ruthless success was a disaster for both the Templars and the Assassins. It represented a major deterioration in their military and political situation. They were now definitively surrounded and vastly outnumbered by an increasingly consolidated Sunni empire.

But, left with no other option, they continued to throw themselves into the fray. They both correctly identified that this new empire posed an existential threat. Both groups tried to kill Saladin several times during the 1170s, each using their own characteristic and dramatic methods of death-dealing.

Saladin became the urgent target of their attentions.

'Be on the lookout for us': Aleppo (1175)

Walter of Mesnil may literally have killed off the possibility of a formal alliance between the crusaders and the Assassins – that had always been the intention of the Templars. But we do know that around the same time, in the winter of 1173–4, the two unlikely allies were still working together to try to neutralise Saladin before he became even more powerful.

A conspiracy to oust – and presumably kill – Saladin in Egypt was set in train. Dissident Fatimid officials were in communication with the Latin kingdom of Jerusalem about what needed to be done. We also know from a letter sent by Saladin to his nominal overlord in Baghdad, written in 1174, that the Fatimid plotters had specifically contacted Sinan to get his support and, inevitably, access to a skilled *fidais* squad.

This was a coalition of mutual interest. All the parties involved in the conspiracy hated Saladin and the threat he represented. And all wanted a Shiite power re-established in Cairo. Saladin's rule had not yet become fully consolidated: the relatives of the last Fatimid caliph were still alive and housed conveniently nearby in Egypt. This was the last good chance to dispose of Saladin before he became so powerful as to be almost untouchable.

But it didn't happen. Whatever plans may or may not have been in place, the plot was uncovered by Saladin and his security teams in the spring of 1174. The Assassins and the crusaders were both implicated in the scheme, alongside many disgruntled remnants from the previous Fatimid regime. Inevitably, bloody repression ensued. The plot failed and Saladin emerged stronger than ever.[4]

As conspiracy had failed, the Assassins turned back to their old ways – the tried and trusted solution of a visit from the *fidais*. Saladin was already high on the Assassins' hit list, but now he moved against the Nizari 'heretics' in a manner which increased his unpopularity still further. While on his way to attack his fellow Sunni rivals in Aleppo at the end of 1174, he still found time to send his men off to raid Ismaili territory in the Jabal as-Summaq, destroying villages and killing their inhabitants. The Sunni historian Ibn al-Jawzi claimed that it was these attacks which sparked the Assassins' animosity.[5]

Plans were immediately set in train by Sinan for a series of retaliatory attacks. The first *fidais* team struck in January 1175, while Saladin was besieging Aleppo. It got close – but not close enough.

Thirteen men, all armed with knives, were chosen to kill him. The size of the team was a direct reflection of the importance of the hit. Saladin was a priority target, and Sinan wanted him definitively eliminated at the first attempt, before his security measures could be ramped up. The team timed the attack to coincide with the communal meal, when servants and guests would be milling around and everyone would be most at ease – and most distracted. Everything was in place for an overwhelming assault.[6]

It was thwarted by a single piece of bad luck. When the *fidais* arrived at Saladin's camp, 'an emir called Khumartakin, lord of the castle of Abu Qubays, saw and recognized them, because he was their neighbour who met and fought with them often. When he saw them, he said to them, "What has brought you here? On what business have you come?"⁷

It was an easy question with no easy answer. Knives were drawn as the Assassins tried to push their way through. They stabbed the emir

> with some deadly blows and one of their number charged towards Saladin to slay him but was killed before he could reach him. The rest of the Ismailis began to fight and killed several persons before they themselves were killed.⁸

The *fidais* team failed, but it killed as many of the Ayyubid soldiers as possible. The Assassin who got closest to Saladin was ferociously cut down and his head hacked off by an emir who came to the sultan's rescue. Saladin's chancellor, Imad al-Din, wrote that 'the others were not killed until they had killed a number of people'. The *fidais* did not die quietly.⁹

Saladin's propagandists had long sought to denigrate their enemies by association with heretics and crusaders. Trying to extract at least something good from what had clearly been a very close call, they claimed that the Assassins had been put up to it by the sultan's rivals in Aleppo. This was not only impossible, but it was also very convenient. The Assassins had plenty of strong motives of their own to kill Saladin. They may have been coordinating their attacks with the sultan's enemies for practical or tactical considerations, but it was not the main driver behind their animosity.¹⁰

Saladin himself was shaken by the attack. He composed a letter while he was still in the freezing siege camp of Aleppo, to his nephew, Farrukh-Shah – the weather was harsh, he wrote, 'but men's minds are hardened by the expectation of victory'. He made it clear that he believed the Aleppans to have been behind the attempt, and that they were working in concert with the Assassins.

The sultan wrote that they had already received large sums of money for the attempted assassination. He advised his nephew to be on his guard at all times, and to surround himself only with men whom he already knew. Above all, Saladin was now fully aware that the Nizaris were coming for him – in a vivid turn of phrase, he told Farrukh-Shah that 'the knives have been distributed'.[11]

After the failure of the attack at Aleppo, there was a period of bluster, threat and bad-tempered diplomacy. It was perhaps after this first attempt on his life that Saladin was said to have

> sent a messenger to [Sinan] with a threatening message, and [Sinan] said to the messenger: 'I will show you the men with whom I will encounter him.' Then he made a sign to a group of the companions to throw themselves off the highest point of the fortress, and they threw themselves one after another and perished.

Regardless of the details of the meeting (and this was, after all, a Sunni account of the episode), the theatre of death was a stock in trade of Nizari diplomacy. The sect was happy to re-emphasise it at critical points.[12]

Kamal al-Din's biography of Sinan includes excerpts from a letter which Sinan is said to have written to Saladin, also in response to a message from the sultan. The correspondence probably dates to this same period of hate-filled 'phoney war'. Saladin had, it seems, demanded Sinan's presence at his court. The demand had been accompanied by insults and threats against the Assassins' castles and lands.

Mysterious as ever, Sinan set the tone of his response by riposting with some suitably menacing poetry:

> O you who threaten me with strokes of the sword,
> May my power never rise again if you overthrow it!
> The dove rises up to threaten the hawk,
> The hyenas of the desert are roused against the lions!
> He tries to stop the mouth of the viper with his finger,
> Let the pain his finger feels suffice him.[13]

SALADIN MUST DIE: ASSASSINS TAKE THE LEAD

Having established the mandatory threatening nature of his reply, Sinan proceeded in characteristic fashion. It is worth quoting the letter in some detail, as it is one of the rare instances in which we get a first-hand glimpse into the mind of a Nizari leader. It shows how he saw the world and, just as importantly – given the Assassins' dependence on the leverage of fear – how he wanted the world to see him.

'We have read the gist and details of your letter,' Sinan wrote,

> and taken note of its threats against us with words and deeds, and by God it is astonishing to find a fly buzzing in an elephant's ear and a gnat biting statues. Others before you have said these things and we destroyed them and none could help them . . . If indeed your orders have gone forth to cut off my head and tear my castles from the solid mountains, these are false hopes and vain fantasies.[14]

Sinan continued in similar vein, setting out self-justifications which verged upon self-pity, alongside supremely accomplished threats. 'We are oppressed and not oppressors, deprived and not deprivers,' he wrote, slightly peevishly:

> [P]repare means for disaster and don a garment against catastrophe; for I will defeat you from within your own ranks and take vengeance against you at your own place, and you will be as one who encompasses his own destruction.

The conclusion to Sinan's letter was all the more menacing for its lack of hyperbole: 'When you read this letter of ours, be on the lookout for us.'[15]

The *fidais* were on their way again.

'Hardly crediting his escape'

In May 1176, Saladin was besieging the castle of 'Azaz, which belonged to one of his Sunni rivals. Here the Assassins launched another – even more ferocious – attempt on his life, with a smaller, but more focused team.

Having failed to inflict a fatal blow on the sultan at the first attempt, this time the *fidais* had strict orders to go for the most vulnerable and critical parts of Saladin's body – his neck and head. On 22 May 1176, wrote Ibn al-Athir, 'while Saladin was in a tent belonging to one of his emirs, [a man] called Jawuli, the commander of the Asadi troop, [an Assassin] leapt on him, struck him on the head with a dagger and wounded him'.[16]

This was close, but again not close enough. The dagger that was launched at his skull encountered iron, rather than bone. Spooked by the previous attempt, Saladin was better protected than before. Under his flowing outer garments, he was almost totally covered in layers of concealed body-armour.

The armour saved Saladin's life. 'Had it not been for the mailed helmet under his cap,' wrote Ibn al-Athir,

> he would have been killed. Saladin grasped the [Assassin's] hand in his, although he was unable totally to prevent him striking a blow. However, he could only give him weak blows. The [Assassin] continued striking him on the neck with his dagger. Saladin was wearing a brigandine and the blows fell on the collar of the brigandine, cutting into it. The chainmail prevented the blows reaching his neck, because his allotted end was still some way off.[17]

Saladin's men immediately rushed to his aid. An emir named Yazkush (an old retainer of Saladin's uncle, Shirkuh) 'came forward and seized the dagger in his hand. The [Assassin] wounded him but he did not let go until the [Assassin] was killed. Another Ismaili advanced and was killed, and then a third, who was also killed.' Saladin was hustled away to his tent 'in a state of shock, hardly crediting his escape'.[18]

The second team member had killed one of Saladin's commanders, a man named Da'ud, before being hacked down in turn. Another *fidais* fought on until he was killed by Saladin's brother. The last surviving Nizari escaped from the tent, but was torn apart by the crowd that had quickly gathered outside.

The *fidais* had got close by being disguised as members of Saladin's own elite guard. After the attack, security had to be tightened still further, with particular attention being paid to the soldiers surrounding the sultan. As the chronicler Ibn Wasil wrote:

> The sultan rode to his tent, terrified by this event, with his blood flowing down his cheek and the collar of his chainmail wet. He hid himself away, took precautions and constructed around his tent something resembling a palisade to cover it. He sat in a wooden house, on his guard against the soldiery. Those whom he did not like [the look of] he sent away and those he recognised he allowed in.[19]

Security measures such as these ruined many careers. Proximity to power was everything, and being deprived of that proximity could be a disaster. In a rather touching HR aside, Imad al-Din, who had been an eyewitness to the attack, wrote that when Saladin 'rode out, if he saw anyone in his entourage whom he did not know, he had them removed. [But] afterwards he would ask about them and if they wanted intercession or help, he would help them.'[20]

It was not just the sultan who was shaken. Shockwaves reverberated throughout Saladin's fragile, personality-based empire. Ibn Abi Tayy, a Shiite chronicler, wrote that 'the army was disturbed and people were afraid of one another'. Saladin quickly sent a reassuring message back to Egypt, in order to discourage any thought of an uprising. 'There was only a scratch with some few drops of blood,' he wrote implausibly. Perhaps more to the point, he was keen to emphasise that 'there is nothing to cause distress'.[21]

But everyone knew that it had been a close-run thing.

Peace without trust

The *fidais* had got to Saladin. Once again, they had almost killed him. And they had wounded or killed several of his bodyguards and senior officers. Another emir named Mankalan died a couple of days after the attack, as a result of wounds received during the fracas with the back-up members of the *fidais* team. But the failure of the murder attempt outside Aleppo in 1175 had given Saladin time to increase his security – and the Nizaris paid the price for that initial failure.[22]

Saladin had plenty of enemies who were higher up his 'to do' list – most notably his Sunni rivals in Aleppo and the Franks of the crusader states. But he knew that he could no longer ignore the Assassins.

Sinan had made personal attacks on the sultan. The sultan would repay the compliment. In July 1176, Saladin moved his armies into the heart of the Nizaris' territory to take his revenge. He was said to have 'ravaged their land, destroying and burning. He besieged the fortress of Masyaf, one of their strongest and most impregnable castles. He set up trebuchets [catapults] and pressed hard on the defenders without any break.'[23]

There is a surviving account of a diplomatic mission sent by Saladin to the Old Man of the Mountain, probably during this counter-offensive. The unlucky diplomat chosen to lead these discussions was a certain al-Muntagib, the son of one of Saladin's accountants. He cannot have relished the job he had to do – his was the high-risk task of taking insults and threats to one of the world's most frightening men.

Perhaps to al-Muntagib's surprise, he lived to tell the tale. He later said that

> Saladin sent me to Sinan, the leader of the Ismailis . . . with threats and menaces the purport of which was 'I will kill you with my own sword' . . . and he wrote a letter to him. Sinan made no reply to the letter but wrote some [threatening] verses of his own composition on the margin of the letter he received.[24]

SALADIN MUST DIE: ASSASSINS TAKE THE LEAD

According to al-Muntagib, Sinan told him: 'Your master rules the externals of his army and I rule the innermost hearts of my army. The proof is what you will now see.' After a suitably dramatic pause, the usual theatre of death was enacted once more. Sinan

> called ten of the young men of the chamber . . . and there was a ventilator overlooking the moat. He took out a knife from under his prayermat and threw it through the ventilator. Then he made them a sign and said: 'Let whoever wants this knife throw himself after it.' At once they all leapt after it and were shattered on the rocks [below].[25]

From the perspective of Sinan (and the *fidais*) this was a costly but effective display. Having witnessed this frightening and bloody demonstration, al-Muntagib was said to have 'returned to [Saladin] and informed him of what had happened, and after that [Saladin] made peace with [Sinan]'.[26]

Most accounts refer to only two attempts on Saladin's life by the Assassins (though even that must have felt like more than enough for the sultan). But al-Muntagib said there were more, and explicitly referred to 'their third attempt on Saladin in Damascus'.[27]

The timing of such an incident is problematic. Saladin did not return to Damascus until August 1176, by which time he and Sinan seem to have papered over their differences. But talk of a third attempt on Saladin's life is supported by another source, which also suggests that a failed attack took place in Damascus. A *fidais* was said to have hidden himself in a walnut tree, waiting along a route where the sultan was expected to ride. The Assassin mistimed his jump, however – landing ignominiously on the horse's bottom, the embarrassed Nizari was cut down by Saladin's guards.[28]

Kamal al-Din, one of our better sources, certainly thought that a third attack took place. It is perhaps more plausible, however, to suppose that this final attempt (if it happened at all) took place during the siege of Masyaf, shortly before peace was agreed with the Assassins – and therefore just a few days before Saladin returned to Damascus.[29]

Kamal al-Din wrote another, not necessarily contradictory, account of the deadly diplomatic interplay at this time. Again presumably during the siege of Masyaf, he reported that

> Sinan sent a messenger to Saladin and ordered him to deliver his message only in private. Saladin had him searched, and when they found nothing dangerous on him he dismissed the assembly for him, leaving only a few people, and asked him to deliver his message.[30]

The Nizari diplomat then said:

> 'My master ordered me not to deliver the message [except in private].' Saladin then emptied the assembly of all save two Mamluks, and then said: 'Give your message.' He replied: 'I have been ordered only to deliver it in private.' Saladin said: 'These two do not leave me. If you wish, deliver your message, and if not, return.' He said: 'Why do you not send away these two as you sent away the others?' Saladin replied: 'I regard these as my own sons, and they and I are as one.' Then the messenger turned to the two Mamluks and said: 'If I ordered you in the name of my master to kill this Sultan, would you do so?' They answered yes, and drew their swords, saying: 'Command us as you wish.' Sultan Saladin was astounded, and the messenger left, taking them with him. And thereupon Saladin inclined to make peace with him and enter into friendly relations with him.[31]

The details, at least as conveyed by Kamal al-Din, were almost certainly not correct – the people who were supposed to be in the room were unlikely to be talking about what happened. But the story conveyed a deeper truth. Fear. And the unstoppable nature of the Assassins' threat of death.

SALADIN MUST DIE: ASSASSINS TAKE THE LEAD

Appropriately enough, Saladin's campaign against the Assassins ended in mystery. It lasted only about a week in total. His army left Aleppo on 31 July, marched to Masyaf (some 95 kilometres away) and was back on the road to Hama on 9 August 1176. The 'siege' of Masyaf was so short that there was barely an opportunity for his engineers to establish a camp and assemble the siege engines. Even at the time, commentators were perplexed as to what had really happened during this brief but brutal demonstration.[32]

Ibn al-Athir, for instance, suggested that the Assassins had blackmailed one of Saladin's relatives into persuading him to call off the campaign. 'Sinan, the leader of the Ismailis,' he wrote,

> sent to Shihab al-Din al-Harimi, lord of Hama, who was Saladin's maternal uncle, asking him to mediate, to settle matters and intercede for him, and adding, 'If you do not, we will kill you and all of Saladin's family and emirs.'

Highly motivated by this direct form of approach, 'Shihab al-Din came to Saladin, interceded for them and asked for them to be pardoned. Saladin agreed to this, made peace with them and then departed.'[33]

But there were other possible reasons for the brevity of the siege. The Aleppan historian Ibn Abi Tayy suggested that posturing by the crusaders, who were gathering an army to march up the Beka'a valley, had contributed to Saladin's decision to bring the siege of Masyaf to a swift conclusion. Alternatively, an Ismaili version of these events argues that Saladin sued for peace with the Assassins because he was intimidated by Sinan's magical powers and his ferocious capacity for revenge. All of these reasons, with suitable provisos, could be true – they are not necessarily mutually contradictory.[34]

There was clearly a convergence of interests. Sinan did not want a huge army camped outside his castle, ravaging the hard-won Nizari lands in Syria. Saladin wanted to preserve his life, and the lives of his family. And he had plenty of other enemies to attend to. The two forces were so asymmetrical, so uneven and unpredictable, that both parties probably wanted to call an end to things as soon as possible.

After this, the Assassins generally remained neutral. They had presumably given reassurances to Saladin about his personal safety. He, too, however much he privately detested them as heretics who had killed his friends and tried to murder him, seems to have pulled back from the brink of further antagonism. He did not involve them or their lands in his attacks on the Franks. And, extraordinarily, he even included them in peace treaties that he drew up which might affect their interests.

An uneasy truce was sustained. Love binds – but so, too, does fear.

'Heresy' as propaganda

The Assassins survived Saladin's invasion of 1176. But the balance of power had shifted. Theirs was a relationship based firmly on hatred and fear, rather than on any real trust or affection. It is clear from Saladin's correspondence at the beginning of 1178 that he was still expecting another attempt on his life. He warned his nephew Farrukh-Shah that he should still be fearful of another attack by Assassins. Saladin continued to write to other Sunni leaders about how much he hated the Nizaris, and boasted that they, and the crusaders, would soon be consigned to the hell fires of history.[35]

Saladin had always been eager to talk of his hatred of the Assassins, and had framed a narrative about them that went as far back as his move into Syria in 1174 – he was keen to explain that he had only taken over the lands of his erstwhile master, Nur al-Din, because he had wanted to clear the region of Nizari 'heretics' and Christian crusaders. Saladin still needed external enemies to explain his own internal treachery – so this PR campaign continued even after he had made his uneasy peace with the Assassins.[36]

In 1179, Saladin wrote to Baghdad to smear his competitors in Aleppo and Mosul by accusing them of having a continuing relationship with the Nizaris of the Jabal Bahra.[37] Several years later, in 1182, he was still accusing the government of Mosul of maintaining contact with the hated Assassins and of using them as go-betweens in their negotiations with the equally hated Franks. The sultan claimed to have written evidence of these secret negotiations with the Assassins and threatened to send the letters to their mutual overlords in Baghdad.[38]

Later that year, he once more accused the Nizaris of accepting money from the Zengid diehards in Aleppo and Mosul to 'take the life of one whose friend and master is the Commander of the Faithful' – this was presumably himself. Nizari 'heretics' and crusaders continued to be the pantomime villains of choice to throw into any such diplomatic offensive.[39]

The mutual animosity remained all too apparent. The Andalusian traveller Ibn Jubayr visited the area soon after the siege of Masyaf, in the early 1180s. This was a time of ostensible peace between the Nizaris and Saladin. But Ibn Jubayr, presumably reflecting the opinions of his Sunni hosts, commented at length on the Assassins' theatrical devotion to death and on the evil nature of their 'perverted' leadership. He described them as 'a sect which swerved from Islam and vested divinity in a man. Their prophet was a devil in man's disguise called Sinan, who deceived them.' The uneasy nature of the truce was plain to see.[40]

For Saladin, the Nizaris were always unfinished business. On their part, however, the more customary and satisfying expression of their hatred was a luxury they could no longer afford. On the contrary, they increasingly behaved as though they were Saladin's creatures.

It is perhaps telling that in 1177, shortly after Saladin's armies had left Nizari territory, a *fidais* team attacked the vizier of Aleppo, a man who had a 'boldness and daring in him'. 'One day when he was in the mosque,' wrote Ibn al-Athir, 'some [Assassins] attacked and killed him. He passed away, a martyr.' The hit allegedly took place at the behest of Gumustekin, the governor of Aleppo. He in turn was arrested and tortured to death shortly afterwards.[41]

The exact purpose of this murder and its highly destabilising consequences was, as the Assassins doubtless intended, shrouded in mystery. But it was perhaps more than a coincidence that Saladin was the major beneficiary of these events. And it all took place suspiciously soon after his rapprochement with the sect.

This somewhat cynical view of events is borne out by Ayyubid diplomatic correspondence shortly after the hit – a letter from 1178 shows that the Assassins continued to put out placatory peace-feelers to Saladin, presumably to ensure that the informal truce would remain in place, and that their independence could be maintained.[42]

They may have hated Saladin – but even the Assassins could no longer afford to show it.

16

Saladin Must Die: The Templars' Turn (1177–1191)

It was 25 November 1177 and a grim winter's day in Palestine – one on which there was a sense of imminent death and destruction. There was also a sense of panic in the air. The enemy stretched out in front of the Frankish lines, largely lost in the dust and sand kicked up by the thousands of horses and baggage animals. Saladin's forces had the numbers, but something was not right. Men were shuffling across the field, trying to force a way into the ranks, and disordering their comrades. Others moved more or less surreptitiously away, perhaps under orders to change position – or perhaps just getting nervous, edging away from a place of danger. A hint of indecision. Maybe even the smell of fear.

Saladin's armies had rolled over the southern frontiers of the Latin kingdom of Jerusalem just a few days earlier – in overwhelming force. The Frankish field army took refuge in its castles, waiting for an opportunity to strike back. Lulled into a sense of complacency by their huge numerical superiority and the inactivity of the crusaders, the sultan's troops, in the words of the chronicler Ibn al-Athir, 'scattered throughout those regions in raiding parties . . . [and] became over eager and relaxed, moving around the country secure and confident'.[1] Overconfident, in fact.

ASSASSINS AND TEMPLARS

Triumph at Mont Gisard

Saladin had fully mobilised his armies in Egypt for the invasion, determined to destroy the Latin kingdom of Jerusalem by sheer weight of numbers. He had an army of over 20,000 men at his command, including a core of some 8,000 well-disciplined household cavalry.

Against such an overwhelming force the Franks could muster just 375 knights, supplemented by infantry and their Turcopole light-cavalry auxiliaries. Overconfidence is rarely helpful; but given the huge mismatch in the size of the two armies, it is easy to see why Saladin's troops had begun to relax.

Now, as they met on the battlefield of Mont Gisard, the crusaders knew they had just one chance. One charge, one roll of the dice. That charge was to be spearheaded by those who were best qualified for the (almost) suicidal task ahead – the Templars.

The Templar brothers took on the most hazardous roles in this and many other battles. However outnumbered they might be, they could still take death to the enemy. A Frankish charge was a brutally effective, almost elemental force – but that single charge had to succeed if there was to be any chance of turning the tide.

The Templar squadron numbered less than a hundred men. They were risking everything in a single attempt to break the centre of the Muslim army. They could see the standards of the enemy commanders. Their focus was precise – Saladin and his inner circle, surrounded by a wall of mounted bodyguards. The stakes could not have been higher – and the outcome was nothing short of extraordinary.

English chronicler Ralph of Diceto, writing from London and drawing on a Templar eyewitness account sent back home to the west, noted the pivotal role played by this assault. He singled out the master of the Templars, Odo of Saint-Amand, who personally led his knights into the very heart of the Muslim army. According to Ralph, the Templars struck with such force that Saladin's men were scattered in all directions, fleeing in disorder:

SALADIN MUST DIE: THE TEMPLARS' TURN

Odo the master of the Knighthood of the Temple, like another Judas Maccabaeus, had eighty-four knights of his Order with him in his personal company. He took himself into battle with his men, strengthened by the sign of the cross. Spurring all together, as one man, they made a charge, turning neither to the left nor to the right. Recognising the body of troops in which Saladin commanded many knights, they manfully approached it, immediately penetrated it, incessantly knocked down, scattered, struck and crushed. Saladin was smitten with admiration, seeing his men dispersed everywhere, everywhere turned in flight, everywhere given to the mouth of the sword.[2]

The Templar knights' sudden, all-out charge sent shockwaves through the Muslim ranks, especially at the centre of the army. Saladin's nephew, Taqi al-Din, and his heavy cavalry tried to slow down the Templar advance. Large numbers of Saladin's bodyguards, including one of his young relatives, died in the attempt. But the Templars still managed to push through.

Saladin became increasingly nervous as 'the Franks crowded him', getting dangerously close. In the chaotic seconds that followed, one knight, braver and stronger than those alongside him, hacked his way through to the front. He could see Saladin just a few yards away and charged forward. He was within striking distance of the sultan.[3]

The Templars' ideology of death now had a chance to change the course of history. So close. But not close enough. The battle of Mont Gisard in 1177 was the Templars' first – and best – chance to kill Saladin. They would never get so close again.

The lone knight within striking distance of the sultan was cut down at the last moment. Once again, as with the *fidais* attacks, it was a very close call. Saladin abandoned his armour and ran, leaving his army to be hunted down over the days that followed. It was a disaster, and it nearly destroyed his empire before it was even fully formed.[4]

But Saladin survived. The Templars had tried and failed, like the Assassins before them, to kill their enemy. They now had to live with the consequences of that failure.

The Assassins tried to get to Saladin several times between 1174 and 1176, but always without success. Now the threat he posed grew greater every year. The Templar ideology of martyrdom and death was needed more than ever. Perhaps, where the subtlety of the *fidais* had failed, the blunter, more direct violence of the order could prevail.

The Templars had been buoyed up by an ideology which taught them, correctly in this case, that one highly motivated man could overpower large numbers of the enemy. The power of their commitment and their elite training had destroyed Saladin's armies – but bad luck (and the racing camel on which he fled the battlefield) meant that they had failed to kill the man himself.

Revenge and retribution

Saladin never forgot and never forgave. He swore to take revenge on the Templars and took every opportunity to do so – on a grand scale. Less than two years later, on 10 June 1179, the Frankish field army was ambushed and badly cut up at Marj Ayun, near the eastern frontiers of the Latin kingdom of Jerusalem. Many Frankish lords were killed or captured, along with their troops. The Templars played a major part in the battle, but their master, Odo of Saint-Amand, the hero of Mont Gisard, was blamed by many of the participants for their defeat. He was taken and died in captivity a year later, 'lamented by no one', as William of Tyre rather unkindly put it.[5]

Worse was to follow. The Templars already had a substantial castle at Safad, guarding some of the eastern approaches to the Latin Kingdom. But, aggressive as ever, they wanted to push their defences still further forward, to a part of the frontier more suitable for launching threatening raids into Muslim territory. Over the winter of 1178–9, at a crossing point on the River Jordan known as Jacob's Ford, they started to build a magnificent, state-of-the-art castle. They called it Chastellet.

The strategic strengths of the location were evident to both sides. This was to be the centrepiece of a new Templar 'principality', poised dangerously on the borders of Damascus and threatening the fertile Hauran region. Saladin felt, entirely correctly, that it would make attacks by the Templars inevitable and that it would destabilise much of his newly acquired possessions. And that could not be allowed.[6]

Work on the inner walls of the castle continued until April 1179, but the ultimate Templar plan was to construct a double line of walls in the classic concentric fashion of later crusader fortifications. Because the building of the outer wall was still unfinished, however, the castle was, for a brief moment, vulnerable.

Saladin was quick to take advantage of this temporary weakness. With morale in the Latin kingdom of Jerusalem still low after its recent defeat at Marj Ayun, Saladin felt confident enough to start a full-scale siege. He and his troops arrived at Chastellet on 24 August 1179.

The Ayyubid engineers quickly 'mined the fort and deepened the mine'. With five gates to defend around the site (always weak spots), the Templar garrison knew that its position was extremely precarious. There were some 700–1,000 men in the castle, but many were non-combatants. Not surprisingly – given that it was still a building site – most of the men were construction workers: a Muslim letter written after the event mentioned the large number of artisans taken prisoner, including architects, blacksmiths, masons and carpenters.

The siege ground on and part of the defences began to give way. As soon as it was clear that a breach was imminent, the Templar garrison positioned wooden barricades behind the walls. As Saladin's men tried to push their way in, the knights set the barricades alight and formed up to make a last stand. There was a short pause in the fighting, with the Muslim assault squads understandably reluctant to fight their way through the flames. But there was no hurry. The fires would die down. And the Templars weren't going anywhere.

The attackers poured through the gap. The fighting, partially obscured by smoke and dying flames, was brief but terrible. The Templar commander provided a horrific example of the order's ideology of death before dishonour: perhaps wounded and preferring a death he could control to the prospect of execution or captivity, he threw himself into what remained of the fires.

The victorious Saladin questioned all the prisoners to determine which of the mercenaries or local Christians might be considered 'Muslim converts' – and he had those killed first. All the Templar prisoners were also singled out for execution – this was an interesting, if unwelcome, testament to their military prowess and the embarrassment they had recently caused him at Mont Gisard. Most of the remaining Christian prisoners were butchered over the next few days.

Ironically, however, the Templars were to wreak their revenge from beyond the grave. Most of the Templar corpses had been dumped in the castle's cistern, where they quietly rotted while the demolition work on the half-built castle was under way. The August heat, the unsanitary siege conditions and the bodies in the water combined to create a lethal cocktail. Disease broke out, killing far more of Saladin's men than had fallen in the assaults. His nephew, Taqi al-Din, fell seriously ill and ten of his commanders died, along with large numbers of the rank and file.[7]

'Christ is our life and death is our reward': Blood and glory

The Assassins had come to an understanding with Saladin. But there could be no such truce for the Templars. In 1119, just as the Templar order was being born, another proto-military order, the elite 'confraternity of St Peter', came to an abrupt end. The scene was a place known, in the endearingly brutal and literal way of the medieval world, as the Field of Blood – Ager Sanguinis. Like the Templars, this order occupied the position of honour: the right of the line and the first into combat. One eyewitness wrote that on the Field of Blood, the confraternity crashed into the Muslim lines to their front, 'giving their horses their heads, brandishing their lances as they made haste to strike the cohort in their path violently and quickly', and succeeded in putting the enemy to flight.[8]

But despite their initial success, the Frankish forces were hopelessly outnumbered and surrounded. Like the rest of the army of Antioch, the brave warriors of St Peter died on the field a few minutes later, wiped out almost to the last man.

Almost seventy years later, in May 1187, a similar bloodbath took place, but this time at the Springs of the Cresson, in the Latin kingdom of Jerusalem. The horror played out on a smaller scale, but for the Templars it was every bit as dramatic. It was a crucible of bloodshed and a drama that came to embody the Templar ideology.

At the Springs of the Cresson, a predominantly Templar cavalry force, unsupported by infantry, crashed into a Muslim raiding party of perhaps 6,000 or 7,000 cavalry. There were only 140 Christian knights on the field, of whom 90 were Templars, led by their master, Gerard of Ridefort, and taken from the order's castles at nearby La Fève and Caco.[9]

As they gathered to attack, we are told,

> the knights of Christ rejoiced, saying: 'the Lord has delivered them into our hands.' And when they came near to the enemy, the latter pretended flight, until those who had been hiding in ambush rose up and surrounded them, and 'they smote them with the edge of the sword'.[10]

The result of the absurdly one-sided battle was catastrophic, but predictable. It was a massacre. The heads of the Templars killed in the battle, together with those of the executed prisoners, were stuck on lances and paraded on the way back to Damascus. In a time and place where bloodshed was commonplace, this encounter was recognised as being something different. Even the Muslim chronicler Ibn al-Athir, a man used to writing about the brutality of warfare, knew that it was 'a battle fit to turn black hair grey'.[11]

It was a shocking defeat. But it was also a sublime moment when theology and military theory met head on – a heady melting pot where the spiritual planes collided with the material world in the most violent manner.

Strangely enough to modern sensibilities, the actions of the Templar brothers that day were felt to be a triumph – a vivid and glorious embodiment of the order's ideology. Descriptions of the battle make it clear that the martyrdom of the individual, as well as the destruction of the squadron as a whole, was felt to be admirable, despite the disastrous outcome of the battle.

Only three men escaped the carnage, all of them Templars. The stories they told of the defeat served to emphasise the nature of Templar martyrdom and the way in which members of the order believed, like the Assassins, that they could achieve victory even in death.

The prodigious bravery of one Templar knight, James of Mailly, was singled out by the survivors. A near-contemporary account of his prowess and martyrdom is worth quoting at length, as it shows vividly how a brother knight would want to be remembered:

> A certain Templar – a knight by profession, of Touraine by nation, [James] de Mailly by name – brought all the enemy assault on himself through his outstanding courage. While the rest of his fellow knights ... had either been captured or killed, he bore all the force of the battle alone and shone out as a glorious champion for the law of his God. He was surrounded by enemy troops and almost abandoned by human aid, but when he saw so many thousands running towards him from all directions he strengthened his resolve and courageously undertook the battle, one man against all.[12]

'His commendable courage', went on the chronicler,

> won him his enemies' approval. Many were sorry for him and affectionately urged him to surrender, but he ignored their urgings, for

he was not afraid to die for Christ. At long last, crushed rather than conquered by spears, stones and lances, he sank to the ground and joyfully passed to heaven with the martyr's crown, triumphant.[13]

For such a man, the Templars believed, death was just a beginning. Despite the horrific violence, his personal last stand was characterised as 'a gentle death with no place for sorrow, when one man's sword had constructed such a great crown for himself from the crowd laid all around him'. Comparisons with the saints of the Christian cause soon followed. It was said that because he had been riding 'a white horse and had white armour and weapons, the Gentiles, who knew that Saint George had this appearance in battle, boasted that they had killed the Knight of Shining Armour, the protector of the Christians'.[14]

Saints need relics and rituals, as well as stories. And inevitably, those followed quickly. 'It is said', wrote one chronicler, 'that there were some who sprinkled the body of the dead man with dust and placed the dust on their heads, believing that they would draw courage from the contact.'[15]

Even his genitals had power. Their masculine strength was believed (with typical male optimism) to be capable of entirely unfeasible potency. One particularly devout Christian was said to have 'cut off the man's genitals, and kept them safely for begetting children so that even when dead the man's members [sic] – if such a thing were possible – would produce an heir with courage as great as his'.[16]

Grim but devout tales such as this tell us much about what constituted an 'ideal' Templar. James of Mailly was subsequently revered as a martyr, and his story seems to have been designed to act, at least in part, as a motivational tool for the brothers in their moments of reflection. James is portrayed as being astonishingly brave, fully committed to the cause of his religion and his order, and explicitly associated with George, the warrior saint.

James made (or so it was said) a conscious decision to fight on against the enemies of Christ, rather than retreat; and to have embraced death, rather than surrender. He was venerated for embodying the highest ambitions of the fighting Templar.[17]

Interestingly, the almost spiritual nature of a Templar cavalry charge was widely recognised, even beyond the order. A letter sent back to Europe a few weeks later, in July 1187, stated that once the brother knights at Cresson realised just how outnumbered they were, they immediately made 'the sign of the cross, and with the words, "Christ is our life and death is our reward", they launched an attack'.[18]

People knew that Cresson was different. The charge of the Templar knights at Mont Gisard was brave and full of risk. They were outnumbered, but they had, literally, a fighting chance of success. The battle at the Springs of the Cresson, almost exactly ten years later, reveals a very different side of the order. Militarily, the Templar decision to charge a clearly overwhelming number of enemy cavalry makes very little sense. At best, one might see it as an act of desperation. At worst, an obviously crazy mistake born of arrogance and overconfidence.

But in ideological terms, one can see how it could happen. These were men who knew that Saint Bernard had exhorted them as warriors of Christ who 'are mindful of the words of Maccabees, "It is simple enough for a multitude to be vanquished by a handful . . . victory in war does not depend on a big army, but bravery is the gift from heaven." '[19]

Even more to the point, Bernard had declared that 'as they have on numerous occasions experienced, one man may pursue a thousand, and two put ten thousand to flight'. This was all too easy to write in the quiet beauty of a French monastery, of course. But with an ideological heritage such as this, an almost incomprehensible catastrophe such as the battle at the Springs of the Cresson becomes far more explicable.[20]

Where others would have seen a bloody defeat (and a foolishly unnecessary one at that), the Templars lingered over the details. This was a brutal conflict, in which the brother knights not only were subjected to what they saw as martyrdom, but were also active agents in the process. They thereby willingly embraced Saint Bernard's maxims of martyrdom.

Despite the gory humiliation of its material outcome, Cresson was cherished as an occasion on which the order grasped spiritual victory through martyrdom – the binary, glorious moment when the knights could show the Christian world their true commitment. The battle was one of the ideological turning points for the order. The brothers could follow Christ's example in the humiliation of death and, like him, rise all the stronger from the ashes of failure.

But Cresson was just the beginning. Over the coming weeks the Templars' bloodletting continued on an unprecedented scale.

Hattin (1187)

Shortly after the intangible glory (and all-too-tangible gore) of Cresson, Guy of Lusignan, the weak and vacillating king of Jerusalem (who only held the throne through his wife), made an appalling decision – he was persuaded to take his troops to the rescue of the castle of Tiberias, besieged by Saladin's armies. Marching along an almost waterless route, surrounded and hopelessly outnumbered by Muslim armies, the Frankish forces were falling apart even before they made serious contact with the enemy. As the doomed crusader army paced slowly towards the village of Hattin on 3–4 July 1187, the Templars were assigned the position of greatest danger, and the one which the Franks knew required most discipline in the face of enemy provocation – the rearguard.

The Templar rearguard was increasingly pushed back, as the weight of enemy numbers began to tell. Eventually it undertook a desperate charge to try to keep Saladin's troops at bay. Afterwards, as recriminations were bandied about, messages sent back to the west after the battle complained that it was only a lack of support from other parts of the army that had caused the Templar charge to fail. One letter sent by the Hospitallers to Italy said that 'at around the third hour the master of the Temple charged with all his brothers. They received no assistance, and God allowed most of them to be lost.'[21]

The battle ground on remorselessly towards its inevitable, shocking conclusion. King Guy did not command the respect of his vassals, so the last stand of the Frankish army, fought around the king's tent, was inevitably a somewhat lonely affair. Some men had already fled or fought their way out. Others had surrendered or taken temporary refuge on a nearby hill. A few of Guy's close allies were still with him – but the core of this final diehard band was the men of the military orders.[22]

There was precious little hope. There was a couple of hundred knights at most, surrounded by tens of thousands. But the Templars fell back on their ideology: they had only the most negligible chance of material success, but they could still go down fighting, inspired by the glorious prospect of sacrifice and martyrdom. Even their Muslim enemies knew what was happening. As Ibn al-Athir later wrote, 'they understood that they would only be saved from death by facing it boldly'.[23]

The Templars chose the same path they had taken at Mont Gisard ten years earlier – they identified Saladin's standards, lowered their lances and charged. Saladin's son, al-Afdal, witnessed what happened next, as he sat with his father towards the end of the battle. He left an extraordinary account of the final desperate assaults:

> I was alongside my father during this battle, the first I had witnessed. When the king of the Franks was on the hill . . . they made a formidable charge against the Muslims facing them, so that they drove them back to my father. I looked towards him and he was overcome by grief and his complexion pale . . . The Muslims rallied, returned to the fight and climbed the hill. When I saw that the Franks withdrew, pursued by the Muslims, I shouted for joy, 'We have beaten them!' But the Franks rallied and charged again like the first time and drove the Muslims back to my father. He acted as he had on the

first occasion and the Muslims turned upon the Franks and drove them back to the hill. I again shouted, 'We have beaten them!' but my father rounded on me and said, 'Be quiet! We have not beaten them until that tent falls.' As he was speaking to me, the tent [of King Guy] fell.[24]

The Templars' last charges were awe-inspiring, and they had caused Saladin some moments of real concern – even though the battle was, for all practical purposes, already over. But now it was time for revenge.

The Frankish army at Hattin, the greatest force ever fielded by the crusader states, had been defeated. Most of the survivors were captured and enslaved. But not the Templars. Saladin had something else in mind for them.[25]

The sultan had the prisoners from the military orders rounded up and killed for the entertainment of his men. Imad al-Din, Saladin's chancellor and secretary, had a grandstand view of how the Templar prisoners of war were slaughtered in an obscenely amateurish fashion by Muslim religious scholars. He left a customarily obsequious and flowery account of the grim event:

> [T]wo days after the victory [at Hattin], the Sultan sought out the Templars and Hospitallers who had been captured and said: 'I shall purify the land of these two impure races.' . . . He ordered that they should be beheaded, choosing to have them dead rather than in prison. With him was a whole band of scholars and sufis and a certain number of devout men and ascetics; each begged to be allowed to kill one of them, and drew his sword and rolled back his sleeve.[26]

Saladin derived huge pleasure from the spectacle of death that he caused to be played out in front of him:

> [H]is face joyful, [he] was sitting on his dais; the unbelievers showed black despair, the troops were drawn up in their ranks, the amirs

stood in double file. There were some who slashed and cut cleanly, and were thanked for it; some who refused and failed to act, and were excused; some who made fools of themselves, and others took their places.

Saladin's revenge for his humiliation at Mont Gisard was elaborate, public and designed to be savoured.[27]

A few days after the battle, the senior surviving Templar, a preceptor named Terricus, wrote about what happened next. He had fought at Hattin, so he described events through the traumatic prism of experience. He was probably part of the small Christian vanguard that had carved its way out through the Muslim lines as the outcome of the battle became clear – he and a small band of comrades escaped to the Christian strongholds on the coast. Coming so soon after the disaster, the horror of the events which he had witnessed was palpable.

Terricus, in his shocked letter back to the west, wrote that 'two hundred and thirty of our [Templar] brothers were beheaded that day . . . the other sixty having been killed on 1 May' – executed after the battle at the Springs of the Cresson. There were a few stunned survivors, but there was a glaring, unavoidable truth.[28]

The Templars in the east were struggling to survive as a fighting force.

17

The Death of Heroes (1192–1193)

It is a hot night in the close, dark streets of medieval Acre. A small, slight man – well dressed, but not ostentatiously so – is walking home. The smell is sickening, with filth overflowing the gutters. But the man does not notice: this is normal. Comforting even. He is in familiar surroundings. And he is happy. He has just dined with his friend, and is buzzing pleasantly. He is relaxed and he feels safe.

As he turns a corner, he notices two young men from his household running towards him. Unusual, but nothing too threatening. Possibly coming to warn him of some problem at home. Maybe bringing news of an overly pushy petitioner.

He has only a second or two to process what is happening before they reach him. Strangely, they do not stop. They both punch him in the stomach and keep moving. Fast. Their master is surprised rather than anything else. He is winded, almost pushed over by the force of their unexpected blows. But he doesn't fall. He just sinks slowly to his knees. And it is only then that he notices how wet he is. There is blood everywhere. It soaks his clothes, mixing slowly with the ordure and offal in the street. The king-elect of Jerusalem is dying.

ASSASSINS AND TEMPLARS

The assassination of Conrad (1192)

In the wake of the disaster at Hattin, the crusaders struggled to rebuild their country. The Third Crusade was launched, led by King Philip II of France and King Richard I of England. Sieges were endured and battles fought. The Frankish coastal cities were largely recovered – but inland, most of the Latin kingdom of Jerusalem was lost. The Templars struggled with the challenges of martyrdom. But for the Assassins, it was business as usual.

The skills of the *fidais* were useful in protecting the sect against bullies, but they also provided it with something to trade. In return for safety and influence, its members could act on behalf of their patrons, making sure that their enemies died in an appropriately unpleasant manner – a manner, moreover, that did not implicate those who had commissioned their death. Perhaps not surprisingly, given the ferocious in-fighting among the Muslim city states of the time, many Turkic leaders availed themselves of this opportunity.

The Nizaris did not have a particular problem with Christians, of course. But ultimately, business was business. In the deadly and pragmatic world of the medieval Holy Land, they occasionally undertook contracts for business reasons, in exchange for money or political advantage.

On 28 April 1192, Conrad, marquis of Montferrat and, for a very short time, the uncrowned king of Jerusalem, fell victim to one such contract.

The attack was shocking. Conrad was greatly admired. He had been brave and quick-thinking in the immediate aftermath of the meltdown that followed the rout at Hattin. He had saved the city of Tyre, and helped lead the initial fight-back. Arguably, it was only because of Conrad of Montferrat that the crusader states were able to struggle on for another century. The impact of his death on the Frankish community was profound.

This high-profile murder was both well documented and yet shrouded in mystery – a lurid 'true crime' murder, full of motives and suspects, and yet still lacking a definitive solution. But while the identity of the ultimate author of the crime remains uncertain, the circumstances of the hit are known in some detail. And luckily for us, they are corroborated by multiple sources, from different cultures and varying perspectives.

That evening, Conrad

> had eaten with the Bishop of Beauvais with great pleasure and joy and the time came for him to take his leave. He was in front of the Exchange [of Tyre] . . . As he went on his way, happy, two young men, without cloaks, carrying two knives, came running up to him, striking him in his body as they ran up, so that he fell.[1]

Conrad's men

> took him gently in their arms and took him from the place where he was hurt . . . He lived for a short time, then died. But first he made confession and said secretly to the marchioness, his wife, in whose eyes he saw tears, that she must turn her mind to the protection of Tyre . . . Then he died and was buried.

People were stunned. It had all happened so quickly.[2]

This was a classic Nizari hit. At least one of the murderers had insinuated his way into Conrad's household, using patience to build up trust prior to the job. Both of the *fidais* had tried to escape, but one of them was immediately grabbed and killed outright. The other sought refuge in a church, vainly seeking sanctuary. He was dragged out and interrogated.

Knowing that he was going to be killed, the Assassin proudly confessed that he and his comrade

> had stayed near to the marquis for a long time in order to do this, that they had for a long time sought successfully to kill him, until

the day came when many tears were shed, and that they had been sent by the Old Man of the Mountain who hated him and who causes all those whom he hates with a [bitter] hatred to be killed in such a way.[3]

But the ultimate perpetrator – the man who had commissioned the act – was never identified. And, as with any good whodunnit, there was a long list of suspects.

Some blamed the English, because Richard the Lionheart had been a fierce opponent of Conrad's candidacy for the throne of Jerusalem. The French, inevitably, were pushing stories that 'King Richard had pursued and sought the death of Conrad through payment'. Even more implausibly, they also suggested that he had hired another *fidais* squad to travel to France. The French army was so shaken that it 'sent [messengers] to the king of France, saying that he should fear and protect himself from the Assassins, because they had killed the marquis and that the king of England had sent four of them to sweet France to kill him'.[4]

The Anglo-Normans, who, like their master, had been consistently hostile to Conrad, were outraged by the accusation. 'God! What a foul thing to say,' wrote Ambroise, the Norman chronicler:

[T]hey did a vile deed when they sent the message [to France]. As a result of it many people were later troubled, angered and grieved . . . For a long time was the king melancholy on account of the news of the marquis, who by such great misfortune had been killed so hideously.[5]

The anonymous author of another English chronicle of the Third Crusade added a couple of different details:

One of the homicides was at once beheaded. The other at once took refuge in a church, but he was pulled out of it and condemned to be dragged through the middle of the city until he died, giving up the spirit which was guilty of such treachery.[6]

Roger of Howden, yet another English chronicler, spoke to some of the men returning from the Third Crusade and seemed to have specific details about how the captured murderers were tortured. 'One of them was immediately put to death', but the other murderer was captured and, as there was more time available for extended attention, he was 'flayed alive'. Alternatively, of course, it may be that the 'flaying' Roger referred to was just a grim commentary on what was left of the man after he had been dragged around Tyre. Either way, it was a bad ending.[7]

Like the French, many local Muslims assumed that King Richard was behind the killing. Conrad had refused to support Richard's campaigning after King Philip of France had returned to Europe – the English king's disputes with Conrad had created bad blood and certainly gave him a possible motive. Beha al-Din, one of Saladin's senior lawyers and historians, was with his master at the time, and got his version of events from Saladin's ambassador to the Franks, who happened to be in Tyre when the Assassins struck. Baha al-Din wrote that

> two of his men attacked him with daggers. He was slight of build. They kept striking him until [he died]. The two men were apprehended and questioned about the affair and who had put them up to it. They replied, 'The king of England put us up to it.'[8]

Given the succession dispute that had been rumbling on, the accusation had its own logic. But commissioning such an attack made little sense for Richard at that point. He had already accepted that Conrad was the only practical choice for king once the crusade had finished, and he was planning to get back to England as soon as possible. Tempers were certainly running high, but Conrad's death was an inconvenience for Richard, rather than an advantage – it merely delayed his return home.⁹

Moreover, the timeline did not fit. Everyone agreed that the murder was the culmination of a long-standing conspiracy – the Assassins seem to have been in Conrad's employ for at least six months before the murder; so, including planning and negotiations about payment, the plot must have been in train for the best part of a year. If he had a major problem, King Richard, as a blunt man of action who had no known connections with the Assassins, would have been far more likely to confront Conrad in person than to enter into extended intrigues.

There were other western suspects, too. The German chronicler, Arnold of Lübeck, extended the list of suspects to include, unconvincingly, the military orders. 'King Conrad of Jerusalem was slain', he suggested, 'through the treachery . . . of certain Templars' – presumably in conjunction with their Assassin neighbours. Arnold, who had heard the elaborate stories of how the *fidais* were trained to accept death, also added (with rather forced irony) that he did 'not know whether [the murderers] found paradise' after they succeeded in their mission.¹⁰

Guy of Lusignan, the unsuccessful contender for the throne of Jerusalem after his wife's death, was Conrad's arch-rival and yet another suspect – he had an obvious motive in seeing his competitor dead. Humphrey of Toron, a local nobleman whose wife (following an annulment) was taken in marriage by Conrad as part of his campaign to legitimise his claim to be king of Jerusalem, was also (unsurprisingly) no fan.

Most glaringly of all, the crusader Henry II, count of Champagne, deserves a prominent place on any list of suspects, if only because of his motive – he became king on Conrad's death and took the latter's pregnant widow as his wife. Henry had most to gain.

Even more suspiciously, however, Henry was the only Frankish ruler known to have had a face-to-face relationship with the leader of the Assassins in Syria. And he was also the only one to personally visit the Assassin castles – he went to Kahf in 1194, just a couple of years after

THE DEATH OF HEROES

Conrad's death. We know that while he was there he had discussions with Sinan's successor, the (new) Old Man of the Mountain. This may have been a courtesy call. Or it may have been an attempt to forge an alliance. But it is also possible that he was there to acknowledge past debts and build on an existing business relationship.

Everyone had a theory. The chronicler Ibn al-Athir thought he knew who was behind the hit. His information was that Saladin had employed the Assassins to kill either Richard or Conrad. Sinan had decided to kill the latter, as he did not want Saladin to have too free a hand in the peace negotiations that he knew could not be too far away.

According to Ibn al-Athir's version of events, Saladin encouraged Sinan

> to send someone to kill the king of England. [Or, alternatively] if he killed the Marquis, he would have ten thousand dinars. They were unable to assassinate the king and Sinan did not see any advantage for them in it, [being eager] that Saladin should not have a mind untroubled by the Franks and thus be free to deal with [the Assassins].[11]

Having a contract against Conrad suited Sinan very well indeed.

Cleverly receiving large sums of much-needed cash, while simultaneously pursuing his own political interests, Sinan was said to have 'sent two men disguised as monks, who became associated with the lord of Sidon and Balian's son the lord of Ramla ... The Marquis became acquainted with them and trusted them.' Ibn al-Athir is clear that the crusaders came to the logical, but possibly false, conclusion that Richard had been responsible, and 'attributed [Conrad's] assassination to the king of England's instigation, for he [Richard] wished to become the sole ruler of the Syrian coastline'.[12]

In the absence of firm evidence, the number of suspects kept multiplying. It is still not clear who ordered the hit on Conrad. Ultimately, although the details of the attack itself were known, all the other evidence was purely circumstantial. Accusations, therefore, centred around motivation, rather than anything more conclusive. The problem was that there were too many suspects and too many motives – but far too little evidence.

Perhaps, as is so often the case with putative conspiracies, the truth lies in the most mundane, and most obvious, answer – that the Assassins killed Conrad because they didn't like him. Prosaically, Sinan had his own disputes with Conrad. In fact, we know that a ship belonging to the Assassins had been seized when it arrived in the port of Tyre and the marquis had refused to return it, despite threats from the Old Man – and to make matters worse, Conrad's men had mistreated the crew. Although Sinan was doubtless glad to accept large sums of money from all or any of the possible suspects, the dramatic assassination itself may have partly been the outcome of a paltry trade dispute, rather than anything of deeper significance.[13]

But there were also far bigger issues at stake – issues that went to the heart of the Assassins' future in Syria. Conrad and Richard had been at loggerheads. This distracted the crusaders and strengthened Saladin's hand at the negotiating table. He had maintained direct diplomatic relations with both Conrad and Richard, and played them off against each other. The last thing the Assassins wanted was an undistracted Saladin with nothing better to do than deal with the 'heretic problem' that the Nizaris posed.

Some of the local Syriac community certainly believed that Sinan had launched the attack on his own behalf. One of the community's chronicles suggested that despite early indications that King Richard was responsible, 'later on it was revealed that it was Sinan, the chief of the Ismailis, who had sent them'.[14] The private tradition among the Assassins themselves certainly suggested that they had been responsible for killing Conrad off their own bat. Abu Firas, for instance, wrote that Sinan had ordered the hit, albeit in cooperation with Saladin, because he was not on good terms with Conrad.[15]

The Assassins were perhaps also trying to make a point. Conrad's murder was both a wake-up call and a way to emphasise their importance at a time of critical change. A new map of the region was being drawn up between the Sunni Muslims of the Ayyubid empire and the Franks of the Third Crusade. A relatively small group such as the Nizaris were in danger of being overlooked and excluded. But death at the highest level, the main bargaining chip in the Assassins' arsenal, inevitably grabbed attention when it was needed most – and instability in the region was very much in their interests.

They had already made (at least) two attempts on Saladin's life – and they had very nearly succeeded. The death of the ruler of Jerusalem served to demonstrate – if any further proof were needed – just how dangerous they were to have as enemies. It may have been a coincidence, but soon after Conrad's death a peace treaty was signed by Richard and Saladin. The truce that was arranged was to run for three years and eight months, and would cover both land and sea. Significantly, Saladin ensured that the treaty covered the Assassins' territories, as well as the crusader states.

No more heroes

The giants of this part of our story all bowed out within a few months of each other. Matters had reached an impasse. Saladin could not completely dislodge the crusaders. But neither could the crusaders recapture Jerusalem. Even the 'wise Templars', completely committed as they were to the cause of the Holy Land, advised Richard

> that in their opinion, in truth, whoever at that time were to lay siege to the city of Jerusalem would be attacked by Saladin, that while our men were at the siege the Turks would take the route that lay between the sea and [Jerusalem] and everything would go badly if [they] took their provisions from the army.

A truce, however grudging, was the only alternative.[16]

On 2 September 1192, Saladin's negotiator handed over a copy of the peace treaty to Richard, but the king was too ill to read the final version. Instead he reached out and said: 'I have made peace: here is my hand.' The Third Crusade was over and, despite expectations, the Assassins and the Templars had both survived to carry on their struggles.[17]

Richard, betrayed by the French king and his own brother John, returned to the west a few weeks later, in October 1192, only to be captured and held hostage on his way home. He was finally ransomed at great expense, but died a few years later, in 1199.

Strangely enough for our story, a Templar named Robert de Sablé died in the Holy Land around this time, too. He was always an unlikely Templar, and he himself recognised the incongruity – his decision to enter the order probably stemmed from a desire to atone for a turbulent past. Robert had been involved in the 1173 rebellion of Henry the Young King against Henry II of England. He had, on occasion, also overstepped the rights of the church. Robert de Sablé had things on his conscience.

He joined King Richard on the Third Crusade; but before doing so, he took care to make public amends for his past sins, founding a monastery and making religious donations. In a gesture of humility and contrition, he knelt before the abbot of Évron at Codoingel castle, refusing to rise until the abbot had served him wine, thus symbolically forgiving his past mistakes. With his affairs in order, Robert embarked on what he must have known would be the final chapter of his life.[18]

King Richard's long-standing relationship with the Templars, fostered through years of personal association at the English court, culminated in Robert's elevation to grand master of the entire order. Robert de Sablé was not a conventional choice from a religious perspective. Like many of his fellow Templars, his strengths lay more in the muscular field of warfare than in abstract spirituality.

As a direct vassal of Richard, he controlled lands in northern Anjou, and their relationship, built on loyalty and mutual trust, spanned many years. Robert had served the king in various crucial roles, including as justiciar of the royal fleet in 1190, and later as one of Richard's key negotiators with King Tancred of Sicily. These duties underscored his value within the army and consolidated his standing as a man of 'high lineage and great nobility'.[19]

Throughout the crusade, Robert and his fellow Templars performed a delicate balancing act, mediating between the rival kings of England and France. The Third Crusade was fraught with tension between Richard and Philip II, and the Templars worked tirelessly to maintain unity, culminating in the Treaty of Messina in October 1190, which papered over the cracks of mutual suspicion, for a time at least.

By the time Robert became grand master, he was already in the twilight of his career. A widower with few remaining ties, he joined the Templars with a sense of finality, dedicating himself to their cause. He died on 28 September 1193 in the Holy Land, having served both his king and Christendom with unwavering dedication – perhaps finally at peace with his God.

Robert de Sablé was dead. But strangely, we shall hear more of him later in this book. Unbeknownst to Robert (and perhaps happily so) his rebirth as a video game icon was still a long way in the future.[20]

Saladin died soon after Richard left the Middle East, just after dawn on 4 March 1193. He was mourned by his many followers. As Baha al-Din later wrote: 'This was a day such as had not befallen the Muslims and Islam since the loss of the rightly guided caliphs . . . The citadel, the city, the world was overwhelmed by such a sense of loss as God alone could comprehend.'[21]

Sinan, too, died at around the same time as Saladin, the man he had tried to kill on multiple occasions. Sinan was not an easy man, but his achievements had been profound. He had joined a small, endangered community with few intrinsic assets, and had turned it into something that inspired fear in its enemies.

He was so mysterious, so secretive in his ways and such a central part of the sect that even his own people refused to believe he was really dead. As one Syriac chronicle wryly noted, the eccentric Sinan had previously hidden 'himself many times, and the report went forth that he was dead, but he very soon reappeared. This was so often the case that when he was dead his slaves did not believe it.'[22]

Once he was gone, even his enemies could not entirely hide their admiration for his unique qualities, or for what he had accomplished. According to the Sunni chronicle of al-Husayn,

> he was an outstanding man, of secret devices, vast designs and great jugglery, with power to incite and mislead hearts, to hide secrets, outwit enemies and to use the vile and the foolish for his evil purposes ... [He] trained himself in the sciences of the philosophers and read many of the books of controversy and sophistry, and of the Epistles of the Sincere Brethren and similar works of the philosophy that persuades and is put forward but not proved.[23]

But his achievements stretched far beyond the arcane. Al-Husayn also acknowledged that Sinan 'built fortresses in Syria for this sect ... Time spared him and kings took care not to attack his possessions for fear of the murderous attacks of his henchmen. He ruled in Syria for thirty odd years.'[24]

He had established the Assassins in Syria as a force to be reckoned with – semi-independent of Persia, secure in their mountain fortresses and embedded in a complex network of political relationships with their Muslim and Christian neighbours. Sinan had, to a large extent, invented the legend of the Assassins. He had honed and professionalised the *fidais*, the tool that gave the sect its unique leverage. The Nizaris might still be hated and detested, but at least they now had a home and status, however ambiguous, in a dangerous world.[25]

18

Contest for the Holy Land (1194–1248)

The Assassins and the Templars had both tried to stop the unification of Sunni Islam in the Middle East. And they had both failed. Saladin succeeded in uniting Egypt, Syria and parts of North Africa under his new regime. His death had been helpful to the Assassins and the Templars alike, as it led to the partial fragmentation of his empire. But they were still surrounded, as well as being greatly outnumbered. It was only a matter of time before they moved to the top of the Sunni Muslim agenda.

The Assassins and the Templars struggled against this increased threat, each in their own deadly ways. Their weakness was not always obvious – and yet with hindsight it is clear that an inexorable process was under way. Both were fading. The threat underpinning their 'promise of death' was becoming perceptibly less credible.

The Assassins came to an accommodation with their much larger Muslim neighbours – they bought an uneasy truce by offering peace, but implicitly continuing to threaten the personal safety of their enemies and their families. The Templars holed up in their castles and continued with their dogged defiance.

Neither had the strength for long-term victory.

Muslim neighbours

The Assassins of Syria had entered a long, slow decline. Despite the overwhelming strength of their powerful Sunni neighbours, however, they were able to retain a modicum of initiative and independence.

After the death of Sinan, efforts were made by the Persian headquarters to bring the Syrian arm of the sect back into line. The authority of Alamut was re-established. Alongside this new hierarchy, there was also a reversion to more traditional forms of worship – internal conformity found its echo in international relations.

In 1211–12, Hasan III, the lord of Alamut, overturned the 'Resurrection' and sent instructions that the Assassins in Syria should return to more traditional practices. From now on, they were expected to avoid forbidden foods and drugs, to fast and to build mosques in which to perform ritual prayers. This was accepted locally and a form of sharia was adopted once more.[1]

Sinan's dangerous and arcane unpredictability was replaced with something altogether more orthodox. There was comfort to be found in this more reasonable, more compromising approach. But it also undermined the threat and implicit danger that lay at the heart of the Assassins' relationship with the outside world.[2]

Some commentators took a cynical view of Hasan III's actions. As one Christian chronicler commented, 'in the beginning of [Hasan's] rule he began by pretending to agree with the Faith of the Muslims, and he fasted and prayed . . . And believing him, they rejoiced in him and honoured him with many gifts and rich presents.'[3]

Such cynicism was not entirely without foundation. This was a rational move on Hasan's part. Moving closer to the mainstream of Islamic thinking was an important part of the sect's attempts to fit into an increasingly threatening world. Not coincidentally, relations with Saladin's Ayyubid successors improved.

The gradual thawing in the Nizaris' doctrinal and political relationships with their Muslim neighbours was a deliberate attempt to defuse tensions in what was (for them) a very dangerous region. Moving towards religious conformism was a reflection of their new strategy – a strategy that demanded they should play a more integrated part in the complex and highly mannered diplomatic connections that governed the area.

There were short-term benefits to conformity. This religious rapprochement was reflected in greater political stability.

But their unique threat was wearing thin.

Frankish friends – and enemies

Much the same was true of their relationship with the Franks. Doctrinal differences were left behind, as the Assassins settled into the pursuit of more local and tactical issues, generally dictated by expediency and self-interest.[4]

As we have seen, Henry of Champagne, ruler of the Latin kingdom of Jerusalem, visited one of the Nizari fortresses in 1194, possibly as part of a diplomatic intervention he was making to negotiate peace between the Christian rulers of Antioch and Armenia. The exact purpose of his meeting is not known, and nor is the nature of the negotiations that took place. But given the foreign policy nature of the entire mission, it is likely that relationship building and improved diplomatic relations were at least on the agenda of this charm offensive.

The Frankish chroniclers inevitably revelled in the possibilities conjured up by such an encounter. They created a rich (and possibly exaggerated) version of what took place. In what was believed to be the traditionally theatrical negotiating stance of the Assassins, the Old Man of the Mountain allegedly told some of the *fidais* to jump to their death from the castle walls, in an attempt to impress and intimidate his western visitor. One version of events speaks of some *fidais* impaling themselves on an iron spike, in an ultra-violent display of power and fanaticism, and of others hurling themselves dramatically from the highest tower.

To further extend his hospitality, the Old Man was also said to have promised, as an upbeat gesture of goodwill, to murder any individual whom Henry should nominate – 'and if there was any man who had done him an injury,' he was alleged to have said, as part of their fond farewells, 'he should let him know, and he would have him killed'.[5]

We do not know if Henry accepted the Assassins' kind offer. Instead, death came to Henry himself soon after, in a bizarre and spectacularly undignified way.

On 10 September 1197, he was in Acre, reviewing his troops. To get a better view of the men, he chose the vantage point of an upper gallery window that would not have passed modern health and safety standards. Henry, nicknamed 'the fat' with good reason, overbalanced. His favourite court entertainer, a dwarf, was standing next to him and bravely leapt forward to stop the fall. What followed was the inevitable triumph of gravity and inertia. Both men fell to their deaths.

We do not know what impact this tragic accident had on Franco-Nizari relations. As always, however, it was far easier for the Assassins to have peaceful relations with the rulers of Jerusalem (who did not share a border with them) than with those Franks who were uncomfortably close neighbours.

In 1212, almost two decades after Henry's mysterious negotiations with the Old Man of the Mountain, a German diplomat and pilgrim named Wilbrand of Oldenburg passed through the area and commented astutely on the situation he found there. As he travelled beyond the Hospitaller fortress of Crac des Chevaliers, he noted that

> on the same side [of the mountains] we saw Chastel-Blanc (*Casteblans*), which is a good strong castle sited in the mountains and on the borders of the Old Man of the Mountain, who is accustomed to kill our princes by means of envoys armed with knives . . . This castle is very injurious to his land because it is held and guarded by the Templars.[6]

The Templars were clearly still at loggerheads with the Assassins. But they were not the only ones. Wilbrand's other comment (that the Nizaris were 'accustomed to kill our princes') was also strangely prescient.

Just over a year later, at the end of 1213, they struck again. The target of the hit was Raymond, the teenage son of Prince Bohemond IV of Antioch–Tripoli (r. 1183–1233). A *fidais* hit squad 'wantonly killed the son of the count of Tripoli, a fine young man'. Raymond's death was deliberately, and provocatively, high profile. He was cut down in a cathedral in the heart of Frankish power in the region, while he was 'prostrate before the altar in the church of the Blessed Virgin at Tortosa'.[7]

The exact motivation behind the killing remained deliberately obscure, as was so often the case with Nizari assassinations. Bohemond, the victim's father, was not an easy man. He had quarrelled with the Church and had been excommunicated by Pope Innocent III a few years earlier. He had also fallen out with many of his fellow Franks. The list of suspects was long.

Bohemond believed that in killing his son, the Assassins had been working for the Hospitallers based at Margat, to whom they also paid tribute. Extraordinary as it seems, he may not have been entirely wrong in this belief: he had fallen out with the Hospitallers and we know that, highly suspiciously, the Assassins gave military assistance to them in a campaign against Bohemond a few years later, in 1230.[8]

Bohemond did not take his son's death well. Not surprisingly, he erupted in a torrent of grief and anger. Whatever his thoughts about the Hospitallers, he knew one group that was definitely involved in the murder. The armies of Tripoli and Antioch were unleashed into the Assassins' lands in the search for revenge. Bohemond's men camped outside their castle of Khawabi and settled down for a siege, doubtless also inflicting as much unpleasantness as they could manage on the surrounding Nizari villages.

The Templars took this as an opportunity to join in and give the Assassins a good kicking. They 'did not cease to pursue them for such a violation of religious liberty, until they were humiliated to the servitude of paying a tribute of three thousand besants annually to the Templars'. Once again, the financial disagreements and power struggles that rumbled on between the Templars and the Assassins came to the fore – they were at the root of much of the occasionally fractious fabric of their relationship with the Franks.[9]

The Assassins were forced to call in help from the Sunni authorities – and however much the Sunnis disliked the Ismailis, it was not in their interests for the crusaders to be in possession of the Jabal Bahra. The Franks fought off a relief force from Aleppo, but were then attacked by an Ayyubid army from Damascus as well. Under pressure on all sides, Bohemond and the Templars were forced to withdraw.

Peace, of a sort, was restored. But the underlying tensions remained. The Assassins had no choice: they continued to pay protection money to the military orders. Mutual antipathy was never far below the surface.

A Franciscan Friar named Thietmar visited the region just a few years later (1217–18) and summed up the enduringly unsatisfactory situation well. He was on a pilgrimage in the Holy Land, and travelled near the Jabal Bahra. The impact of the 'Resurrection' was even now being felt, and many still did not believe that the Nizaris were practising Muslims. Thietmar wrote, with the usual blend of rumour and realism, that 'the Ismailis . . . are called Assassins. They are descended from the Jews, but do not observe the Jewish law. They eat pork.' In the aftermath of the Templar revenge for the killing of Prince Raymond, he also made a point of stressing that 'the Templars have annihilated them in great part and have devastated their land for a distance of more than ten days' travel'.[10]

Clearly, the Templars still hated the Nizaris with a passion, and that feeling was undoubtedly reciprocated – many still found their practices so extreme that they were not felt to qualify as true Muslims.

The jostling for money, power and influence continued. The Assassins were always eager to escape from the overbearing demands of the Templars and the Hospitallers. One way they tried to do this was to impress foreign visitors and get them on their side – preferably before they had a chance to establish where the real balance of power lay.

This was largely a reflection of the differing patterns of self-interest: the secular authorities, and particularly those who were not their neighbours, sometimes wanted to form alliances with the sect. The military orders, on the other hand, impervious to their strong-arm tactics, were keen on intimidating them.

A few years later, in 1227, Emperor Frederick II was planning to come east on crusade. He sent envoys to give the Assassins a large gift (some 80,000 dinars), in return for which he wanted unobstructed access to march across their lands. Frederick probably saw this as a simple and very cost-effective way of ensuring safe passage for his men. But the Assassins, however unrealistically, chose to present the payment as a form of tribute.[11]

When the Hospitallers heard that such large sums of money were being bandied around, they in turn demanded vastly increased tribute from the Nizaris – in effect, pressurising the Assassins to share the new 'tribute' with them. Refusing, the Assassins were said to have disingenuously protested: 'your king the Emperor gives to us; will you then take from us?' The Hospitallers, not surprisingly, remained unconvinced.[12]

They quickly sent an army into the mountains to destroy some of the local Assassin villages. Nizari castles were attacked and the expedition came back laden with booty. The Assassins caved in, and from 1228 onwards they seem to have made payments to both the Templars and the Hospitallers.[13]

Echoing the suspicions of Prince Bohemond about the attack on his son, there were hints that the Nizaris had even been coerced at this point into becoming allies of the Hospitallers. This was a step too far for the more conservative elements of the Catholic Church, who feared that an alliance such as this would draw the dangerous Muslim sect too closely into the already murky waters of internecine Frankish politics.

Pope Gregory IX (1227–41) wrote an outraged note to the order in 1236, railing against such a relationship and expressing his horror at the unhealthily close relations that had developed between the 'Assassins, the enemies of God and of the Christians' and the Hospitallers. He ordered the military orders to take a more arm's-length approach in their dealings with the Nizaris.[14]

The pope's suspicions were not entirely unfounded. Closer dealings between the Assassins and the local crusaders were even reflected in their active diplomatic relations. By 1238, the Assassins were felt to have such a close relationship with the Franks that they were apparently chosen to lead a joint Muslim mission to the heartlands of Europe, in order to seek help against the Mongol invasion of the Middle East. The English chronicler Matthew Paris wrote that Nizari diplomats 'asked assistance from the western nations, the better to be able to repress the fury of the [Mongols]'.[15]

The European powers were, perhaps not surprisingly, underwhelmed by this request for help from their old enemies. Many hoped that the new entrants into the Middle East would be more favourably inclined towards the Christian cause; or, at the very least, that they would distract and weaken the Franks' Ayyubid enemies. As the bishop of Winchester rather uncharitably put it: 'Let us leave these dogs to devour one another, that they may all be consumed, and perish.'[16]

Despite the Assassins' attempted transformation into international diplomats, westerners continued to have a rather jaundiced view – their reputation for death-dealing mystery and fanaticism may originally have been useful, and deliberately cultivated, but it was now coming back to haunt them. Matthew Paris's *Itinerary from London to Jerusalem* (a map drawn not long afterwards, in *c.* 1250–9) tellingly included the following notes about the Assassins' reputation: 'there lives there [in the Jabal Bahra] the Old Man of the Mountain, that is to say the ruler of the High Assassins, who carry knives and kill . . . They are capable of all kind of outrageous lies, spells (*cuntementz*) and evil deeds.'[17]

The Nizari 'brand' was still powerful – but not always helpful.

19

Egypt, Saints and Sinners (1248–1254)

Richard the Lionheart and the Third Crusade had saved the crusader states from complete destruction. The rump that could be salvaged, however, was a sad parody of what had once been proud and vibrant communities.

The native Christian villages had mostly been overrun. The inland Frankish settlements were in ruins – the survivors had either taken refuge in the remaining coastal cities or had shipped themselves and their families back to Europe. The scattered remnants clung to the coast in increasingly small and threatened pockets. The Frankish interior had almost entirely disappeared, reduced to just a few (barely inland) suburbs of the coastal towns. Just as unhelpfully, the fractious local crusaders turned in on themselves, arguing more and more about less and less.

But the crusading movement refused to admit defeat. There was still one possible way of resuscitating the dying communities of the Christian East: Egypt.

Crusading and Egypt: The Templars' last hope

The large-scale crusades of the thirteenth century were focused on bringing Egypt back into Christian hands. As the Frankish settlers of the previous century had astutely identified, it was only with Egypt's wealth and lands that the Latin East could have a sustainable future. The Fifth Crusade (1217–21) and the Seventh Crusade (1248–54) were both major military expeditions by the European powers, and both temporarily captured the important Egyptian port of Damietta.

Yet while their strategic objectives might have been correct, they ultimately lacked the resources to make a long-term breakthrough. And even if they had done so, it is hard to see how it could have been held against the inevitable Muslim counter-attacks. Recovering Egypt was always a forlorn hope.[1]

The Lateran Council of 1215 had called for a crusade to set off to the Holy Land in the summer of 1217. The ensuing expedition, known to history as the Fifth Crusade, was beset with problems. The army was relatively small, at least compared to the Muslim powers it faced. It arrived piecemeal in the eastern Mediterranean. Even more unhelpfully, it was ill-disciplined and ignorant of local affairs.

The crusaders, supported by a large Templar contingent, invaded Egypt and besieged the coastal city of Damietta from 1218 to 1219. By October 1219, hostilities were still grinding on, with neither side gaining the upper hand. The Muslim authorities offered to give back Jerusalem, large parts of central Palestine and western Galilee, if only the crusaders would leave Egypt.

This was undoubtedly tempting. But it was the same strategically awkward possibility of retaking Jerusalem that had faced Richard the Lionheart twenty years earlier. The Templars, despite being famous for their reckless ferocity in battle, once again counselled caution. In the absence of a viable population and a permanent army, they knew that the Holy City was still virtually indefensible.

While the Templars were exercising restraint in their advice (or so it must have seemed to many observers), it is interesting to see that the Assassins' propaganda was successfully moving in the opposite direction. European crusaders were aware of their work, long before they arrived in the east. Even when campaigning as far afield as Egypt, hundreds of kilometres away from the Assassins' strongholds, the Franks were wary of their reputation.

During the siege of Damietta, on the Nile delta, in 1218, Oliver of Paderborn wrote that the crusaders were nervous about Nizari attacks. He reported that the entire Christian army was relieved that God 'defended our leaders from the murderers of our persecutors in the siege of Damietta. For the Assassins and their chief, the Old Man of the Mountain, had the custom of [using] knives against the Christians.' The army's anxiety was exaggerated, but it was not entirely without just cause. There was a collective memory in the camp of the assassination of Prince Bohemond's son in 1213, just two years before the crusade was proclaimed – the army of the Fifth Crusade still talked about it and was suitably intimidated.[2]

By the summer of 1221, the expedition had collapsed. There was, however, one significant gain from this frustrating and debilitating episode. The Templars were astute (as always) when it came to identifying the real drivers of local politics and warfare. The order managed to extract a tactical gain, even in the midst of this strategic failure. It – and some of the crusaders – had used the opportunity of a significant European military intervention to build what became one of the defining fortifications of the thirteenth century: the castle known as Château Pèlerin, or 'Atlit. It was never taken by siege.

The crusaders inevitably went home. But the Templars still had their new castle – and, aggressive as ever, they refused to just sit around on the defensive. In June 1237, for instance, large numbers of Templars and their soldiers were killed while making a characteristically bold, but overly ambitious, raid on Turkic-held Darbsak, hundreds of kilometres to the north. Once the force was deep in enemy territory, local Christians and escaped prisoners of war gave the Templar leaders advance warning that overwhelming numbers of Muslim cavalry were approaching from Aleppo. But William of Montserrat, the order's preceptor of Antioch and the overall commander of the force, was having none of it.

Displaying the ideology that could create religiously induced overconfidence, he 'despised their warnings'. Insultingly, William called those of his own men who wanted to proceed more cautiously 'timid people'. Casualties in the ensuing battle were horrific, as 'more than a hundred knights of the Temple fell, and three hundred crossbowmen, not including some other secular [troops] and a large number of foot-soldiers'.[3]

William of Montserrat was duly castigated for his intransigence. Significantly, however, one of the Templars was singled out for the way he behaved, embracing martyrdom during the battle. This was an example to be remembered. 'In this unlucky conflict,' wrote Matthew Paris,

> an illustrious English Templar knight, named Reginald of Argenton, who was [the Templar] standard-bearer on that day, was slain; but he, as well as others who fell, left a most bloody victory to their enemies, for he unweariedly defended the standard until his legs and arms were cut off.[4]

The situation was eventually just about stabilised. But things remained distinctly unpromising for the Templar brothers who were left manning the front line. The grand master of the order, Armand of Périgord, was, not surprisingly, based in the east. He wrote to the brothers in England in July 1244 to warn them about the worsening military position, and to ask the English master, Robert of Sandford, for aid. The Templars, he wrote, along with

> a few of the barons, who offer us whatever help they can, carry the burden of defending the land . . . But, unless [the west can give] us effective protection there is no way we can hold out for long in defence of those castles we have against the sultan, who is extremely powerful and intelligent.[5]

Armand was not exaggerating. Just three months later, most of the Templar knights in the Holy Land were killed or captured at the battle of La Forbie (17 October 1244).

The order had, with great difficulty, scraped together an army. It had pulled precious troops out of its castle garrisons. But even that was nowhere near enough. The Templar troops, stationed (as ever) in the front ranks and fighting with an ideology that embraced martyrdom, were almost wiped out.

The patriarch of Jerusalem, who was with the army and barely 'escaped half dead to Ascalon', wrote shortly after the event that 'only thirty-three Templars, twenty-six Hospitallers and three Teutonic brothers escaped, the others being killed or captured'. No one was safe. Casualties cascaded from the top of the order downwards. They included, according to the chronicle of Eracles, even the prescient 'Armand of Périgord, master of the Temple, who [later] died in prison'.[6]

A saint in Egypt: The Seventh Crusade (1248–54)

The shocking disaster at La Forbie helped galvanise support for the crusader states in the west, for a time at least. After the usual protracted bouts of political manoeuvring and painful fundraising, the Seventh Crusade eventually set off, led by King (later Saint) Louis IX of France. But the crusade turned out to be a disaster. Decision-making was poor and relations between the different contingents of the Christian army were even worse.[7]

The Templars did their best to keep the expedition on track. They were always in the thick of the fighting, taking the vanguard when circumstances required aggression, or leading the rearguard when the discipline of defence was needed instead.

At the battle of Mansurah on 8 February 1250, the order was engulfed in a frantic vanguard action. The previous day, entrepreneurial Bedouin tribesmen had offered to help the crusaders find a river crossing, in return for a large cash payment. One of them 'told the king that there certainly was a ford further down the Tanis; it was rather deep but he was sure the king would be able to cross there'. Eager to maintain his army's momentum, King Louis led a large mounted contingent from the crusader army, including most of the knights, to try to find the ford and outflank the enemy.

The orders of the day were strict. Louis specifically commanded that 'when the first contingent had got across the river, they must wait on the bank until the king and all the others had crossed'.

Robert, the count of Artois and the king's brother, was in charge of the vanguard. Having crossed the river, however, Robert chose to ignore his clear, but irritatingly unglamorous orders. Instead, he and his troops 'rode fast up river as far as the place where the Saracen engines were set up opposite the causeway'. They stormed the Egyptian camp and Fakhr al-Din, the enemy commander, was killed in the fighting. The Muslim army routed back towards the town of Mansurah.

Despite Robert's insubordination, all was going well. But the crusader knights were overexcited. The taste of success encouraged even more reckless behaviour. Trying to take advantage of their opponents' temporary weakness, they succumbed to the adrenaline rush of a bloody pursuit.

The master of the Templars could see disaster looming. He knew that street fighting on horseback would not end well. He was also acutely aware of the need to reorder their ranks, and to ensure that the knights had clear ground in front of them, across which to charge at the enemy. The Mamluk encampment, strewn with tents, baggage and bulky siege engines, was not the kind of environment in which he wanted his cavalry to operate.

He was right on both counts, of course. But instead of pausing to regroup and wait for the army, the arrogant and overconfident Robert of Artois decided to launch a highly unorthodox mounted charge on the town of Mansurah. Unable to persuade him of the folly of his plans, the Templars threw themselves into the vanguard, as 'they believed they would be dishonoured if they were to allow the count of Artois to stay ahead of them'.[8]

The Templars' bravery and ideological commitment meant that they were at the forefront of the crusader army. They hacked their way straight through the town, engaged with enemy cavalry outside, and then attempted to retrace their steps in order to help extricate their comrades who had got bogged down fighting in the town behind them.

But, 'when they decided to turn back, the Turks flung beams and pieces of timber on them as they went through the narrow streets of Mansurah'. The outcome was never in doubt. Isolated in the narrow streets, the brothers were almost entirely wiped out, much as they had been at Ascalon, almost a hundred years earlier. Urban fighting, where infantry were at a significant advantage, was not the right environment for mounted – and vastly outnumbered – knights. However brave and well trained, they could not fight to best effect.[9]

The Frankish survivors broke and fled back towards the river. Matthew Paris wrote that the losses included

> all the Templars who were present, so that only four or five Templars survived. Very many of our lords, knights, crossbowmen and mounted sergeants, the most valiant, most hardy, the best of all our host – all these were lost and nothing definite was ever known about them.

The chronicler added despondently that 'out of all that glorious and distinguished body of knights there escaped only two Templars . . . who swam the river naked and brought word to the French king and the rest of the army'.[10]

John of Joinville, a participant in the army, later wrote that 'the Temple, so the master told me later, lost 280 armed men, all of them mounted'. The casualties taken in the crazy attack were appalling.[11]

The shock back in the west was profound – and profoundly discouraging.

ASSASSINS AND TEMPLARS

Bullying, bluff and bluster

The disaster at Mansurah was just the beginning. As the situation deteriorated, the Frankish position became irretrievable and the entire army surrendered on 6 April 1250. King Louis of France was only released from captivity in Egypt after paying a huge ransom. Disoriented and despondent, he led the sad remnants of his army to the Holy Land, arriving there in May 1250.

The Assassins felt that this was an opportune time to make their presence felt in the maelstrom of Syrian politics. Envoys were sent to see what advantage they could extract from the battered Frankish states. They hoped, not unreasonably, to find the king in a vulnerable position. He had only just escaped torture or execution by his Egyptian captors, and they wanted him to be cowed by their unique form of political leverage as quickly as possible – and ideally before the much depleted military orders could stiffen his resolve.

The timing was propitious, but this was a naïve and desperate gambit – it harked back to 'happier' times when the threat of murder by the Assassins was taken altogether more seriously. Luckily for us, John of Joinville, one of Louis's close companions, left an account of the meeting. It provides a rare and fascinating insight into Nizari negotiating tactics and foreign policy.[12]

The Assassins, according to this account, were blunt to the point of rudeness: in the classic manner of aggressive negotiators, their opening gambit was to put their opponents on the back foot. Threats were in the air before substantive discussions had even begun.

First, the theatre of death was rolled out. 'Envoys from the Old Man of the Mountain', wrote Joinville,

> came to the king while he was at Acre . . . there was an emir in front . . . and behind this emir was an impressively equipped young man who held three knives in his hand; the blade of each knife fitted inside the handle of another. If the king had rebuffed the emir the

young man would have presented these three knives to the king as a token of defiance. Behind the man holding the knives was another who had a length of linen wound round his arm; if he had refused the Old Man of the Mountain's request, this too would have been presented to the king, as a burial shroud.[13]

King Louis politely but noncommittally mentioned that 'he had never met [the Old Man], but he certainly had heard talk of him'. The Assassins' envoy chose to interpret this politeness as weakness. He went straight onto the offensive:

> Since you have heard talk of my lord, I am greatly amazed that you haven't sent him sufficient of your wealth to secure his friendship. The emperor of Germany, the king of Hungary, the sultan of Egypt and the other rulers do so every year; they are well aware that they will not survive unless it is pleasing to my lord.[14]

The true objectives of this aggressive negotiating stance quickly became apparent, however, and they were far less impressive: the Assassins wanted help in getting the military orders to stop bullying them and extorting money. Deliberately changing pitch and moving the talks onto an altogether more reasonable note, the envoy suggested to Louis that 'if you are not willing to [pay tribute], then have [the Old Man of the Mountain] acquitted of the tribute he owes to the Hospital and the Temple, and he will deem himself to have been paid by you'. The king was not to be cowed or fooled, however. He 'replied to the emir that he should return in the afternoon' and in the meantime conferred with the Templars and the Hospitallers.[15]

Louis called the Assassins' bluff. When the emissary returned,

> he found the king seated with the master of the Hospital on one side of him and the master of the Temple on the other. The king then told him to repeat what he had said that morning, but the emir said

he was not inclined to repeat himself in front of anyone except those who had been with the king earlier. The two masters told him, 'We order you to speak.' And he said that he would repeat himself, since they commanded it. Then the two masters had him told in the Saracen language to come and speak to them the following day in the Hospital, and so he did.[16]

A third meeting took place. And it was very different from the first two. The military orders were inevitably unimpressed by the Assassins' clumsy attempt to go behind their backs. Menace was met with menace. The two masters went swiftly on to confirm what they saw as the natural order of their relationship – one in which the Nizaris showed due deference and subordination to the military orders. They told the envoy that the Old Man of the Mountain 'was very bold to dare to send such harsh words to the king'.[17]

In an appropriately Assassin-like way, both masters, speaking in Arabic, threatened the envoys' physical safety. With a wonderfully demeaning and menacing turn of phrase, they said that had they not been 'concerned about the honour of the king to whom the emir and his companions had come as envoys, they would have drowned them in Acre's filthy waters in defiance of his lord'. The Assassin diplomats were dismissed with an instruction 'to return to [the Old Man] and to be back here in two weeks, bringing such letters and jewels from him that the king will deem himself satisfied and pleased with you'.[18]

The Assassins had tried to intimidate, but it had all been bluster. They did as they were told. Within two weeks they were back and had 'brought the king the Old Man's chemise and on their lord's behalf they told the king of its significance: just as the chemise is closer to one's body than any other piece of clothing, so the Old Man wanted to keep the king closer in love than any other king'.[19]

More intriguingly from a diplomatic perspective, the Old Man also 'sent the king his ring, which was made of very fine gold and had his name engraved on it; their lord informed them that with this ring he formed a union with the king, wishing them to be as one from this time forwards'. Louis could perhaps be forgiven for thinking that there was now, as there had been in the 1170s, some prospect of a genuine and enduring alliance with the Assassins. Bluff and bullying had been replaced by an almost embarrassingly fawning display of friendship.[20]

The overtures were accompanied by rich and exotic gifts, as they had been instructed. Treasures were delivered in fine chests of sweet-smelling wood. Nizari craftsmen had made fruits and animals, finely carved out of crystal. Ambergris decorations were fixed to the crystal with fine gold settings. There were rare backgammon and chess sets. The Franks were suitably impressed. Diplomatic discussions could now continue.[21]

The Assassins had approached Louis at a vulnerable time for him. They had tried to make an impression with threats and intimidation. But their efforts had failed. The proper hierarchy of the relationship had been re-established, at least to the satisfaction of the Templars and Hospitallers. Both sides moved towards establishing some level of cooperation around mutual interests.

Friars and *fidais*

King Louis sent his own envoys, including a friar named Yves the Breton, to exchange gifts with the Assassins – and, as the king was of a saintly disposition, to explore theological areas that they might have in common.[22]

Brother Yves travelled to the Assassins' domains, and there, in the strongholds of the Jabal Bahra – probably at the castle of Masyaf – he had a series of meetings with the Old Man. Discussions resumed in a less highly charged atmosphere. Alongside the friar, who was fluent in 'the Saracen language', Louis also sent 'a great quantity of jewels, lengths of scarlet, gold cups and silver bits for [the Old Man's] horses'. After a rocky start, both sides were now turning on the charm.[23]

The exact objectives of these talks are unclear. As one Frankish chronicler blandly put it, presumably because he did not know the details, 'the Old Man of the Mountain, lord of the Assassins . . . sent envoys to the king . . . The king sent his own envoys . . . [back] accompanying theirs.' Ultimately, all this diplomatic manoeuvring came to naught.[24]

Luckily for us, however, an insider account of these diplomatic discussions has survived. On his return to Acre, Yves talked in detail to John of Joinville, who wrote down some of the highlights of the conversations. The surviving notes make for fascinating reading.

The reputation of the Assassins among the Franks was partly based on exaggeration and distortion. Some of this was encouraged by the Assassins; other elements were not. But it is not easy to fully disregard Joinville's account of the Assassins' beliefs and practices: it is, after all, based on a debriefing with someone who had first-hand knowledge of the sect, who had been welcomed into the Syrian Nizari community and who had spent, it appears, a significant amount of time with the Old Man himself. If there was distortion, it was just as likely to have come from the Assassins themselves as it was from the retelling of the events that had taken place.

Despite efforts to project a more mainstream image onto their Sunni neighbours, the reverberations of the Nizari 'Resurrection' were still in evidence – and they were substantial enough to make a major impression on outsiders. Importantly, the continuing differences between the sect and the rest of the Islamic world seem to have been actively emphasised by the Nizaris themselves when educating a foreign visitor about the nature of their religious beliefs. Doubtless influenced by a good dose of wishful thinking, aided perhaps by some manipulation on behalf of their hosts, the Frankish envoys returned having 'discovered that the Old Man of the Mountain did not believe in Muhammad'.[25]

'Instead,' Yves reported back, the Old Man

> believed the law of Ali, who was Muhammad's uncle . . . it is still the case that all those who follow the law of Ali say that all those who follow the law of Muhammad are unbelievers, while all those who

follow the law of Muhammad say that all those who follow the law of Ali are unbelievers.[26]

This was clearly a simplistic attempt to articulate the Sunni–Shiite split. But there were other, deeper, religious differences which the Old Man was happy to share. It was stressed that a belief in the transmigration of the soul was a fundamental point of their theology, coupled with a sense of predestination. 'Because of this,' Joinville wrote,

> the Assassins are unperturbed by facing death when their lord commands it, since they believe they will be happier once they have died than they had been previously. Another point is this: they believe no man can die before the day appointed for him.

These two strands of belief were distinct, but mutually supportive.[27]

Gregory Bar Hebraeus, a Syriac Orthodox historian writing around the same time, was also convinced that transmigration was a central part of Nizari philosophy. He wrote that Sinan

> was well instructed in the wisdom of the foreigners and transmigration of souls, and he taught the doctrine of Plato to the men of his own party. And therefore they held death in contempt, and [believed] that they did not go forth from the world even though they were killed.[28]

This should not just be written off as a misunderstanding by ignorant Christian observers. The Sunni historian al-Umari, writing in the early fourteenth century, carefully investigated many aspects of the Nizaris' beliefs and was likewise convinced that they believed in the transmigration of the soul:

> It became clear to me that the sect considers that souls are imprisoned in earthly bodies with the duty to obey the one who they claim

is the Sanctified Imam. If the soul passes on in a state of obedience, it is released and migrates to the celestial lights, but if it passes on in rebellion, it falls into the lower darknesses.[29]

The practical consequence, of course, was that those sent off on *fidais* assassination missions could expect a happy ending to their high-risk (probably fatal) efforts. It is hard to know whether the friar's interpretation of what he was being told was strictly accurate. Nonetheless, it had its own logic. And as a philosophy with which to inspire men undertaking the most dangerous tasks, it certainly had much to recommend it.

It is not clear which came first. Was this an ideology gradually built up to justify and motivate semi-suicidal hit squads? Or had it pre-dated and empowered the formation of the *fidais* teams? It is hard to prove either way; but there certainly seems to have been a continuing and organic linkage between the sect's religious beliefs and its levels of comfort with the consequences of murder.

However, the drama of death was visual, as well as philosophical. Both aspects played their part in this intoxicatingly idiosyncratic cocktail. Brother Yves witnessed the Old Man on his travels within the Jabal Bahra, presumably still following the peripatetic management style of previous Nizari leaders. The effect was electric. 'When the Old Man rode out,' he reported to Joinville, 'he had a crier ride in front of him who carried a Danish axe that had a long handle covered with silver and with many blades embedded in it. He called out, "Make way for the man who holds the death of kings in his hands."' No one would forget a visit from the Old Man.[30]

Even among the Nizaris, the theatrics of the promise of death were prominent. It is interesting that this procession, and the wandering lifestyle that underpinned it, accords well with what we know of the itinerant government of Sinan and his successors. This corroborating evidence, even of something so ostensibly outlandish, adds credence to Yves's other testimony.

Even more interestingly from a Catholic and diplomatic perspective, Brother Yves told Joinville that there was 'a book beside the head of the Old Man's bed in which were written several of Our Lord's sayings to Saint Peter during his time on Earth'. The Old Man of the Mountain had made a point of stressing to Yves that Saint Peter was revered by the Nizaris because Abel's soul had passed by transmigration into Saint Peter's body, via Noah and Abraham along the way. The foundational texts of the Assassins at this point were still eclectic and eccentric – the Old Man was clearly proud (rather than embarrassed) to emphasise their profound differences from mainstream Islam.[31]

So, unlikely though it may seem, there is a possibility that the Assassins were in some ways not too distant from Catholicism in viewing Saint Peter as being the first 'pope'. It might be tempting to suggest that these texts were deliberately placed next to the Old Man's bed, in order to encourage Brother Yves into imagining that some form of religious rapprochement with the Assassins was possible (such as had been attempted in the 1170s with King Amalric of Jerusalem). Certainly, the friar was given the run of the Old Man's household quarters, and was allowed to engage in religious and philosophical debate with him.

But this rather cynical view of events does not accord well with the evidence. Far from encouraging a deceptive commonality of thought, the two men seem, more plausibly, to have disagreed. We know that when Brother Yves was told about the transmigration of Abel's soul into Saint Peter's body, he 'explained that this belief was not good, and he passed on much sound doctrine, but the Old Man did not want to believe it. Brother Yves related these things to the king when he returned to us.'[32]

The views of the Assassins were idiosyncratic and remained characteristically their own.

✧

Dealings with the Assassins were always tinged with mistrust; but diplomacy and the search for common ground against their Sunni enemies continued. The crusaders' knowledge of the sect was tainted by legend and myth, deliberately planted or otherwise. But there were increasing hints that they were aware of the extreme theological differences between the Nizari Ismailis and mainstream Islam.

The history of the sect was full of mystery, intrigue and misrepresentation. The death cult image that its members cultivated so assiduously succeeded in permeating the imagination of their enemies. One thirteenth-century Frank, for instance, still described them as 'unbelieving Muslims [who] ate pork and lay with their own mothers, sisters, daughters and all the women they could get, contrary to the laws of Muhammad'. The way in which they were viewed was sometimes a travesty of their true belief systems, and there were aspects of this description that would probably have been deeply offensive. But it showed what a long and intimidating shadow the cult had cast.[33]

In fact, far from being unduly targeted, there were occasions when the crusaders could barely disguise their admiration for the Assassins. These were, after all, men who were brave and personally devoted warriors. Joinville's views were sometimes mistaken and garbled. Groups like the Assassins (and the Bedouin) were highly exotic and almost legendary – they were the object of much ill-informed, but fascinated speculation by newcomers from the west. But it is clear that, however much he might disagree with them in theory, there was a part of Joinville the soldier that admired the Assassins – as impressive, loyal men who would willingly die for their lord. These were virtues that a western knight such as he would have understood and aspired to.[34]

The reputation of the Assassins, like that of the Templars, cast a far bigger shadow than their numbers would ever have justified. On one occasion, when King Louis was in Sidon, helping to refortify the city, he came across an ancient church out in the fields nearby, and saw a priest celebrating mass. Louis said to Joinville, who was in charge of his bodyguard that day, that he wanted to 'go inside to listen to the Mass begun by the priest'.[35]

Joinville was completely unnerved by this request – not because he was fearful of Muslim armies, but because he thought that the Assassins were masters of disguise, and could be hiding anywhere. When King

Louis entered the church, Joinville 'noticed that the clerk who was assisting in singing the Mass was large, dark, thin and hairy'. He was concerned that 'it might turn out that he was one of those wicked Assassins and that he would be able to kill the king'.[36]

It transpired that he was worrying needlessly. Louis stopped for a quick mass, and the crusading party went on its way. But it does show the pervasive level of fear the Assassins had created. More prosaically, it also shows the stereotypical view of what a newly arrived Frenchman thought the undercover *fidais* looked like. 'Wicked' – and scary.

20

Assassins: Holocaust and horror (1255–1291)

Scary or not, time was running out for both the Assassins and their Frankish neighbours. The era when bluster, intimidation and threats could be a decisive factor was rapidly coming to an end. They were finally confronted with opponents who embraced death even more comprehensively than themselves – the Mongols.

Even by the appallingly low, war-torn standards of the medieval Middle East, the Mongols were different. They were a semi-mystical force of death-dealing horror. This was the stuff of nightmares, the medieval equivalent of a zombie apocalypse. Stories about the Mongols' cruelty and almost superhuman, borderline psychopathic tendencies abounded. These tales helped to create a feeling of powerlessness and panic among their enemies. Intense fear created its own form of almost hypnotic paralysis.

Two stories, true or not, speak volumes for the impact of this tsunami of terror on those who were at the receiving end of this unwelcome attention. The chronicler Ibn al-Athir wrote what were, in effect, warnings from a collapsing world to future generations:

> I have been told stories about [the Mongols] that the hearer can scarcely credit, about the fear of them that God Almighty cast into

people's hearts. It has even been said that one of them would enter a village or a quarter, where there was a large number of people, and he would continue to kill them one by one, while nobody dared to raise his hand against that horseman.[1]

In a similar nihilistic vein of fear and panic, he wrote that

one of them captured a man but the [Mongol] had nothing to kill him with, so he said to him, 'Put your head on the ground and do not move.' The man put his head on the ground, the Mongol left, fetched a sword and killed him with it. Another man told me the following: 'I was travelling on a road with seventeen men. A [Mongol] horseman came to us and told us to tie one another up. My companions began to do what he had ordered them. I said to them, "This is one man. Why do we not kill him and run away?" They said, "We are afraid." I replied, "This man is intending to kill you this minute. Let us kill him. Perhaps God will save us." By God, not one of them dared to act, so I took a knife and slew him. We ran away and were safe. There were many incidents like this.'[2]

There was a shocking, almost debilitating, effect in the Mongol eruptions. Entire communities were stunned. 'For several years,' wrote one Muslim chronicler,

I continued to avoid mention of this disaster as it horrified me and I was unwilling to recount it. I was taking one step towards it and then another back. Who is there who would find it easy to write the obituary of Islam and the Muslims?[3]

The crusader states were just as scared and confused. One of the Frankish chronicles of the time told of how the Mongols conquered all the lands they came to and destroyed all sorts of peoples – heathens, Muslims, Jews and Christians – without distinction . . . So many people did they slaughter, heathen Muslims more than others, that it was hard to believe it was happening, it all seemed a fable.[4]

For those of a religious disposition – which was almost everyone – this was the end of days.

Shadow of the Mongols

Fable or (more likely) nightmare – it was all shocking. The Assassins and the Templars – groups whose foundations depended on the implicit promise of death – had met their match.

At first, some of the rulers of the western Islamic states (those who had least interaction with the Mongols) were more concerned about the Franks than the Mongols. This was largely because the Franks, as a sedentary society, would occupy land permanently, whereas the Mongols (or at least so they mistakenly thought at the time) were merely disruptive raiders, albeit on a massive scale.[5]

That comforting ignorance did not long survive contact with the reality of dealing with the new invaders from the steppes.

The Mongols had erupted like a force of nature at the beginning of the thirteenth century. In 1219, the armies of Genghis Khan had crossed into Muslim territory, devastating the Khwarazmian state and moving relentlessly westward, into Transoxiana and Khorasan. By 1220, they had captured Bukhara and Samarkand, and in 1221 eastern Persia fell.

Genghis died in 1227, but for the Mongols this was just the beginning. By 1240, they had conquered what was left of Persia and had moved on to invade northern Mesopotamia, Armenia and Georgia – Muslims and Christians alike were shocked at the enormity of what they were facing. To do nothing meant instant submission to an alien culture – but to resist almost invariably meant a violent death.[6]

ASSASSINS: HOLOCAUST AND HORROR

The Assassins were initially ambivalent about the nature of the Mongol threat and tried to play a waiting game. They might be fearsome, but, so the Nizari logic ran, anyone who killed that many Sunni Muslims could not be all bad. The Assassins were said to have been in communication with the Mongols even before the invasion of Persia. Relations with Genghis Khan were friendly at first. Perhaps, the Assassins thought, the Mongols might even be useful. Soon after Khan's death, for instance, we find them trying to persuade the Mongols in Transoxiana to invade and destroy their Sunni enemies. This loose, one-sided alliance between the Assassins and the Mongols seems to have survived into the 1240s. But the true balance of power was becoming more apparent.[7]

Perhaps inevitably given the nature of the two protagonists, the relationship deteriorated. The Mongol general Chaghadai, ostentatiously known as 'the Greater', made himself an enemy of the Assassins. They responded in the time-honoured fashion – by murdering him. Not only may this have been a satisfying reflex action on their part, but it was also a profound mistake.

The Assassins found that they had finally got the Mongols' attention, but not in a good way. In 1252, the Mongol prince, Hulegu, a grandson of Genghis Khan, was sent to destroy the Nizari castles in Quhistan and the Alburz mountains.[8]

A detachment from Hulegu's army, a vanguard of some 12,000 men, was dispatched against the Nizaris in August, under the command of the Christian general Kitbuqa. It crossed the River Oxus in March 1253 and by May was launching a series of attacks on the Assassins' fortresses in Quhistan. Things did not go according to plan, however. The Mongol army was too small for the objectives it had been given. Some smaller castles were taken, but the major Nizari centres were able to withstand the desultory Mongol sieges that rumbled on throughout the rest of the year.[9]

A stalemate set in. The Mongols were not present in sufficient strength to finish the job. But the Assassins were outraged at the assault on their homelands. There are hints in the sources that they may have tried to take the battle to the enemy in the way they knew best.

In May 1254, William of Rubruck, a Christian friar and emissary at the court of the Mongol Khan, reported that he had been particularly carefully questioned, because there were suspicions that the Assassins were about to launch a retaliatory attack. As William wrote, the Mongols

> began to enquire carefully where we were from, for what purpose we had come, and what was our occupation. This interrogation was being conducted because [Mongke Khan] had been informed that four hundred Assassins in various disguises had made their way in with the aim of killing him.

Like John of Joinville at almost the same time, the khan and his security team thought that the Assassins could assume an almost infinite range of disguises. Not unreasonably, they were taking no chances.[10]

The Assassins were still posturing with one of the most dangerous enemies in history – but the struggle was far more uneven than they realised. Minority groups such as the Assassins and Templars were becoming ever more minor: both had always been tiny in number, but now they were so outclassed that they were rapidly becoming irrelevant.

By the second half of the thirteenth century, what remained of the Nizari homelands in Syria and the Templar fortresses in the Latin East were in a permanent state of crisis – but the Templar brother knights and the Assassins' elite *fidais* death squads still fought on against the Mamluks and the Mongols, substituting bravery and sheer stubbornness when hope ran out. Death or redundancy were the only futures left to them.

We are all alone in death. The twin cults, Assassins and Templars, were similarly on their own when they faced their end – on a similar path, at a similar time and facing similar forces. But ultimately on their own.

ASSASSINS: HOLOCAUST AND HORROR

The end in Persia

In 1256, Hulegu arrived in force, and with an army big enough to do the job that Kitbuqa had failed to finish. He parked his army in the heartlands of the Nizari state.[11]

The timing was not good for the Assassins (or 'knife-murderers', as Hulegu, with typical bluntness, used to call them). Just a few months before Hulegu's arrival, their leader, who had been in control for thirty-four years and was in favour of maintaining an aggressive stance against the Mongols, died in post – appropriately enough, he had been murdered by his own people. His youthful son, Rukn al-Din Khurshah, the Assassins' new leader in Persia, was far more conciliatory. He vacillated in the face of overwhelming force.

Khurshah soon made it clear that he had a policy of appeasement in mind. Immediately after his accession, he sent an envoy to the Mongols to offer his submission. Ominously, they responded by saying that he needed to come in person. Faced with the prospect of such a complete surrender, Khurshah played for time and tried to string the Mongols along. He made desultory attempts to reduce some of his castles' fortifications. He sent a stream of envoys and relatives to the Mongols, many of whom were detained as hostages. And he repeatedly requested a year's grace, on different pretexts, when he was asked to come and give submission.[12]

This was the worst of all worlds. Khurshah was weak and diffident – but at the same time he frustrated and angered his enemy. He was leading his people to a noiseless smothering, rather than to victory or even the glory of a brave ending. The only thing that might be said in Khurshah's favour was that he was probably holding an unwinnable hand.

The Mongols had all the leverage, and they dominated the negotiations. Undistracted by the delaying tactics, the Mongols secretly killed the hostages that Khurshah had given them, and in October 1256 their troops started to besiege his fortress of Maymundiz.

An extended artillery bombardment, including long-range Chinese ballistae, provided an appropriately impressive display of power. The *fidais* in the garrison wanted to keep fighting. They had achieved some success with their own catapults, and had kept the besieging forces at a distance. They argued that if they could hold on until the weather got worse, they might be able to wear down their Mongol besiegers.

But their leader wavered. On 19 November, Khurshah left his castle and went down to enter impotently into negotiations. The following day, he ordered his family, advisers and other occupants of the castle to destroy the fortifications and join him in the Mongol camp. Displaying a glimmer of their old pride and aggression, the *fidais* still refused to surrender: in a hopeless act of defiance, they fought on for another three days, until they were destroyed.[13]

Khurshah had been in power for just one year. He was not the leader that the Assassins needed at this time of crisis.

Khurshah turned towards collaboration with the Mongols, perhaps justifying it to himself with the thought that submission and cooperation had worked well in the past. He sent his teams out one last time – this time not to kill, but to order his own people to destroy their fortresses and surrender. Some forty Nizari castles were quietly, even shamefully, evacuated and slighted.

Only the commanders of the great castles of Alamut and Lamasar stood out in the midst of this quiet catastrophe: they refused to capitulate. Disgracefully, Khurshah went in person with his new Mongol friends to try to persuade the garrison of Alamut to surrender. They initially refused, but were eventually pounded into submission by the end of December 1256. The Mongols occupied the site, accompanied by their creature Khurshah, and started the process of destruction.

The Sunni historian Juwayni was with the Mongol army. Amidst the destruction, he took a few choice manuscripts and scientific instruments from the famous library of Alamut – the rest were thrown onto a bonfire. Juwayni settled down to compose a gloating epitaph for the sect that he had always despised.[14]

ASSASSINS: HOLOCAUST AND HORROR

The castle of Lamasar was the last major hold-out. The commander of the garrison was made of sterner stuff than his leader. Despite being ordered to surrender by Khurshah, he and his men held out for a year against the overwhelming Mongol forces that surrounded them. The few survivors only gave up when they had been ravaged by cholera.[15]

The Ismaili state in Persia was effectively at an end. Khurshah did not long outlive his usefulness. He may have thought that he had charmed his way into a position of influence. For a while the Mongols humoured his naïve predilections for watching camels mating and, more practically, for the attractions of young Turkic women. But he soon found that his status as 'honoured guest' among his new Mongol friends was a sham.[16]

Khurshah asked if he could travel to the court of Mongke Khan, presumably to make obeisance and a case for his continued role at the heart of the Mongol administration. Permission was granted, and he set off with nine companions and an entourage of Mongol soldiers, ostensibly there for his protection.

Khurshah was determined to continue to do anything he could to ingratiate himself with his overlords. On the way to Mongolia, he made a detour to visit the castle of Girdkuh, where a group of Nizari diehards continued to hold out. He once more ordered them to surrender – and the *fidais* once more refused. The dejected group continued on its journey to court but, having made the hard and degrading journey, Mongke refused to see him.[17]

Khurshah had nothing useful left to offer. As he was being taken back to Persia, his guards

> led him away from the road on the pretext of a feast they had prepared for him, and then caused him to taste the punishment for all that his forefathers had done to the people of God. He and his followers were kicked to a pulp and then put to the sword; and of him and his stock no trace was left . . . So was the world cleansed which had been polluted by their evil.[18]

It was a sordid and deliberately petty end to the Assassins' state in Persia.

This was not just a 'political death', however. In the traditional Mongol way, Khurshah's death was followed by genocide and massacre. The blood-letting began with Khurshah's family, which was already living with the Mongols: it was ordered that his 'sons and daughters, brothers and sisters and all of his seed and family should be laid on the fire of annihilation'.[19]

Some of his family were singled out for a more lingering death. 'Two or three of them' were handed over to the son of the Mongol commander Chaghadai (a victim of the *fidais*) and they endured a lingering death by torture. But the killing was genocidal as well as personal – not 'one of their race was spared . . . Orders were also sent to . . . the commander of the army of Khorasan, who was dealing with Quhistan, that he too should drive out such of those people as were obstinately attached to the Heresy on the pretext of raising a levy.' The male Nizaris were mustered to join a fictitious militia before being slaughtered, and 'in this way 12,000 people were put to death'.[20]

As one Mongol chronicler put it, definitively and with satisfaction, 'they destroyed them wherever they were'.[21]

The Mongols in Syria

The collapse of the Nizaris' state in Persia was a source of joy for the mainstream Islamic world, but was shocking for their coreligionists in Syria. They had jockeyed for autonomy from Alamut, with greater or lesser degrees of success, for over 150 years. But to achieve independence in this way was profoundly disturbing. Fresh from their victories in Persia, the Mongols were inevitably heading towards Syria – and that did not bode well for the remaining Assassins.

In 1257, Hulegu was given an army and told, with sublime simplicity, to conquer the Middle East. His troops devastated Persia once more and reached Baghdad, the capital of Sunni Islam, in January 1258.[22]

ASSASSINS: HOLOCAUST AND HORROR

The Mongols were, as ever, remorseless. Baghdad was put under siege. The inhabitants mounted a defence, but the end came quickly. On 10 February, the caliph came out from the city to surrender, along with his sons and his family. The destruction of Baghdad began in earnest shortly afterwards. The Mongol army entered the city, raping and killing, burning and stealing on an industrial scale. Hulegu wrote proudly to King Louis IX of France that he had killed 200,000 men in the course of the sack, 'and a host of others too many to count'. Rotting corpses and a contaminated water supply finished the job that Mongol swords had started.[23]

The caliph begged for mercy and offered submission – but it was too late. There had been some resistance. The attempt to surrender had been insufficiently speedy and obsequious – an example needed to be made. Once he had handed over his harem and his treasury, the caliph's use was at an end. Hulegu had the caliph and one of his sons killed in the traditional Mongol way – wrapped in felt and beaten to death. Another son was executed in Baghdad at the same time.[24]

The shock and awe of the Mongol invasions continued. At the end of 1259, Hulegu attacked northern Syria. Aleppo fell to his armies on 25 January 1260 after a siege of just seven days, and the inhabitants were massacred. The citizens of Damascus were, as he had intended, suitably cowed. They sent the keys of the city as a sign of their prompt submission. In March 1260, a Mongol army entered Damascus, the prize that had evaded the crusaders for so long.[25]

But that was the high-water mark. Hulegu had been forced to return to the Far East within a few weeks of capturing Aleppo – news had arrived of Mongke Khan's death in China, and a ferocious bout of internecine politics had erupted as a result. Kitbuqa was left behind with an inadequate army of perhaps under 10,000 men to guard the newly conquered territories.[26]

The Mamluk rulers of Egypt were quick to take advantage of this hiatus. Pausing only to end diplomatic discussions by killing the Mongol envoys at their court, the Mamluk army, consisting of some 12,000 cavalry, left Cairo on 20 July 1260.[27]

The Franks had not been unhappy to see their old Muslim enemies massacred by an enemy so fierce that it could be regarded as the retribution of God. And there was still a genuine possibility that the Mongols would become Christian. Indeed, the Christian population of Baghdad had specifically been spared from the recent massacres by the influence of Hulegu's Christian mother and wife.[28]

A quick dose of reality intervened soon after, however. The crusader city of Sidon was attacked and destroyed by Kitbuqa, just a few weeks after Hulegu returned east. The Franks entered into an unenthusiastic alliance with the Mamluks, offering them supplies and safe conduct as their army travelled north into the Holy Land. This was the correct call. On 3 September 1260, the Mamluk forces defeated the Mongols and their allies at the battle of 'Ayn Jalut. Kitbuqa was killed and his armies destroyed or dispersed. Although it was not immediately clear to everyone at the time, the Mongol advance had been stopped.[29]

Unsurprisingly, given the holocaust to which the sect had been subjected in Persia, the Assassins had chosen to ally themselves with the Mamluks. The Nizari leader at the time had already established diplomatic relations – he had gone on a conciliatory mission to Cairo in 1258, shortly after he took over as leader. The Nizaris therefore helped the Mamluks against the Mongols, providing whatever assistance they could. They were rewarded after the climactic battle of 'Ayn Jalut with the return of four of their castles that had previously been lost to the Mongols.[30]

If the Assassins in Syria were relieved by the Mongols' misfortunes, their celebrations were short lived. Sultan Qutuz, the victor of 'Ayn Jalut, was killed by his own officers a few weeks after the battle. By the time the Mamluk army got back to Cairo, someone even more ruthless had taken command. The Mamluks had a new sultan – his name was Baybars.[31]

Baybars and the Mamluk menace

The Assassins had survived thanks to their use of bluster, intimidation and the tangible threat of violence. In Baybars, however, they were dealing with someone who was prepared to face them down.

ASSASSINS: HOLOCAUST AND HORROR

The first few years of Baybars's reign, while he was consolidating his position, were deceptively calm. The balance of power had been irredeemably altered, however. The Nizaris had survived in part because of their position on a warring frontier. They had been irritating, but, as a buffer state against the Franks, they fulfilled a useful function for their much bigger Sunni neighbours. Now even that usefulness was gone. As the Franks were forced back to their last enclaves on the coast, the Assassins looked increasingly anomalous – a Shiite nuisance in the midst of victorious Sunni orthodoxy.

The Assassins' fate increasingly lay in the hands of a ruthless killer who was dedicated to the destruction of anyone who threatened himself or Sunni Islam. This included the Mongols, the crusaders and, most ominously for the Nizaris, those Baybars considered to be heretics. Tellingly, soon after his bloody accession Baybars was reported to have assigned the future income from the Assassins' lands to one of his generals, the lord of neighbouring Hama, as a bribe to gain his support. The ultimate agenda may not have been made public, but it was already clear in the sultan's mind.[32]

By the time a new Old Man, Najm al-Din, took over as leader of the Assassins in 1261–2, the military situation reflected their political weakness. Khariba had been lost and the sect's network of fortifications in the Jabal Bahra seems to have been reduced to only eight castles – Kahf, Masyaf and Qadmus, alongside Ullayqa, Qulay'a, Khawabi, Rusafa and Maniqa.[33]

Surviving fragments of a letter written by Baybars in *c.* 1265 show the contempt in which he held them. 'This Assassin trash', he wrote, 'failed to realise that riding well-bred horses is better than [hiding] in mountain peaks, and that sheets of metal are a better protection than sheets of paper.' He despised them and their increasingly hollow threats.[34]

Power was ebbing away from the Assassins. In 1266 and 1267, Baybars drew up treaties with the Hospitallers in which he forced them not only to relinquish the money they received from their Sunni Muslim tenants, but also to include the Assassins in the new arrangement: no longer, it was said, would they be required to give the Hospitallers 1,200 dinars each year, alongside quantities of wheat and barley.

This was not to benefit the Nizaris, however. The tribute was merely being transferred to their new master, Baybars. The Assassins' diplomats knew what they had to do and, grudgingly,

> messengers from the Ismailis came [to Baybars], bringing with them a quantity of gold. They said: 'This is the money which we used to contribute as a toll to the Franks and we have now brought it to the treasury of the Muslims that it may be spent on those who are fighting in the holy war.'

The identity of the bully had merely changed. The Assassins were still being squeezed.[35] After this, Baybars took over control of Nizari internal politics. He seems to have been able to dismiss and appoint the sect's leaders at will – he was in de facto command of the Assassins. In 1270, Baybars deposed the Old Man, Najm al-Din, because of his uncooperative attitude. Najm al-Din had made the mistake of not presenting himself quickly enough in person to pay homage to Baybars. The sultan was not amused. Misreading the situation and compounding his mistake, Najm al-Din sent envoys to the sultan soon afterwards to try to reduce the tribute they paid him.[36]

Baybars appointed another man, Sarim al-Din, in his place, while simultaneously confiscating the vital castle of Masyaf. The new Old Man was instructed not to take up residence there; but, disappointingly from Baybars's perspective, he disobeyed in spectacular fashion – instead of handing over the castle, he took control of Masyaf and killed those who had been collaborating with the Mamluks. Sarim was eventually captured and taken to Cairo, where he was imprisoned and poisoned. Najm al-Din, now suitably chastened, was allowed to take back his position as Old Man, alongside his son Shams al-Din; but inevitably, only on condition that they paid tribute to Baybars.[37]

ASSASSINS: HOLOCAUST AND HORROR

The two sides were on a collision course, however. Baybars suspected that the Assassins were scheming with the Franks, providing them with military information and plotting to kill him. In February or March 1271, while Baybars was besieging the Hospitaller castle of Crac des Chevaliers, two *fidais* from Ullayqa were arrested and charged with conspiring to murder the sultan. The Nizari leaders, Najm al-Din and his son, had to come in person to secure their release. The two *fidais* were freed suspiciously easily.

Baybars was not known for his affability, particularly where matters of personal security was concerned. Their quick release almost certainly implies that the *fidais* were innocent – it seems likely that this was really a case of hostage-taking and intimidation, and that they were just pawns with which to bully the Nizari leadership. But Baybars's plan succeeded. The Assassins were forced to surrender their castles to the sultan and Najm al-Din was taken away as a 'guest' to Cairo. He died in exile there in 1274.[38]

Shams al-Din realised that the end was near. He managed to get to the Nizari castle of Kahf and started to organise resistance. But it was all far too late. Baybars captured Ullayqa in May 1271 and Rusafa a few weeks later. Shams al-Din surrendered, and he and his household were sent, like his father, into exile in Cairo. Khawabi was taken by the Mamluks soon after. By the spring of 1273, Qulay'a, Maniqa and Qadmus had also surrendered. Kahf, the last of the Assassins' castles fell in July.[39]

While the Nizari state was being dismantled, the Assassins were browbeaten into supplying money and the precious services of the *fidais* as the price of their continued, albeit stunted, existence. This gave Baybars a new weapon of intimidation, and he used it to the full.

The chronicle of Qirta al-'Izzi tells a vague story of a Frankish lord from the county of Tripoli named Arnaud of Gibelet who had made the mistake of allying himself with the Mongol forces of Hulegu and raiding Muslim lands in conjunction with them. Baybars got his revenge by having his Assassin squads murder Arnaud, presumably in *c.* 1265. As

259

a strange aside, the sultan allegedly then tried to arrange for the Templars to provide a boat to take the successful *fidais* to safety.[40]

The attack on Philip of Montfort, the lord of Tyre, in 1270 (see chapter one) was similarly instigated by Baybars, and in April 1271 he felt confident enough of his new creatures to threaten the count of Tripoli with assassination. He was clearly enjoying using the Nizaris' services.[41]

Extraordinarily, the same simple method used to kill Philip of Montfort continued to deliver results for the Assassins. A small squad of *fidais* would be sent in. They would ask for conversion and employment. Then, when the target was at his most vulnerable, they would strike with daggers.

Only two years later, on 18 June 1272, an almost identical plot emerged, this time involving the heir to the English throne. Once again, the Christians, short of manpower and desperate to take mercenaries of any ethnicity into their service, were seduced into making a major mistake.

Prince Edward of England (later better known as King Edward I, 'Longshanks') had led an army on crusade to the Holy Land. The numbers of troops involved were far too small to make a significant military difference. But Baybars knew a good general when he saw one. He did not want Edward to come back with a bigger army – and the Assassins could make sure that would not happen.

The final arrangements for the hit were organised by the governor of Ramla, a certain Ibn-Shawar. He inserted an Assassin, 'who courted [Edward's] friendship', into the Christian camp. When a Turkic cavalryman appeared at Acre, apparently looking for work, the English prince was only too eager to oblige.

The mercenary had extremely valuable local knowledge and language skills. To further increase his appeal, he had pretended to be an apostate. The Assassin asked to change his religion and was duly 'baptised at Acre'. He was engaged as a Turcopole light cavalryman and (more appropriately than anyone knew) as a spy – the man was so trusted that 'the Lord Edward had made him into a Christian, and retained him in his own quarters'. As sponsor, Edward probably also became the Assassin's godfather.[42]

The *fidais* waited for the signal to be activated and to murder the prince. 'One night', wrote the anonymous chronicler we now refer to as the 'Templar of Tyre', the Assassin 'came to the chambers where the Lord Edward was sleeping ... and let it be known that he had just come from spying and that he wanted to speak to the Lord Edward'.[43]

Edward opened the door to his bedroom 'dressed only in an undershirt and braie [a loose-fitting pair of trousers]'. The prince was off guard, unarmoured and unarmed. The *fidais* seized his chance and lunged forward. But he could not land a killer blow. Instead, he cut the prince 'on the hip with a dagger, making a deep, dangerous wound' – presumably Lord Edward had made a reflex blocking action, and parried the dagger downwards. With an impressively quick recovery, Edward 'struck the Saracen a blow with his fist, on the temple, which knocked him senseless to the ground for a moment'.[44]

These were violent times and, luckily for Edward, he had a weapon of his own near to hand. Before his attacker had time to get up, he 'caught up a dagger from the table which was in the chamber, and stabbed the Saracen in the head and killed him'.[45]

There is another near-contemporary version of events. William of Tripoli, a Dominican friar who was in Acre at the time, wrote an account of the incident for Pope Gregory X. In it he corroborated most of the details set out by the Templar of Tyre, with one main exception: he claimed, entirely plausibly, that Edward had grabbed the Assassin's knife from him while he lay stunned on the floor (rather than picking up his own bedside weapon), and killed his assailant with it.[46]

Whatever the exact circumstances, the Assassin's dagger was poisoned and the Templar master rushed to administer an antidote. The cure consisted of persuading Edward to drink a liquid which contained a precious stone that had been ground up. But the Templars' skills were better suited to the battlefield than the infirmary: the remedy, not surprisingly, did not work. An English doctor stepped in and saved Edward by cutting away the edges of the wound.[47]

While 'the alarm was raised throughout the household', Edward's men 'saw that their lord was injured, and the cry went out through the city of Acre'. They took the lazy but traditional retaliatory measures – targeting the usual suspects, they 'mounted their horses and killed a few of the [local] Muslims' and, in all likelihood, some of the Arab Christians – they looked, to their eyes, all too similar.[48]

Tellingly, just a few hours after the attack, and presumably as soon as Edward was well enough to articulate his wishes, he made his will (dated 18 June 1272). It was witnessed by, among others, 'brother Thomas Bérard master of the Temple', who attached his seal to the document. Perhaps there were still concerns that he might die of the after-effects of the wound inflicted by the poisoned dagger. Or perhaps he had just had an all-too-dramatic reminder of his own mortality. But either way, Edward and his men had had enough. Most of the English crusaders returned home soon afterwards. They were glad to be on their way.[49]

The deposition of Najm al-Din in 1271 had taught the Assassins that they needed to be fully cooperative with their new master, if they were to survive in any form at all. Even with their active submission to their new masters, Nizari Ismailism from this time on was reduced to the status of a minor heresy, which survived only at the whim of the Mamluk overlords. Echoes of this strange master–servant relationship eventually entered folklore. The *Sira of Baybars*, an Egyptian folk epic constructed by professional storytellers, portrays the Assassins as Baybars's trusty cat-burglars, side-kicks eager to help him in any criminal enterprise. This was a sad parody, but, in spirit, close to the truth.[50]

Even more anti-climactically than with their co-religionists in Persia, the Syrian Assassins went out with a compliant whimper, rather than a bang.

Unlike their comrades in Persia, they were not wiped out. Instead, they proved they still had value, and were allowed to survive. They traded blood for their continued existence. It is interesting to see that the entire group were now sometimes referred to in Sunni texts as '*fidais*'. This was technically incorrect, of course, but perhaps understandable: delivering death, albeit in someone else's interests rather than their own, was now their only remaining value, and lay at the heart of what kept their community in existence. The Assassins' 'brand' was now unhelpfully boiled down to its essence.

The Assassins bought their freedom of worship with other people's lives. Baybars's successor, Sultan al-Malik al-Mansur, was blatant in the way he used them as tame contract killers to threaten his neighbours. In establishing a treaty with Margaret, the Lady of Tyre, in 1285, he made sure to tell her that although he would not murder her himself, he reserved the right to send in his *fidais* hit squads to do the job for him.

Clause 17 of the treaty was shocking in its brutality:

> None of the soldiery shall make an attempt against the Lady, Dame Margaret, the Lady of Tyre . . . except the Ismailis who are under the jurisdiction of our lord the Sultan. Our lord the Sultan may despatch whom of them he wishes to the Lady of Tyre with evil and injury when he wishes.

Lady Margaret's husband (Philip of Montfort) had already been murdered by Assassins sent by Baybars in 1270. She knew the threat was real.[51]

Acting as hired murderers on behalf of their Mamluk masters was the price the Assassins had to pay. 'They are the arrows of al-Malik al-Nasir [the Mamluk sultan, d.1341],' reported Ibn Battuta,

> by means of whom [sic] he strikes down those of his enemies . . . and they receive fixed emoluments. When the sultan desires to send one of them to assassinate some foe of his, he pays him his blood-money. If he escapes after carrying out what is desired of him, the money is his, but if he is caught it goes to his children. They

have poisoned knives, with which they strike the victim of their mission, but sometimes their devices do not succeed and they themselves are killed.[52]

Al-Umari, writing around the same time, had a similarly jaded view of the way in which the Assassins continued to obey murderous orders on behalf of their new masters. The *fidais*, he wrote, submit themselves to the Old Man

> and they think it right to lose their lives in his obedience for the very great bliss that is the resulting reward. By the adherence of these people the [Mamluk] ruler of Egypt acquires an advantage that makes him feared by his enemies, for from such men he may send out assassins who are heedless of their own possible death.[53]

Ironically, the Assassins were now reduced to a role which strangely presaged their distorted image in modern popular culture: they were hired killers who launched near-suicidal attacks for money.

21

Templars: Death in the East (1255–1291)

It was the morning of 22 July 1266 at Safad, in Galilee. The dry, rocky landscape, punctuated by smallholdings and hardy olive trees, was already searingly hot and strangely quiet. A castle, still impressive, but with towers and battlements damaged, cast its jagged shadow over the men below.

The survivors of the Templar garrison at Safad rode out in defeat. They made a self-conscious, almost theatrical effort to keep their heads high, looking straight ahead. The men did not want to give their victorious enemies the pleasure of eye contact. The Templar commander handed the castle over to their Muslim besiegers. As had been arranged, they prepared to make the journey back to the order's headquarters.

Their Mamluk guards were accommodating. Strangely relaxed even. Perhaps too relaxed, given that their hated Templar adversaries were about to ride off to freedom and, inevitably, to fight another day. But the garrison's horses were jittery and disoriented, coming out of the shadows for the first time in many days. The highly strung animals were like their riders – nervously liberated after their confinement in the claustrophobic conditions of a castle under siege.

They sensed something was not right.

Slaughter at Safad

By the middle of the thirteenth century, what remained of the Latin East was in a permanent state of crisis. But the Templar brothers still fought on, brave in the face of hopelessness. Matters came to a head in 1266. Their state-of-the-art castle at Safad, one of the Franks' last remaining inland fortifications, was besieged by the Mamluk sultan, Baybars.

Given the size of the Muslim armies, no relief force was feasible. Negotiations were opened up with Baybars in order to minimise casualties on both sides. He eventually agreed that the brothers of the garrison would be given safe conduct. Armed with cast-iron guarantees, the Templars 'came out of the castle with all their equipment loaded onto mules, ready to go at once to Acre'. They were going to ride off towards their fellow brothers on the coast.[1]

Or at least that was the plan. Like other Middle Eastern dictators in more modern times, Baybars sometimes employed body doubles to stand in for him for security purposes. He later asserted that it was one such imposter who had sworn to guarantee the safety of the Templar garrison. He claimed he was personally not bound to honour the agreement. True or not, it no longer mattered.[2]

Once the members of the garrison were clear of the castle gates, Baybars had them all seized and bound. The horror of their fate became clear. A couple of brave monks, not of the order, rose to the occasion. As the brother knights were led off for ritualistic execution, 'there were two Franciscans with them, who kept them firm in the faith by preaching to them'. Baybars had them taken to 'a small hillock about half a league away, and there he put them to death, beheaded. Then he had a circular wall erected around them', in which, as one Christian chronicle sadly put it, 'their bones and their heads may still be seen'. The lost garrison of Safad at least died with a final prayer to help maintain their resolve.[3]

The loss of Safad was catastrophic and demoralising. But there were other reverses, too. In February 1261, for instance, the Templars had launched an attack on Turcoman tribesmen near Tiberias. Things went badly wrong. The knights' vital charge failed, and they were heavily defeated. Casualties included the local Templar commander, a Brother Matthew Sauvage, and 'many sergeants, both horse and foot, [who] were also killed or captured'.[4]

The Templar marshal, Stephen of Sissey, was in charge on the battlefield that day. He survived, only to be accused of having executed the attack on the enemy very poorly, presumably because of bad timing. Even worse, it was suggested that he had 'turned back without striking a blow, either because his courage failed him, or else voluntarily, because (they said) he bore ill-will to the lord of Beirut, urged on by a mad jealousy over a woman of his country'. The in-fighting rumbled on long after the debacle had ended. The 'master of the Temple ordered him back to the west and stripped him of his habit'. But Stephen was later reinstated at the direct behest of the pope.[5]

This was obviously a very controversial encounter. The Templar marshal, who would have led and coordinated the charge, was felt to have mismanaged things. But it cannot have been clear cut. He harboured a massive sense of grievance about the way he had been treated, and was eventually pardoned.

Whatever the cause of the defeat, however, the consequences were once more grievous. Sixteen Templar captives were later ransomed. But that was it – the rest were dead and 'no more could be found alive'.[6]

It was increasingly obvious that not only did crusading remain cripplingly expensive, but it was also able to deliver fewer and fewer rewards – and that the fragile survival of the lordships of the Latin East now depended more on the political vagaries of their Muslim neighbours than on the military strength of the Templars and the Frankish colonies.

The Templars were fighting against enemies who far outmatched them: they were struggling to keep the order alive.

ASSASSINS AND TEMPLARS

Catastrophe at Tripoli

In 1275, William of Beaujeu, the newly appointed Templar grand master, arrived in Acre. He immediately wrote from his base in the city to King Edward I of England:

> Amid all this we have found the state of the House of the Temple weaker and more fragile than it ever was in the past; food is lacking, there are many expenses, revenues are almost non-existent. Your majesty is not unaware of the fact that all the brothers' goods or the greater part of them in these regions have been pillaged by the powerful sultan. And revenues from beyond the sea [in the west] cannot suffice to keep us alive; we have countless costs in defending the Holy Land and strengthening the castles that have remained for the Christians overseas.[7]

William was not exaggerating. By 1289, even the great crusader city of Tripoli was under direct threat. The Templars had obtained some forewarning of the attack through their network of spies and contacts. The Frankish authorities in Tripoli could not bring themselves to believe the worst. But even if they had, there was little they could do. At the end of March, Muslim armies took up position outside the city walls and began a ferocious siege. Templar reinforcements were sent to the garrison, but the defenders were vastly outnumbered. The huge Mamluk siege engines, employed in a battery of some nineteen machines, pounded the defences remorselessly.

By the end of April, at least two of Tripoli's towers had been severely damaged by the artillery barrage. The besiegers launched a full-scale assault and successfully stormed the city. Templar casualties in the fighting were appalling. Senior figures were singled out for special mention in the chronicles: 'Brother Peter of Moncada, the Templar commander, was killed in the battle,' we are told, 'as was William of Cardona, a Templar brother. Brother Reddecoeur was taken prisoner, as was Brother Hugh, son of the count of Ampurias and a Templar brother.' But casualties in the other ranks were crippling, too.[8]

The final test for the Templars and their ideology of martyrdom was fast approaching.

The last charge

That moment came on 18 May 1291. Thousands of Mamluk soldiers forced their way into Acre, the last major crusader city. The Templars hurried to try to seal off the gap in the wall and stop the flow of enemy soldiers into the port.

William of Beaujeu, the Templar master, 'gathered ten or twelve [brother knights] and his own household troops and headed for the St Anthony Gate, right between the two walls' of Acre, where the breach had occurred.[9]

There was no real chance of victory, but at least they could buy more time for civilians to run down to the port and escape – and they could go down fighting. The Templars frantically strapped on whatever armour they had to hand and ran towards their horses. This was a gallant but forlorn gesture – a bitter hope and the prospect of martyrdom thrown against an unstoppable tide of jubilant soldiery. The men saddled up and rode off towards the sound of the fighting.

The knights 'found the Saracens coming in on foot, and they counter-attacked them. But it was all to no effect . . . for there were too many Saracens.' When they charged against the Mamluk assault squads, one eyewitness wrote that 'it seemed as if they hurled themselves against a stone wall'.[10]

The Templar counter-attack had been extremely hurried, a mad rush in response to a dire emergency. The brothers had leapt on their horses at speed, without pausing to put on their full armour. This sense of urgency was not only essential, but it also had consequences. During one of the repeated charges and the hand-to-hand melees which followed, 'a javelin came at the master of the Temple, just as he raised his left hand'.

It struck him at a critical point under the armpit – his arming had taken place so hastily that there was a 'gap where the plates of the armour were not joined'. The shaft sank deep into his body. William paid the ultimate penalty for rushing to do his duty so quickly.[11]

The last fighting master of the order fell from his horse, mortally wounded. His Templar comrades gave no thought to their own safety: they dismounted and laid him, appropriately enough, on a large shield which they found discarded on the ground. Crouching under continual enemy fire, they dragged him back to what was left of the Christian lines.[12]

William clung to life for the rest of that day. Even at the end, he tried to keep a grip on how the battle was unfolding. When 'he heard the clamour of men fleeing death, he wanted to know what was happening. They told him that men were fighting, and he commanded that they should leave him in peace. He did not speak again, but gave his soul up to God.'[13]

William's charge had bought some time, but it could not stem the assault: thousands more Muslim troops were pouring into the city. It did, however, give the civilians a chance to dash for safety. The Templar compound formed the last fall-back position for the Frankish capital, and it was said that 'more than ten thousand persons sought refuge' there.[14]

Negotiations for surrender took place in bad blood and with bad grace. Mamluk negotiators arrived in the compound, with four hundred cavalry to guard them and make preparations for the surrender. But, exhilarated by victory, their discipline broke down and they started to rape young boys and women in the fortress. Provoked beyond endurance, the Christian defenders turned on the Muslim troops and full-scale fighting broke out. Discussions reached a definitive end.

The Templar marshal, Peter of Sevrey, was the senior surviving officer and the man leading the defence of the city. He tried to revive the negotiations and ventured out for discussions under a guarantee of safety. But he and his men were tied up and beheaded when they reached the enemy lines. There was no more talking.

Some ten days after the rest of the city had fallen, the last Templar defences were mined. The end was approaching. Appropriately enough for a bloody two-hundred-year history, the last tower collapsed 'outwards towards the street, and crushed more than two thousand mounted Turks'. There were no survivors from this last, desperate garrison of Templars.[15]

East and west: A reckoning looms

Shortly before the fall of Acre, Theobald Gaudin, the Templar commander, managed to escape to the coastal town of Sidon with the order's treasure and some of his fellow knights. The town itself and its citadel, 'the Castle on the Land', were soon recognised as being indefensible. The Templars quickly withdrew to their stronger 'Castle on the Sea', linked to the town by a narrow bridge. There they elected Gaudin as their new grand master.

Gaudin was an obvious choice. He was the most senior surviving official in the east and had had a long military career in the order. He had fought in the crusader states for over thirty years, during which time he had served both as a brother knight and as the 'Turcopolier' of the order, in charge of the light cavalry.

The trouble was that he was too old. His nerves were shot after the horrors he had seen at Acre. Gaudin sailed off to Cyprus, leaving his men behind. He claimed he was going to gather reinforcements with which to defend Sidon and the handful of remaining fortresses. The men on the front line waited. But Gaudin never returned. Only one thing came back – a less than inspiring message suggesting that they should get out while they still could.

This defeatist attitude was unwelcome, but not unrealistic: the Franks, and their Templar military elite, had indeed been defeated.

Sidon was abandoned in a night-time withdrawal on 14 July 1291. The order's last strongholds were left with no choice but to follow suit. Tortosa was evacuated on 3 August. 'Atlit was now the only base left on the mainland. The last Templar ships left port on 14 August. Mamluk troops moved in to dismantle the fortifications that they had never been able to take by force.[16]

The brother knights had given their lives and their treasure to defend the Latin East. But it was gone.

22

Afterlife: From Intimidation to Entertainment

You can't have it both ways.

You can try to portray the Assassins as deeply misunderstood, but fundamentally ordinary folk. You might say that they were an oppressed minority doing the best they could to survive in a world that was overwhelmingly hostile to their beliefs and way of life.

Or you can see them as super-human psychopaths, two-dimensional, brainwashed, drug-addled fanatics with acute homicidal tendencies.

And it is the same with the Templars. You can talk about them as a group of dedicated clerics, doing a difficult job under trying circumstances – kindly, devout souls, safeguarding pilgrims and defending the Holy Land. Or, more fashionably at the moment, you can see them as remorseless ultra-nationalists, elite military killers with a cheery sideline in satanic worship and treasure hunting.

These caricatures have an element of plausibility about them. Each is attractive, at least to some people. But all are fundamentally false. And they are inevitably mutually incompatible.

Both groups instinctively grasped the opportunities presented by reputation and 'corporate branding'. A vital part of 'the brand', the narrative they needed to impose, was the 'legend'. They were small, but, in the time-honoured evolutionary strategy of the animal world, they understood the advantages of looking – and acting – big. Both needed to punch above their weight. In a time of big armies and mass violence, they knew that they had to behave in a way that was far more clever and focused. If their opponents were the blunt instrument of a sawn-off shotgun, the Assassins and Templars were the precision sniper rifle.

The threat was real – both groups were genuinely fearsome. Templar warriors were indeed terrifying and elemental, something that deserved to be feared on the battlefield. If they turned their attention to you and the standards that betrayed your position in the battle line, you knew you were in trouble. Similarly, if the Assassins had you and your family in their sights, you had a significant problem – and a problem that might never go away.

The promise of death, and the fear that went with it, lay at the heart of what made both groups special. Their stories became distorted (often deliberately so) while they were still in their prime. Propaganda and 'brand-building' were used by both the Assassins and the Templars – and by their enemies. Everyone had a hand in creating the enduring legends and conspiracy theories that surrounded them from the very beginning and which persist to this day. Both ideologies were founded on fear and needed 'legend' to act as a multiplier for their threat.

Legend and brand were always key. But the Templars lost control of the narrative . . .

Unlucky for some

The suppression of the Templars was the biggest tabloid story of the Middle Ages.

King Philip of France was short of money. But he had a well-established method of dealing with this irritating problem: isolate a vulnerable group; accuse them of outrageous crimes; rob them blind.

He also had an extensive track record of raiding the assets of outsiders in his kingdom. He attacked the Italian ('Lombard') banking communities in France twice – first in 1291 and again in 1311 – in order to get some

AFTERLIFE

quick cash. And the Jewish community had been treated likewise in 1306. Tellingly, Philip not only made money from their persecution, but also seemed to genuinely believe that they had desecrated the Christian host.[1]

The Templars were vulnerable because they were the institution most closely linked to the defence of the Latin East. But the Holy Land, as most astute observers were aware, had been definitively lost in 1291. So the order was tarnished with undeniable failure. The Hospitallers fell back on their caring activities, and carved out a role for themselves on Rhodes as the Christian defenders of the eastern Mediterranean. But the Templars, inflexible and poorly led, had just one idea to sell – a vast, implausible invasion of the Middle East that no one in the west had any appetite for. Although they did not recognise it, they were clearly redundant.[2]

On 14 September 1307, King Philip sent out secret orders to his men. They were to arrest the Templars throughout France. It had been discovered that the brothers were committing ghastly crimes. Among other things, they were accused of denying Christ, running a secret satanic cult and worshipping the devil. This was the deepest betrayal of Christendom. Their treachery was, according to Philip, 'horrible to contemplate, terrible to hear of, a heinous crime'.[3]

Philip had a crude, but rational financial motive for attacking the Templars: he needed money. But, as with the Jewish community, he may really have believed his own propaganda – even the most far-fetched of the charges. In the suppression of the Templars, it is perhaps more realistic to see greed and superstition as natural, but dangerous bedfellows, rather than as alternative explanations.

Dawn raids were carried out against the order a month later. The blow fell on Friday, 13 October. Unlucky for almost everyone involved.

The arrests were meticulously planned and successfully executed – after all, the king's men had previous experience in such matters. This was a well-oiled machine of repression and extortion.[4]

Torture, and the threat of torture, were present from the very beginning. In the immediate aftermath of the arrests, justice was replaced with terror. The rack was used, and men were hanged. Weights were attached to their penis or testicles. Feet were burnt in fires. Bernard of Vado, a Templar priest from Albi, had the bones seared off his feet – he later carried them around with him in a bag to explain why he had confessed. Men said anything to stop the pain.

A couple of examples serve to show the brutal and literal methods of corporeal (and corporate) dismemberment at work. The preceptor of Cyprus, Raimbaud of Caromb, was questioned in Paris. He said he knew nothing of the charges or of any other wrong-doing in the order. Torture was applied. The following day, with no end to the pain in sight, he confessed to everything.[5] Another brother in Caen similarly denied all the charges when he was first questioned. The following day, after a visit from the torturers, he remembered that he was guilty of all the accusations.

Even compliance brought no end to this nightmare world of pain. Ithier of Rochefort, the Templar preceptor of Douzens, confessed but was still repeatedly tortured afterwards – the French inquisitors were probably drunk (as many were) or possibly just enjoyed their work too much. Perhaps both.

It is not surprising that confessions were quick and fulsome. The only surprise was that so many of the Templar brothers held out for so long. Many died under torture rather than perjure themselves.[6]

People still remembered the Templars' commitment to the possibility of martyrdom. But any public display of support was dangerous in the extreme – to be seen helping heretics was tantamount to heresy itself. Even so, anonymous documents circulated around Paris, harking back to the order's old ideology.

One such text, the *Lamentacio quedam pro Templariis*, claimed that thirty-six Templar brothers had already died under torture in Paris alone. It also pointed to the ferocious commitment to Christendom shown by the order – a hundred brother knights, it claimed, were still waiting to die in the prisons of Cairo, rather than betray their Christian faith. The king of France might want the order's money, but the Templars' acceptance of martyrdom in defence of the faith had not been forgotten.[7]

Others, too, remembered the Templars' heroism. During their trials in France, in the last days of the order, the Templar priest Peter of Bologna described those who died under torture by French officials as being 'like Christian martyrs' in their death and commitment. Many remembered that the Templars had a proud past – but their future was far less clear.[8]

The master of the Templars at the time of the suppression, Jacques de Molay, was old and inflexible. Shocked by the way events had unfolded, he had not been an impressive leader in the final days of the order. But even he rose to the occasion in the end, and died as a martyr should. At his final hearing, Jacques shouted that all the accusations against the order were false, and

> upon these words a sergeant struck him with his hand across the mouth, so that he might speak no further, and he was dragged by his hair into a chapel ... And then the master and the commander of Gascony were placed in a small boat and taken onto an island in the river, and there a fire was burning ... So they took him and cast him into the fire, and he was burnt.

As one chronicler succinctly put it, 'they are martyrs before God'.[9]

Even at this time of political hysteria and propaganda, the people of Paris recognised what was happening. 'The night after the said master and his companion had been martyred,' it was said, 'their ashes and bones were collected as sacred relics by the friars and other religious persons, and carried away to holy places.'[10]

The last Templar master was burnt on 18 March 1314. The order was gone. Although most in the Church were eventually convinced of the Templars' innocence, their reputation was indelibly tainted – the brand was now beyond redemption.

Gone but not forgotten

The consequences of having such a tainted reputation have reverberated through the ages. The Templars were unfairly, absurdly, maligned during their trials. But the stories were so outrageous, so garish, that a lot of the craziness they were accused of has since found resonance in the public imagination. To paraphrase a more modern totalitarian brand manager, 'if you tell a lie, tell it big, and make it stick'. They are now possibly among the most misrepresented groups in history.

The Templars were founded around an extraordinary, but fundamentally rational premise – they had a defensive strategy for protecting the Christian communities of the Holy Land and developed an intimidating ideology of selfless bravery to help them do so. But because of the outlandish manner of their dissolution, they have become the target for any number of conspiracy theories and what one might generously call 'special interest groups'.

Conspiracies, secrets and the desire to explain events that we cannot control have long captivated our collective imagination. The modern world is replete with icons upon which to base bizarre conspiracy theories. Aliens, Cathars, Illuminati, John Dillinger, Prince Philip. The list is endless – it's a competitive market.

The process of turning history into conspiracy often involves transforming the mundane into something that crudely resembles 'magic'. The Templars, in this context, are a perfect vehicle. They were closed down on the basis of false, but beguiling stories of satanism and supernatural knowledge. And the loss of their archives means that they can serve as both a blank canvas and a cipher. Even the less intellectually gifted conspiracists can use them to construct a 'code' that promises to make sense of the chaos that surrounds us all.[11]

The internet now serves as an obvious engine for these conspiratorial stories. But the origins of this Templar mythology stretch back long before our digital age. The eighteenth century proved particularly fertile. Freemasonry began to flourish and sought legitimacy. The Masons tried

AFTERLIFE

to establish a lineage that linked their movement to the chivalric traditions of the Middle Ages, and this required a grand, albeit fabricated, heritage. The Templar narrative of dissolution was perfect for the task. All the elements were there – mysticism and esoteric knowledge, magic and a healthy dose of secrecy, all brought together by brave, upmarket people doing extraordinary things. The Templars were the ideal backstory.

By the 1760s, German Freemasons were actively engaged in retrofitting their supposed connections to the Templars. Drawing on the spurious accusations levelled against the order's members during their trials, they created a story in which the order had long been a bastion of secret wisdom and profound insights. They suggested that just prior to his arrest, Jacques de Molay managed to transmit all this coveted knowledge to his Masonic 'successor', thus tying the Templars directly into the lineage of modern Freemasonry.

None of this is encumbered by evidence, of course. That would be too obvious. But it fulfils several needs simultaneously. A new, prosaic institution gets an upmarket and mystical makeover. Individuals get a story that fits nicely with their need to find order in a frighteningly chaotic universe. And the Templars, of course, are no longer able to defend themselves from such fantasies. It's a perfect fit.[12]

Fast forward to today, and the internet has become a facilitator and multiplier for these and other elaborate conspiracy theories. The Templars have an aspirational place in the thinking of many groups, other than the Masons. Most of them are harmless, but others are decidedly less so. Some members of far-right organisations, including those on the terrorist fringe, have taken up the military dedication and trappings of the order's branding (clothes, crosses and so on) as part of their racial, cultural and nationalistic agendas.

AI-generated images on the internet often now show the Templars looking like Aryan cage-fighters, with clothes taken from a medieval dressing-up box. Some right-wing extremist groups occasionally dress up in Templar costumes and claim to be members of their own proto-military order. Several branches of the Ku Klux Klan (which, bizarrely, manages to be simultaneously anti-Catholic) even offer members different levels of 'knighthood' in their own imitation 'chivalric orders'.[13]

This is particularly ironic, given that the Templars were founded as an internationalist organisation – nationalism and provincialism in Europe were among the centrifugal forces that they and their papal masters were working against. They also had no racist objectives, ideologies or doctrine. On the contrary, one of the main aims of the order was the protection of the local Christian communities (Arabs, Armenians and Syrians) who constituted the majority of the populations of the crusader states. A typical front-line Templar army was a multi-ethnic, multinational force, with large numbers (often a majority) of their troops being ethnic Arabs or Armenians.[14]

But irony is lost on extremists.

'Aladdin Sane': The Assassins' medieval myths

The Templars' reputation changed overnight. One minute they were Christendom's bravest and most pious defenders. The next, they were crazed satanists and conspiratorial treasure hunters. This was a branding meltdown of unprecedented proportions, propelled by greed and redundancy.

The Assassins were more fortunate. They had largely been destroyed in Persia, but in Syria they struggled on. They remained a vulnerable religious minority, and they still carried out occasional assassinations, albeit for their new Mamluk masters, rather than on their own account. But they had never become redundant in the way that the Templars had. There was no blank page for conspiracists to work with.

Perhaps not surprisingly, however, the Assassins have also had countless brushes with unhelpful mythology and distortion. They have always retained their singular capacity for controversy. The modern Egyptian TV drama, *Al-Hashashin* (2024), for instance, based on the life of

AFTERLIFE

Hasan Sabbah, shows the continuing interest in their history and mythology. The series is hugely popular across the Middle East, but is banned in Iran. The Assassins' capacity for polarising opinion remains as strong as ever.

But modern legends are propelled by their medieval 'brand-building'. Larger-than-life tales were told of the sect, even in its prime. And – as the sect intended – outsiders exaggerated the Assassins' capabilities. Sunni accounts were coloured by hatred, horror and contempt. Western descriptions often contained a breathless mixture of truth, exaggeration and misunderstanding – only the balance between the three changed, according to the perspective of the commentator.

Marco Polo was a Venetian merchant writing, probably with collaborators, at the end of the thirteenth century. This was after the Assassins had been crushed as an independent entity, but his account still showed the strength of their corporate brand. And, as his work was so famous, it has become the archetypal summary of how the medieval west viewed the Assassins.

Their leader, he proudly informed his readers, was 'the Old Man', who was also called 'Ala' al-Din'. The Old Man was said to be focused on developing the *fidais* and kept with him 'all the youths of the country between twelve and twenty years old – that is, those who seemed men-at-arms'.[15] When he wanted someone murdered, 'he gave the nod to those he thought the best of his assassins. He sent several out in the surrounding country nearby, ordering them to kill some men. They would immediately go and carry out their lord's command, then return to court.'[16]

The *fidais*, according to Marco Polo, carried out the Old Man's orders with blind obedience and 'in this way, no one escaped being killed, when the Old Man of the Mountain desired it. I tell you in all truth that several kings and several barons paid him tribute and maintained good relations with him for fear that he might have them killed.'[17]

Marco Polo's account also contained several of the more or less legendary tropes associated with the Assassins – their supposedly widespread drug use; the way in which the *fidais* were sequestered away from the world; their 'secret garden' which resembled an earthly paradise, designed to give them a spurious taste of their reward in the afterlife; their unswerving commitment to the wishes of the Old Man, and so on. So far, so predictable.

It is tempting to write off this account as part of a naïve and patronising early form of western 'orientalism'. But that would be far too easy. Marco Polo had spent much of the period between 1271 and 1295 on the Eurasian steppes, in the service of the Mongols' great khan. And he had clearly spoken to men who had helped destroy the Nizaris in Persia.

'Around the year 1262,' Marco Polo wrote rather simplistically,

> Hulegu, lord of the Tartars of the East, found out all the bad things this Old Man was doing and said to himself that he would destroy him. Then he took some of his barons and sent them to this castle with a lot of people. They besieged the castle a good three years without succeeding in taking it . . . But after three years, they had nothing left to eat. So the Old Man, whose name was Alā' al-Dīn, was, along with all his men, taken and killed. From that Old Man until now, there has been no Old Man and no Assassin; with him, the rule and all the evils that Old Men of the Mountain had committed in former times came to an end.[18]

Overblown prose aside, there is much in the core of Marco Polo's account that is accurate. The committed young men, the secrecy of an isolated sect, the death-dealing missions at their master's command, the spiritual rewards the *fidais* (like the Templars) believed they would receive for their bravery in defence of their community – all these core elements are true. Even the commemoration and feting of the *fidais* after their missions finds resonance in Marco Polo's account. 'When those who had escaped returned to their lord,' he wrote, 'they told him that they had carried out their task. The Old Man showed them great joy and great celebration.'[19]

In the absence of all the facts, Marco Polo makes up some detail. And the language is flowery (he is, after all, trying to sell a book). But it is clearly an enemy's view of the Assassins and, as always, that reputation for cold-blooded killing was promulgated just as much by the Assassins as by those they fought. This was the 'promise of death' that they needed to survive, and it lived on long after their political demise.[20]

Reunited at last: *Assassin's Creed*

In the course of the nineteenth century, Europe became more interested in studying Islam in general, and the Assassins in particular. Scholars were guided (or perhaps misguided) in their research into the Nizaris by their reliance on two groups of sources. Both of them were problematic. Most historical references to the sect were in newly discovered texts written by Sunni writers, who generally hated them. And these references were inevitably supplemented by the views of medieval Christian sources, which often misunderstood them. This did not make for the happiest historiographical development.[21]

One easy and colourful way of interpreting the group was to envisage the Nizari Ismailis as some kind of extreme 'religious order'. The first European book devoted entirely to them (published in 1818) made continual reference to 'the Order of the Assassins', as if they were a mirror of the European military orders. Structural comparisons with the Templars, however implausible, were imported wholesale. The Nizari leaders were referred to as 'Grand Masters', and the sect was a 'secret society'. Ironically, and in ways they would never have imagined, the Assassins and the Templars were moving back together.[22]

So the pairing of the Assassins and the Templars has its own two-hundred-year history in the west. And, like all good legends, the separate and conjoined stories of the Assassins and the Templars say far more about us, and our deeper fears, than they do about any historical truth.

Video games are one of the defining media of our age, so it is perhaps not surprising that it is in this sphere that the two groups have once

ASSASSINS AND TEMPLARS

more coalesced. And neither should it be surprising that one of the most popular and iconic games of modern times brings our two groups of 'heroes' together in one place and defines much of their current mythology – *Assassin's Creed*.

The classic *Assassin's Creed* (2007) was a ground-breaking video game that has spawned a plethora of other games, novels and art books. The numbers speak volumes about our voracious appetite for the Assassin–Templar mythology – the franchise has sold around 230 million copies and continues to successfully refresh and reinvent itself.[23]

We are all creatures of our time. *Assassin's Creed* is no exception. Development on the original game began in 2003 and was inevitably shaped by the momentous political and cultural events that had unfolded around it. The attacks on the World Trade Center took place on 11 September 2001. They caused, as the perpetrators had wanted, a backlash of monumental proportions. The ensuing conflicts helped validate (for extremists at both ends of the spectrum) the idea that there is an enduring war between the Muslim world and the west. Casual misappropriation of words such as 'crusade' and 'jihad' by politicians on all sides made a difficult situation still worse. The impact of that attack and response still reverberates around the world.

The 'war on terror' in turn sparked off a reaction in certain parts of the media. Some, such as Ridley Scott's movie homage to the crusader states, *Kingdom of Heaven*, tried to pursue, however clumsily, a more conciliatory agenda. The movie was released in 2005, but development and production work had inevitably been taking place in the immediate aftermath of the 9/11 maelstrom.

Kingdom of Heaven is at pains to take a moderate path, and was deeply influential in the development of *Assassin's Creed*. The movie's narrative avoids easy cultural stereotypes, attempting instead to take an even-handed approach to the conflicts in both the twelfth and the twenty-first centuries. Our 'hero' is a crusader, but there are empathetic characters on all sides – the forces of reason and fanaticism each have their champions, and are on both sides of the supposed cultural divide.

AFTERLIFE

Quite apart from this macro-mood setting, however, there are two areas in which *Kingdom of Heaven* provided inspiration for *Assassin's Creed*. Most obviously, there is the visual backdrop of the world it creates. Whatever one's views of the historical accuracy of the movie (and it is, after all, a piece of entertainment, rather than a lecture series), the visualisation of place and time is bold and sumptuous. We are completely drawn into this semi-alien environment. And, of course, in video-gaming, as in the cinema, immersion is everything.

Perhaps even more importantly, as part of the drive to make the movie more politically neutral, the Templars are pitched as exemplars of the 'dark side' of the crusading movement. Unlike the Hospitallers, they use their malign influence to push the weak and bullying King Guy of Lusignan into making a series of rash, and ultimately disastrous, decisions. If the Assassins are the obvious anti-heroes of Islam, *Kingdom of Heaven* helped cement the Templars' place as their natural opponents – an equivalent sect of secrecy and arcane malevolence living among the Franks.

Assassin's Creed draws on these influences, but gives them its own twists. Like the movie, it is heavily fictionalised, but authentically presented. And the *Kingdom of Heaven*'s plotline provides an easy, chronologically seamless introduction for *Assassin's Creed*'s video-gaming audience.

The movie helpfully sets out the immediate back history of several of the main characters from the original *Assassin's Creed*. Distorted versions of Saladin and Guy de Lusignan both feature in the movie, and the Muslim conquest of the Latin kingdom of Jerusalem creates the context for the crusaders' counter-offensive. The very last scene introduces Richard the Lionheart and his English knights travelling south through France, heading off on the Third Crusade.

Assassin's Creed picks up the narrative just a few months after the events portrayed in *Kingdom of Heaven*. Richard and his men have arrived in the east. Richard's admiral and diplomat, Robert de Sablé, has become the master of the Templars. It is the perfect moment to introduce the Assassins as anti-heroes playing a dramatic counterpoint to their Templar nemesis.

Assassin's Creed was launched in the emotionally heightened political atmosphere of 2007. But one of the most satisfying aspects of the game is the way in which it avoids the obvious clichés. The Assassins have often been simplistically caricatured as 'terrorists'. Playing comfortably to the crowd in this febrile time, such a distortion would have been an easy route to take.

It would also have been tempting to pose the game's narrative as an early variant of the temporarily fashionable idea of a 'clash of civilisations' – video-gaming could have been used as yet another shallow excuse to pitch Islam and the west against each other, with the Assassins and the Templars positioned as avatars for their respective cultures.

Once again, this would have been a facile and ultimately false premise. And it would, of course, have been particularly ironic – the main axis of conflict for the Assassins was the enduring hostility they encountered from other parts of Islam, particularly their Sunni neighbours.

Assassin's Creed takes neither route. It eschews the easy win of crowd-pleasing prejudice – and instead blends the protagonists into an overarching sci-fi premise. Its emphasis on imagination and problem-solving is more engaging than the cheap, politicised shoot-em-up premise that it could have taken.[24]

Our 'heroes' are truly reunited in imagination.

Living the Assassins and Templars

Instead of the obvious prejudices, irony permeates the game, much as it did in real life. As Templar and Nizari ideology would also have claimed, the gamer tries to achieve peace through murder. As players, we seek the triumph of love through bloodshed.

The Templars in the original version of *Assassin's Creed* are the 'evil' force, following much of the same narrative arc that we see in their

AFTERLIFE

reputational meltdown as the order was suppressed. They are revealed to include Muslim members and they exist to pursue goals which supersede the strictures of the Abrahamic religions – the 'Templars' of *Assassin's Creed* have their own agenda of power, one that transcends the more prosaic beliefs of the uninitiated.[25]

The game is set in the period soon after July 1191, when the crusaders recovered much of the Holy Land from Saladin. The main figure in the game, the player's avatar, is a fictional character named Altaïr Ibn-La'Ahad (1165–1257), who is involved in the real events of the Third Crusade. Following the Third Crusade motif, most of the gameplay takes place in the atmospheric locations of medieval Acre, Jerusalem, Damascus and the Assassins' castle at Masyaf.

The timing is deliberate. The historical Assassins and the Templars of the early 1190s were in their prime. Their leaders were both powerful and impressive characters – Sinan and Robert de Sablé were individuals of huge ability, with depth, charisma and power. Their communities were under threat, but it was not entirely hopeless – they still had something to play for. This moment in time is an appropriate introduction to our main protagonists.

It also allows the narrative arc of the game to include other famous and recognisable historical characters. Although they are relatively minor characters in the game, the historical Saladin and Richard the Lionheart have each had their own reputational arcs in modern times, veering from hero to zero and back again. And in some ways they mirror the mythological trajectory of the Assassins and the Templars. Light turns to dark, and then back again. Like our two groups of 'heroes', they have become almost one in the popular imagination, figures moving in a timeless dance so closely entwined that they blur, conjoined as a single mythic entity.[26]

Our avatar is similarly conjoined. Altaïr is the son of a Christian English woman and a Nizari diplomat who is executed by Saladin – he is part Christian, part Muslim, part western, but partly from the Middle East. He is recruited as a *fidais* by Sinan, but is then thwarted by Robert de Sablé when he attempts to steal an ancient artefact from the Templars' old headquarters in Jerusalem.

Altaïr's punishment for failure is that he must kill nine Templar (or 'secret Templar') characters – some of these are fictional, but others are historical figures who did actually die in the period 1191–3. The latter include Hospitaller master Garnier de Nablus, William V of Montferrat and, ultimately, Templar master Robert de Sablé.[27]

As well as having these genuine figures, the game is populated with historical scenery and references. The depiction of medieval Syria is convincing. The costumes are similarly based on historical dress, albeit slightly exaggerated for dramatic effect. The objective is to create what a player might think has the right 'feel', rather than being creatively governed by the restrictions of surviving evidence. *Assassin's Creed* plays to what the gamer feels to be 'authentically' medieval, rather than, of course, that which is factual.[28]

But before we get too carried away, we need to remind ourselves of its context.

Assassin's Creed's backstory has a grounding in real history, but it quickly develops in a different direction. Instead of participating in a period drama (worthy but potentially dull), the gamer discovers a premise that is based in fantasy-fiction rather than historical fact. As Ubisoft, the game's developers, have said, *Assassin's Creed* 'is not a historical game. It is a sci-fi universe in which you play in a historical setting'. It is unfair to be too judgemental. *Assassin's Creed* is unambiguously positioned as a game, not a history lecture, and needs to be treated as such.[29]

The core premise is that 'genetic memories' allow us to tap into the experiences of our ancestors – and much of the attraction derives from the way in which the game combines that with an epic historical sweep. Gameplay takes place primarily in the 1190s in the Middle East, but also in contemporary Rome (2012). The player is a double avatar, both Desmond Miles, a modern bartender, and his Anglo-Nizari ancestor, Altaïr.[30]

AFTERLIFE

At its core, *Assassin's Creed* is set firmly in our own world of ambiguities, embellished with a veneer of historicity. Reflecting our own experience, full of fake news and without definitive touchstones for right and wrong, everything is grounded in ambiguity and mystery. We are unsure of ourselves, we operate within a complex, shifting moral framework, and so too do our gaming characters. Modern heroes, and the modern avatars of *Assassin's Creed*, are morally agnostic. Patterns of good and evil, political right and wrong, are redrawn as shades of grey.

The characters labelled 'Templars' and 'Assassins' in *Assassin's Creed* inevitably follow this trajectory of uncertainty. The Templars are recruited from both the Christian and Muslim faiths. The Assassins are mainly, but not exclusively, Muslim. Even Sinan himself is revealed as a secret Templar, a man who wants the artefact for himself, and is at odds with both groups.

Uncertainty is shown most fully in the way in which religion is treated within *Assassin's Creed*. The tension at the core of this ambivalence is reflected in the game's maxim – 'nothing is true, everything is permitted'. This is a world with no absolutes, and where Godhead is often seen as the ultimate (missing) absolute. Our avatars reflect our own confusion.[31]

The Assassins and Templars are portrayed as groups of conspiracy and extreme ability, fitting easily into whichever shape we want to mould them. Mirroring our current obsessions, rather than the mores of the twelfth century, they are morally neutral, ethnically diverse and 'spiritual' rather than sectarian. Perhaps inevitably, given our own views, the Templar order and the Nizari Ismailis of the video game are no longer even particularly 'religious'. We are less pious than our medieval ancestors – so too, necessarily, are the sects of *Assassin's Creed*. Religion is viewed as a primal device for controlling the masses, rather than anything more substantive.[32]

It is not hard to see why *Assassin's Creed* had some success. The Templars are an instantly recognisable (albeit heavily distorted) cultural icon in the modern world. Their inclusion in the game, particularly in the context of their post-medieval reputation for secrecy, arcane arts and martial arts skills all find a natural home in a sci-fi fantasy game.

The Templars in *Assassin's Creed* are a mixture of many previous conspiracy theories. They, like the Illuminati, have access to ancient, secret knowledge. They are a threatening deus ex machina, with unaccountable power. Comforting or not, the Templars of *Assassin's Creed* provide a kind of supra-religious proof, for those who need it, that there is purpose and order in the universe: they may be amoral, but in the absence of God, there is still someone in charge. We may no longer have higher beings, but we can at least access what has been called 'the consolation of paranoia'.[33]

The Assassins have likewise left an exotic legacy. So why not match the two together? They are similarly mysterious, intimidating and deadly – two monstrous, ostensibly ultra-violent groups fighting to the death, bound together in blood. And why not add a heavy carapace of post 9/11 moral ambivalence as well?

Assassin's Creed is, in part, just that – the *Aliens vs. Predator* rematch of the medieval world, played out as a video game. It inevitably reflects the world of its audience, and their impressions of the medieval Middle East, rather than the historical facts. And that is why it has become popular. It not only provides imaginative puzzles set in an immersive and authentic environment, but it also plays to our real fears, representing our world as a place bereft of moral certainty and full, instead, of danger.[34]

We all have our own need for understanding and conspiracy, redemption and salvation. And we find it in the ways most appropriate to our time. The mythology of the Templars and the Assassins allows us to pursue the mirage of ultimate knowledge. We encounter 'secret' societies, men dedicated to extremes of discipline and performance, combined with a hint of arcane knowledge and magic arts. It is easy to see why both groups fit so easily into a role at the epicentre of our conspiracist fantasies.[35]

AFTERLIFE

As individuals, we pursue a forlorn quest for certainty. Much the same seems to be true of societies as a whole. Conspiracy theories traditionally enjoy a resurgence during periods of intense social change or crisis. The tradition of paranoia and intrigue finds a home in the media most appropriate to its age. The cheap novels of the early nineteenth century, with all its revolutionary fervour, became the thrillers and movies of the horror-filled twentieth century. They in turn gave way to the internet, AI and the interactive gaming environment of *Assassin's Creed* in the troubled landscape of the twenty-first century.[36]

Perhaps, unlike the real Templars and Assassins, each generation gets what it needs – and what it deserves.

23

Ending and Beginning

We can't finish like this.

There is more to the memory of the Assassins and Templars than conspiracies and chaos, cultist wannabes and video games. Too much blood has been spilt. Too much commitment, so generously given and so carelessly spent. They deserve better than plastic daggers and cosplay outfits.

No one would pretend that they were angels. Ultimately, they all dealt in death – and they exploited the power that gave them. But there was also an honesty and a bravery about them.

It is hard to be definitive about success or failure. Both groups were, from our comfortable standpoint almost one thousand years in the future, a failure. The Templars were formed to defend the Christian communities of the Middle East, but they failed to do so: all the crusader states were destroyed. The Assassins and their revolutionary religio-political doctrines did not overthrow the Seljuk Turks or their successors. They carved out a couple of minor principalities for a time, but little more. They did not even hold any major cities. Both sects were eventually brushed aside by their much larger military opponents.[1]

But we should not be too harsh. Everything comes to an end. We all die. Even the biggest empires fall. Against all the odds, the Templars helped keep the crusading movement, and the settlements of the Latin East, alive for almost two hundred years – most modern states don't last that long. The Assassins similarly survived far longer than one might have expected. Outnumbered and with few natural resources to call on, they made themselves heard, hated and feared. Assassins and Templars carved out a space for their communities in a time of supreme danger.

Both failed. But both also exceeded most expectations. In doing so, they pushed the bounds of dedication and commitment to new limits. And it is that extraordinary legacy, with all its faults, which deserves to be remembered.

Acknowledgements

The Latter-day Saints have responded well to the tongue-in-cheek lashing they receive every night in the musical comedy *The Book of Mormon*. Instead of instigating pointless lawsuits, they take the mature approach and advertise in the programme. Mockery is transformed into affection and profile-raising.

Neither the Assassins nor the Templars had a lively sense of humour. In the (monumentally unlikely) event that they had, however, both groups might likewise have embraced the iconic reputation that video games have now given them. But I doubt it.

My own interest in the strange relationship between the Templars and the Assassins did not originate in the gaming world, but in the rich primary source material which I encountered when writing two previous books.

With *Templars: The knights who made Britain* (Yale University Press, 2023), I quickly became aware of the professionalism, commitment and focus (some might say fanaticism) of the order. It was also clear that the disproportionate impact that the members of this relatively small group had on their world was no coincidence – it was shaped by sheer force of will, and through the undaunted commitment of generations of young men who bought into the ideals and objectives of the Templars.

ACKNOWLEDGEMENTS

I came across the Assassins in a very similar way. Writing a book called *Crusader Criminals: The knights who went rogue in the Holy Land* (Yale University Press, 2024) about the criminal underworld of the ironically named 'Holy Wars', I naturally needed to investigate a lot of murders. And with murders in the medieval Middle East, it is only a matter of minutes before the subject of the Assassins arises. In the event, I dropped the Assassins from the book, as they were clearly using murder as a political act, rather than as a more narrowly defined expression of 'criminality'. But their extraordinary *modus operandi* stuck with me.

The more I learnt about both groups, the more I realised that they had elaborate strategies and patterns of behaviour in common. And, having spent much of the non-academic part of my career in the business of crafting brands and corporate reputations, I recognised fellow professionals when I saw them.

✦

Writing a history of the Assassins and Templars is not straightforward. We have to be aware of all the usual provisos about medieval evidence. Much of it is anecdotal and ultimately unverifiable, and the chronicles have a charming, but irritating, tendency to suggest numbers that are suspiciously round and large. On top of that, both the Templars and the Assassins are encased in legend. They are mythologised now, but even at the time they created and enjoyed their own mystiques. And with the Assassins we encounter an additional layer of problems – evidence about the sect is often provided by people who both feared and hated them, and followed an obvious agenda in painting their actions in the most negative light.

But many people have helped in the delicate task of sifting through the evidence. The academic world continues to uncover new insights.

Ronan O'Reilly of Royal Holloway, University of London, has been enormously generous in his help with the Templars, and particularly with regard to what we might nowadays call their 'group ideology'. Professor Malcolm Barber, the ever-amiable doyen

ACKNOWLEDGEMENTS

of Templar historians and a charming voice of good-natured sanity (Brentford FC supporters have to be well grounded, of course), has been his usual kind and professional self.

The marvellous Professor Peter Edbury has similarly brought his encyclopaedic knowledge of the crusades to bear, especially with regard to the Templars, Cyprus and the Frankish states. Professor John France has very kindly allowed me to use his excellent, unpublished, translation of Kamal al-Din. My dear friend Dr Chris Marshall has added his deep understanding of the thirteenth century to the mix. And Dr Mohamad El-Merheb, the renowned Mamluk expert, has been particularly kind, bringing his knowledge of Middle Eastern historiography and first-hand experience of Nizari castles to the book.

The lovely Peter Konieczny, Dr Rory McClellan and Dr Mike Horswell have likewise been incredibly helpful with the more modern aspects of memory and legend. My brother Andrew and nephews Freddie and Alfie, alongside my brother-in-law Philip, have similarly helped with the transition from legend to gameplay, particularly with regard to *Assassin's Creed*.

They have all been far too generous with their insights – residual mistakes remain resolutely my own.

Most of all, however, I would like to thank my wife, Dr Faith Tibble, for her love and support. She guided me through the writing process, encouraging me when things were difficult, taking the worst edges off what passes for my humour and helping to edit and adjust the final manuscript. It would not have been the same, or such fun, without her.

London and Herefordshire, 2025

Notes

Abbreviations used in the notes

IA	Ibn al-Athir, *The Chronicle of Ibn al-Athır for the Crusading Period from al-Kamil fi'l-Ta'rıkh*, parts 1, 2 and 3, tr. D.S. Richards, Aldershot, 2006, 2007, 2008
Joinville	Joinville and Villehardouin, *Chronicles of the Crusades*, tr. C. Smith, London, 2008
L&J	M.C. Lyons and D.E.P. Jackson, *Saladin: The politics of the Holy War*, Cambridge, 1982
Letters	*Letters from the East: Crusaders, pilgrims and settlers in the 12th–13th centuries*, tr. M. Barber and K. Bate, Crusade Texts in Translation, 18, Farnham, 2010
Qal	Ibn al-Qalanisi, *The Damascus Chronicle of the Crusades*, tr. H.A.R. Gibb, London, 1932
RHC Or	*Recueil des Historiens des Croisades: Historiens orientaux*
TTT	Paul Crawford (ed.), *The 'Templar of Tyre': Part III of the 'Deeds of the Cypriots'*, Abingdon, 2016
Usama	Usama ibn-Munqidh, *The Book of Contemplation*, tr. P.M. Cobb, London, 2008
WT	William of Tyre, *A History of Deeds Done Beyond the Sea*, tr. E.A. Babcock and A.C. Krey, 2 vols, Records of Civilization, Sources and Studies, 35, New York, 1943

Chapter 1

1. *TTT*, p. 63. Tyre was one of the most important coastal cities in the Latin kingdom of Jerusalem. It is now part of modern Lebanon.
2. *TTT*, p. 63.
3. *TTT*, p. 64.

4. *TTT*, p. 64.
5. *TTT*, p. 64.
6. *TTT*, p. 64.
7. *TTT*, pp. 64–5.
8. *TTT*, p. 65.
9. *TTT*, p. 65.
10. *TTT*, p. 65.
11. *TTT*, p. 65.
12. *TTT*, p. 65.
13. *TTT*, p. 65.
14. *TTT*, pp. 65–6.
15. The one exception may have been the quick-witted William of Picquigny. It was notoriously difficult to break into the ranks of the famously clannish Frankish nobility of Cyprus, but William later made that difficult transition. In so doing, he was possibly being rewarded for his bravery by John of Montfort's wife, who was the sister of the king of Cyprus. Edbury, 2015, pp. 81–2.
16. *TTT*, p. 66.

Chapter 2

1. See Tibble, 2024, pp. 5–48 for the shocking social effect which this demographic distortion had on local communities.
2. Daftary, 2007, pp. 1–22; Saleh, 1995, pp. 35–43.
3. Hillenbrand, 2022a, p. 342.
4. Tibble, 2018, pp. 67–98.
5. Tibble, 2024, pp. 5–48.
6. See Poor, 2019 for an excellent rebuttal of the simplistic charges of 'terrorism' often levelled against the Assassins.
7. Eddé, 2011, pp. 17–18.
8. Daftary, 2007, pp. 243–4; Eddé, 2011, p. 18.
9. Hodgson, 1955, pp. 25–6.
10. Letter from Sinan, quoted in Lewis, 1966, p. 235.
11. Qal, p. 180.

Chapter 3

1. Mirza, 1997, p. 2; Hillenbrand, 2022a, p. 337.
2. Lewis, 2003, p. 27. For the concept of *Taqiyya* (caution, or concealing religious beliefs) which underpins much of this, see Lewis, 2003, p. 25 and Mirza, 1997, p. 4.
3. Lewis, 2003, pp. 28–9. The more junior *da'is* within the sect, depending on their task, might be called 'missionaries', or, as Bernard Lewis described them, as 'something like an ordained priesthood'; Lewis, 2003, p. 48.
4. Lewis, 2003, p. 23.
5. Lewis, 2003, pp. 30–1.
6. Barber, 2012, pp. 47–8.
7. Daftary, 2012, p. 69.

8. Hodgson, 1955, pp. 41–5. Our understanding of Hasan's early life is largely speculative. It is not known if he ever met the Fatimid imam-caliph of the time, al-Mustansir, but we know that the vizier Badr al-Jamali opposed him. It is not entirely clear what Hasan was able to achieve or do while in Egypt.
9. Daftary, 2007, pp. 343–4.
10. Lewis, 2003, pp. 42–4.
11. IA I, pp. 42–3; Lewis, 2003, pp. 42–4; Daftary, 2005, pp. 129–30; Hodgson, 1955, pp. 48–50. The owner of Alamut was said to have been given 3,000 gold dinars to sweeten the deal and ensure that matters proceeded peacefully.
12. Juwayni, pp. 720–1; Hodgson, 1955, pp. 50–1; Daftary, 2005, p. 130.
13. Another translation is 'Eagle's Nest'.
14. IA I, p. 42; Lewis, 2003, pp. 43–4.
15. Daftary, 2005, p. 132; Daftary, 2007, pp. 313–16.
16. Daftary, 2005, p. 131.
17. Lewis, 2003, pp. 61–3; Daftary, 2007, pp. 343–4.
18. Daftary, 2005, pp. 133–4.
19. Juwayni, quoted in Lewis, 2003, p. 44; Daftary, 2005, p. 133.
20. Daftary, 2005, pp. 134–5; Daftary, 2007, pp. 327–8.
21. Daftary, 2007, p. 329.
22. Daftary, 2007, p. 329.
23. Hodgson, 1955, pp. 82–4; Lewis, 2003, pp. 133–4; Daftary, 2005, pp. 135 and 149–50.
24. IA I, p. 40; Lewis, 2003, pp. 45–6.
25. Lewis, 2003, p. 47; Ibn al-Athir, *Annals*, pp. 253 and 253 n.88.
26. Lewis, 2003, pp. 47–8.
27. Lewis, 2003, pp. 34–5.
28. Daftary, 2012, pp. 123–4; Lewis, 2003, pp. 34–5.
29. Ibn Nazif, p. 45; Ambroise, p. 150 n.565; Daftary, 1994, pp. 1–48; Phillips, 2019, p. 101.
30. Daftary, 2007, pp. 241–3 and 324–5; Daftary, 2012, p. 152; Willey, 2005, pp. 16–17. After the death of al-Mustansir, the caliph, in 1094, the Fatimid Ismailis split into two main groups: the Mustalis and the Nizaris. The Nizaris regarded Nizar and his descendants as their legitimate imams. But, until the appearance of the Imam Hasan II at Alamut in 1162 and the proclamation of the 'Resurrection' in 1164, authority in the community was represented by the chief *da'is* of the time; Mirza, 1997, pp. 19–20.
31. Daftary, 2005, pp. 136–7 and 149; Hodgson, 1955, pp. 62–9.
32. Daftary, 2005, p. 143.
33. Lewis, 2003, pp. 62–3.
34. Hillenbrand, 2022b, pp. 145–62.

Chapter 4

1. Tyerman, 2006, pp. 12 and 126–9.
2. Cobb, 2014, pp. 78–81; Tibble, 2018, pp. 9–11.
3. Lewis, 2003, pp. 98–9. Note that the Turkish invasions of Syria did not all take place after the Turkish incursions into Anatolia – for a more detailed view of this period, see Wilson, 2023.

4. Tibble, 2020, pp. 18–22.
5. Daftary, 2005, p. 138.
6. Lewis, 2003, p. 98.
7. Daftary, 2007, pp. 331–3; Hodgson, 1955, pp. 70–2.
8. Lewis, 2003, p. 27.
9. Lewis, 2003, pp. 98–100.
10. Daftary, 2005, pp. 141–2 and 150–1.
11. Lewis, 2003, pp. 130–2.
12. Daftary, 2005, p. 150; Daftary, 2007, p. 328.
13. Lewis, 1966, p. 235.
14. Daftary, 2005, p. 136.
15. IA I, p. 40; Hodgson, 1955, pp. 82–3.
16. Hodgson, 1955, pp. 82–3; Lewis, 2003, pp. 130–1.
17. Daftary, 2005, p. 150; Daftary, 2007, pp. 328–9.
18. Daftary, 2007, p. 328; Lewis, 2003, p. 48.
19. IA I, p. 44.
20. Daftary, 2007, pp. 331–5; Hodgson, 1955, pp. 89–92; Mirza, 1997, pp. 8–11.
21. Kamal al-Din, France tr. of *RHC Or*, 3, pp. 590 and 604.
22. Daftary, 2007, pp. 332–3; Willey, 2005, p. 42.
23. Daftary, 2007, pp. 331–5.
24. Qal, pp. 57–8; Barber, 2012, p. 383 n.108.
25. Qal, pp. 57–8; Kamal al-Din, *RHC Or*, 3, pp. 590–1; Azimi, quoted in Lewis, 1952, p. 485; Daftary, 2007, pp. 332–3.
26. Lewis, 2003, p. 100.
27. Asbridge, 2000, pp. 34–46.
28. Lewis, 2003, pp. 100–2; Daftary, 2007, pp. 331–5.
29. Cobb, 2005, p. 11; Daftary, 2007, pp. 333–5; Lewis, 2003, pp. 100–2.
30. Usama, p. 244.
31. Usama, pp. 244–5.
32. Qal, pp. 72–4; Usama, pp. 244–5.
33. Qal, p. 73.
34. Qal, p. 73.
35. Qal, p. 73; Lewis, 2003, pp. 102–3.
36. Qal, p. 74; Daftary, 2005, p. 152; Lewis, 2003, p. 102.
37. Asbridge, 2000, pp. 47–68.
38. Daftary, 2007, p. 334; Hodgson, 1955, p. 92.
39. Hodgson, 1955, p. 107 n.27; Asbridge, 2000, p. 62.
40. Lewis, 2003, p. 103; Daftary, 2007, p. 334.
41. Qal, p. 115.
42. Qal, pp. 114–15. See Hodgson, 1955, pp. 92–3 for Ridwan's use of Assassin troops in this period.
43. Qal, p. 140; Barber, 2012, pp. 101–3; Lewis, 2003, p. 103; Daftary, 2007, p. 334.
44. Qal, p. 140.
45. Qal, p. 140.
46. Qal, pp. 140–2; IA I, pp. 162–3.
47. WT I, pp. 495–6.
48. Albert of Aachen, pp. 850–3; Fulcher of Chartres, p. 211; Matthew of Edessa, p. 214.

49. IA I, pp. 162–3.
50. Bar Hebraeus, pp. 245–6.
51. Barber, 2012, pp. 101–3.
52. Daftary, 2007, pp. 334–5; Lewis, 2003, pp. 103–4; Hodgson, 1955, p. 94.
53. Qal, p. 145.
54. Kamal al-Din, France tr. of *RHC Or*, 3, pp. 603–4.
55. Kamal al-Din, France tr. of *RHC Or*, 3, pp. 604–5.
56. Qal, pp. 145–6; Kamal al-Din, France tr. of *RHC Or*, 3, p. 604.
57. Qal, pp. 145–6; IA I, p. 164.

Chapter 5

1. Cobb, 2005, pp. 1–24.
2. Daftary, 2007, p. 335; Lewis, 2003, p. 104.
3. Qal, p. 148.
4. Kennedy, 2012, pp. 2–25.
5. Kennedy, 2012, pp. 4–7.
6. Qal, pp. 147–8.
7. Usama, pp. 135–6.
8. Usama, pp. 135–6.
9. Usama, p. 257; Qal, pp. 147–8.
10. Usama, p. 137.
11. Usama, p. 137.
12. Usama, p. 137.
13. Qal, pp. 147–8.
14. Usama, pp. 257–8 and 330 n.51; Cobb, 2005, pp. 6–7.
15. Usama, p. 137; Qal, p. 148.
16. Usama, p. 129.
17. Usama, p. 129.
18. Usama, p. 129.
19. Usama, p. 173.
20. Usama, p. 173.
21. Usama, p. 173; Mitchell, Nagar and Ellenblum, 2006, pp. 145–55.
22. Usama, p. 176.
23. Usama, pp. 176–7.
24. Qal, p. 148; IA I, p. 146.
25. Usama, pp. 157–8; Tibble, 2024, pp. 106–7.
26. Christie, 2004, pp. 75–6.
27. Christie, 2004, pp. 71–87.

Chapter 6

1. Kamal al-Din, France tr. of *RHC Or*, 3, p. 616.
2. Kamal al-Din, France tr. of *RHC Or*, 3, p. 616; Lewis, 2003, p. 104.
3. Lewis, 2003, p. 59.
4. Qal, p. 163. Ismaili chronicle, cited by Rashid al-Din and the Persian historian Kashani, quoted in Lewis, 2003, p. 59 (see also pp. 62–3 and 108); Daftary, 2007, pp. 342–3; Barber, 2012, p. 141.

5. Qal, p. 179; Lewis, 2003, pp. 104–5; Mirza, 1997, pp. 11–13.
6. Qal, p. 179.
7. Qal, pp. 179–80.
8. Qal, pp. 174–6.
9. Daftary, 2007, pp. 347–8.
10. Kamal al-Din, France tr. of *RHC Or*, 3, pp. 654–5.
11. Michael the Syrian, in Matthew of Edessa, p. 349 n.4.
12. Ibn al-Qalanisi, in Matthew of Edessa, p. 349 n.4.
13. Kamal al-Din, France tr. of *RHC Or*, 3, pp. 654–5.
14. Kamal al-Din, France tr. of *RHC Or*, 3, pp. 654–5; IA I, pp. 261–2.
15. IA I, p. 262.
16. IA I, p. 262.
17. Matthew of Edessa, p. 236.
18. IA I, p. 262.
19. Kamal al-Din, in Lewis, 2003, pp. 104–5.
20. Qal, pp. 177–80; Daftary, 2007, pp. 348–9; Daftary, 2012, p. 29; Hodgson, 1955, pp. 104–5.
21. Barber, 2012, pp. 164–5; Pringle, *The Churches*, I, 1993, p. 108; Pringle, 1997, p. 30; Mukaddasi, p. 24.
22. Qal, p. 180.
23. Qal, pp. 179–80. Ibn al-Athir had a similarly jaundiced view of events: IA I, pp. 260–1.
24. Daftary, 2007, p. 348; Lewis, 2003, pp. 105–6.

Chapter 7

1. Tibble, 2023, pp. 15–17.
2. Tibble, 2020, pp. 18–26.
3. Barber, 2012, pp. 37–49.
4. Phillips, 2009, p. 15; Cobb, 2014, pp. 9–123.
5. Riley-Smith, 2014, pp. 71–4.
6. Tibble, 2023, pp. 17–19.
7. It is worth noting that – perhaps inevitably, given the circumstances of the time – the process by which the Templars and the other military orders came to take on a structural military role within the defence of the crusader states was gradual. Tibble, 2023, pp. 20–1.
8. Barber, 1994, pp. 6–7; Tibble, 2023, pp. 20–5.
9. Walter Map, pp. 54–5. Map is, of course, having a bit of monkish slapstick fun with the Latin word for 'pagan' here as well.
10. Walter Map, pp. 54–5.
11. The importance of the Council of Nablus in the foundation and acceptance of the Templars is likely, but ultimately unprovable. The order was not mentioned by name in the decrees of the Council, for instance. Barber, 1994, pp. 9–10.
12. WT I, pp. 524–7; Barber, 1994, pp. 6–7; Bernard of Clairvaux, *In Praise*, p. 10.
13. Michael the Syrian, in Barber, 1994, p. 7. For the Templars' relationship with the kings of Jerusalem, see the excellent Burgtorf, 2017, pp. 25–37.
14. Possibly thirty men, if one believes Michael the Syrian, pp. 629–30 – in any event, hardly an army. Barber, 1994, pp. 9–10.

15. Tibble, 2023, pp. 25–30.
16. WT II, p. 40; Phillips, 1996, pp. 39–43.
17. Rother, 2014, pp. 169–71.
18. Rother, 2014, p. 171; Purkis, 2008, pp. 98–111.
19. Barber, 1994, pp. 12–16.
20. Barber, 1994, p. 13; Bulst-Thiele, 1992, pp. 58–9.
21. The Rule was similar to the Rule of Saint Benedict. It seems to have been partly written the previous year and then discussed, revised and appended to the Council minutes.
22. Barber, in Bernard of Clairvaux, *In Praise*, pp. 12–13; Rother, 2014, p. 171; Purkis, 2008, pp. 98–111. Bernard's ideas did not, of course, achieve general approval overnight.
23. Bernard of Clairvaux, *In Praise*, p. 40.
24. Bernard of Clairvaux, *In Praise*, pp. 33–4; Grabois, 1992, pp. 49–56.

Chapter 8

1. Rother, 2014, p. 178. For the religious activities of the Templars, see Schenk, 2017, pp. 199–211.
2. Rother, 2014, p. 183.
3. Rother, 2014, pp. 175–6.
4. Bernard of Clairvaux, *Opera*, quoted in Rother, 2014, p. 173.
5. Rother, 2014, p. 173.
6. Bernard of Clairvaux, *Opera*, quoted in Rother, 2014, pp. 172–3.
7. Rother, 2014, pp. 173–4.
8. Walter Map, pp. 54–9.
9. Walter Map, pp. 58–9.
10. Walter Map, pp. 58–9.
11. Anonymous text of *c.* 1130 quoted in Barber, 1994, p. 42.
12. Barber, 1994, pp. 44–6.
13. Bernard of Clairvaux, *In Praise*, p. 65 (see also pp. 34 and 39).
14. See Purkis, 2008 for an excellent discussion of how the Templars self-consciously became 'Imitatores Christi'; Cassidy-Welch, 2023, pp. 61–2.
15. Schenk, 2017, pp. 205–6.
16. Barber, 1994, pp. 56–7; Purkis, 2008, p. 107.
17. Rother, 2014, pp. 181–2.
18. Rother, 2014, pp. 181–3.
19. Rother, 2014, pp. 179–83. See, for example, *The Rule of the Templars*, p. 34.
20. Rother, 2014, p. 183.
21. Kirch, 2021, p. 88; Smith, 2003, pp. 189–96; Dunbabin, 1985, pp. 31–41. For Muslim views of martyrdom in this period, see Talmon-Heller, 2002, pp. 131–9.
22. Kirch, 2021, pp. 88–91.
23. Rother, 2014, pp. 179–80.
24. Tamminen, 2011, p. 301; Lapina, 2012, pp. 147–59; Schatkin, 1974, pp. 97–113; Morton, 2017, pp. 409–11. The Templars were not priests (except for their chaplains, who were generally priests *before* they joined the order). The brothers took vows of obedience and chastity, but, unlike Benedictines and Cistercians, not vows of 'stability' (which bound a monk for his whole life to his

monastery). So the idea of the Templars as 'armed monks' is a good approximation of their standing.
25. Tamminen, 2011, p. 302.
26. Morton, 2010, pp. 275–6.
27. *Letters*, p. 59; Morton, 2010, pp. 283–4.
28. *The Conquest of the Holy Land*, pp. 114–15; Morton, 2010, p. 286. See also: John of Salisbury, *The Statesman's Book*, pp. 313–14; James of Vitry, *History of Jerusalem*, pp. 51–2; Cole, 1993, pp. 22–6; Wilson, 2022, pp. 9–10; Rother, 2014, pp. 176–7.
29. Quotation from Bernard of Clairvaux, *In Praise*, p. 34. More fully: 'Truly a fearless knight . . . stands up for Christ, but he would prefer to be dissolved and to be with Christ, by far the better thing.'
30. James of Vitry, *Exempla*, pp. 39 and 171.
31. James of Vitry, *Exempla*, pp. 39 and 171–2; Throop, 2011, p. 151.
32. James of Vitry, *Exempla*, pp. 39 and 171–2.
33. Rother, 2014, p. 191.
34. Rother, 2014, pp. 174–5.
35. Bernard of Clairvaux, *In Praise*, p. 35.
36. See Sandler, 2018, pp. 46–54, 65–9 and 107–9.
37. Barber, 1994, p. 18; de Ayala Martínez, 1998, pp. 225–33.
38. Tibble, 2018, pp. 111–31.
39. Kennedy, 1994, p. 196.
40. Upton-Ward, 1994, pp. 179–81.
41. Upton-Ward, 1994, pp. 181–2.
42. Upton-Ward, 1994, pp. 186–7.
43. Upton-Ward, 1994, p. 188.

Chapter 9

1. Lewis, 2003, pp. 105–6; Hodgson, 1955, pp. 104–5; Daftary, 2007, pp. 347–9.
2. IA I, p. 277.
3. Qal, pp. 180 and 187–8.
4. Qal, pp. 187–8.
5. Qal, p. 189.
6. Qal, p. 190.
7. Qal, p. 190; IA I, p. 277.
8. Qal, pp. 190–1.
9. Qal, pp. 190–1; IA I, p. 277; Ibn Nazif, p. 85.
10. Asbridge, 2013, pp. 86–93; Barber, 1994, pp. 11–19; Phillips, 1994, pp. 141–7; Phillips, 1996, pp. 40–3; Tibble, 2020, pp. 81–8.
11. Fulcher of Chartres, pp. 288–92; WT II, pp. 27–30; Qal, pp. 174–7.
12. WT II, p. 40.
13. Qal, p. 183.
14. Qal, p. 191.
15. Qal, p. 191.
16. IA I, pp. 277–8.
17. Lewis, 2003, p. 108.
18. IA I, pp. 277–8; Asbridge, 2013, pp. 88–91.

19. Qal, pp. 191–2; Ibn Nazif, p. 85.
20. IA I, p. 278.
21. Qal, p. 193.
22. Qal, p. 193.
23. Qal, p. 193; Lewis, 2003, pp. 106–7; Daftary, 2007, pp. 348–9; Mirza, 1997, pp. 11–13.
24. IA I, pp. 277–8.
25. Qal, p. 194.
26. Qal, p. 194; Smarandache, 2012, pp. 221–39.
27. IA I, p. 278.
28. Qal, p. 195.
29. Qal, pp. 196–7.
30. Qal, p. 199.
31. Qal, p. 199; IA I, pp. 278–9.
32. WT II, p. 40.

Chapter 10

1. Qal, pp. 202–3.
2. Qal, pp. 202–3.
3. Qal, p. 203.
4. Qal, p. 203.
5. Qal, pp. 208–9.
6. IA I, p. 295; Lewis, 2003, p. 107; Daftary, 2007, p. 349.
7. Daftary, 2007, p. 352.
8. Daftary, 2005, p. 153; Willey, 2005, p. 217.
9. Willey, 2005, p. 219.
10. Tibble, 2018, pp. 31 and 200.
11. Tibble, 2018, p. 200.
12. Tibble, 2018, pp. 185–6.
13. Tibble, 2018, pp. 200–3.
14. Kamal al-Din, *RHC Or*, 3, p. 665; Willey, 2005, pp. 43–4 and 220; Daftary, 2007, pp. 349–50; Hodgson, 1955, p. 106.
15. Benjamin of Tudela, p. 17; Willey, 2005, pp. 228–30.
16. Lewis, 2017, p. 112; Barber, 2012, p. 153. Though note that IA I, p. 277 puts the acquisition slightly earlier, in the late 1120s.
17. Lewis, 2003, pp. 108–9; Willey, 2005, pp. 233–7; Daftary, 2007, p. 350.
18. Willey, 2005, p. 234.
19. Willey, 2005, p. 237.
20. Willey, 2005, pp. 235–7.
21. Daftary, 2005, p. 153.
22. Daftary, 2005, p. 153.
23. Qal, p. 263; Daftary, 2007, p. 350.
24. Willey, 2005, pp. 220–2.
25. Willey, 2005, pp. 222–3.
26. Willey, 2005, p. 224.
27. Willey, 2005, p. 226.

28. Willey, 2005, pp. 227–8; Hillenbrand, 2022a, pp. 337–8; Mirza, 1997, p. 14. Several other castles were acquired at around the same time as Masyaf, including Rusafa, Maniqa, Khawabi and Qulay'a.
29. See, for example, Lewis, 2003, pp. 131–2.
30. *De Constructione Castri Saphet*, p. 41; Kennedy, 1994, p. 196.
31. *De Constructione Castri Saphet*, p. 41; Kennedy, 1994, p. 196.
32. Burchard of Strasbourg, in Arnold of Lübeck, p. 280.
33. Juwayni, p. 717; Lewis, 2003, pp. 95–6.

Chapter 11

1. WT II, p. 175.
2. John of Salisbury, *Historia Pontificalis*, p. 54; Phillips, 2007, pp. 199–202.
3. WT II, p. 175.
4. Odo of Deuil, pp. 116–17; WT II, pp. 176–7.
5. Odo of Deuil, pp. 124–7; Phillips, 2007, p. 202.
6. WT I, p. 526; Barber, 1994, p. 66.
7. For the Templars at war, see the excellent France, 2017.
8. Nicholson, 2024, pp. 197–207.
9. Note that concentric defences were not entirely unprecedented in the Middle East before the construction of such castles by the Templars and other military orders.
10. Bennett, 1992, pp. 175–88; Tibble, 2018, pp. 133–49.
11. WT II, p. 196.
12. *Cartulaire général de l'Ordre du Temple*, p. 66, translated in Barber, 1994, p. 37.
13. Only the walled town and citadel of Caesarea itself remained in secular hands (though note that ownership of two small castles is unknown). Tibble, 1989, pp. 99–152; Barber, 1994, p. 89.
14. Tibble, 2020, pp. 110–17.
15. *Letters*, pp. 47–9; Barber, 1994, pp. 70–2. See Mallett, 2013, pp. 48–60.
16. Qal, p. 292; IA II, p. 31; Barber, 2012, pp. 193–4; Lewis, 2003, pp. 109–10; Daftary, 2007, p. 352.
17. *Letters*, p. 48.
18. *Letters*, p. 48.
19. *Letters*, pp. 48–9; Barber, 2012, pp. 193–5.
20. Barber, 1994, pp. 65–70.
21. Kennedy, 1994, pp. 141–4.
22. Riley-Smith, 1978, pp. 92–5; Barber, 1994, pp. 77–9.
23. John Kinnamos, p. 24; Barber, 1994, p. 77.
24. Barber, 1994, p. 79.
25. Barber, 1994, p. 35.
26. WT II, pp. 103–5. For Thecua, see the excellent study in Pringle, *The Churches*, II, 1998, pp. 347–50.
27. WT II, p. 104.
28. WT II, pp. 104–5.
29. WT II, p. 105; Barber, 1994, p. 35.
30. WT II, p. 104; Barber, 1994, p. 36.
31. Barber, 1994, pp. 76–7.

32. Barber, 1994, p. 86.
33. Barber, 1994, pp. 87–8.
34. Barber, 1994, pp. 87–8.
35. Barber, 2012, p. 201; Tibble, 2020, pp. 123–32.
36. WT II, p. 203.
37. WT II, p. 203.
38. Usama, pp. 24–6.
39. WT II, p. 203.
40. WT II, p. 203; Barber, 1994, pp. 34–5.
41. WT II, pp. 217–34.
42. WT II, pp. 226–8; Barber, 1994, pp. 73–5; Nicholson, 1998, pp. 112–13.
43. WT II, pp. 226–8; Matthew of Edessa, p. 270.
44. Barber, 2012, pp. 210–11 and 213–14.
45. Barber, 1994, p. 95.
46. *Letters*, p. 61. Bertrand of Blancfort, master of the Templars, to King Louis VII of France, November 1164.
47. Tibble, 2020, pp. 176–220. For the Frankish campaigns in Egypt in the 1160s and beyond, see the excellent Fulton, 2022, pp. 45–146.
48. *Letters*, pp. 57–61; Barber, 1994, p. 97.
49. Barber, 1994, p. 97.
50. Richard of Poitou, *Chronica*, in MGH SS, vol. XXVI, p. 80; Barber, 1994, p. 36.

Chapter 12

1. Orderic Vitalis, VI, pp. 496–7; WT II, pp. 87–8; Barber, 1994, p. 35.
2. Tibble, 2018, pp. 200–2.
3. Riley-Smith, 2012, pp. 29–31.
4. Barber, 1994, pp. 79–85; Riley-Smith, 1969, pp. 278–88.
5. Tibble, 2018, pp. 200–4; Barber, 2012, p. 198; Riley-Smith, 1969, pp. 278–88.
6. Barber, 1994, p. 83.
7. WT II, p. 214; Barber, 2012, p. 199.
8. WT II, p. 214; Lewis, 2017, pp. 170–3.
9. Daftary, 2005, pp. 153–4; Daftary, 2007, p. 352.
10. Joinville, p. 257; see also William of Newburgh, pp. 364–5.
11. Lewis, 2017, pp. 170–2.
12. Willey, 2005, pp. 43–4; Lewis, 2003, p. 129.

Chapter 13

1. Hillenbrand, 2022a, pp. 340–1.
2. Daftary, 2012, pp. 144–5.
3. Kamal al-Din, in Lewis, 1966, p. 231; Daftary, 2007, pp. 367–8; Hillenbrand, 2022a, pp. 338–42; Lewis, 2003, pp. 110–12; Hodgson, 1955, pp. 185–6; Mirza, 1997, pp. 22–36.
4. Kamal al-Din, in Lewis, 1966, p. 231.
5. Kamal al-Din, in Lewis, 1966, p. 231.
6. Kamal al-Din, in Lewis, 1966, pp. 231–2; Lewis, 2003, pp. 71–2.
7. Kamal al-Din, in Lewis, 1966, pp. 231–2.

8. Kamal al-Din, in Lewis, 1966, p. 232; Lewis, 2003, pp. 110–11; Mirza, 1997, pp. 26–7.
9. Kamal al-Din, in Lewis, 1966, p. 229.
10. Kamal al-Din, in Lewis, 1966, p. 231; Daftary, 2007, pp. 367–8.
11. Daftary, 2005, p. 154.
12. Willey, 2005, pp. 230–1.
13. Daftary, 2007, p. 368; Lewis, 1966, p. 248.
14. Hillenbrand, 2022a, p. 341; Mirza, 1997, pp. 27–8. See Edgington, 1996 for a fascinating paper on communications by pigeon in the crusades.
15. Abu Firas, quoted in Hillenbrand, 2022a, p. 338.
16. Hillenbrand, 2022a, pp. 340–1.
17. Hodgson, 1955, pp. 196–7.
18. Buckley, 1984, pp. 137–65; Daftary, 2007, pp. 370–1.
19. Rashid al-Din, quoted in Buckley, 1984, pp. 142–3.
20. Buckley, 1984, p. 143.
21. Rashid al-Din, quoted in Buckley, 1984, p. 143.
22. Hamilton, 2000, pp. 72–3; Lewis, 1966, pp. 239–42; Lewis, 2003, p. 111; Daftary, 2007, p. 371.
23. Kamal al-Din, in Lewis, 1966, pp. 230 and 239–42; Ibn Nazif, p. 90.
24. Lewis, 1966, p. 240.
25. WT II, pp. 391–2.
26. John Phocas, in *Jerusalem Pilgrimage, 1099–1185*, p. 317. His trip was in 1185.
27. Benjamin of Tudela, pp. 16–17.
28. Benjamin of Tudela, pp. 17 and 53–4.
29. Daftary, 2005, pp. 162–3.
30. Kamal al-Din, in Lewis, 2003, p. 111; Kamal al-Din in Lewis, 1966, pp. 230 and 241–4; Mirza, 1997, pp. 30–1.
31. Willey, 2005, p. 46.
32. Al-Husayn (or al-Hasan), quoted in Lewis, 1966, pp. 230–1 and 251–3; Mirza, 1997, pp. 28–30.
33. WT II, p. 391.
34. *Crusader Syria*, p. 35.
35. Kamal al-Din, in Lewis, 1966, pp. 234 and 253–4. The original verses are by Abu Tammam al-Ta'i (d.845 or 846).
36. Bar Hebraeus, p. 343.
37. John Phocas, in *Jerusalem Pilgrimage, 1099–1185*, p. 317.
38. Arnold of Lübeck, p. 162.
39. Arnold of Lübeck, p. 162.
40. The letter of Burchard of Strasbourg (1175) is quoted at length in Arnold of Lübeck, pp. 272–83. This quote is from Arnold of Lübeck, pp. 280–1.
41. Arnold of Lübeck, pp. 280–1.
42. WT II, p. 391.
43. Lewis, 2003, pp. 129–31.

Chapter 14

1. *The Templars – Selected Sources*, p. 74.
2. WT II, p. 391; *The Templars – Selected Sources*, p. 74. For William of Tyre's intelligence-gathering role in the multiple invasions of Egypt, see Tibble, 2020, pp. 204–5.

3. *The Templars – Selected Sources*, p. 75.
4. WT II, p. 392; *The Templars – Selected Sources*, p. 75.
5. WT II, pp. 392–3.
6. WT II, p. 393.
7. WT II, p. 393.
8. WT II, p. 393; *The Templars – Selected Sources*, p. 76.
9. Hamilton, 2000, p. 74; Forey, 2002, p. 11. For the killing of the Assassins' envoys, see also: Hamilton, 2007, pp. 13–24; Edbury, 2007, pp. 25–38; Barber, 1994, pp. 100–5; Barber, 2012, pp. 259–60; Daftary, 2007, pp. 368–9; Mirza, 1997, pp. 38–9.
10. Walter Map, in *The Templars – Selected Sources*, pp. 76–7.
11. WT II, pp. 298 and 300.
12. Ellenblum, 2007, p. 177.
13. WT II, p. 312.
14. WT II, p. 297.
15. WT II, p. 312.
16. Fulton, 2022, pp. 82–101 and 114.
17. Barber, 1994, p. 105.
18. WT II, p. 394.
19. WT II, p. 394.
20. Michael the Syrian, p. 638.
21. Hamilton, 2000, pp. 70–5.
22. Barber, 2012, pp. 259–60.

Chapter 15

1. See Lewis, 2005, pp. 131–7 for a discussion of the sources for Saladin's relationship with the Assassins; Beben, 2017, pp. 1–23.
2. Abu Firas, quoted in Hillenbrand, 2022a, p. 343; Daftary, 2007, p. 369; Hodgson, 1955, pp. 187–8.
3. Tibble, 2018, pp. 293–4; Lewis, 2003, pp. 112–15; Hillenbrand, 2022a, pp. 343–4.
4. For the 1174 conspiracy, see: Hamilton, 2000, p. 81; Lewis, 2003, pp. 114–15; Lewis, 2005, pp. 134–5; Eddé, 2011, p. 58; L&J, pp. 66–7; Phillips, 2019, pp. 83–5.
5. Lewis, 2003, pp. 113–15; Lewis, 2005, pp. 133–4; Hillenbrand, 2022a, pp. 343–4.
6. L&J, pp. 87–8.
7. IA II, p. 234.
8. IA II, p. 234.
9. L&J, pp. 86–8.
10. Lewis, 2003, pp. 113–15; Lewis, 2005, pp. 131–7; Phillips, 2019, pp. 102–3; Daftary, 2007, pp. 369–70; Eddé, 2011, pp. 71–2.
11. L&J, pp. 86–8.
12. Kamal al-Din, in Lewis, 1966, pp. 230 and 238–9.
13. Kamal al-Din, in Lewis, 1966, p. 234.
14. Lewis, 1966, pp. 234–5.

15. Lewis, 1966, p. 235; Lewis, 2003, pp. 115–16. Other, slightly different versions of this letter also exist. Aspects of its authenticity and dating are the subject of scholarly debate. See Lewis, 1966, pp. 254–7.
16. IA II, p. 243.
17. IA II, p. 243.
18. IA II, p. 243; Hillenbrand, 2022a, p. 346.
19. Ibn Wasil, quoted in Hillenbrand, 2022a, p. 346; Phillips, 2019, pp. 110–11.
20. Imad al-Din, quoted in L&J, p. 106.
21. Ibn Abi Tayy, quoted in L&J, p. 106; Michael the Syrian, p. 711; Daftary, 2007, p. 370.
22. Phillips, 2019, pp. 110–11; Hillenbrand, 2022a, p. 346; Lewis, 2003, pp. 113–14.
23. IA II, p. 249; Michael the Syrian, p. 711.
24. Kamal al-Din, in Lewis, 1966, p. 236.
25. Kamal al-Din, in Lewis, 1966, p. 236.
26. Kamal al-Din, in Lewis, 1966, p. 236.
27. Kamal al-Din, in Lewis, 1966, p. 236.
28. Lewis, 1966, pp. 258–9; Hamilton, 2000, p. 108.
29. Kamal al-Din, in Lewis, 1966, pp. 258–9; Hamilton, 2000, p. 108.
30. Kamal al-Din, in Lewis, 1966, p. 236.
31. Lewis, 1966, pp. 236–7 and 259–67; Lewis, 2003, pp. 116–17.
32. Hamilton, 2000, pp. 106–8; L&J, pp. 108–9. Lewis, 2005, p. 132 suggests the siege of Masyaf started on 30 July.
33. IA II, p. 249.
34. Hamilton, 2000, p. 107; Phillips, 2019, pp. 111–12; Lewis, 2003, p. 115; Lewis, 2005, pp. 135–6; Daftary, 2007, p. 370; Hillenbrand, 2022a, pp. 346–7; Mirza, 1997, pp. 31–6.
35. L&J, p. 128.
36. L&J, pp. 193–4.
37. L&J, pp. 133–4.
38. L&J, pp. 161–3.
39. L&J, pp. 171–2.
40. Ibn Jubayr, p. 284.
41. IA II, p. 255; Daftary, 2007, p. 370; Lewis, 2003, p. 117; L&J, p. 126.
42. L&J, p. 131.

Chapter 16

1. IA II, p. 253. See Phillips, 2019, pp. 116–22.
2. Nicholson, 2004, p. 48; Ralph of Diceto, I, pp. 423–4.
3. IA II, p. 253; Tibble, 2018, pp. 300–13; Ehrlich, 2013, pp. 94–105.
4. Tibble, 2023, pp. 92–4; Ehrlich, 2013, pp. 94–105.
5. WT II, pp. 442–3.
6. Schenk, 2010, pp. 44–5 and 48–9; Ellenblum, 2007, pp. 258–74; Raphael, 2023. Note that Chastellet, despite causing Saladin and his advisers much consternation, was much further away from Damascus than Banyas – the latter's strategic position was clear to all parties, and explains its central role in the frontier fighting from 1128 until it was captured by Nur al-Din in 1164.

7. Barber, 2012, pp. 271–3; Tibble, 2020, pp. 246–54.
8. Walter the Chancellor, p. 126; Tibble, 2020, pp. 283–5.
9. Barber, 2008, pp. 111–19. A further ten knights were Hospitaller brothers.
10. Arnold of Lübeck, p. 139.
11. IA II, p. 319; Tibble, 2020, pp. 1–7; Barber, 2012, pp. 297–9; Pringle, 2001, pp. 231–40; Edbury, 2011, pp. 45–60.
12. *Chronicle of the Third Crusade*, p. 25.
13. *Chronicle of the Third Crusade*, p. 26.
14. *Chronicle of the Third Crusade*, p. 26.
15. *Chronicle of the Third Crusade*, p. 26.
16. *Chronicle of the Third Crusade*, p. 26; *The Conquest of the Holy Land*, pp. 126–31.
17. Rother, 2014, pp. 185–6; Nicholson, 2014, pp. 105–9.
18. *Letters*, p. 76.
19. Bernard of Clairvaux, *In Praise*, pp. 47–8; Rother, 2014, pp. 185–6.
20. Bernard of Clairvaux, *In Praise*, p. 48; Rother, 2014, pp. 185–6.
21. *The Conquest of Jerusalem*, pp. 160–2.
22. France, 2015, p. 99.
23. IA II, p. 322.
24. IA II, p. 323; L&J, p. 263.
25. France, 2015; Barber, 2012, pp. 302–6.
26. *Arab Historians*, pp. 82–3.
27. *Arab Historians*, p. 83.
28. *Letters*, p. 78.

Chapter 17

1. Ambroise, p. 150.
2. Ambroise, p. 151.
3. Ambroise, pp. 150–1.
4. Ambroise, p. 152; Barber, 2012, pp. 337–8 and 351–2.
5. Ambroise, pp. 152–3.
6. *Chronicle of the Third Crusade*, pp. 305–6.
7. Roger of Howden, *The Annals*, 2, p. 267; Roger of Howden, *Chronica*, 3, p. 181; Mitchell, 2004, p. 131.
8. Baha al-Din Ibn Shaddad, pp. 200–1; Ibn Nazif, p. 104.
9. Ambroise, p. 152 n.571.
10. Arnold of Lübeck, p. 162.
11. IA II, p. 396.
12. IA II, p. 397.
13. *The* Chronique d'Ernoul, 1, pp. 357–60 and 2, pp. 198–9; *Chronicle of the Third Crusade*, pp. 384–5; Croizy-Naquet, 2011, pp. 242–57; Daftary, 2007, pp. 372–3; Williams, 1970, pp. 381–9; Harari, 2007, pp. 91–108; L&J, pp. 348–9; Lewis, 1952, pp. 487–8; Mirza, 1997, pp. 36–7.
14. Bar Hebraeus, p. 339.
15. Lewis, 2003, pp. 117–18.
16. Ambroise, pp. 135–6.
17. L&J, pp. 359–60.

18. For Robert de Sablé, see: Tibble, 2023, pp. 120–2; Barber, 2012, pp. 340–1; Barber, 1994, pp. 119 and 122–3.
19. Ambroise, p. 43; *Chronicle of the Third Crusade*, pp. 164–5.
20. Ambroise, p. 43 and n.75. Frustratingly, we know far more about Robert as a lord in Anjou than as a Templar master. Even the year of his death is not entirely clear – it is possible that he died on 28 September 1192.
21. Baha al-Din Ibn Shaddad, pp. 243–4; Phillips, 2019, pp. 301–3.
22. Bar Hebraeus, p. 343. Most sources report that the Old Man died in Masyaf. Some sources, and an enduring legend, however, suggest that he died in Kahf, where visitors are still shown his alleged tomb. At this distance, it is impossible to be sure. Willey, 2005, p. 227; Mirza, 1997, p. 39.
23. Al-Husayn, in Lewis, 1966, pp. 230–1 and 244–9.
24. Al-Husayn, in Lewis, 1966, pp. 230–1 and 250–3.
25. Daftary, 2007, p. 373.

Chapter 18

1. Lewis, 2003, p. 119; Daftary, 2007, p. 389.
2. Daftary, 2007, p. 389.
3. Bar Hebraeus, p. 366.
4. Daftary, 2005, pp. 158–9.
5. *The* Chronique d'Ernoul, 1, pp. 23 and 394–5 and 2, pp. 24 and 209; Lewis, 2003, p. 5; Willey, 2005, p. 234; Williams, 1970, pp. 381–9. Note that the episode with Henry appears only in the Ernoul/Eracles account of events and should be treated with appropriate caution.
6. Wilbrand of Oldenburg, in *Pilgrimage to Jerusalem*, pp. 68–9. Wilbrand was in the area in 1211–12.
7. That is, the Cathedral of Our Lady of Tortosa. Oliver of Paderborn, pp. 91–2.
8. Riley-Smith, 2012, p. 91; Lewis, 2003, p. 119; Daftary, 2007, p. 389; Daftary, 2005, p. 157.
9. Oliver of Paderborn, pp. 91–2; Humphreys, 1977, p. 137.
10. *Pilgrimage to Jerusalem*, p. 132.
11. Daftary, 2007, p. 390; Mirza, 1997, pp. 48–9.
12. Muhammad al-Hamawi, quoted in Lewis, 2003, pp. 119–20; Ibn Nazif, pp. 167–8 and 172.
13. Daftary, 2007, p. 390.
14. Daftary, 2005, pp. 157–8; Daftary, 2007, p. 390.
15. *Matthew Paris's English History*, I, pp. 131–2.
16. *Matthew Paris's English History*, I, p. 132.
17. *Pilgrimage to Jerusalem*, p. 200.

Chapter 19

1. Riley-Smith, 2014, pp. 197–207 and 216–23.
2. Oliver of Paderborn, pp. 91–2.
3. *Matthew Paris's English History*, I, p. 63.
4. *Matthew Paris's English History*, I, pp. 62–3; Matthew Paris, *Chronica Majora*, III, pp. 404–6; Nicholson, 1992, pp. 68–85.

5. *Letters*, pp. 140–2.
6. *Letters*, pp. 142–6; *Crusader Syria*, p. 133; Berkovich, 2011, pp. 9–44; Lotan, 2012, pp. 53–67. The losses were so great that the military capacity of the Latin East never fully recovered from the debacle.
7. Tyerman, 1988, pp. 108–10; Tyerman, 2006, pp. 770–802.
8. Joinville, p. 200.
9. Joinville, p. 200.
10. *Matthew Paris's English History*, II, pp. 366–73.
11. Joinville, p. 200. Joinville's inference that the Templars pushed their way through the town, but then retraced their steps into Mansurah to help others who had become bogged down in the fighting, is confirmed by Muslim sources – conversation with Mohamad El-Merheb on the subject of Ibn al-Khazrajī, *Tārīkh dawlat al-Akrād wa-al-Atrāk*, Istanbul, Suleymaniye, MS Hekimoglu 695.
12. Lewis, 2003, pp. 5–6 and 120–1; Daftary, 2007, pp. 390–1; Willey, 2005, p. 234; Mirza, 1997, pp. 51–3. At the time, the Assassins were probably led by Taj al-Din Abu'l-Futuh, the 'Old Man' whose name is mentioned in an inscription at Masyaf dated February–March 1249.
13. Joinville, p. 256.
14. Joinville, p. 257.
15. Joinville, p. 257.
16. Joinville, p. 257.
17. Joinville, p. 257.
18. Joinville, pp. 257–8.
19. Joinville, p. 258.
20. Joinville, p. 258.
21. Joinville, p. 258.
22. Daftary, 2005, pp. 158–9.
23. Joinville, p. 258. The talks probably took place at Masyaf, but possibly at one of their other castles in the Jabal Bahra, such as Kahf. See Willey, 2005, p. 234.
24. *Crusader Syria*, p. 109.
25. Joinville, p. 258.
26. Joinville, p. 258.
27. Joinville, pp. 208 and 258–9.
28. Bar Hebraeus, p. 343.
29. Al-Umari, p. 46.
30. Joinville, p. 259.
31. Joinville, p. 259.
32. Joinville, p. 259.
33. *Crusader Syria*, p. 35.
34. Joinville, pp. 208 and 369–70 n.1.
35. Joinville, p. 292.
36. Joinville, pp. 292–3.

Chapter 20

1. IA III, p. 307.
2. IA III, pp. 307–8.
3. IA III, p. 202.

4. *Crusader Syria*, pp. 62–3.
5. IA III, pp. 230–1.
6. Lewis, 2003, pp. 89–90.
7. Jackson, 2017, pp. 74 and 91; Daftary, 2007, pp. 382–3; Lewis, 2003, pp. 90–1; May, 2004, pp. 231–9.
8. Jackson, 2017, pp. 125–6.
9. Daftary, 2007, p. 391; Lewis, 2003, p. 91.
10. William of Rubruck, p. 222; Jackson, 2017, p. 126.
11. See Morton, 2022 for an excellent overview of the Mongol campaigns.
12. Daftary, 2007, pp. 391–4; Lewis, 2003, pp. 91–3.
13. Daftary, 2007, pp. 394–6; Jackson, 2017, p. 127.
14. Juwayni, p. 666.
15. Daftary, 2007, p. 396.
16. Juwayni, pp. 722–3; Lewis, 2003, p. 93.
17. Daftary, 2007, p. 397.
18. Juwayni, pp. 724–5; Lewis, 2003, pp. 94–5.
19. Juwayni, p. 723; Mirza, 1997, pp. 53–8.
20. Juwayni, pp. 723–4.
21. Juwayni, pp. 723–4; Daftary, 2007, p. 397. Despite the Mongols' undoubted enthusiasm, there was some level of Ismaili continuity in Persia, albeit in a non-politicised or demilitarised sense. See Jamal, 2002.
22. Lewis, 2003, pp. 89–90; Jackson, 2017, p. 128.
23. *Letters*, p. 158; Morton, 2022, p. 163.
24. Lewis, 2003, pp. 89–90; Jackson, 2017, p. 128.
25. Daftary, 2007, pp. 398–9; Jackson, 2017, pp. 130–1.
26. Jackson, 2017, pp. 131–2.
27. Jackson, 2017, p. 132.
28. Jackson, 2005, p. 176; Jackson, 2017, pp. 41 and 168–9.
29. Jackson, 2017, pp. 132–3.
30. Daftary, 2007, pp. 399–400.
31. Jackson, 2017, p. 133.
32. Daftary, 2007, pp. 401–2; Lewis, 2003, pp. 121–2; Hodgson, 1955, pp. 272–3; Mirza, 1997, pp. 59–63.
33. Daftary, 2007, pp. 399–400.
34. Ibn ʿAbd al-Zahir, pp. 574–5; Thorau, 1992, pp. 164–5.
35. Ibn al-Furat, pp. 98, 100 and 104; Lewis, 2003, p. 121; Holt, 1995, pp. 34–40 and 48–57. For the Muslim sources for Baybars's relationship with the Assassins, see Lewis, 1952, p. 488.
36. Ibn al-Furat, p. 140; Daftary, 2007, p. 400.
37. Ibn al-Furat, p. 140; Lewis, 2003, p. 122; Daftary, 2007, pp. 400–1.
38. Ibn al-Furat, p. 146; Lewis, 2003, pp. 122–3; Daftary, 2007, p. 401.
39. Daftary, 2005, pp. 159–60; Daftary, 2007, p. 401; Lewis, 2003, pp. 122–3.
40. Irwin, 1989, p. 237.
41. Daftary, 2007, p. 402; Mirza, 1997, pp. 59–63.
42. *TTT*, p. 68; Ibn ʿAbd al-Zahir, pp. 776–7; Prestwich, 1997, pp. 77–9; Beebe, 1971, pp. 82–4; Lloyd, 1984, pp. 120–33; Tibble, 2023, pp. 197–204.
43. *TTT*, p. 69.
44. *TTT*, p. 69.

45. *TTT*, p. 69.
46. Edgington, 2023, pp. 177–8.
47. Ibn al-Furat, p. 159. See dear Jonathan Riley-Smith's characteristically masterly footnotes on p. 244. You can still hear the great man's voice.
48. *TTT*, p. 69. Ibn ʿAbd al-Zahir, pp. 776–7.
49. Edgington, 2023, pp. 186–90.
50. Irwin, 1989, pp. 234–6; Daftary, 2005, pp. 159–60; Daftary, 2007, pp. 401–2; Lewis, 2003, pp. 123–4.
51. Holt, 1995, pp. 108 and 116.
52. Ibn Battuta, pp. 106–7; Daftary, 2007, pp. 400–2.
53. Al-Umari, p. 45.

Chapter 21

1. *TTT*, pp. 50–1 and 51 n.2; Ibn ʿAbd al-Zahir, pp. 587–600.
2. *TTT*, p. 51.
3. *TTT*, p. 51; Barbé, 2015, pp. 45–84.
4. *TTT*, p. 36.
5. *TTT*, p. 36.
6. *TTT*, pp. 36–7; *Crusader Syria*, p. 142; Barber, 1994, pp. 158 and 187–8.
7. *Letters*, pp. 162–3.
8. *TTT*, pp. 98–101; Marshall, 1992, pp. 232–4.
9. *TTT*, pp. 110–11.
10. *TTT*, p. 111.
11. *TTT*, pp. 111–12.
12. *TTT*, p. 112.
13. *TTT*, pp. 112–13.
14. *TTT*, p. 114.
15. *TTT*, pp. 116–17; Barber, 2006, p. 7.
16. Barber, 1994, pp. 163 and 177–8.

Chapter 22

1. Barber, 1981, pp. 1–17.
2. The Templars attempted, but failed, to regain the offensive from time to time, for instance through their disastrous intervention on the isolated island of Ruad in 1302. Barber, 1994, pp. 286 and 293–4.
3. *The Templars – Selected Sources*, p. 244; Barber, 2006, pp. 59–60.
4. Barber, 2006, p. 60.
5. It is worth noting that in Cyprus, where the Templars who were on active service were stationed, there was no torture and, not coincidentally, no confessions. Importantly, those lay witnesses brought forward, even those who had been opposed to the Templars in the recent political upheavals, refused to endorse the charges.
6. Barber, 2006, pp. 69–72.
7. Barber, 2006, pp. 93–4.
8. Barber, 2006, p. 160.
9. *TTT*, pp. 180–1.

10. Barber, 2006, p. 282; Luttrell, 2015, pp. 365–72.
11. Walker, 2010, pp. 347–57; Walker, 2017, pp. 360–71.
12. See Barber, 1994, pp. 314–34.
13. See the excellent case studies in MacLellan, 2019; Elliott, 2017, pp. 132–82; Cassidy-Welch, 2023, pp. 87–8. For medieval western views of the Assassins, see Pagès, 2014.
14. Tibble, 2018, pp. 67–98; Tibble, 2023, pp. 281–95.
15. Marco Polo, pp. 33–6.
16. Marco Polo, pp. 33–6.
17. Marco Polo, pp. 33–6.
18. Marco Polo, pp. 33–6.
19. Marco Polo, pp. 33–6.
20. Daftary, 2005, pp. 33–5 and 46–8; Daftary, 2013, pp. 5–16.
21. Daftary, 2006, pp. 71–3.
22. Hammer, 1818; Daftary, 2006, pp. 77–81.
23. Horswell, 2022, pp. 48–51.
24. Horswell, 2022, pp. 51–2.
25. Horswell, 2022, pp. 52–3.
26. Bosman, 2016, pp. 6–8; Horswell, 2021, pp. 75–94. This also has echoes in the way they are handled in the *Kingdom of Heaven*.
27. Bosman, 2016, pp. 13–14.
28. Horswell, 2022, pp. 58–60.
29. Chirilă, 2021, p. 54; Horswell, 2022, pp. 51–2; Buzay and Buzay, 2015, pp. 119–22.
30. Buzay and Buzay, 2015, pp. 114–15.
31. Buzay and Buzay, 2015, pp. 117–18.
32. Bosman, 2016, pp. 23–4.
33. Horswell, 2022, pp. 54–5; Brown, 2013, pp. 227–8 and 237–8. For the meta-history of the Templars, see also: Walker, 2012, pp. 439–47; Wood, 2012, pp. 449–60.
34. Buzay and Buzay, 2015, pp. 124–8.
35. Brown, 2013, pp. 237–8.
36. Brown, 2013, pp. 237–8.

Chapter 23

1. Lewis, 2003, pp. 139–40.

References and Further Reading

Primary sources

Abu Firas, French trans. Stanislas Guyard, 'Un grand maître des Assassins au temps de Saladin', *Journal Asiatique*, 7:9 (1877), pp. 387–489

Albert of Aachen, *Historia Ierosolimitana*, ed. and tr. S.B. Edgington, Oxford, 2007

Ambroise, *The History of the Holy War*, ed. and tr. M. Ailes and M. Barber, 2 vols, Woodbridge, 2003

Arab Historians of the Crusades, comp. and tr. F. Gabrieli, tr. from the Italian by E.J. Costello, Berkeley and Los Angeles, 1969

Arnold of Lübeck, *The Chronicle of Arnold of Lübeck*, tr. G.A. Loud, Crusade Texts in Translation, Abingdon, 2019

Baha al-Din Ibn Shaddad, *The Rare and Excellent History of Saladin*, tr. D.S. Richards, Crusade Texts in Translation, 7, Aldershot, 2001

Bar Hebraeus, Gregory, called Abu'l Farag, *Chronography*, tr. E.A.R. Budge, Amsterdam, 1932

Benjamin of Tudela, *The Itinerary of Benjamin of Tudela*, tr. M.N. Adler, London, 1907

Bernard of Clairvaux, *Sancti Bernardi opera*, vol. 3, ed. J. Leclercq, Rome, 1963

—— *In Praise of the New Knighthood*, tr. M.C. Greenia, Piscataway, NJ, 2010

Cartulaire général de l'Ordre du Temple 1119?–1150: Recueil des chartes et des bulles relatives à l'ordre du Temple, ed. Marquis d'Albon, Paris, 1913

Chronicle of the Third Crusade: A translation of the Itinerarium Peregrinorum et Gesta Regis Ricardi, tr. H. Nicholson, Crusade Texts in Translation, 3, Aldershot, 1997

The Chronique d'Ernoul *and the* Colbert-Fontainebleau Continuation *of William of Tyre*, vols 1 & 2, ed. Peter Edbury and Massimiliano Gaggero, Leiden, 2023

The Conquest of Jerusalem and the Third Crusade: Sources in Translation, tr. P.W. Edbury, Aldershot, 1996

The Conquest of the Holy Land by Salah al-Din – A critical edition and translation of the anonymous Libellus de expugnatione Terrae Sanctae per Saladinum, ed. K. Brewer and J.H. Kane, London, 2019

REFERENCES AND FURTHER READING

Crusader Syria in the Thirteenth Century: The Rothelin *Continuation of the* History of William of Tyre *with part of the* Eracles *or* Acre *text*, tr. J. Shirley, Crusade Texts in Translation, 5, Aldershot, 1999

De Constructione Castri Saphet: Construction et fonctions d'un château fort franc en Terre Sainte, ed. R.B.C. Huygens, Amsterdam, 1981

Fulcher of Chartres, *A History of the Expedition to Jerusalem, 1095–1127*, tr. F. Ryan, ed. H. Fink, Knoxville, 1969

Ibn ʿAbd al-Zahir, 'A critical edition of an unknown Arabic source for the life of *al-Malik al-Ẓāhir Baibars*', vol. 2, ed. A.A. Khuwaytir, Unpublished PhD thesis, London University, 1960

Ibn al-Athir, *The Annals of the Saljuq Turks: Selections from al-Kāmil fi'l-Ta'rīkh of ʿIzz al-Dīn Ibn al-Athīr*, tr. D.S. Richards, Abingdon, 2002

— *The Chronicle of Ibn al-Athir for the Crusading Period from al-Kamil fi'l-Ta'rıkh*, parts 1, 2 and 3, tr. D.S. Richards, Aldershot, 2006, 2007, 2008

Ibn Battuta, *The Travels of Ibn Battuta, A.D. 1325–1354*, vol. 1, tr. H.A.R. Gibb, Cambridge, 1958

Ibn al-Furat, *Ayyubids, Mamlukes and Crusaders: Selections from the Tārīkh al-duwal wa'l-Mulūk of Ibn al-Furāt*, vol. 2, ed. and tr. U. Lyons, M.C. Lyons and J.S.C. Riley-Smith, Cambridge, 1971

Ibn Jubayr, *The Travels of Ibn Jubayr*, tr. R.J.C. Broadhurst, London, 1952

Ibn al-Qalanisi, *The Damascus Chronicle of the Crusades*, tr. H.A.R. Gibb, London, 1932

Ibn Nazif, *Ibn Naẓīf's World-History: Al-Tā'rīkh al-Manṣūrī*, tr. D. Cook, Abingdon, 2021

James of Vitry, *The Exempla*, ed. T.F. Crane, London, 1890

— *History of Jerusalem*, tr. A. Stewart, Palestine Pilgrims' Text Society, London, 1896

Jerusalem Pilgrimage, 1099–1185, tr. J. Wilkinson, Hakluyt Society, series II, 167, London, 1988

John Kinnamos, *The Deeds of John and Manuel Comnenus*, tr. C.M. Brand, Records of Civilization, Sources and Studies, 95, New York, 1976

John of Salisbury, *The Statesman's Book of John of Salisbury*, tr. J. Dickinson, New York, 1927

— *The* Historia Pontificalis *of John of Salisbury*, ed. M. Chibnall, London, 1956

Joinville and Villehardouin, *Chronicles of the Crusades*, tr. C. Smith, London, 2008

Juwayni, *The History of the World-Conqueror*, tr. J.A. Boyle, Manchester, 1997

Kamal al-Din, 'Extraits de la Chronique d'Alep par Kemal ed-Din', in *RHC Or*, vol. 3, Paris, 1872, pp. 571–690

Letters from the East: Crusaders, pilgrims and settlers in the 12th–13th centuries, tr. M. Barber and K. Bate, Crusade Texts in Translation, 18, Farnham, 2010

Marco Polo, *The Description of the World*, tr. S. Kinoshita, Indianapolis, IN, 2016

Matthew of Edessa, *Armenia and the Crusades. Tenth to the Twelfth Centuries: The Chronicle of Matthew of Edessa*, tr. A. Dostourian, Lanham, MD, 1993

Matthew Paris, *Matthew Paris's English History*, 2 vols, tr. J.A. Giles, London, 1852 and 1853

— *Chronica Majora*, ed. H. Richards Luard, Rolls Series, 57, 7 vols, London, 1872–83

Michael the Syrian, *The Syriac Chronicle of Michael Rabo (The Great): A universal history from the creation*, tr. M. Moosa, Teaneck, NJ, 2014

REFERENCES AND FURTHER READING

Mukaddasi, *Description of Syria, including Palestine*, tr. G. le Strange, Palestine Pilgrims' Text Society, 3, London, 1886

Odo of Deuil, *De profectione Ludovici VII in Orientem*, ed. and tr. V.G. Berry, New York, 1948

Oliver of Paderborn, *Capture of Damietta*, in E. Peters (ed.), *Christian Society and the Crusades, 1198–1229*, Philadelphia, PA, 1971

Orderic Vitalis, *Ecclesiastical History*, vol. VI, ed. and tr. M. Chibnall, Oxford, 1978

Pilgrimage to Jerusalem and the Holy Land, 1187–1291, tr. D. Pringle, Crusade Texts in Translation, 23, Abingdon, 2012

Ralph of Diceto, *The Historical Works of Master Ralph de Diceto*, ed. W. Stubbs, 2 vols, Rolls Series, 68, London, 1876

Richard of Poitou, *Chronica*, in MGH SS, vol. XXVI

Roger of Howden, *The Annals of Roger de Hoveden*, tr. H. Riley, vol. 2, London, 1853

— *Chronica*, vols 1–3, ed. W. Stubbs, Rolls Series, 51, London, 1869

The Rule of the Templars: The French text of the Rule of the Order of the Knights Templar, tr. J.M. Upton-Ward, Woodbridge, 1992

The Templars – Selected Sources, tr. M. Barber and K. Bate, Manchester Medieval Sources, Manchester, 2002

al-Umari, *Egypt and Syria in the Early Mamluk Period: An extract from Ibn Faḍl Allāh Al-'Umarī's Masālik Al-Abṣār Fī Mamālik Al-Amṣār*, ed. D.S. Richards, Abingdon, 2017

Usama ibn-Munqidh, *The Book of Contemplation*, tr. P.M. Cobb, London, 2008

Walter the Chancellor, *The Antiochene Wars*, tr. T.S. Asbridge and S.B. Edgington, Crusade Texts in Translation, 4, Aldershot, 1999

Walter Map, *De Nugis Curialium or Courtiers' Trifles*, tr. M.R. James, rev. C.N.L. Brooke and R.A.B. Mynors, Oxford, 1983

William of Newburgh, *Historia Rerum Anglicarum*, in R. Howlett (ed.), *Chronicles and Memorials of the Reigns of Stephen, Henry II and Richard I*, vol. 4, Rolls Series, 82, London, 1884

William of Rubruck, *The Mission of Friar William of Rubruck: His journey to the Court of the Great Khan Möngke 1253–1255*, Hakluyt Society, 2nd series, 173, Cambridge, 1990

William of Tyre, *A History of Deeds Done Beyond the Sea*, tr. E.A. Babcock and A.C. Krey, 2 vols, Records of Civilization, Sources and Studies, 35, New York, 1943

Secondary sources

Asbridge, T., *The Creation of the Principality of Antioch, 1098–1130*, Woodbridge, 2000

— 'How the crusades could have been won: King Baldwin II of Jerusalem's campaigns against Aleppo (1124–5) and Damascus (1129)', *Journal of Medieval Military History*, XI (2013), pp. 89–91

Barbé, H., 'Safed (Zefat), Jerusalem Street: Crusader-period remains in the vicinity of the castle', *'Atiqot*, 81 (2015), pp. 45–84

Barber, M., 'Lepers, Jews and Moslems: The plot to overthrow Christendom in 1321', *History*, 66:216 (1981), pp. 1–17

— 'Supplying the crusader states: The role of the Templars', in B.Z. Kedar (ed.), *The Horns of Hattin*, London, 1992, pp. 314–26

REFERENCES AND FURTHER READING

— *The New Knighthood: A history of the Order of the Temple*, Cambridge, 1994
— *The Trial of the Templars*, 2nd edn, Cambridge, 2006
— 'The reputation of Gerard of Ridefort', in J. Upton-Ward (ed.), *The Military Orders*, Vol. 4: *On Land and by Sea*, Aldershot, 2008, pp. 111–19
— 'The challenge of state building in the twelfth century: The crusader states in Palestine and Syria', *Reading Medieval Studies*, 36 (2010), pp. 7–22
— *The Crusader States*, London, 2012
Beben, D., 'Remembering Saladin: The crusades and the politics of heresy in Persian historiography', *Journal of the Royal Asiatic Society*, Series 3, 28:2 (2017), pp. 1–23
Beebe, B., 'Edward I and the crusades', Unpublished PhD Thesis, University of St Andrews, 1971
Bennett, M., 'La Règle du Temple as a military manual or how to deliver a cavalry charge', in *The Rule of the Templars: The French text of the Rule of the Order of the Knights Templar*, tr. J.M. Upton-Ward, Woodbridge, 1992, pp. 175–88
Berkovich, I., 'The Battle of Forbie and the Second Frankish Kingdom of Jerusalem', *Journal of Military History*, 75 (2011), pp. 9–44
Bosman, F.G., ' "Nothing is true, everything is permitted": The portrayal of the Nizari Isma'ilis in the *Assassin's Creed* game series', in S. Heidbrink and T. Knoll (eds), *Religion in Digital Games Respawned*, Heidelberg, 2016, pp. 6–26
Brown, H.J., 'The consolation of paranoia: Conspiracy, epistemology, and the Templars in *Assassin's Creed*, *Deus Ex*, and *Dragon Age*', in D.T. Kline (ed.), *Digital Gaming Re-imagines the Middle Ages*, London, 2014, pp. 227–39
Buckley, J.J., 'The Nizârî Ismâ'îlîtes' abolishment of the sharî'a during the "Great Resurrection" of 1164 A.D./559 A.H.', *Studia Islamica*, 60 (1984), pp. 137–65
Bulst-Thiele, M.L., 'The influence of St Bernard of Clairvaux on the formation of the Order of the Knights Templar', in M. Gervers (ed.), *The Second Crusade and the Cistercians*, New York, 1992, pp. 57–65
Burgtorf, J., 'The Templars and the kings of Jerusalem', in K. Borchardt, K. Döring, P. Josserand and H.J. Nicholson (eds), *The Templars and Their Sources*, Abingdon, 2017, pp. 25–37
Buzay, E.H. and E. Buzay, 'Neomedievalism and the epic in *Assassin's Creed*', in H. Young (ed.), *The Middle Ages in Popular Culture: Medievalism and Genre*, Amherst, NY, 2015
Cassidy-Welch, M., *Crusades and Violence*, Amsterdam, 2023
Chirilă, O.-A., ' "Show this fool knight what it is to have no fear": Freedom and oppression in *Assassin's Creed* (2007)', in R. Houghton (ed.), *Playing the Crusades*, Abingdon, 2021, pp. 53–70
Christie, N., 'Just a bunch of dirty stories? Women in the "memoirs" of Usamah ibn-Munqidh', in R. Allen (ed.), *Eastward Bound: Travel and travellers, 1050–1550*, Manchester, 2004, pp. 71–87
Cobb, P.M., *Usama ibn-Munqidh: Warrior poet of the age of crusades*, Oxford, 2005
— *The Race for Paradise: An Islamic history of the crusades*, Oxford, 2014
Cole, P.J., 'Christian perceptions of the Battle of Hattin (583/1187)', *Al-Masāq: Journal of the Medieval Mediterranean*, 6 (1993), pp. 9–39
Croizy-Naquet, C., 'Légende ou histoire? Les assassins dans l'Estoire de guerre sainte d'Ambroise et dans la Chronique d'Ernoul et de Bernard le Trésorier', *Le Moyen Age*, 2:CXVII (2011), pp. 237–57
Daftary, F., *The Assassin Legends*, London, 1994

REFERENCES AND FURTHER READING

—— *Ismailis in Medieval Muslim Societies*, London, 2005
—— 'The "Order of the Assassins": J. von Hammer and the orientalist misrepresentations of the Nizari Ismailis', *Iranian Studies*, 39:1 (2006), pp. 71–81
—— *The Ismāʿīlīs: Their history and doctrines*, 2nd edn, Cambridge, 2007
—— *Historical Dictionary of the Ismailis*, Lanham, MD, 2012
—— *A History of Shi'i Islam*, London, 2013
de Ayala Martínez, C., 'The *Sergents* of the Military Order of Santiago', in H.J. Nicholson (ed.), *The Military Orders*, Vol. 2: *Welfare and Warfare*, Aldershot, 1998, pp. 225–33
Dunbabin, J., 'The Maccabees as exemplars in the tenth and eleventh centuries', *Studies in Church History*, 4 (1985), pp. 31–41
Edbury, P.W., 'The Old French William of Tyre, the Templars and the assassin envoy', in K. Borchardt, N. Jaspert and H.J. Nicholson (eds), *The Hospitallers, The Mediterranean and Europe*, Aldershot, 2007, pp. 25–38
—— 'Gerard of Ridefort and the Battle of Le Cresson (1 May 1187): The developing narrative tradition', in Helen J. Nicholson (ed.), *On the Margins of Crusading: The military orders, the papacy and the Christian world*, Farnham, 2011, pp. 45–60
—— 'Knights, nobles and the rule of Amaury of Tyre, 1306–1310', *Epeterida*, 38 (2015), pp. 9–93
Eddé, A.-M., *Saladin*, London, 2011
Edgington, S.B., 'The doves of war: The part played by carrier pigeons in the crusades', in M. Balard (ed.), *Autour de la Première Croisade*, Paris, 1996, pp. 167–76
—— 'The attempted assassination of Lord Edward of England at Acre, 1272', in R.G. Khamisy, R.Y. Lewis and V.R. Shotten-Hallel (eds), *Exploring Outremer*, vol. I, Abingdon, 2023, pp. 177–90
Ehrlich, M., 'Saint Catherine's Day miracle: The Battle of Montgisard', *Journal of Medieval Military History*, XI (2013), pp. 94–105
Ellenblum, R., *Crusader Castles and Modern Histories*, Cambridge, 2007
Elliott, A.B.R., *Medievalism, Politics and Mass Media: Appropriating the Middle Ages in the twenty-first century*, Cambridge, 2017
Forey, A.J., *The Templars of the 'Corona de Aragón'*, Oxford, 1973
—— 'The military orders and the conversion of Muslims in the twelfth and thirteenth centuries', *Journal of Medieval History*, 28:1 (2002), pp. 1–22
France, J., *Hattin*, Oxford, 2015
—— 'Templar tactics: The order on the battlefield', in K. Borchardt, K. Döring, P. Josserand and H.J. Nicholson (eds), *The Templars and their Sources*, Abingdon, 2017, pp. 156–65
Fulton, M.S., *Contest for Egypt: The collapse of the Fatimid caliphate, the ebb of crusader influence, and the rise of Saladin*, Leiden, 2022
Gatti, I., 'The relationship between the Knights Templar and the kings of England: From the order's foundation to the reign of Edward', Unpublished PhD Thesis, Reading University, 2005
Gilmour-Bryson, A., 'Testimony of non-Templar witnesses in Cyprus', in M. Barber (ed.), *The Military Orders*, Vol. 1: *Fighting for the Faith and Caring for the Sick*, Abingdon, 1994, pp. 205–11
Grabois, A., 'Militia and malitia: The Bernardine vision of chivalry', in Michael Gervers (ed.), *The Second Crusade and the Cistercians*, New York, 1992, pp. 49–56

REFERENCES AND FURTHER READING

Hamilton, B., *The Leper King and his Heirs: Baldwin IV and the crusader Kingdom of Jerusalem*, Cambridge, 2000
— 'The Templars, the Syrian Assassins and King Amalric of Jerusalem', in K. Borchardt, N. Jaspert and H.J. Nicholson (eds), *The Hospitallers, The Mediterranean and Europe*, Aldershot, 2007, pp. 13–24
Hammer, J. von., *Die Geschichte der Assassins aus morgenländischen Quellen*, Stuttgart and Tübingen, 1818
Harari, Y.N., *Special Operations in the Age of Chivalry, 1100–1550*, Woodbridge, 2007
Hillenbrand, C., *The Crusades: Islamic perspectives*, Edinburgh, 1999
— 'The Assassins in fact and fiction: The Old Man of the Mountain', in *Islam and the Crusades: Collected papers*, Edinburgh, 2022a, pp. 334–51
— 'The power struggle between the Saljuqs and the Ismailis of Alamut, 487–518/1094–1124: The Saljuq perspective', in *The Medieval Turks: Collected papers*, Edinburgh, 2022b, pp. 145–62
Hodgson, M.G.S., *The Order of Assassins: The struggle of the early Nizârî Ismâî'lîs against the Islamic world*, The Hague, 1955
Holt, P.M., *Early Mamluk Diplomacy (1260–1290)*, Leiden, 1995
Horswell, M., 'Saladin and Richard the Lionheart: Entangled memories', in M. Horswell and K. Skottki (eds), *The Making of Crusading Heroes and Villains*, Abingdon, 2021, pp. 75–94
— 'Historicising *Assassin's Creed* (2007): Crusader medievalism, historiography and digital games for the classroom', in R. Houghton (ed.), *Using, Modding and Creating Games for Education and Impact*, Berlin, 2022
Humphreys, R.S., *From Saladin to the Mongols: The Ayyubids of Damascus, 1193–1260*, Albany, NY, 1977
Irwin, R., 'The image of the Byzantine and the Frank in Arab popular literature of the late Middle Ages', in B. Arbel, B. Hamilton and D. Jacoby (eds), *Latins and Greeks in the Eastern Mediterranean after 1204*, Abingdon, 1989, pp. 226–42
Jackson, P., *The Mongols and the West, 1221–1410*, London, 2005
— *The Mongols and the Islamic World: From conquest to conversion*, London, 2017
Jamal, N.E., *Surviving the Mongols: Nizārī Quhistānī and the continuity of Ismaili tradition in Persia*, London, 2002
Kennedy, H., *Crusader Castles*, Cambridge, 1994
— 'An historical overview', in C. Tonghini, *Shayzar I: The fortification of the citadel*, Leiden, 2012
Kirch, S., 'The Templars as *Milites Christi* and martyrs in God's Army (1180–1307)', in J. Burgtorf, S. Lotan and E. Mallorquí-Ruscalleda (eds), *The Templars: The rise, fall, and legacy of a military religious order*, Abingdon, 2021, pp. 81–102
Lapina, E., 'The Maccabees and the battle of Antioch', in G. Signori (ed.), *Dying for the Faith, Killing for the Faith: Old-Testament faith-warriors (1 and 2 Maccabees) in historical perspective*, Leiden, 2012, pp. 147–59
Lewis, B., 'The sources for the history of the Syrian Assassins', *Speculum*, 27 (1952), pp. 475–89
— 'Kamal al-Din's biography of Rasid al-Din Sinan', *Arabica*, 13 (1966), pp. 225–7
— *The Assassins: A radical sect in Islam*, London, 2003

REFERENCES AND FURTHER READING

— 'Saladin and the Assassins', in G.R. Hawting (comp.), *Muslims, Mongols and Crusaders: An anthology of articles published in the* Bulletin of the School of Oriental and African Studies, Abingdon, 2005, pp. 131–7

Lewis, K.J., *The Counts of Tripoli and Lebanon in the Twelfth Century: Sons of Saint-Gilles*, Abingdon, 2017

Lloyd, S., 'The Lord Edward's crusade of 1270–2', in J. Gillingham and J.C. Holt (eds), *War and Government in the Middle Ages*, Woodbridge, 1984, pp. 120–33

Lord, E., *The Knights Templar in Britain*, 2nd edn, Abingdon, 2013

Lotan, S., 'The battle of La Forbie (1244) and its aftermath: Re-examination of the military orders' involvement in the Latin kingdom of Jerusalem in the mid-thirteenth century', *Ordines Militares*, 17 (2012), pp. 53–67

Luttrell, A., 'The election of the Templar Master Jacques de Molay', in J. Burgtorf, P.F. Crawford and H.J. Nicholson (eds), *The Debate on the Trial of the Templars (1307–1314)*, Farnham, 2010, pp. 21–31

— 'Observations on the fall of the Temple', in P. Josserand, L.F. Oliveira and D. Carraz (eds), *Élites et ordres militaires au Moyen Âge: Rencontre autour d'Alain Demurger*, Madrid, 2015, pp. 365–72

Lyons, M.C. and D.E.P. Jackson, *Saladin: The politics of the Holy War*, Cambridge, 1982

MacLellan, R., 'Far-right appropriations of the medieval military orders', *The Medieval Journal*, 9:1 (2019), pp. 175–98

Mallett, A., 'The battle of Inab', *Journal of Medieval History*, 39 (2013), pp. 48–60

Marshall, C., *Warfare in the Latin East, 1192–1291*, Cambridge, 1992

May, T., 'A Mongol–Isma'ili alliance? Thoughts on the Mongols and Assassins', *Journal of the Royal Asiatic Society*, Series 3, 14:3 (2004), pp. 231–9

Mirza, N.A., *Syrian Ismailism: The ever-living line of the imamate, AD 1100–1260*, London, 1997

Mitchell, P.D., *Medicine in the Crusades: Warfare, wounds and the medieval surgeon*, Cambridge, 2004

Mitchell, P.D., Y. Nagar and R. Ellenblum, 'Weapon injuries in the 12th century crusader garrison of Vadum Iacob Castle, Galilee', *International Journal of Osteoarchaeology*, 16 (2006), pp. 145–55

Morton, N., 'The defence of the Holy Land and the memory of the Maccabees', *Journal of Medieval History*, 36 (2010), pp. 275–93

— 'Walls of defence for the House of Israel: Ezekiel 13:5 and the crusading movement', in E. Lapina and N. Morton (eds), *The Uses of the Bible in Crusader Sources*, Leiden, 2017, pp. 403–20

— *The Mongol Storm*, London, 2022

Nicholson, H., 'Steamy Syrian scandals: Matthew Paris on the Templars and Hospitallers', *Medieval History*, 2:2 (1992), pp. 68–85

— 'Before William of Tyre: European reports on the military orders' deeds in the east, 1150–1185', in H. Nicholson (ed.), *The Military Orders*, Vol. 2: *Welfare and Warfare*, Aldershot, 1998, pp. 111–18

— *The Knights Templar, 1120–1312*, Oxford, 2004

— '"*Martyrum collegio sociandus haberet*": Depictions of the military orders' martyrs in the Holy Land, 1187–1291', in S. John and N. Morton, *Crusading and Warfare in the Middle Ages*, London, 2014, pp. 101–18

REFERENCES AND FURTHER READING

— 'The Rule of the Temple and the military-religious orders', in J.D. Hosler and D.P. Franke (eds), *Routledge Handbook of Medieval Military Strategy*, London, 2024, pp. 197–207

Pagès, M., *From Martyr to Murderer: Representations of the Assassins in twelfth- and thirteenth-century Europe*, Syracuse, NY, 2014

Phillips, J., 'Hugh of Payns and the 1129 Damascus crusade', in M. Barber (ed.), *The Military Orders*, Vol. 1: *Fighting for the Faith and Caring for the Sick*, Abingdon, 1994, pp. 141–62

— *Defenders of the Holy Land: Relations between the Latin East and the West, 1119–1187*, Oxford, 1996

— *The Second Crusade: Extending the frontiers of Christendom*, London, 2007

— *Holy Warriors: A modern history of the crusades*, London, 2009

— *The Life and Legend of the Sultan Saladin*, London, 2019

Poor, D.M., 'Secular/religious myths of violence: The case of Nizārī Ismailis of the Alamūt period', *Studia Islamica*, 114 (2019), pp. 47–68

Prestwich, M., *Edward I*, London, 1997

Pringle, D., *The Churches of the Crusader Kingdom of Jerusalem: A corpus*, 4 vols, Cambridge, 1993–2009

— *Secular Buildings in the Crusader Kingdom of Jerusalem: An archaeological gazetteer*, Cambridge, 1997

— 'The Spring of the Cresson in crusading history', in M. Balard, B.Z. Kedar and J. Riley-Smith (eds), *Dei gesta per Francos*, Abingdon, 2001, pp. 231–40

Purkis, W.J., *Crusading Spirituality in the Holy Land and Iberia, c.1095–c.1187*, Woodbridge, 2008

Raphael, K., *The Excavation of the Templar Fortress at Jacob's Ford (1993–2009)*, Jerusalem, 2023

Riley-Smith, J., 'The Templars and the castle of Tortosa in Syria: An unknown document concerning the acquisition of the fortress', *English Historical Review*, 74 (1969), pp. 278–88

— 'The Templars and the Teutonic Knights in Cilician Armenia', in T.S.R. Boase (ed.), *The Cilician Kingdom of Armenia*, Edinburgh and London, 1978

— 'Crusading as an act of love', *History*, 65:214 (1980), pp. 177–92

— *The Knights Hospitaller in the Levant, c.1070–1309*, Basingstoke, 2012

— *The Crusades: A history*, 3rd edn, London, 2014

Rother, J., 'Embracing death, celebrating life: Reflections on the concept of martyrdom in the Order of the Knights Templar', *Ordines Militares*, 19 (2014), pp. 169–92

— *Das Martyrium im Templerorden: eine Studie zur historisch-theologischen Relevanz des Opfertodes im geistlichen Ritterorden der Templer*, Bamberger historische Studien, Bamberg, 2017

Saleh, S., 'The use of Bāṭinī, Fidāʾī and Ḥashīshī', *Studia Islamica*, 82 (1995), pp. 35–43

Sandler, T., *Terrorism: What everyone needs to know*, Oxford, 2018

Schatkin, M., 'The Maccabean martyrs', *Vigiliae Christianae*, 28 (1974), pp. 97–113

Schenk, J., 'Nomadic violence in the first Latin kingdom of Jerusalem and the military orders', *Reading Medieval Studies*, 36 (2010), pp. 39–55

— 'The documentary evidence for Templar religion', in K. Borchardt, K. Döring, P. Josserand and H.J. Nicholson (eds), *The Templars and their Sources*, Abingdon, 2017, pp. 199–211

REFERENCES AND FURTHER READING

Smarandache, B.C., 'The Franks and the Nizari Ismailis in the early crusade period', *Al-Masāq*, 24:3 (2012), pp. 221–39

Smith, C., 'Martyrdom and crusading in the thirteenth century: Remembering the dead of Louis IX's crusades', *Al-Masāq*, 15:2 (2003), pp. 189–96

Talmon-Heller, D., 'Muslim martyrdom and quest for martyrdom in the crusading period', *Al-Masaq*, 14:2 (2002), pp. 131–9

Tamminen, M., 'Who deserves the crown of martyrdom? Martyrs in the crusade ideology of Jacques de Vitry (1160/70–1240)', in C. Krötzl and K. Mustakallio (eds), *On Old Age: Approaching death in antiquity and the middle ages*, Turnhout, 2011, pp. 293–313

Thorau, P. *The Lion of Egypt: Sultan Baybars I and the Near East in the thirteenth century*, trans. P.M. Holt, London, 1992

Throop, S.A., *Crusading as an Act of Vengeance, 1095–1216*, Farnham, 2011

Tibble, S., *Monarchy and Lordships in the Latin Kingdom of Jerusalem, 1099–1291*, Oxford, 1989

— *The Crusader Armies*, London, 2018

— *The Crusader Strategy*, London, 2020

— *Templars: The knights who made Britain*, London, 2023

— *Crusader Criminals: The knights who went rogue in the Holy Land*, London, 2024

Tyerman, C.J., *England and the Crusades, 1095–1588*, Chicago, IL, 1988

— *God's War: A new history of the crusades*, London, 2006

Upton-Ward, J., 'The surrender of Gaston and the Rule of the Templars', in M. Barber (ed.), *The Military Orders*, Vol. 1: *Fighting for the Faith and Caring for the Sick*, Abingdon, 1994, pp. 179–88

Virani, S.N., *The Ismailis in the Middle Ages: A history of survival, a search for salvation*, Oxford, 2007

Walker, J., '"The Templars are everywhere": An examination of the myths behind Templar survival after 1307', in J. Burgtorf, P.F. Crawford and H.J. Nicholson (eds), *The Debate on the Trial of the Templars*, Farnham, 2010, pp. 347–57

— '"From the Holy Grail and the Ark of the Covenant to Freemasonry and the Priory of Sion": An introduction to the "after-history" of the Templars', in P.W. Edbury (ed.), *The Military Orders*, Vol. 5: *Politics and Power*, Farnham, 2012, pp. 439–47

— 'Sources for the Templar myth', in K. Borchardt, K. Döring, P. Josserand and H.J. Nicholson (eds), *The Templars and their Sources*, Abingdon, 2017, pp. 360–71

Willey, P., *Eagle's Nest: Ismaili castles in Iran and Syria*, London, 2005

Williams, P.A., 'The assassination of Conrad of Montferrat – Another suspect?', *Traditio*, 26 (1970), pp. 381–9

Wilson, C.C., *The Battle Rhetoric of Crusade and Holy War, c.1099–c.1222*, Abingdon, 2022

Wilson, J., *Medieval Syria and the Onset of the Crusades: The political world of Bilad al-Sham, 1050–1128*, Edinburgh, 2023

Wood, J., 'The myth of secret history, or "It's not just the Templars involved in absolutely everything"', in P.W. Edbury (ed.), *The Military Orders*, Vol. 5: *Politics and Power*, Farnham, 2012, pp. 449–60

Index

Abdullah, Nizari diplomat 171
Abraham 243, 287
Abu ʿAbdallah ibn Hashim 57
Abu'l-Fath 42–3
Abu Firas 156–7, 180, 216
Abu Mansur Nizar 25
Abu Muhammad 153
Abu Qubays castle 182
Abu Tahir al-Saʾigh, the 'Persian goldsmith' 40–1, 43, 48, 63
Abu Tammam al-Taʾi 308n35
Acre 95, 130, 136, 209–11, 224, 236, 238, 240, 260–2, 266, 268–9, 271, 287
al-Afdal, Saladin's son 206
al-Afdal, vizier of Egypt 14, 26, 62
Ager Sanguinis 200
Ahamant 136
Alamut, castle and valley 20–4, 26, 30, 35, 62, 120, 153–4, 162, 222, 252, 254, 299
Alawis 30
Albara 40
Albert of Aachen 46
Albi 276
Alburz mountains 249
Aleppo 14, 27, 29, 32, 36–44, 47–50, 52, 61–3, 65, 68, 102, 106, 111, 116, 129, 140, 152–3, 181–4, 188, 191–3, 226, 231, 255
Alfonso-Jordan, count of Toulouse 128
Ali, Muhammad's cousin 18
Alp Arslan, sultan 28
Alp Arslan al-Akhras, son of Ridwan 47–8
Altaïr Ibn-Laʾ Ahad 287–8
ʿAlwan ibn Harar 54
Amadeus II of Maurienne 123
Amalric, king of Jerusalem 170–8, 243
Amanus mountain range 95, 133
Ambroise, Norman chronicler 212
Anatolia 27, 72–3, 299n3
Andalusia 193
Andrew of Montbard 130–1
Anjou 78, 107, 218, 312n20
Antioch, principality and city 29, 40, 42, 67, 95, 103, 106, 111, 113–14, 128–34, 140–3, 146, 170, 201, 223, 225, 231
Apamea 41–3, 51–2, 96
al-Aqsa mosque 76
Aquitaine 71, 123
Arab, Arabs 2, 19, 24, 28, 41, 50–3, 58, 99–100, 164, 166, 168, 177, 262, 280
Aral Sea 27

INDEX

al-'Arimah 146
Armand of Périgord 232–3
Armenia, Armenians 52, 129, 133, 223, 248, 280
Arnaud of Gibelet 259
Arnold of Lübeck 164–5, 214
Artah 141
Ascalon 91–2, 134–41
Assassin's Creed 283–91, 296
'Atiyya 27
'Atlit, *see* Château Pèlerin
Augustine, saint 86
'Ayn Jalut 256
Ayyubids 9, 183, 194, 199, 217, 222, 226, 228
'Azaz 68, 185

Baalbek 113
backgammon 239
Badr al-Jamali 299n8
Baghdad, city and caliph of 27, 44–8, 64, 181, 192–3, 254–6
Bahram 63–4, 69–70, 98–9, 101, 105, 111
Baldwin I, king of Jerusalem 46
Baldwin II, king of Jerusalem 76–9, 100–3, 107
Baldwin III, king of Jerusalem 137
Balis 50
Baniyas 116
Banyas 68–70, 97–101, 105–8, 111, 116, 140, 310n6
Basil II, Byzantine emperor 52
Basra 152
Batiniyya 12
Baybars, sultan of Egypt 1, 95, 256–60, 262–3, 266, 314n35
Beauvais, bishop of 211
Bedouin 98–9, 111, 138, 233, 244
Beha al-Din 213, 234
Beirut 3, 5, 267
Beka'a valley 191
Belqa 136
Benedict, saint 80, 303
Benjamin of Tudela 114–15, 160–1
Bérard, Thomas 262
Berengar of Collo 88

Bernard of Clairvaux, saint 79–87, 90, 93, 130, 204–5, 304n29
Bernard of Tremelay 139–41
Bernard of Vado 276
Bertrand of Blancfort 140–2, 175, 307n46
Bethany 86
Bethlehem 86, 134
Bethsan 136
al-Bira 52
Bohemond III, prince of Antioch 142
Bohemond IV, prince of Antioch and count of Tripoli 225–7, 231
Bonable, Frankish lord 43
Book of Mormon, The 294
Bukhara 248
Buqaia 136
Burchard of Strasbourg 165, 306–8
Burgundy, Burgundian 79
al-Bursuqi 47, 63–8
Bustan al-gami 159
Bu Tahir Arrani 24
Byzantium, Byzantines 27, 29, 52–3, 72–3, 100, 117, 133–4, 140, 142, 160, 164

Caco 136, 201
Cadmus, mountain 123
Caen 276
Caesarea 128, 306n13
Cairo 19, 25–6, 31, 181, 255–9, 276
Calixtus II, pope 80
Caspian Sea 27
Casteblans, see Chastel-Blanc
Celestine II, pope 90
Chaghadai 'the Greater' 249, 254
Champagne 75, 214, 223
Chastel-Blanc 146, 224
Chastellet 58, 198–9, 310n6; *see also* Jacob's Ford
Château Pèlerin, or 'Atlit 231, 271
chess 239
Cilicia, Cilician Armenia 133
Cistercians 80, 303n24
Cîteaux 80
Clermont, Council of 71–2
Codoingel 218

327

INDEX

concentric castles 117, 126–7, 146, 199, 306n9
Conrad, marquis of Montferrat and king-elect of Jerusalem 210–17
Conrad III, king of Germany 122
Crac des Chevaliers 145–6, 224, 259
Cresson, battle at the Springs of the 90–1, 201–5, 208
Crete 160
Cyprus 271, 276, 296, 298n15, 315n5

Dahhak ben Jandal 111
da'i 19, 298n3, 299n30
Damascus 29, 32, 39, 44–8, 63–4, 68–70, 97–111, 134, 136, 143, 152, 189–90, 199, 201, 226, 255, 287, 297, 310n6
Damietta 230–1
Darayya 107
Darbsak 133, 231
Da'ud, Ayyubid commander 186
Daylam, Daylami 21, 45
De laude novae militiae ('In praise of the new knighthood') 81, 86–7
Dorylaeum 122
Douzens 276
Druze 30
Duqaq 29

Edessa, county and city 29, 107, 128–9, 142, 144
Edward, prince and later King Edward I of England 260–2, 268
Egypt 14, 19, 21, 25–31, 41, 52, 62–3, 71–3, 99–101, 137–8, 141–2, 175, 180–2, 187, 196, 221, 229–31, 233–7, 255, 262, 264, 280, 299n8, 307n47, 308n2
England, English 80, 123, 173, 196, 210, 212–13, 215, 218–19, 228, 232, 260, 262, 268, 285, 287
Eracles, chronicle 233, 312n5
Eudes de Montfaucon 135
Eugenius III, pope 125
Euphrates river 28, 62, 129
Everard des Barres 130

Fahd, local leader 153–4
Fakhr al-Din 234
Farrukh-Shah 183–4, 192
Fatima 19
Fatimid 14, 19, 21, 25–6, 28, 30–1, 37, 41, 52, 62–3, 73, 99–100, 134–5, 137–8, 141, 181–2, 299n8, 299n30
fidais 11, 14, 17, 32–41, 45, 48, 62, 64–8, 77, 83–4, 92–6, 109–11, 118, 132, 148–9, 155, 157, 161–7, 179–89, 193, 197–8, 210–12, 214, 220, 223, 225, 239, 242, 245, 250, 252–4, 259–64, 281–2, 287
Field of Blood, battle of, *see* Ager Sanguinis
Fifth Crusade 230–1
First Crusade 6, 27–9, 51, 72–4, 90
France, French 89, 115, 130, 210, 212–13, 219, 233, 236, 255, 274–5, 277, 285
Frederick II, German emperor 227
Frederick Barbarossa, German emperor 165
Freemasons, Freemasonry 278–9
Fulcher, Geoffrey 142
Fulcher of Chartres 46
Fulk, count of Anjou and king of Jerusalem 78, 107, 114, 135
Funun 55

Galilee 69, 97, 136, 141, 230, 265
Garnier de Nablus 288
Gaston 95–6, 133
Gaudin, Theobald 271
Gaza 137–41
Genghis Khan 248–9
Geoffrey de Rancogne 123
George, saint 203
Georgia 248
Gerard of Rideford 90–1, 201
Girdkuh 253
Godescalous of Turout 172
Godfrey of Saint-Omer 75
Golan 70, 97–101, 107, 116
Gregory IX, pope 227
Gregory X, pope 261

INDEX

Gregory Bar Hebraeus 46, 164, 241
Gumustekin, governor of Aleppo 193–4
Guy of Lusignan, king of Jerusalem 205–7, 214, 285

Hajar Shughlan, mountain pass 133
al-Hakim, the 'doctor-astrologer' 37–40, 48
Hama 112–13, 116, 136, 145, 191, 257
Hammam the Pilgrim 57
Harran 43
Hasan II 153–4, 158–9, 162
Hasan III 222,
Hasan Sabbah 18–26, 30, 62, 281, 299n8
Hattin 205–8, 210
Hauran 69, 199
Henry II, count of Champagne 214, 223–4, 312n5
Henry II, king of England 218
Henry the Young King, son of Henry II, king of England 218
Holy Sepulchre 72, 76, 87, 131
Homs 39, 113–14, 116, 145
Hospitallers 79, 99, 127–8, 132, 134, 144–9, 154, 161–2, 175, 205, 207, 225–7, 233, 237–9, 257–9, 275, 285, 288, 311n9
Hugh, Templar brother, son of the count of Ampurias 269
Hugh of Payns, 'Paganus' 75–80, 101, 134–5
Hulegu 249, 251, 254–6, 259, 282
Humphrey of Toron 214
al-Husayn 152, 220, 308n32

Ibn Abi Tayy 187, 191, 310n21
Ibn al-Athir 24, 67–8, 98, 103–4, 106, 186, 191, 193, 195, 201, 206, 215, 246, 302n23
Ibn al-Jawzi 182
Ibn al-Munira 56
Ibn al-Qalanisi 39, 45–6, 53, 64, 66, 70, 98, 109, 116
Ibn-Badi 47, 62

Ibn Jubayr 193
Ibn-Shawar 260
Ibn Wasil 187
Ibrahim al-Ajami 50
Iliya Lane, Mosul 67
Imad al-Din 183, 187, 207
Inab 129, 133
Innocent II, pope 87
Innocent III, pope 225
Iran 19, 21, 26, 281
Iraq 152
Iron Gate, Damascus 104
Isfahan 23–5, 34
Ismail the Missionary 48, 101–16
Israel 29
Italy, Italians 205, 274
Ithier of Rochefort 276

Jabal as-Summaq 29, 37, 40, 43, 49, 69, 161–2, 182
Jabal Bahra (Jabal Ansariyya) 29, 37, 112, 114, 116, 143–4, 150, 154–5, 160–1, 193, 226, 228, 239, 242, 257, 313n23
Jacob's Ford 140, 198
Jacques de Molay 277, 279
Jaffa 76
James of Mailly 202–4
James of Vitry 90–1, 125
Janah al-Daula 38–40
Jawuli, commander of the Asadi troop 186
Jawuli of Mosul 36
Jerusalem 29, 46, 68, 71–9, 85, 91, 100, 102–3, 106–8, 113–14, 128, 130, 134–8, 140–1, 143, 166, 170, 173–5, 178, 180–1, 195–9, 201, 205, 209–10, 212, 214, 217, 223–4, 228, 230, 233, 243, 285, 287–8, 297n1, 302n13
John, king of England 218
John of Joinville 235–6, 240–5, 250
John Kinnamos 134
John of Montfort, the Young Lord of Tyre 3–5, 298n15
John Phocas 160, 308n26
John of Salisbury 123

329

INDEX

Judas Maccabeus (Maccabaeus) 90, 197
Julian of Grenier, lord of Sidon 1–5
Juwayni 120–1, 252

Kafartab 40, 43
Kahf 112, 114–17, 151, 153, 155, 162, 214, 257, 259, 312n22, 313n23
Kamal al-Din 65, 68, 154, 161, 163, 184, 189–90, 296
Kashani 301n4
Kella 43
Khalaf ibn Mulaʿib 41–2
Khariba 112, 116, 257
Khawabi 112, 154, 225, 257, 259, 306n28
Khumartakin, lord of Abu Qubays castle 182
Khurasan, Khurasanis 45, 109
Khurshah, Rukn al-Din 251–4
Kingdom of Heaven 284–5, 316n26
Kitbuqa 249, 251, 255–6
Ku Klux Klan 280
Kurds, Kurdish 180

La Fève 136, 201
La Forbie 233
La Roche Guillaume 133
La Roche de Roussel 133
Lamasar 252–3
Latakia 30, 116
Lateran Council (1215) 230
Lebanon 29–30, 73, 166, 168, 297
Le Mans 78
Lombardy, Lombards 274
Louis VII, king of France 122–4, 130
Louis IX, king of France 115, 233–9, 244–5, 255, 307n46

Maʾarrat-al-Nuʾman 40
Maʾarrat Masrin 51
Maccabees 89–91, 197, 204
Mahdi 19
Malahida 12
al-Malik al-Mansur, sultan 263
al-Malik al-Nasir, sultan 263
Malik Shah, Seljuk sultan 28

Mamluks 6, 9, 95, 190, 234, 250, 255–6, 258–9, 262–6, 268–70, 272, 280
Mankalan, emir 188
Maniqa 113, 257, 259, 306n28
Mansurah 233–6, 313n11
Manuel, emperor of Byzantium 140
Manzikert 52
Marco Polo 281–3
Mardin 62
Marj Ayun 198–9
Margaret, lady of Tyre 263
Margat 225
Masyaf 112, 116–17, 150, 155, 162, 188, 190–1, 193, 239, 257–8, 287, 306n28, 310n32, 312n22, 313n12
Mattathias, father of Judas Maccabeus 90
Matthew of Edessa 67, 140
Matthew Paris 228, 232, 235
Matthew Sauvage 267
Mawdud 44–7, 64
Maymundiz 251
al-Mazdaghani 101, 103, 106
Melisende 78
Mesopotamia 248
Messina, Treaty of 219
Michael the Syrian 66, 76, 302
Miles, Desmond 288
Mongke Khan 250, 253, 255
Mongols 121, 228, 246–64, 282, 314n21
Montferrand 144
Mont Gisard 196–8, 200, 204, 206, 208
Montsaunès 89
Mosul 36, 44, 47, 64, 113, 115, 128, 144, 192–3
Mount Lebanon 30
muezzin 24, 34
Munqidh, Banu Munqidh clan 43, 50–60, 138; *see also* Usama
al-Muntagib 188–9
al-Muqaddasi 69
al-Mustansir biʾllah 25, 299n8

INDEX

Nablus, Council of (1120) and town 76–7, 302n11
Najm al-Din 257–9, 262
Nazareth 86
neo-Platonism 31
Nile river and delta 141, 231
Nizam al-Mulk 24
Noah 243
Norman, Normans 40, 212
Nur al-Din 117, 129, 138, 140–2, 155, 162, 174, 178, 180, 192, 310n6
Nusayris 30

Odo of Saint-Amand 141, 172–3, 196–8
Old Man of the Mountain, title 148, 215, 223–4, 228, 231, 236–8, 240, 243, 257, 281–2; *see also* Sinan
Oliver of Paderborn 231
Orontes river 51, 53, 55
Oultrejourdain, *see* Transjordan
Oxford 75
Oxus river 249

Palestine 27–8, 72–3, 113, 128, 195, 230
Paris 124, 276–7
Paul, saint 89
Persia, Persians 18–32, 36, 39–41, 61–3, 67, 106, 112, 120, 153, 158, 162, 168, 222, 248–56, 262, 280, 282, 301n4, 314n21
Peter, saint 89, 243
Peter, saint, confraternity of 200–1
Peter of Bologna 277
Peter of Moncada 268
Peter of Sevrey 270
Philip II, king of France 210, 213, 219
Philip IV, king of France 274–5
'Philip' the Assassin 1–5
Philip of Milly 136
Philip of Montfort, lord of Tyre 1–6, 260, 263
Picardy 75
Pons, count of Tripoli 114
posterns 117
Pyrenees 89

Qadmus 98, 112, 114–16, 154–5, 157, 259
Qirta al-'Izzi 259
Qom 19
Quhistan 249, 254
Qulay'a 257, 259, 306n28
Quran 31, 177
Qutuz, sultan 256

Raimbaud of Caromb 276
Ralph of Diceto 196
Ralph de Merle 147
Ramla, town and lord of 215, 260
Raphaniya 144
Raymond II, count of Tripoli 147, 178
Raymond III, count of Tripoli and *bailli* of Jerusalem 178
Raymond, son of Bohemond IV 225–6
Raymond of Poitiers, prince of Antioch 129, 133
Raymond of Vichiers, bishop 89
Reddecoeur, Templar brother 268
Reginald of Argenton 232
Resurrection (of 1164) 157–62, 177, 222, 226, 240, 299n30
Reynouard of Maraclea 145
Rhodes 275
Richard I, the Lionheart, king of England 210–19, 229–30, 285, 287
Richard of Poitou 142
Ridwan 29, 36–47, 102
Robert, count of Artois 234
Robert of Craon 135
Robert de Sablé 218–19, 285–8, 312n18
Robert of Sandford 232
Roger of Howden 213
Ruad 315n2
Rudbar 21, 26
Rugia 114
Ruj valley 40
Rukn al-Din Khurshah, *see* Khurshah
Rule of the Templars 81, 88, 94, 126, 303n21
Rusafa 112, 154, 257, 259, 306n28

Safad (Saphet) 94, 119–20, 136, 198, 265–6

INDEX

St Anthony Gate 269
St Peter, confraternity of 200–1
Saladin 9, 58, 174, 179–208, 213, 215–19, 221–2, 285, 287, 309n1, 310n6
Samarkand 248
Sarim al-Din 258
Sarmin 43, 51
Saveh 24
Scotland 80
Scott, Ridley 284
Second Crusade 122–3, 125–7
Seiher of Mamedunc 172
Seljuk 21, 24–31, 37, 41, 64–5, 100, 102, 122, 292
Seventh Crusade 122–5, 127
Shabib ibn-Munqidh 53–4, 59
Shadhi the Freedman 105
Shaizar 43, 49–61, 63, 96, 111–13, 138, 163
Shams al-Din 258–9
Shihab al-Din al-Harimi, lord of Hama 191
Shiite 6, 10–11, 18–19, 23, 25, 30–1, 37, 40–1, 48, 52, 67, 73, 112, 129, 138, 152, 180–1, 187, 241, 257
Shirkuh, Saladin's uncle 186
Sidon 1, 3, 176, 215, 244, 256, 271
Sinai 137
Sinan, the Old Man of the Mountain 9, 15, 33, 116, 151–67, 170–1, 173, 177–8, 181–5, 188–91, 193, 215–16, 219–20, 222, 241–2, 287, 289, 298n10
Sira of Baybars 262
Stephen, saint 89
Stephen of Sissey 267
Sufi 24, 39, 207
Sultan ibn-Munqidh 52–5
Syria 6, 14–15, 26–51, 59, 61, 63, 65–6, 70–3, 79, 98–106, 111–14, 118–20, 128, 133, 136–7, 143, 150, 152–64, 177, 180, 191–2, 214–16, 219–22, 236, 240–1, 250, 254–6, 262, 280, 288, 299n3
Syrian Gates, mountain pass 133

Tahir, carpenter of Isfahan 24
Taj al-Din Abu'l-Futuh 313n12
Taj al-Muluk Bori 101–4, 109–10
Ta'limiyya 12
Tancred, king of Sicily 219
Tancred, regent of Antioch 40–3
Tanis 234
Taqi al-Din 197, 200
Taqiyya 298n2
Templar of Tyre 261
Terricus, Templar preceptor 208
Thecua 134–5, 306n26
Thietmar, Franciscan Friar 226
Third Crusade 210, 213, 217–19, 229, 285, 287
Tiberias 136, 205, 267
Tortosa 145–6, 225, 271, 312n7
Touraine 202
Transjordan (Oultrejourdain) 134, 136, 174
Transoxiana 248–9
Tripoli, county and city 29, 106–7, 111–16, 128, 141–7, 161, 173, 178, 225, 259–61, 268–9
Troyes, Council of 80
Tughtigin 44–7, 64, 68–70, 97, 101–2
Turcopoles 2, 5, 94, 120, 126–7, 139, 142, 196, 260, 271
Turk, Turkic 1, 6, 9, 14, 16, 19–21, 24–32, 36–9, 41, 43–7, 52, 64, 68–9, 72–3, 100, 102, 108, 110, 113, 122, 124–5, 128–9, 133–8, 143, 177, 180, 210, 217, 231, 235, 253, 260, 271, 292, 299
Turkey 27, 29
Tutush 28
Tyre 1–5, 63, 68, 103, 107, 130, 176, 210–11, 213, 216, 260–1, 263

Ulger of Angers 89
Ullayqa 112, 154–5, 161–2, 257, 259
al-Umari 241, 264
Urban II, pope 71–2
Usama ibn-Munqidh 50–60, 138

INDEX

Wadi al-Taym 99, 105, 111
Walter Map 75, 84, 173, 302n9
Walter of Mesnil 168–9, 172, 176, 181
Warmund of Picquigny 76
Wilbrand of Oldenburg 145, 224–5
William V, marquis of Montferrat 288
William of Beaujeu 268–9
William of Cardona 268
William of Montserrat 231–2
William of Picquigny 3–4, 298n15
William of Rubruck, friar 250
William of Tripoli, friar 261
William of Tyre 46, 76, 84, 125, 127, 138–9, 166, 170, 173, 175–7, 198
World Trade Center 284

Yazkush, emir 186
Yemen, Yemeni 151
Yves the Breton, friar 239–43

Zengi, atabeg of Mosul 113, 115, 117, 128–9, 144, 155, 193